GW01019067

SPEARMEN

THE HISTORY OF THE 9TH/12TH ROYAL LANCERS

(PRINCE OF WALES'S)

Published by 9th/12th Royal Lancers Charitable Association

First published in Great Britain in 2010 by 9th/12th Royal Lancers Charitable Association

ISBN 978-0-9566572-0-6

Design: Craig Stevens and Nick Heal

Printed and bound in Great Britain by Butler, Tanner and Dennis Ltd

SPEARMEN

THE HISTORY OF THE 9TH/12TH ROYAL LANCERS
(PRINCE OF WALES'S)

Richard Charrington

ACKNOWLEDGEMENTS

There are a huge number of people to whom I owe a great deal for all the assistance that they have given me in bringing this history to its present form. The earlier Regimental histories have inevitably been the source of much material, but I have also made extensive use of the Marquis of Anglesey's *History of the British Cavalry* for both background and balance.

In compiling the more recent chapters I am grateful to all the Commanding Officers who have found time to make contributions, in particular Generals Mike Swindells, Robin Searby, James Short and Martin Rutledge, Brigadiers Hugh Pye and Richard Nash and Colonels David Maitland-Titterton, Jamie Martin, Tim Robinson and Will Fooks. Other valuable help has come from John Robson, Freddie Hunn and Nick Peto, while Roger Burgess has provided a great deal for the Cold War period and Patrick Lort-Phillips and others the detail about aviation.

Jonathan Miles and his staff at the Trumpington Gallery have provided several of the images of Regimental pictures, while Regimental Sergeant Major Robert Millar has done a considerable amount of photographic research. I owe Corporal William Foster a huge debt for all the effort he has put in to provide the majority of the photographs of Regimental pictures and property. Mike Galer, the curator of the Regimental Museum at Derby, has also offered great practical support in providing many images from the collection there and allowing me to take up much of his time in searching the archives. Other illustrations are reproduced with the kind permission of the National Army Museum, the Imperial War Museum, the Victoria & Albert Museum, The Tank Museum, the National Gallery of Scotland, The Conway Library/The Courtauld Institute of Art and the Trustees of Edward Ardizonne's Estate. The maps are the work of Richard Stewart, from the Media Support Wing at Bovington, who has managed to fit in their production amidst a host of competing priorities.

In helping to bring the book together I should single out Bobby Collins and David Pritchard, both of whom have read several drafts and offered advice. The latter should probably have his name on the front of the history as he took over the final stages of production on my deployment to Afghanistan. Alexander Stilwell, who has edited the book, has dealt with constantly changing timescales as have Caroline Donald, Craig Stevens and Nick Heal who have proof read and designed the finished work. David Chappell, Joe Hardy and Suresh Mamnani at Home Headquarters have been a strong base to lean on for help and information, while without the support and generous backing of the Regimental Trustees the project would never have seen the light of day.

Finally, I should apologise to those who have forgiven me when my mind should have been on other things. Foremost amongst those are my children, Henry, Camilla and Sophie, and my wife, Mary Anne, whose appointment as the first female Regimental Trustee may have had some bearing on the support given by that body.

BATTLE HONOURS AND VICTORIA CROSS RECIPIENTS

Salamanca | **Peninsula** | **Waterloo** | **Punniar**
Sobraon | **Chillianwallah** | **Goojerat** | **Punjaub**
South Africa 1851–1853 | **Sevastopol** | **Delhi 1857**
Central India | **Lucknow** | **Charasiah** | **Kabul 1879**
Kandahar 1880 | **Afghanistan 1878–1880** | **Modder River**
Relief of Kimberley | **Paardeberg** | **South Africa 1899–1902**

THE FIRST WORLD WAR

Mons | Le Cateau | **Retreat from Mons** | **Marne 1914**
Aisne 1914 | La Bassee 1914 | **Messines 1914**
Armentieres 1914 | **Ypres 1914, 1915** | Neuve Chapelle
Gravenstafel | St Julien | Frezenberg | Bellewaarde
Somme 1916, 1918 | Pozieres | Flers-Courcelette
Arras 1917 | Scarpe 1917 | **Cambrai 1917, 1918**
St Quentin | Rosieres | Avre | Lys | Hazebrouck
Amiens | Albert 1918 | Hindenburg Line | St Quentin Canal | Beaurevoir | **Sambre** | **Pursuit to Mons**
France and Flanders 1914–1918

THE SECOND WORLD WAR

Dyle | Defence of Arras | Arras Counter Attack
Dunkirk 1940 | **Somme 1940** | Withdrawal to Seine
North-West Europe 1940 | **Chor es Sufan**
Saunnu | **Gazala** | Bir el Aslagh | Sidi Rezegh 1942
Defence of Alamein Line | Ruweisat | Ruweisat Ridge
Alam el Halfa | **El Alamein** | Advance on Tripoli
Tebega Gap | **El Hammas** | Akarit | El Kourzia
Djebel Kournine | **Tunis** | Creteville Pass
North Africa 1941–1943 | Citerna | Gothic Line
Coriano | Capture of Forli | Lamone Crossing
Pideura | **Defence of Lamone Bridgehead**
Conventello-Comacchio | **Argenta Gap** | **Bologna**
Sillaro Crossing | Idice Bridgehead | **Italy 1944–1945**

THE INDIAN MUTINY

JONES, Lieutenant AS
HARTIGAN, Sergeant H
HANCOCK, Private T
PURCELL, Private J
BLAIR, Lieutenant R
KELLS, Lance Corporal R
ROBERTS, Private JIR
DONOHOE, Private P
FREEMAN, Private J
SPENCE, Troop Sergeant Major D
GOAT, Lance Corporal W
RUSHE, Troop Sergeant Major D
NEWELL, Private R

THE SECOND AFGHAN WAR

ADAMS, The Reverend JW, Chaplain to the 9th Lancers

THE ZULU WARS

BERESFORD, Captain The Lord William Leslie de la Poer

THE FIRST WORLD WAR

GRENFELL, Captain Francis Octavius

SUBSCRIPTION LIST

Major General MJ Rutledge OBE
Major General RV Searby CB
Major General JHT Short CB OBE
Major General GMG Swindells CB
Brigadier J R St D Mackaness MBE
Brigadier LJR Nash
Brigadier HWK Pye OBE
Colonel RA Charrington
Colonel AP Gilks DL TD
Colonel DHSL Maitland-Titterton
Colonel JM Martin
Colonel NMT Stafford CMG
Lieutenant Colonel AC Brodey
Lieutenant Colonel NC Everard
Lieutenant Colonel WJO Fooks
Lieutenant Colonel J Hutchins
Lieutenant Colonel PGF Lort-Phillips
Lieutenant Colonel RJ Mackaness
Lieutenant Colonel RH Peaver TD
Lieutenant Colonel TP Robinson OBE
Lieutenant Colonel IR Woodbridge MBE
Major TB Andrews MBE
Major ARF Arkwright
Major MHS Ayshford Sanford
Major DN Chappell
Major GA Charrington DL JP
Major TR Clapton
Major RM Collins
Major NS Croft
Major SP Doherty
Major SC Enderby LVO
Major MD Everett
Major JEJ Fuller
Major JR Gasson-Hargreaves
Major DM Goggs
Major B Hartwell
Major RKB Hitchcock MC
Major MML Hudson OBE
Major F Hunn MBE
Major EHS Inglefield
Major AJ Jones
Major TSR Mort
Major PE Mugliston
Major DR Pritchard
Major GS Reid
Major HG Robertson
Major PGE Sebag-Montefiore
Major JA Simpson BEM
Major PA Watson
Major MC Wilkinson
Major WH Wright JP
Major T Wynne
Captain HFA Arbuthnott
Captain AJ Barnett
Captain GR Bellamy
Captain JD Bottomley
Captain E Broadhurst
Captain D Burns
Captain GH Caldecott
Captain N Clifford-Jones
Captain SJ Clitheroe
Captain JJ Dawson
Captain RJT Farmer
Captain JRK Farrer
Captain DA Fleetwood
Captain JM Franklin
Captain CD Glyn-Jones CBE
Captain CW Going
Captain WNC Greig
Captain The Hon CJ Guest
Captain M Guyatt
Captain LGM Hannen MC
Captian EPA Harden
Captain SP Hardy
Captain PHG Harris
Captain CS Hatton
Captain TR Hercock
Captain FTC Inglefield
Captain DGA Jarrett
Captain TG Kappler
Captain AD King
Captain CM Knight
Captain MD Linnell
Captain MR Lowe
Captain CJ Miles
Captain WJ Minards
Captain J Mitchell
Captain PH Norman LVO
Captain JFB Panter
Captain JW Parry
Captain CAG Perry
Captain NJ Peto
Captain JA Rathbone
Captain WJR Richmond
Captain JE Robson MC
Captain RM Sankey
Captain ONG Scholte
Captain EJA Smith-Maxwell
Captain EDS Stiles
Captain MJ Sutton
Captain NA Tapping
Captain OA Tickner
Captain S Tripuraneni
Captain ML Welborn
Captain AJ Winter
Captain MHJ Woodward
Lieutenant AJ Champion
Lieutenant GJN Duffield
Lieutenant TR Gooch
Lieutanant AJ Grant
Lieutenant AJ Horsfall
Lieutenant TP Hughes
Lieutenant JET Davis
Lieutenant CA Luke
Lieutenant RH Willing
Second Lieutenant RES Aitken
Second Lieutenant CD Fisher
Second Lieutenant NJ Groome
Second Lieutenant WG Locke
Second Lieutenant EJ Minards
Second Lieutenant RA O'Shea
Second Lieutenant AJW Robinson
Second Lieutenant FWH Taylor-Dickson
WO1 (RSM) R Millar
WO1 (RSM) J Rickett
WO11 (RQMS) L Beuttell
WO11 N Saul
WO11 PM Savage
WO11 CR Whitehead
SSgt S Bennison
SSgt DC Dalton
SSgt J South
SSgt N Ulliott
Sgt KJ Bagshaw
Sgt J Canning
Sgt JA Cassidy
Sgt R Clarke
Sgt MA Flint
Sgt DT Gibson
Sgt J Mawhinney
Sgt K Rowley
Sgt J Webb
Cpl A Barwick
Cpl S Champkins
Cpl JA Ellis
Cpl WA Foster
Cpl ARJ Hale
Cpl F Hancock
Cpl J Hobson
Cpl DS Murrell
Cpl CRN Parker
Cpl DJ Reid
Cpl B Rushton
Cpl F Spencer
LCpl Brewster
LCpl A Butler
LCpl C Carter
LCpl A Ferla
LCpl A Heighton
LCpl D Horne
LCpl R Miles
LCpl C Reeve
LCpl G Roe
LCpl R Smith
Sir Alastair Aird GCVO
Mr RCM Andrews
Mr P Aspinall
PW Barrows Esq
Mr R Bassett
The Hon RD Beckett
DH Boag Esq
JR Boughey Esq
Mr M Bradford
Mr J Bridge
Mr E Bussingham
Mr RC Chandler
Mr TAJ Chiverton
EG Clifton-Brown Esq
Mr MJ Collins
Mr I Craddock
MG de Burgh Esq
NA De Zoete Esq
Mr M Dodsworth
Mr WK Draper
Mr JT Dulson
Mr J Edmonds
Mr S Finn BEM
JA Fooks Esq
Mr BR Funnell
Mr E Gamble
Mr T Gent
PN Gerrard Esq CBE
AQ Goggs Esq
Mr B Greenham
Mr R Greenwood
Sir Basil Hall KCB MC TD
Mr LJ Harper
Mr K Hayter
D Hayward Esq
HM Henderson Esq DL
CP Hook Esq
Mr J Hudson
CS Inglefield Esq
DGC Inglefield Esq
Mr RH Inglis
Mr AM Isdale
HL Kennedy Esq
Mr G Kerridge
Mr MJ Lewis
RMR MacDonnell Esq
DR Marlow Esq
Mr MA McGrath
Mr A McIntyre
NAH Milne-Home Esq
Mr V Moore
AD Motion Esq
JO Mountney Esq
Mr J Muir
Mr J Mulvihill
ES Nelson Esq
Reverend Canon William Norman
Mr JA Ogden
Mr RC Oldfield
P Owen Esq
DEH Panter Esq
Mr HVR Parish
Mr JD Pearce
LA Ponsonby Esq
Mr GF Porter
Mr D Probert
Mr T Reid
Mr WJ Rogers
Mr RSJ Rowland
Mr D Savory
Mr B Scrase
Fr DGS Smith RAChD
JW Smith Esq
Mr JW Smitherman
Mr V Spencer
Mr RJ Stockwell
Mr D Stratford
RJW Sutcliffe Esq
Mr HJ Teague MBE
Mr MF Todd
ZJA Tyszkiewicz Esq CMG
Mr EJ Walsh
Mr RK Walton
Mr L Ward
Mr R Ward
WA Warre Esq
Mr PA Watchorn
DC Watney Esq
Mr J Westhead
Mr CC Whitehead
Mr M Willey
NC Wright Esq
Mr LGF Yates
Mrs Molly Bonsor
Mrs L Bryan-Brown
Mrs RA Charrington
Mrs A Cornwall
Mrs VM Davies
Elizabeth, Lady Grimthorpe DCVO
Marianna, Viscountess Monckton of Brenchley
The Lady Pym
Mrs V Sims

CONTENTS

Dedicated to

past, present and future
9th/12th Royal Lancers
and their families

BUCKINGHAM PALACE

The 9th Queens Royal Lancers and the 12th Royal Lancers were amalgamated 50 years ago; coincidentally the year that I was born and it is both an honour and a pleasure to be asked to write the Foreword to the first History of the 9th/12th Royal Lancers in this, the Fiftieth Anniversary Year of the Amalgamation.

Both Regiments were raised in 1715. Since then, they have made numerous transitions: from Dragoons to Lancers, then mechanisation between the two World Wars, to Main Battle Tanks and most recently to Armoured Reconnaissance.

They have given loyal and distinguished service around the world for 295 years and participated in most of our nation's decisive battles during that time, including Waterloo and El Alamein; this outstanding service is reflected in the Battle Honours and 16 Victoria Crosses they have been awarded. In 2011 they deploy once again to Afghanistan, where they last served in 1880.

My wonderful Grandmother, Queen Elizabeth the Queen Mother was Colonel in Chief of the Regiment from 1960 until her death in 2002. As her Grandson, I am proud to be her successor and in this 50th Year of the Amalgamated Regiment wish you all continuing good fortune for the future.

INTRODUCTION

The 50th anniversary of the amalgamation of the 9th and 12th Lancers in 1960 is a clear and very obvious occasion to mark with the publication of a new history of the current Regiment and it would have been relatively easy to produce a book that covered only that period. That I have written a history that starts from the Regiments' foundation in 1715 might be regarded as something of a conceit, especially as much more detailed accounts have previously been written. It is therefore worth explaining the motives that led to this publication.

In the first instance, although I am the third generation of my family to have served in the Regiment or in one of its forebears, I have often been acutely aware I knew very little about much of what had been done in the past. This feeling had been heightened when meeting Old Comrades and escorting them on battlefield tours to France and Italy and listening to their tales. My embarrassment was compounded when asked questions by visitors to the Regiment about its history and traditions, to which I frequently found myself fumbling for a reply, often at a loss as to where to find the answer.

Accessing the history of the Regiment became a major task in itself and not one that anyone but the most dedicated researcher would bother with. The two excellent histories of the 9th Lancers to 1945 were extremely hard to come by, while the history of the 12th covering the same period required yet another lengthy volume to be found and then digested. Since 1945, several shorter records have been added, but nowhere was there a single history that would provide an overview of the whole picture for anyone coming to the Regiment for the first time.

Equally important was the wealth of new material that has been written in the last few years, telling of the human side of Regimental life, in particular as it relates to the experiences of those serving before and during the Second World War. These works add colour to the bare bones of the narrative, while modern histories of other periods have given balance to the somewhat biased accounts of the Regiments' earlier historians, who by and large were reluctant to find fault in any aspect of its behaviour. I hope that, while displaying justifiable pride in the history of our Regiments, I have at least done so with an acknowledgement of their occasional shortcomings.

Finally, the Regiment possesses a tremendous collection of art, photographs and other material, much of it with the serving Regiment or in the newly refurbished Museum in Derby. The opportunities provided by modern printing have allowed considerable use of illustration to display the collection and to bring the narrative to life.

Inevitably there will be omissions but, if they are from the modern era, it is either because many of the stories I have been told remain libellous, or because we have become careless at recording them consistently and reliably – a fault this history might spur us to correct if we are vain enough to wish to be remembered. Despite the gaps, I hope this publication contributes to our sense of pride in a great institution that, despite fads, financial crises and interference from only occasionally well-intentioned busy-bodies, continues to serve our country with distinction.

RICHARD CHARRINGTON | KABUL, APRIL 2010

FOUNDATION AND THE EARLY YEARS

1715–1792

KING GEORGE I might have counted himself lucky that, nearly 300 years ago, it was considerbly easier to expand an army quickly than it would be today. Faced with an imminent Jacobite threat, the process in 1715 proved comparitively efficient and allowed him not only to hang on to his throne, but also provided the start point for the two Regiments that would eventually emerge as the 9th/12th Royal Lancers.

With a standing army kept deliberately small and about which there was, following the Cromwellian period of recent memory, a considerable degree of distrust, the King and Parliament now needed another seven thousand men in short order. The problem was resolved by the creation of eight new regiments of foot and 13 of dragoons using the well-tried method of directing trusted men of military experience to raise a regiment each, granting them the Colonelcy and paying for the costs of foundation.

Simple and effective in meeting the needs of the day, the system saw the despatch of two identical letters dated 22nd and 23rd July 1715 to Major General Owen Wynne and Brigadier General Phineas Bowles, commissioning them to raise dragoon regiments of six troops each, a task they were able to complete quickly enough to be operational within three months. Their instructions were short and to the point: '*Whereas we have thought fit that a Regiment of Dragoons be forthwith raised under your Command for Our Service which is to Consist of six Troops of One Serjeant, Two Corporals, One Drummer, One Hautbois, and Thirty private Dragoons, including the Widdows men in Each Troop; These are to Authorize by you by beat of Drummer otherwise to raise so many Volontiers as shall be wanting to*

1 **THE COMMISSION OF MAJOR GENERAL OWEN WYNNE** BRINGING HIM OUT OF RETIREMENT IN MARCH 1715. FOUR MONTHS LATER HE WAS ORDERED TO RAISE THE REGIMENT THAT WOULD BECOME THE 9TH LANCERS.

2 **MAJOR GENERAL OWEN WYNNE.** WYNNE WAS FIRST COMMISSIONED IN 1688 AND COMMANDED THE 5TH ROYAL IRISH DRAGOONS IN THE NETHERLANDS, LATER RAISING A REGIMENT OF INFANTRY IN 1705 ONLY TO FIND IT DISBANDED AFTER THE TREATY OF UTRECHT IN 1713. A SIMILAR FATE HAD BEFALLEN BRIGADIER PHINEAS BOWLES, OF WHOM THERE IS NO EXISTING PORTRAIT, WHO FOUNDED WHAT WAS TO BECOME THE 12TH LANCERS. HE HAD FOUGHT WITH DISTINCTION DURING THE WAR OF THE SPANISH SUCCESSION UNTIL ITS CONCLUSION SAW HIS INFANTRY REGIMENT DISBANDED, LEAVING HIM EFFECTIVELY UNEMPLOYED.

1	2

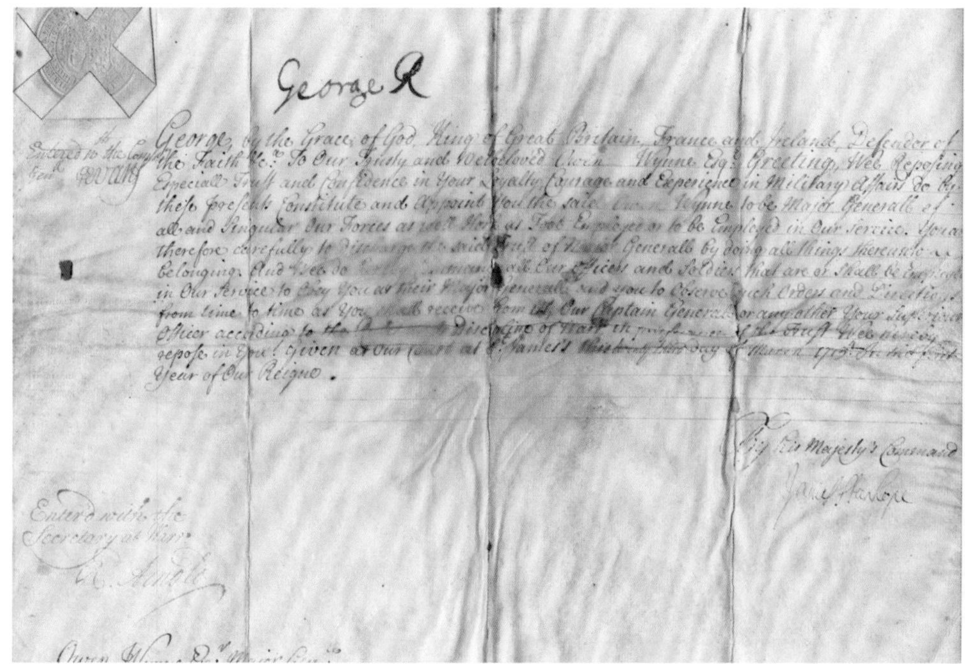
George R

George, by the Grace of God King of Great Britain, France and Ireland, Defender of the Faith &c. To Our Trusty and Welbeloved Owen Wynne Esq. Greeting. Wee Reposing Especiall Trust and Confidence in Your Loyalty, Courage and Experience in Military Affairs do by these presents Constitute and Appoint You the said [illegible] Wynne to be Major Generall of all and Singular Our Forces as well Horse as Foot Employed or to be Employed in Our service. You are therefore carefully to Discharge the said [illegible] of [illegible] Generall by doing all things thereunto belonging. And Wee do [illegible] Command all Our Officers and Soldiers that are or shall be Employed in Our Service to Obey You as their Major Generall, and you to Observe such Orders and Directions from time to time as You shall receive from [illegible] Our Captain Generall or any other Your Superior Officer according to the [illegible] Discipline of Warr in pursuance of the Trust Wee hereby repose in You. Given at Our Court at St. James's [illegible] day of March 1715 In the first Year of Our Reign.

By His Majesty's Command
[illegible]

Entered with the Secretary at Warr
[illegible]

THE BATTLE OF PRESTON ON 12TH–14TH NOVEMBER 1715. WYNNE'S DRAGOONS PROVIDED 50 SOLDIERS FOR THE ASSAULT IN THE EAST, WHILE THE BULK OF THE REGIMENT ATTACKED ON FOOT FROM THE NORTH-WEST.

Compleat the said Regiment to the above Numbers. And when you shall have Listed fifteen Men fitt for service in any of the said Troops, You are to give Notice to Two of Our Justices of the Peace of the Town or Country wherein the same are who hereby authorized and Required to View the Said Men and certify the Day of their so doing, from which Day the said fifteen Men and the Commission and Non Commission Officers of Such Troops are to Enter into our Pay. And you are to Cause the said Volontiers to be raised and Levy'd as aforesaid to March under the Command of such Commission Officers as you shall direct to Reading in Berkshire appointed for the Rendezvous of the said Regiment, And all Magistrates, Justices of the Peace, Constables and Other of Our Officers whom it may Concern, are hereby requir'd to be assisting unto you in providing Quarters, Impressing Carriages and otherwise as there shall be Occasion.'

THE JACOBITE REBELLION

The threat to the State that had precipitated the crisis came from sympathisers of the Stuart, or Jacobite, cause which sought to put a Catholic monarch back on the throne. The cause of the open rebellion was the snubbing of a Scottish nobleman by the King. The immediate military problem came from a rebel army that had advanced from Scotland and the north of England with the intention of seizing London. By 10th November the rebels had captured Preston, but weak leadership and dissent in the rebel ranks prevented further progress, the town itself presenting apparently compelling reasons to stay: *'the ladies of Preston are so very beautiful and so richly attired that the gentlemen soldiers from Wednesday to Saturday minded nothing but courting and feasting.'*[1] Wynne and Bowles had by now established and recruited their Regiments, Wynne joining five other regiments of dragoons and one of foot in Cheshire as part of a force of nearly 2,000 men sent to defeat the rebels at Preston while, elsewhere, a further three dragoon regiments advanced on Lancaster.

Arriving at Preston on 12th November, Wynne's rebels were rapidly forced back into the town as plans were made to attack it from both the east and the north. The eastern assault would be made by the regiment of foot and an *ad hoc* grouping of 50 dismounted men from each of the dragoon regiments, led by the Second-in-Command of Wynne's Dragoons and supported by a further dragoon regiment that would remain mounted. The attack on the northern gate would be mounted by two of the dragoon regiments (including Wynne's), bolstered by an additional squadron, which would conduct a dismounted attack supported by the remaining two mounted regiments. For the bulk of the Regiment, it was on its feet, and in an urban environment, that its first action would be fought.

The rebels' defence preparations were such that, while the initial assaults gained footholds, musket fire and barricades in the streets slowed momentum. By nightfall, some of the town had been set alight to burn out the rebels, though this met with only limited success, while sporadic musket and carbine fire continued as the rebel leadership became more divided and increasing

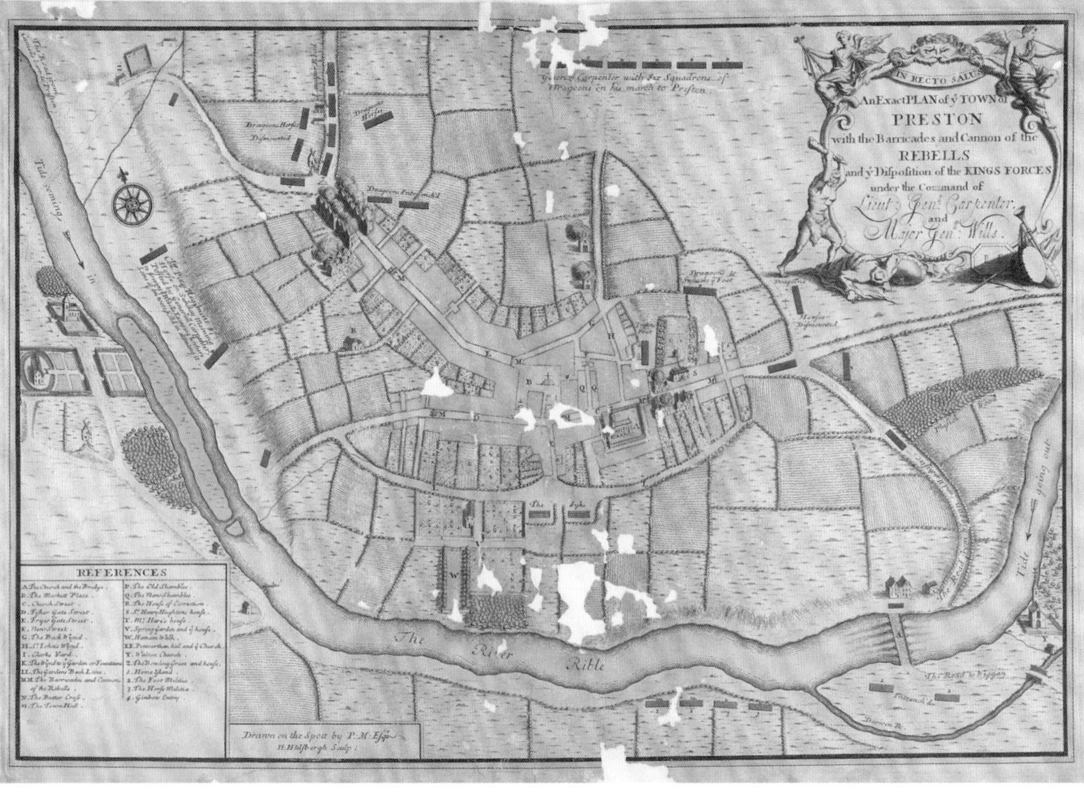

numbers deserted. Despite this, by midday on the 13th, few further gains had been made and only with the arrival of the three dragoon regiments from the force at Lancaster was the initiative regained. The rebel leaders lost their nerve and surrendered that afternoon, though many of their soldiers only agreed to lay down their arms, after serious in-fighting, on the morning of the 14th. In total, 1,500 Jacobites surrendered, the loyalist forces losing 56 men killed, 90 wounded and 72 horses lost. Wynne's Dragoons suffered six privates killed with three officers and 21 privates wounded and 15 horses killed or lost. Bowles' Regiment had enjoyed a less dramatic time, with orders to police the area in which they had been raised, before acting as escorts for the rebel prisoners from the scene of their capture to their final end in London.

Success at Preston had effectively ended the conflict south of the border, while loyalist victory in Scotland forced the rebels further and further north until the rebellion petered out early the next year. While the Crown had been saved, the cost of victory was paid for by the Army with reductions in the size of the standing force. Amongst other measures, all but six of the 13 newly raised Dragoon regiments were disbanded.

IRELAND

Escape from their first brush with defence cuts was achieved by both Regiments joining the Irish Establishment. Wynne's arrived there in June 1717 and Bowles' in October 1718. Money and politics would dictate that they would remain there for the bulk of the century. Financially, the lower pay and greater number of barracks made Ireland a sensible place to send troops, especially mounted soldiers, where forage was a fraction of that in England. As a result, four of the eight regiments of horse and six of the 14 regiments of dragoons were stationed there from 1720 onwards. Politically, their presence not only kept a lid on the frustrations of the populace but also reduced the size of the standing army in England, about which there was a natural suspicion. The Government was able to keep large forces a short distance away but out of the public eye.

The Irish Establishment was a semi-independent organisation, with its own Commander-in-Chief and War Office, the two combining effectively to keep even the limited reforms of the 18th century army on mainland Britain at arm's length. Increasingly, officers and soldiers were of Irish descent, with only the occasional addition from England; the 12th having 16 Irish officers from its total of 18 in 1767, while the Irish soldiers numbered 134 out of 135. These low numbers reflected the requirement to cardreise regiments to keep the total size of the Army below the maximum permitted establishment for Ireland. The 9th Dragoons' returns from 1768 to 1792 never showed more than 25 officers and 200 men, dramatically increasing in 1797 to 31 officers and 699 men when war again threatened.

Soldiering was unrecognisable by today's standards. The standing army was in essence a police force used on duties such as riot control and anti-smuggling operations. It was kept as small as possible and only augmented by additional troops when danger threatened, at which point trustworthy individuals, such as Wynne or Bowles,

1 **A PRIVATE OF BRIGADIER PHINEAS BOWLES' REGIMENT OF DRAGOONS** (LATER THE 12TH LANCERS) IN 1715. DRAGOONS CARRIED BOTH A SWORD AND A MUSKET FOR MOUNTED AND DISMOUNTED ACTION.

2 **COLONEL BROWN'S DRAGOONS** (LATER 9TH LANCERS) IN 1742. THE REGIMENTS WERE ON THE IRISH ESTABLISHMENT FOR MUCH OF THE 18TH CENTURY WHERE COSTS TO THE STATE WERE CHEAPER.

A 9TH DRAGOON OF 1752. THE REGIMENTS HAD CEASED TO BE CALLED BY THEIR COLONELS' NAMES IN THE PREVIOUS YEAR.

would be contacted. Recruiting was largely a matter of personal contacts. While the Colonel was often assisted by an agent to help find officers, friends or previous colleagues were usually selected as captains who would, in their turn, select their friends as the subalterns. No formal leadership training was deemed necessary, so long as they could be assumed to be gentlemen, their trade being learnt from their peer group. While such a self-selecting process might appear at best elitist to the modern mind, to a country with a constant fear of a standing army such a concentration of power in the hands of its upper echelons had its attractions. As argued Henry Pelham in 1744, '*our liberties are in no danger from our standing army because it is commanded by men of the best families and fortunes*'.[2]

To the junior officers fell the task of finding private soldiers, the normal procedure being to turn to their tenants or those of their family to provide. Failing this, recruiting parties would be sent out to cajole, coax – or simply con – likely volunteers. W C Sydney stated that '*by lies they lured them, by liquor they tempted them, and when they were dead drunk they forced a shilling into their fists*'.[3] Even then, at moments where demand outstripped supply and recruits could not be found at the official rate (the Colonel was given 'levy money' for every soldier enlisted), the costs of raising troops could be expensive. Cornet Lewis Folliott of Wynne's Dragoons complained in September 1715 that, of the 33 men he had enlisted, six had deserted on arrival, leaving him with expenses of £47 for which he received £35 of levy money. Despite these apparent disincentives, filling the ranks does not appear to have been a problem and high physical standards could be set, soldiers in the 9th in 1765 averaging five feet nine inches, while the 12th's recruiting instructions stated that they should be '*light and straight made (by no means gummy) broad shoulders, long thighs, a good face, and every way well made. No man to be enlisted who cannot wear his hair or who has the least defect….all recruits are [to be] examined by a knowing surgeon.*'[4] Reflecting these criteria, the familiarity with horses and the physical state of the urban poor, most of the recruits came from the countryside.

Finding officers keen to join was also relatively easy. A young gentlemen parted with £500 to buy a cornetcy (equivalent to about £70,000 today), with a further £100 a year required to keep him in his new profession. The willingness to part with these sort of sums indicated not only the position in society that membership of a 'crack' cavalry regiment conferred but also the slowly increasingly esteem with which the army was held after the low points of the earlier century.

New recruits were issued on arrival with a plethora of kit for both themselves and their horses, most of which would be paid for from money that they were owed, and basic training could now begin. Consisting largely of formal drill movements and the basics of weapon handling (in particular the carbine), rules covered almost everything including posture, the Standing Orders of the 12th requiring soldiers '*to walk in that light, airy manner (but with a firm and lengthy step) which should distinguish the soldier from the awkward, Sheepish Clown*'.[5] The orders to draw a pistol involved six long-winded words of command. Daily routine revolved around stable duties that, while repetitive, were predictable and not overly demanding, and which were eased by the horses being out to grass for up to six months of the year. Leave could be taken as a privilege after completion of a year of service, the last six months without having been 'crimed'. While desertion was commonplace, the average age of the two Regiments increased throughout the 18th century, indicating that many were happy to remain, becoming Non-Commissioned Officers and Quartermasters (the rough equivalent of the current Warrant Officer) in time.

Management of the Regiments consisted largely of institutionalised fraud at all levels. While war might produce rewards of prize money and plunder for the Colonel, in peace his pickings had to be found by cheating the system, or the men, or both; a system connived at by the state which, in order to hide the true cost of keeping a standing army, shifted much of the responsibility onto the Colonels' shoulders, making them proprietors of their regiments. Charged therefore with producing

military capability, those who had purchased their commissions and had invested in their regiments expected a return. The regiment became a personal profit-making exercise in which the Colonel acted as an absentee landlord, with the day-to-day running and training of the troops left to his Lieutenant Colonel as managing director; the financial affairs devolved to the Colonel's agent, a civilian servant of the Colonel who acted as a clerk and go-between with the Government.

To produce a healthy return on his investment, the Colonel could extract revenue in a number of ways. The lack of checks on money provided for the purchase of arms, equipment and uniforms allowed contractors to produce shoddy goods cheaply, leaving the Colonel to take the profit, while false muster rolls, including names of those who had died, allowed claims for non-existent soldiers. In this last practice the authorities connived, reflecting the reality that, without such practices, no regiment could hope to exist. The 'widdows men' and the 'hautbois', mentioned in the orders to raise the Regiments, were non-existent soldiers whose pay was drawn and, in the former case, put into a pension fund for wives of officers who might die in war; in the latter it would go into the regimental administrative fund.

If the Colonel was taking his share, then so too were the rest of the officers, who were effectively partners in a joint enterprise. By paying for their commission and every subsequent promotion, they made a commitment from which it was folly to retire while a living could still be made. One officer of the 12th served for 36 years without rising higher than captain, while another spent 14 years as a cornet and a similar period as a lieutenant. An officer's pay acted as little more than a retainer that would not keep them in peacetime, as, like their soldiers, deductions removed most of their official income.

Pay was subject to more highly dubious practices that started at the highest levels, the Paymaster General even taking one shilling of every pound earned as a sort of transaction fee. All ranks lost large amounts through enforced deductions, while the annual payment of arrears was seldom prompt or in cash. Soldiers' pay, like officers', was reduced by a subsistence element that was taken at source

DRAGOONS

The establishment of a regular army by the Parliamentarians during the Civil War formalised the roles and equipment of the Regiments of horse and dragoons (from the French *dragon* for a short musket or carbine), the latter originally being no more than mounted infantry. To distinguish them in their role, dragoons wore the infantry colour of red (though with the facings of their tunics in their colonel's colours) until 1782 when light dragoon regiments changed to blue and a lighter boot than the longer, heavy jacked boots of the horse regiments. By the time of the regiments' formation in 1715, the distinction in role between horse and dragoon regiments was beginning to reduce and dragoons used the terminology of the cavalry (troops rather than companies, cornets not ensigns), though they continued to wear no armour.

The first role assigned to dragoons had been to seize defiles or secure flanks, dismounting once in position to then fight on foot (as Wynne's Dragoons had done at Preston), using their principal weapon of the carbine and bayonet. This developed into a wider use to provide a screen forward of the main body or to disrupt or delay the enemy, shaping them for subsequent engagement by heavier forces. By the second half of the 18th century, the value of light cavalry had been recognised and both regiments became Light Dragoons, though in reality neither equipment nor role changed significantly and they continued to have to prepare to charge and fight mounted and so carried a sword, as well as conducting raids and patrols. They were, therefore, a particularly hard-worked arm. Although distinctions between heavy and light cavalry continued both in dress and the size of horse they used, by 1844 Queen's Regulations admitted their capabilities should be the same: 'the number of Cavalry being small in reference to the Amount of Force annually voted by Parliament, it is of the utmost importance…that both the Heavy and Light Cavalry should be equal to the Charge in Line, as well as to the Duties on Out-Posts.' [16]

In the social pecking order both in Britain and elsewhere, while anything on a horse was considered superior to the infantry, 'heavy cavalry', a term now regarded as a slight, was considered more prestigious than being a dragoon, the logic being that, with their armoured chests and helmets, they were a more direct link to armoured knights of the Middle Ages. One thing was for certain however, and that was either was better than being a hussar – a term derived from the Hungarian *huzar*, itself derived from a word meaning a pirate, leading one French officer to remark that 'hussars are little more than bandits on horseback.'[17]

A 12TH DRAGOON OF 1742. DRAGOONS CONTINUED TO WEAR RED COATS (THE INFANTRY COLOUR) UNTIL 1782 AND ALWAYS CARRIED A MUSKET OR CARBINE.

A 12TH LIGHT DRAGOON OF 1778 FIGHTING AN IRISH REBEL. THE 12TH HAD BEEN RE-TITLED LIGHT DRAGOONS IN 1768 ALTHOUGH THERE WAS LITTLE DIFFERENCE IN EITHER TRAINING OR EQUIPMENT. THE 9TH WERE RE-STYLED LIGHT DRAGOONS IN 1783.

to pay for billeting, food and for the upkeep of his horse. Throughout the 18th century, it accounted for about 1 shilling 2d out of his 1 shilling 6d pay. The remaining 4d, known as 'gross off reckonings', were due to be paid at the end of the year in much the same way as the officers' arrears. These should have come to about £6 a year but, after various deductions by the Paymaster General and others for miscellaneous 'donations', the result was closer to £4 10 shillings. All off reckonings were then paid to the Colonel, who should then have issued them to the men after payments for uniforms, arms and equipments had been settled. Needless to say, as there were no fixed costs for these items, further abuse was possible with the result that a soldier, at the year's end, might see nothing in his hand at all.

'I found this Regt very good, both men and horse.. under good discipline, performing their Exercise both on foot and horse back perfectly well.'

The shortage of barracks required most soldiers to be accommodated in dispersed billets in isolated troop locations, which, either as a punishment or a deterrent, were often taken at no payment to the understandably reluctant hosts and with little attempt not to abuse their hospitality, especially if there to keep the peace. '*The paradise has in all ages been free quarters – to live in somebody else's house, to call for the best, to have plenty of meat to eat and wine to drink and coal to give warmth, to make the owner perform the office of a servant or at best an inn-keeper; to eat, to drink, to sleep, to make love and to have nothing to pay; to be utterly free from all cares, to be under no necessity to take thought for the morrow what he shall eat and what he shall drink, and wherewithal he shall be clothed; to enjoy the sweetness of stolen goods without any fear of the penalties – this is the meaning of free quarters to soldiers, his summum bonum of military bliss.*'[6]

Although cheap and a preventative against mutiny, the dispersion brought about by the billeting policy – in 1725 the 9th were spread over an area 45 miles by 50 – resulted in few opportunities for anything other than low-level training, the exception being the annual inspection by a visiting general – '*a vital element in creating an atmosphere of gentlemanly competition between individual units*'.[7] To prepare for this review, officers and men would come together for about two months, though, with friends meeting for the first time in many months, the atmosphere more closely resembled a reunion than a serious piece of military training: '*the morning was usually devoted to rehearsals for the review, and all the rest of the day to more interesting matters, such as concerts, private theatrical performances, balls, dinners, suppers, drinking and wenching.*'[8] Perhaps inevitably the reports indicate a varied level of performance. One of the earliest, from 1725, comments of the 9th: '*I found this Regt. very good, both men and horse.. under good discipline, performing their Exercise both on foot and horse back perfectly well. I heard no complaints and found the men regularly paid and Cleared pursuant to ye last order.*'[9] While the 12th's report of the same year stated: '*That men and horses are good, well disciplined, performing their Exercise well. Their accoutrements good, their arms bad. The non-commissioned officers and private men are regularly paid. I heard no complaints. They have no tents or camp necessaries.*'[10] Others were less complimentary, the 9th's of 1772 recording that manoeuvres had been performed 'indifferently' and the 12th's of 1769 seemed amazed that they were 'surprisingly steady and attentive'.

A low standard of training was by no means exceptional and reflected the requirements of the nature of warfare at the time, as well as the

Government's abiding fear of a well-prepared standing army and the desire to invest as little as possible in it. In operational terms, the military's tasks at home, in the absence of a police force, were almost exclusively to quell disorder and enforce the revenue laws and this produced an attitude to soldiering that is reflected in the attendance rates, with up to two-thirds of officers on leave or extended absence at any one time, leaving one at regimental headquarters and perhaps one or two at each of the six troops. The Commander-in-Chief's inspection of 1724 only managing to induce six of the 27 Colonels to appear. Government attempts to check on the efficiency of the army and levels of abuse were, at best, weak, with only six, part-time commissaries for all of England, Wales and Scotland. If action was required, then Ireland was not the place for it, and while volunteers did serve abroad, there was already a tradition growing of off-loading the weak elsewhere, an order for Flanders in 1744 requiring that '*No man to be drafted either as a Volunteer or otherwise who is lame, bursten, or disqualified for His Majesty's Service. Nor any horses which are disqualified for the Service, nor above the Age of Nine Years last Grass.*'

Discipline was not helped by the poor accommodation, absentee officers and a stagnating routine. There were some notable lapses, a troop of the 9th based in Rathdowney in 1770 killing several members of the village in a quarrel over supply prices, which led to the cashiering of the troop officers. Continuing what was an unhappy period for the 9th, five years later the Adjutant was himself court-martialled for behaving disrespectfully to the Commanding Officer but given a light punishment as the Lord-Lieutenant, when referring the case to the King for decision, found that the Commanding Officer had himself been guilty of dereliction of duty and deserved punishment. Needless to say the Annual Report for that year found the Regiment '*in extremely bad order and very unfit for service*',[11] a recommendation following that they should be converted to Light Dragoons on account of low efficiency. Despite these lapses, later records indicate that discipline in all of the light cavalry regiments was less dependent on the threat of punishment than elsewhere, with soldiers treated with a greater degree of respect by those in command.

Quite possibly contributing to the lapses in discipline were the duties that the Regiments were called on to perform. Primarily present as an internal security force, these involved police duties, revenue collection, anti-smuggling duties and 'still-hunting', this final task involving the seeking out and destruction of the various illegal distilleries across the country.

Away from the purely military, a decision was taken to number regiments that, until this time had been known by the name of their Colonel. The Royal Warrant of 1st July 1751 establishing the 9th Dragoons from the Regiment founded by Wynne and the 12th Dragoons from Bowles' Regiment, while for the first time regulating their clothing, standards and colours. Further change followed in 1768 when the 12th, as a result of lobbying of the King by the Colonel of the time, were restyled the 12th or Prince of Wales's Regiment, adopting several familiar devices to reflect the connection, including the motifs of the three ostrich feathers, the rising sun, the Red Dragon and the motto 'Ich Dien'.

THE DUKE OF WELLINGTON, THEN THE HONOURABLE ARTHUR WELLESLEY, SERVED AS A LIEUTENANT IN THE 12TH LIGHT DRAGOONS FROM 1789-1791 BEFORE PURCHASING HIS CAPTAINCY IN AN INFANTRY REGIMENT.

Coinciding with this change in nomenclature came the decision to become a Regiment of light dragoons, the initiative probably coming from the Commanding Officer of the time, Lieutenant Colonel Burton, who petitioned that '*a Regiment of Light Cavalry…will be of particular advantage…in marching with much greater celerity than Heavy Dragoons from one part of the kingdom to the other, in case of invasion, and which appears… will be very advantageous to His Majesty's Service and of particular utility to the Kingdom of Ireland.*'[12] The thinking behind the change was not entirely new, the Duke of Kingston having earlier raised such a regiment '*upon an entire new plan, to imitate the Hussars in foreign service, to act regularly or irregularly, as occasion required, without adhering to the strict rules of the heavy horse, but to co-operate with them*'.[13]

Conversion of the 9th followed in 1783, though, as with the 12th, it proved to be in name only, the desire being largely to reduce costs rather than overcome the military limitations of the slower, more ponderous heavy regiments. Although dress was slightly altered and a lighter saddle introduced, the basket-hilted sabre and flintlock pistols remained, while the heavy infantry musket was replaced by a carbine: '*a weapon which exerted a greater moral than physical effect and which, when the length of the*

barrel was reduced from 21 to 15 inches, was as near useless as any fire-arm has a right to be.'[14] More significantly, no doctrine or training for the new role, particularly scouting and reconnaissance, was received and it was not until 1778 that a book by a Captain Hinde titled *Discipline of the Light Horse* appeared, giving instructions such as, *'Care should be taken to post officers to the Light Troops who are distinguished for activity and address, and above all by a spirit of enterprise…The spirit of this corps should be always to try, by which great things can only be achieved.'*[15]

Hinde's book was perhaps an indication of the increasing interest being shown at all levels by the end of the century. As unsuccessful campaigns in America and against France galvanised change, the Duke of York, who assumed the role of Commander-in-Chief from 1795, adding extra weight to the undercurrents already set in motion. Administration in particular was tightened up as a result of a Board of Generals in 1796 that did much to improve, train and regulate the cavalry. Regimental Paymasters replaced the Colonel's agent to try to reduce fraud, while vets, armourers and saddlers were also established, though the provision of clothing and uniform remained with the Colonel (and could still produce a profit), a problem partially offset by an increase in pay for soldiers in 1797 and the earlier abolition of many of the deductions from source.

The Board's purely military recommendations advocated a lighter horse and adopted a uniform pattern of sword for light dragoons (a curved, flat-bladed pattern, better for cutting than thrusting and said to have been based on a 9th Light Dragoon design), complemented by the newly introduced 'Instructions for the Formations and Movements of the Cavalry' in June 1796, setting out in considerable detail the doctrine for every eventuality, from the march to the charge. Improvements in theory were slow to turn into practice, with training remaining unsatisfactory at anything but the lowest levels, resulting in an army in Ireland that was described by Lieutenant General Sir Ralph Abercromby, when he assumed command in 1797, as *'in a state of licentiousness rendering it formidable to everyone but the enemy'*. The British cavalry remained less effective than their Continental counterparts and there was much to learn before they would become true light cavalry, *'with their eyes and ears always open and their horses always fit, cunning as foxes in the matter of ground, enterprising and with no lack of dash upon occasion; as handy on foot as in the saddle, terrible in the charge and cunning and handy with firearms'*.

GUIDONS

From 1715–1743 guidons were designed by the Colonel of the Regiment to reflect his personal taste, with the 1st or Colonel's troop having his coat of arms, crest or other device in the centre, with the colour that of his livery. In 1743 the first 'true' guidon had been introduced, made of the King's crimson silk, with the crown, rose and thistle in the centre beneath 'Dieu et mon droit', and in 1751 Colonels were prohibited from placing their own coat of arms on their guidons. Troop guidons were carried by a junior officer and were originally called standards.

Guidons were not carried during the Peninsular War, and even before this their use would have been largely restricted as dragoons, acting independently over large distances, would have had little requirement for a line to rally to in battle. Guidons seemed to have ceased being carried by either Regiment following their conversion to the lance in 1816. The lance pennon originated from the personal banner of a Polish nobleman carried on his lance, which would have negated the need for a separate colour.

Although there are reports of sergeant-majors carrying them in 1822, in 1834 standards and guidons were abolished for all but the Household Cavalry, regiments of Dragoon Guards and three regiments of Dragoons. Guidons were finally carried again in 1958 by the 12th and the 9th in 1960, having been authorised for regiments of hussars and lancers only a short time before.

THE FIRST OR KING'S GUIDON OF THE 9TH DRAGOONS FROM ABOUT 1751.

THE GUIDON OF THE 9TH/12TH ROYAL LANCERS PRESENTED TO THE REGIMENT BY HM QUEEN ELIZABETH THE QUEEN MOTHER IN JULY 2000.

WAR WITH FRANCE
1792–1811

Egypt

REVOLUTION IN FRANCE IN 1792 proved the catalyst that brought both Regiments out of their near-suspended animation in Ireland and caught them up in a struggle to deal with a country that, having rid itself of its monarchy, emerged first as a rampant republican state and then an acquisitive empire, threatening Britain's institutions to a far greater degree than the previous regime. The Regiments' employment reflected Britain's strategic dilemma of the time. Although clear in the requirement for a powerful navy and an army strong enough to protect both the homeland and an already far-flung empire, there remained a reluctance to engage on the Continent on a scale comparable to the other great powers. Sir John Moore was told in 1808 that his 32,000-strong army for the Peninsula was *'not merely a considerable part of the disposable force of this country. It is, in fact, the British army'.*[1]

To add to the troop shortages, incompetence and a lack of clear priorities resulted in a series of apparently unrelated campaigns that too often ended in ignominy. Tactically, recent wars in India, Canada, Europe and the West Indies had provided Britain's military with some experienced field commanders and a degree of self-confidence, but any advantage this brought was largely undone by a confused command structure and the organisation of defence at the time. Up to five departments were needed to launch a single operation and this resulted in a plethora of competing strategies while resources were insufficient for even one. As George III commented *'the misfortune of our situation is that we have too many things to attend to and our force must consequently be too weak at every place'.* Only with the decision to invest in the Peninsula would Britain finally produce a coherent strategy for dealing with France but, until their commitment there in 1811, the 9th and 12th Light Dragoons were to find themselves involved in a very mixed bag of far-flung military adventures; the 9th, in particular, suffering in two of the worst.

CORSICA AND ITALY

The 12th Light Dragoons were to be the first of the two Regiments to venture away from Britain. Of four entirely unconnected campaigns launched against France in 1793 (the others included expeditions to Belgium where the 'Grand Old' Duke of York was losing an army; to the West Indies, and finally to mainland France to help Royalists), the 12th found themselves sent to reinforce Admiral Hood at Toulon in southern France, where he had initially secured the port as a British base in the Mediterranean. Although their last report in Ireland described them as *'a remarkably even and good Body of Men… but not well on horseback. By the system now established for the Management and Discipline of this Regiment it is likely soon to be in perfect Order'*, such perfection was to be of little immediate use. By the time of their arrival in the Mediterranean in late 1793, Toulon had already been lost and Hood's attentions had switched to securing Corsica. The subsequent campaign, waged in support of the island's anti-French nationalist party and with the intent of providing Britain with a naval base, is chiefly remembered for costing Nelson his eye during the siege of Calvi. The 12th's part in it was distinctly limited, with only one squadron landed in 1794 as the rest of the Regiment continued on to Italy. Even a single

A 12TH LIGHT DRAGOON OF 1806 WEARING THE UNIFORM, INCLUDING A TARLETON HELMET, WORN BETWEEN 1788 AND 1812.

squadron of cavalry can have been little more than a hindrance on the rocky, barren island where it was present at, but unable to contribute materially to the capture of the port of Bastia.

The rest of the Regiment had sailed straight to the port of Civita Vecchia near Rome to help protect the Papal States against the French. Here the conduct of the 12th in unknown and unspecified military activity appeared to have earned widespread praise, even coming to the attention of the Vatican. The Secretary of State to Pope Pius VI wrote before they left at the end of 1794: '*The marked consideration which the Holy Father has always entertained, and never will cease to entertain, for the generous and illustrious English nation, induces him not to neglect the opportunity of giving proof of it which is now attended by the stay of a British Regiment at Civita Vecchia. As His Holiness cannot but applaud the regular and trustworthy conduct of the Troops in question, he has determined to evince his entire satisfaction by presenting a gold medal to each of the officers.....and since these medals, twelve in number, are not at the present moment, in readiness, nor can be provided before the departure of the regiment from Civita Vecchia, the Holy Father will be careful that they shall be sent, as soon as possible to Sir John Cox Hippesly, who will be pleased to transmit them to the respective officers, making them acquainted, at the same time... with the feelings by which His Holiness is animated, and with the lively desire which he entertains of manifesting, on all occasions, his unalterable regard, whether it be towards the nation in general, or towards every individual Englishman...*'

From Italy, the 12th travelled back to Britain in January 1795, moving from Tavistock to Nottingham a year later where, together with a yeomanry regiment, they helped put down a food riot, for which they were awarded the freedom of the city. In the same year, a Board of General Officers looked into the deficiencies that had been revealed in recent campaigns and, although making changes in uniform, saddlery, weaponry, sword drill and horses, shied away from the wholesale reforms that might have undermined the Colonels' profits or improved training. Light cavalry continued to ignore the basics such as scouting and dismounted work, leaving them unable to do anything other than simply charge, while lacking sufficient discipline to form efficiently for it or reform after it.

THE REGIMENTAL HYMNS

Three officers were given an audience with Pope Pius VI at the Vatican in 1793. Northcote's painting depicts a helmet being placed on Captain Browne's head, while the Pope prayed 'that Heaven would enable the cause of Truth and religion to triumph over injustice and infidelity'. For the officers present, the blessing appears to have been beneficial, for they all ended their careers as generals. The picture also shows the officers wearing the medals presented by the Pope, although the letter sent to the Regiment at the time states that these were not yet ready and would be sent later.

It is said that on the same occasion the Pope presented the Regimental Hymns, comprising The Sicilian Vespers, Spanish Chant and the Russian Hymn, though an alternative tale suggests that they were a quixotic punishment from the Duke of Wellington at the end of Peninsular campaign in 1813 or 1814 for raiding a nunnery after crossing from Spain into France. Both stories appear unlikely to be true as at the time of both incidents the 12th were without a band, which was only reformed at Ponsonby's request after Waterloo and even then was only reluctantly agreed to by the Colonel of the Regiment. The nunnery incident appears to have gained some notoriety, even only as gossip, John Vandeleur writing from Spain that 'your correspondent who told you a story about nuns is rather partial to drawing the long bow' and no mention is made of a punishment. Whatever the origin, all three of the hymns were played regularly until the demise of the Regimental Band, though the Russian Hymn, played to the tune of the Imperial Russian National Anthem, was suspended during the Crimea.

THE PRESENTATION OF THREE OFFICERS OF THE 12TH LIGHT DRAGOONS TO POPE PIUS VI IN 1793 FOLLOWING THE REGIMENT'S SERVICE IN THE PAPAL STATES TO PROTECT THEM FROM THE FRENCH. EACH RECEIVED A PAPAL MEDAL AND A BLESSING AND ALL WENT ON TO BECOME GENERALS.

DEFENCE OF LISBON

In Europe, the decision by Spain to enter the war on France's side forced the evacuation of all British ground forces in the Mediterranean and left Lisbon, which was vital to the maintenance of the blockade of Cadiz, vulnerable to attack. To assist with its security, three regiments of infantry and the 12th Light Dragoons were despatched from Britain, fewer than 2,000 men arriving in June 1797. The quality of the force clearly failed to impress their plain-speaking commander General Stuart, who remarked of the infantry battalions, '*I never in the course of my service saw two regiments so disgraceful to the British name as Roll and Dillon,*' before continuing to offer the Secretary of State for War his own views of his orders: '*I am determined to be guided by your instructions so long as they are in the reach of my comprehension*'. Stuart's difficulties were compounded by the demands of multi-nationality and the requirement to serve under three independent Portuguese Commanders-in-Chief, while lamenting the 12th's contribution, which arrived with 85 soldiers and 114 horses down on their return of 600 men and '*risks them being annihilated in the course of one campaign*'.[2]

Although the defence was rapidly organised and training completed, the threat to Lisbon never materialised, constant patrolling forming the 12th's principal occupation for the four years they remained in Portugal. Almost inevitably the most noteworthy incident, '*a trifling disturbance that might give some cause for uneasiness to His Majesty's Ministers,*' filled the newspapers. In this, a bar-room brawl clearly erupted into a first-class fight between members of the Regiment and their Portuguese allies, the subsequent investigation attaching no blame to the British side, perhaps a result of its being conducted by Brigadier General James St Clair Erskine of the 12th Light Dragoons. More extraordinarily, the officers and NCOs of the regiment raised money to donate to their own government for the prosecution of the war against France, the former collecting over £300, the latter offering seven days' pay. The time in Portugal nevertheless served to raise professional standards, the Prince of Brazil finding much to admire in 1798, while Stuart's successor, General Frazer noted in 1801 that: '*no Corps can be fitter for service, no Dragoons more masters of their Horses...they do credit to Colonel Archdale's close attention and assiduity,*'[3] a compliment that would soon be tested in Egypt.

IRISH REBELLION 1798

While the 12th had been abroad opposing French aspirations, the 9th Light Dragoons, who had remained in Ireland, found themselves in an increasingly unstable situation. As a result of the war with France, the garrison in Ireland had been reduced from 15,000 to 5,000, offering the Catholic majority an opportunity to address their grievances directly, ideally timed to coincide with an invasion.

THE 9TH LIGHT DRAGOONS WERE HEAVILY INVOLVED IN THE SUPPRESSION OF IRISH REBELLION OF 1798, WHICH WAS MARKED BY VICIOUS ACTIONS BY BOTH SIDES. THE WORDING ON THE LINTEL OF THE DOOR 'TRUE FRENCH SPIRITS' REFLECTS THE TIMING OF THE REBELLION IN WHICH FRANCE WAS TO HELP.

Despite this latent threat, the 9th remained dispersed in small detachments in billets across much of the county of Leinster, with their centre of mass just to the south-west of Dublin, tasked with looking for weapons and signs of disorder.

When it came, the rebellion of 1798 proved largely ineffective, the principal leaders having been arrested and Ulster all but disarmed. Momentum was achieved in the south-eastern counties however, where its outbreak caught most of the Army by surprise with many detachments attacked. In one well-documented instance, a troop of 30 9th Light Dragoons and 10 militia based in eight houses throughout Ballymore Eustace were assaulted at one in the morning on the 24th May when the rebels burst in on the sleeping troops. A mixture of bravery, good fortune and rebel incompetence only just managed to save the day, as a house was turned into a defended position. It survived for two hours before a counter-attack routed the rebels, though not before seven troopers had died at a reported cost to the rebels of 100 of their 800 strong force.

Similar engagements took place elsewhere, including a more traditional cavalry action in which a troop of 40 from the 9th, part of a larger force based at Naas, was ordered to conduct a head-on charge against a rebel position across a road. The troop's frontage limited to six abreast by the fences and dykes either side of the narrow road. Leading the charge, Captain Erskine declared that *'neither he nor his men would breakfast till they had breakfasted on the Croppies'* but on three occasions they were beaten back, Erskine dying on the fourth attempt, *'thrust through with a pike…cutting furiously with his sabre at the staff of the weapon imbedded in his body'*. The action had cost the troop nine dead and seven wounded, though the rebel follow up was in its turn defeated, which allowed the survivors to launch their own pursuit.

The main body of the 9th secured the town of Carlow where it was stationed in barracks. Their defensive duties were made easier by the rebels' bad luck and ill-discipline, which alerted the garrison to their attack. The rebels were ambushed as they entered the town, the survivors fleeing into buildings which caught light, killing most of them. Several hundred died in the fighting in Carlow and 200 more were captured, tried by drumhead court-martial and then hanged or shot. Such severity typified the actions of both sides and little credit reflected anywhere. The murder of Quartermaster King of the 9th, an old man of 70, who was captured and then shot out of hand, helped to fuel the reprisals that followed.

Further south in Wexford, four large columns of rebels achieved varying degrees of success. In one assault, reportedly numbering 30,000 men, the New Ross garrison of 1,200 soldiers, including a troop from the 9th, managed to hold the rebels in fierce fighting before the attackers eventually lost heart and many returned to their homes. The arrival of strong reinforcements in the south left the rebels little room to manoeuvre, while those that were left were harried around the country in a series of engagements in which the 9th played their part. The rout at Kilcomney on 29th June effectively ended the military threat posed by the rebellion.

Although other smaller disturbances continued, including a landing by the French, these failed to take hold and by the end of 1798 an uneasy peace existed, leaving the 9th to reflect on the campaign. Not only had the bitterness of another civil war been at hand but, from a military standpoint, they had had little to boast of. The country and the narrow roads offered few opportunities for consolidated action and left them largely operating against beaten and fleeing enemies. In the longer term, both Regiments were profoundly affected by the rebellion which ushered in the Act of Union in 1800. This created a single parliament for both countries and ended the separate military establishment in Ireland, of which both Regiments had been so long a part.

EGYPT

The 12th's stay in Portugal, where they had been stationed since 1797, was ended by the decision to eject the French forces that had been left in Egypt under the command of General Menou since the destruction of the French fleet at the Battle of the Nile in 1798. The plan saw simultaneous assaults by a large Turkish army through Palestine and two British landings, one on the Red Sea coast and the other near Alexandria, which would then advance on Cairo. The Regiment would form part of Sir Ralph Abercromby's army, which they joined in February 1801 at a staging area in the Bay of Marmorice. The expedition gave every appearance of being ill-fated. Illness had already reduced the 17,000-strong army by 1,500, whereas optimistic assessments of the enemy strength put them at 12,000 rather than a more accurate 18,000. British difficulties were compounded by the inability of the fleet to launch more than 6,000 men at any one time, while on land matters would not be much better, with little transport to be had and water apparently only available from the ships.

Another difficulty lay in the Turkish allies, or lack of them, who should have joined the expedition at this point. Their absence was especially felt by the 12th, which represented a large part of the 1,100 cavalry on the expedition who were relying, for over two-thirds of their mounts, on Turkish resources. Those horses that had been brought from Portugal, though the best available, were in poor condition after their journey and, though local purchase produced an extra 300, these were found to be so unsatisfactory that the Regiment declined them, generously offering them to the Gunners instead. When the Commanding Officer asked to fight on foot, the offer was rejected and another 300 horses were found from across the Army, though by the time the fleet left the Bay for the invasion itself, the total cavalry force mustered 51 officers and 1,055 men but only 320 horses. The 12th found 28 officers, 527 men and 128 horses. the troops had been brought ashore and a patrol of 20 men from the 12th despatched to the Rosetta ferry to the east while, for the next four days, the force offloaded supplies, rested and carried out reconnaissance, the results of which were unexpected: '*we discovered a general error. We landed in Egypt expecting to find a country without woods or heights and were deceived. Between Aboukir and the entrenched camp outside Alexandria are innumerable palm woods and sandhills and our enemy knew well their advantage.*'[5]

THE BATTLE OF ALEXANDRIA ON THE 21ST MARCH 1801. AFTER A SUCCESSFUL AMPHIBIOUS LANDING THIS VICTORY, IN WHICH THE 12TH LIGHT DRAGOONS WERE EMPLOYED AGAINST THE FRENCH CAVALRY AND CAMEL CORPS, EFFECTIVELY SEALED THE FATE OF THE FRENCH FORCES IN EQYPT. IT REPRESENTED ONE OF THE FEW SUCCESSES OF THIS STAGE OF THE WAR AGAINST FRANCE (NAM).

'We landed in Egypt expecting to find a country without woods or heights and were deceived.'

Storms prevented surprise as the fleet, having arrived off Alexandria on 1st March, could not land until the 8th, and then on the eastern side of the Aboukir peninsula. The value of the rehearsals on the beaches of the Bay of Marmorice was proved in the landings, which proceeded without a hitch, the infantry beating off determined French opposition and quickly securing a beach-head. Lieutenant Caton of the 12th recalled: '*at ten minutes after ten the first boats touched the shore; at half past ten the enemy were driven from the hills in every direction and our own troops formed upon them.*'[4] By nightfall, all

The French had by now taken up a position along the heights between the bay and Alexandria, with Roman Camp the key to their line on the left edge of the high ground. Although Abercromby's attack on 13th March was initially successful and took Roman Camp, he proved unable to get around the French flank. In the battle the 12th were limited to supporting the advance guard when French cavalry threatened, successfully deterring their attack and remaining in that role throughout the day. Suffering their first casualties of the campaign, they also discovered the tricks that the land could

ON 17TH MAY 1801 LIEUTENANT COLONEL BROWNE MANAGED TO BLUFF A MUCH LARGER FRENCH FORCE, WHICH INCLUDED A DROMEDARY CAMEL CORPS, CAPTURING 600 MEN AND 500 CAMELS AS A RESULT.

play – a small force ordered to pursue some Arabs into some water discovering after a chase of five miles that the 'water' was a mirage.

Holding Roman Camp, Abercromby elected to observe the road along which French reinforcements from Cairo had to come, an enemy patrol finally being reported on the 18th March. Colonel Archdale, the Commanding Officer of the 12th, immediately rode out to engage with 80 men. At about three miles distant, Archdale came upon a mixed force of infantry and hussars over twice his party's size, which he immediately attacked. Successfully sending a party of 12 to work around the flank, the main body charged, breaking up the French infantry as they tried to form while the hussars behind fled. This might have been a sensible time to break off the engagement, but a pursuit began which was only abandoned when the freshness of the French horses began to tell. The 12th returned via the scene of their charge, where the impetuousness of their pursuit revealed itself. The French infantry, which had not been dealt with in detail, were found to have reformed into a position along a sand hill from where they poured fire into the returning dragoons, who were unable to react swiftly with exhausted horses. Thirty-three officers and men were either killed, missing or wounded, the last figure including the unfortunate Colonel Archdale, who had to have his arm amputated. Almost as seriously for the poorly equipped cavalry force, 42 horses were also killed or injured.

The imminent arrival in Egypt of the other two forces in the Allied invasion at last forced the French to attempt a concerted effort to dislodge the landing and an attack was launched on 21st March. In the subsequent battle, a feint by the enemy cavalry and camel corps, against which the 12th were employed, failed to distract attention from the main enemy infantry assault, which was successfully repulsed. Although the British victory at the Battle of Alexandria proved that the hitherto invincible French columns could be beaten, the gloss was taken off the day by the death of Abercromby.

Bolstered by 4,000 Turks, the new commander, General Hutchinson, left the French garrison in Alexandria and prepared to advance on Cairo. In the meantime the 12th, two regiments of infantry and some Turks were sent to help take control of the mouth of the Nile, the fort at Rosetta falling in early April without a shot being fired after a three-day siege. Moving south, on 9th May they rejoined Hutchinson and his army near Ramanieh to follow the French withdrawal to Cairo. By now cracks in the enemy's morale were beginning to show, 30 men from the 12th capturing 40 French dragoons and an ADC without a fight in an earlier skirmish. Despite these successes, the advance along the Nile continued in conditions that Lieutenant Caton remembered were far from ideal: *'at all times we slept in our cloaks in the sands, over-run with scorpions, centipedes, tarantulas, and a thousand other noxious reptiles, never without our clothes except to change, nor any other bed than a rough mat…What we most regret is the want of wine or spirits; I can speak positively for ourselves and believe the want pretty general'.*

On 17th May, the 12th, on the right flank of the army, were informed by a Bedouin of a French convoy in the desert nearby. This intelligence led to the despatch of a brigade, together with the 12th and 26th Light Dragoons, with orders to intercept them. By now, Lieutenant Colonel Browne, the Regiment's new Commanding Officer, had already acted, sending out a scouting party to find and track the enemy, while giving the rest of the Regiment and some guns the order to 'stand-to', the two groups being linked by a liaison party to pass information. Having successfully located the enemy, the reconnaissance party was now joined by an officer from Hompesche's Horse, who immediately galloped forward to offer terms of a safe passage to France for the enemy in return for their surrender. The offer was rejected by the French commander who could only see a small British force matched against his 108 dragoons, 200 infantry, two guns and a Dromedary Camel Corps. The lure of a return to France seemed more attractive to the enemy rank and file, especially when Lieutenant Colonel Browne, who had just appeared with more troops, decided to call their bluff: *'I ordered the column to deploy into line and 'form rank entire', extending their distance of troops to as great a front as possible, still advancing. This I conceived might impose on the enemy; and the stratagem, assisted by the deception of the mirage, succeeded.'*[6]

The effect was nearly instantaneous. A French ADC overtook Major Wilson on his return journey to accept the terms, though eagerness quickly turned to anger when the deception was revealed. Only with the arrival of the infantry to add weight to the British cause was a fight prevented and a neat victory secured: *'thus, by a happy manoeuvre we obtained without the loss of a single man the means of transporting the baggage of the army…mounted one hundred and eight more cavalry, then much wanted, and obtained upwards of five hundred baggage camels, besides taking from the enemy's effective fighting strength nearly six hundred men.'*[7]

Finally reaching at Cairo on 21st June with numbers depleted by disease, a short siege ensued before the 13,000-strong French garrison capitulated and on 27th June agreed to evacuate all their troops from Egypt. The garrison in Alexandria still remained to be dealt with and the Army set off north again, resolution coming on the 2nd September when they too surrendered after a more protracted siege.

Alexandria's capture and the conclusion of the campaign marked the end of Napoleon's dream of an Empire in the east, while the highly successful campaign not only proved that the French were not invincible but significantly boosted Britain's

'EGYPT, WITH THE SPHINX' WAS THE FIRST BATTLE HONOUR TO BE GAINED BY EITHER REGIMENT. THE AWARD OF BATTLE HONOURS DID NOT BECOME COMMON PRACTICE UNTIL 1800 AND THIS WAS THE FIRST CAMPAIGN AWARD. EARLIER BATTLE HONOURS WERE 'BACKDATED' FOLLOWING A DECISION IN 1881.

confidence in her army. For the 12th Light Dragoons the final chapter was the award of their first battle honour, only the second to be issued, while 'Egypt, with the Sphinx' was permitted to be used on guidons and standards from its announcement in the Gazette on 6th July 1802, *'as a lasting memorial acquired…by the zeal, discipline and intrepidity of his troops in that arduous and important campaign.'*[8]

SOUTH AMERICA, 1806

Although the Treaty of Amiens in March 1802, which had been signed before the victory in Egypt was known, brought a brief period of peace, hostilities recommenced the following year. Britain again concentrated on the maritime operations that would culminate at Trafalgar, while land forces were largely confined to dealing with the threat of invasion. The 12th, with the exception of two years spent in Ireland from 1803–1805, remained in England after their return from Egypt in 1802, mainly in small detachments along the Kent and Sussex coast, before assuming royal escort duties at Hounslow and Hampton Court in 1808. The 9th joined them from Ireland in 1803 after 86 years of unbroken service, the move coinciding with their finally being equipped as a light dragoon regiment after many years as one in name only. By 1805 the establishment had been raised to the strongest they would ever be. The Regiments numbered a total strength of 49 officers, 114 Warrant Officers and Non-Commissioned Officers and 962 other ranks.

Following two years at Hounslow on royal escort duties, the 9th moved to Thanet in 1806, from where they left later that year as part of an ambitious plan to seize Montevideo and Buenos Aires in South America. The origins of the expedition lay in a largely unauthorised campaign the previous year to secure these Spanish possessions which, while initially successful, had ended in embarrassing failure and surrender. The brief success had, however, raised both political and commercial hopes in Britain, which now sent further forces in support of a wildly ambitious scheme. Four thousand men were stood by to travel to Buenos Aires, to be followed shortly afterwards by a further 5,000 who would land on the west coast of South America to capture Chile. They would between them establish *'a chain of communicating posts between Chile and Buenos Aires'*, a task that would have been daunting for a much larger force and was made near impossible by the mountains that covered the 900 miles between the two countries.

Embarking the manpower of eight of its 10 troops (the horses were left behind as they were expected to be in plentiful and ready supply in South America), the 9th began on the first of several sea voyages in its history that would be dogged by misfortune. Delays prevented their sailing until 12th November 1806, nearly six weeks after the planned date and a month after the rest of the expedition. A slow passage resulted in the Regiment finally joining the expedition in Montevideo harbour on 21st March 1807, three days after one of the few successes of the campaign had captured the town. The campaign now stalled. With no authority to offer protection to the population if they rose against the Spanish, and with an army only large enough to hold onto the gains already made, rather than maintain the momentum to Buenos Aires, little more could be done until

reinforcements arrived. Fortuitously, this happened earlier than planned when the second expedition to Chile was abandoned and its forces were diverted to assist the assault on Buenos Aires.

While preparations were being made for the advance 90 miles along the coast to their objective, the British outposts at Montevideo came under various attacks. The 9th, most of whom were still dismounted, provided six troops to cover a withdrawal to Montevideo while, in a separate incident, two mounted troops were involved in a pursuit. These distractions could not hide the problems facing the cavalry for which it was proving impossible to procure horses, either by purchase or requisition. Those that could be found went to the artillery and transport while the remainder, about 160, were issued to the 17th Light Dragoons with all the other cavalry regiments remaining dismounted. To make matters worse, an order was issued for all remaining horse equipment to be destroyed. In the face of objections that there would be no chance to replace it, to say nothing of the financial loss, a bizarre compromise was reached in which 60 sets of equipment were thrown out but all cavalry soldiers were instructed to carry snaffle bridles.

By the end of June, the assault on Buenos Aires was ready to be launched. A landing 45 miles south-east of the capital would be followed by an approach march across high ground, with the final assault to be accompanied by a naval bombardment. The landing on the 28th June was soon in difficulty as troops struggled to cross the four miles of swampland that stretched from the shore. While the leading forces managed to cross, those behind bogged down in the chewed-up ground, with the wheeled transport and artillery particularly affected – only 11 of the 16 guns made it. Equally disastrously, the pack mules, which were untried, bolted as soon as they were loaded, taking with them much of the baggage and stores, including all but half a day's ration of food and, more seriously for morale, resulting in the destruction of the entire spirit ration, which could no longer be carried.

Buenos Aires was finally reached on 3rd July after a difficult march, the driving rain of the coming wet season accompanying the troops as they moved, as did the Spanish cavalry who maintained constant observation to prevent any element of surprise. An initial skirmish by the advance guard on the outskirts of the city secured the abattoir, the stench staying with the army as it spent an unhappy night there to prepare. The assault would come from the west, the orders apparently oblivious to the fact that this was directly towards the supporting naval gunfire, which they would not be able to see. Broken down piecemeal into 13 half-battalion sized columns which were each given a street to advance down, the dispersion was made worse by the architecture of the city. Flat-roofed houses with high balustrades or parapets made perfect firing points from which defenders could fire down the wide, straight streets, while the grid of the town plan was easily raked by cannon fire.

Four troops of the 9th and the bulk of the 6th Dragoon Guards with an overall strength of 500 men formed one of the central columns with orders to advance towards the Plaza Mayor. Two other troops were held with the 1,100 strong reserve, while the remainder of the Regiment and the rearguard remained on the southern flank of the city. A signal gun sounded the advance at 6.30am on 5th July, with the column formed by the 9th and 6th Dragoons Guards, dismounted and armed with carbines, bayonets and between 30 and 40 rounds per man, moving forward with an artillery piece in support. Conducted in silence as firing had been forbidden and muskets were not loaded, they looked, said a Spanish General, like *'ten thousand sheep come to present their throats to the knife'*.

Few casualties were suffered until the column tried to cross an open square, where they were instantly caught in a crossfire. Despite the heavy losses, further progress for two more blocks was made, but by now the 6th's Commanding Officer and Second in Command were out of action and the attack began to stall. Fresh impetus came from the officer commanding the 9th's leading squadron who renewed the attack down another street before again being checked. Consultation with the 6th's senior surviving officer resulted in withdrawal from their impossible position back to the square, where the rest of the main body of the column, under command of the 9th's Colonel, established a defensive position and began to come under sniper fire. Orders to push on arrived with an ADC but were soon countermanded when he saw the situation, and for the rest of the day and night the column remained fixed in its position. Every attempt to skirt round the enemy ended in failure due to sniper fire, while the lack of equipment to break down doors prevented systematic clearance of the houses.

If this part of the attack had been unsuccessful, the rest was a disaster. Although the extreme

Flat-roofed houses with high balustrades or parapets made perfect firing points from which defenders could fire down…

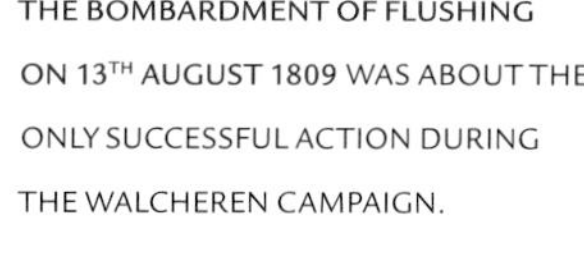
THE BOMBARDMENT OF FLUSHING ON 13TH AUGUST 1809 WAS ABOUT THE ONLY SUCCESSFUL ACTION DURING THE WALCHEREN CAMPAIGN.

northern and southern columns had made some progress, it had been accomplished with heavy losses, while many of the columns in the centre had been surrounded and forced to surrender, or had been destroyed. General Whitelocke, the British commander, who had stayed on the western edge of the town, knew nothing of these debacles and it was only on the following day when a letter from his Spanish opponent outlined the situation to him and offered terms for surrender that his knowledge improved.

By now, the Spanish had over 1,000 prisoners to add to those taken from the previous expedition and they demanded that, in exchange for the release of all the prisoners, the British would withdraw immediately from all Spain's South American territories. General Whitelocke, in no position to refuse, returned to England where he was dismissed, while within six weeks the 9th had also left South America, hurried out with the rest of the army in order to prevent too many desertions. Even now their troubles were not at an end. One transport ship carrying two troops and some of the soldiers' families was dashed onto the rocks at Mounts Bay in Cornwall, with the loss of all the stores and equipment and 29 members of the Regiment, 10 crew and two children.

WALCHEREN CAMPAIGN 1809

Partly as a result of such ill-judged expeditions, by the early summer of 1809 Napoleon's dominance of Europe was near complete, leaving Britain, which had kept a comparatively small army in Portugal since 1808, to continue the fight in conjunction with Spanish nationalists. However, Austria, keen to re-enter the fight, had been calling on the British government to launch an attack that would more directly threaten the heart of the French Empire and draw off French troops. Only two options for such an attack were open. The first lay in western Germany, where there were rumours of an uprising. The second was an amphibious attack in Holland and the naval base at Antwerp, which represented a constant threat to Britain's maritime interests and its coast. After months of dithering, the latter course was chosen, even though by now the Austrians had been knocked out at the Battle of Wagram, thereby removing the rationale for the ultimately disastrous adventure that was to follow.

Forming part of an enormous expeditionary force of 40,000 soldiers, including 2,000 cavalry, the 9th left Hounslow and its King's Messenger and escort duty, while the 12th gave up their coastal protection task in the south of England to embark on the largest armada yet to leave Britain. Despite its size, which, with a similar-sized army in Spain, represented the only occasion on which Britain

A CONTEMPORARY VIEW OF THE DISASTROUS WALCHEREN CAMPAIGN. BOTH REGIMENTS WERE EMBARKED, THOUGH THE 9TH LIGHT DRAGOONS WERE THE ONLY CAVALRY REGIMENT TO GET OFF THEIR SHIPS, LOSING NEARLY HALF OF THEIR 500 MEN AS CASUALTIES – PRINCIPALLY TO FEVER.

committed two substantial forces to the Continent throughout this period, the expedition seemed doomed from the start. A complete lack of secrecy rendered surprise impossible, while the naval and military commanders – the latter, Lord Chatham, *'indolent beyond any man I have ever seen'*[9], according to one officer, failed to work together and engendered delay throughout the campaign.

The British plan aimed to capture or destroy a new enemy fleet being built on the River Scheldt at Antwerp and to secure and permanently garrison the island of Walcheren and its key fort at Flushing. This fort dominated all approaches to the Scheldt and would render traffic to Antwerp impossible. The capture of Walcheren and Flushing would therefore be the first phase of an operation to provide access to the Scheldt and a secure base for the subsequent attack on Antwerp. Roompot on the farthest, most northerly point of Walcheren, was judged to be the only practical place for the army to land, but would give time for enemy reinforcements to reach Flushing. Further landings would therefore be made at Cadzand to block reinforcements from Ghent and Bruges, and at Beveland to block the approach from Antwerp. The 9th were to be the only cavalry included in the landing at Roompot and were ordered to march south to Flushing, while the 12th would stay on their boats to form part of the main force that would advance to Antwerp.

Although Beveland was seized with no opposition, bad weather stopped the other blocking force and allowed Flushing to be reinforced (the garrison doubled during the siege). The main landings at Roompot on 30th July proved successful, the forces marching south to begin the siege of Flushing within 48 hours. The 9th landed on 9th August and immediately found the land unsuited to cavalry, being flat, wet and inhospitable and criss-crossed by dykes and poor roads. With no obvious or suitable role, they were soon employed as messengers and escorts. A change of weather and wind direction on 13th August finally allowed the British fleet to come within range of Flushing. The massive bombardment that followed forced the surrender of the garrison of 4,000 within 48 hours, allowing preparations for the next phase to begin. On 23rd August, the 9th were ferried across to South Beveland but, while the route to Antwerp was clear, the expedition's other problems had begun to escalate, with ships bringing the follow-on forces making slow progress, no funds available to buy local supplies and the resulting delay allowing the French ample time to prepare for the defence of Antwerp. Worse still, the marshy ground, which had been flooded by the French, also proved the perfect breeding ground for mosquitoes. Soon 3,000 men were either dead or incapacitated by the virulent 'Walcheren fever', which, at its worst, was killing 100 men every day.

Realising that even a scaled-down attack on Antwerp's outlying fortresses was now beyond its capability, the forces assigned to take them were sent home. They took with them the 12th Light Dragoons, who had never disembarked, and the main body of the 9th, the latter suffering again as bad winds condemned them to a month spent at sea while making the short crossing. A residual garrison of seven infantry brigades supported by artillery and cavalry, including two troops of the 9th, remained to hold Walcheren indefinitely.

The condition of those left on Walcheren continued to deteriorate, with poor nutrition and low resistance to infection: *'We catch colds and fevers as if we were so many women – a few days rain or soaking mist will invalid a whole British Army', the fever producing bright, livid, spots before it killed so that 'every ditch, every field and every street [was] full of dying and dead.'*[10] By 27th October half of the small party of the 9th were sick or dead and a further troop of dismounted men was sent out to fill the ranks, the conditions apparently requiring two men for every horse. Within days, the soaring death rate led to an order, on 4th November, to destroy all the island's defences and abandon the expedition completely, the original garrison of 9,500 having reduced to fewer than half who were fit for duty. Although 106 had been killed in action, 4,000 had died from disease, while 11,000 others returned with a sickness that took ages to clear. The 9th Light Dragoons' contingent of 500 had been reduced by 200 dead or ill.

THE PENINSULA AND WATERLOO

1811–1815

Salamanca | Peninsula | Waterloo

WITHIN TWO YEARS of the disastrous Walcheren campaign both Regiments were again caught up in the war to defeat Napoleon and France on the Continent. The result this time would be happier as, in the summer of 1811, the 9th Light Dragoons, having barely recovered from the experiences and attendant sickness of the Walcheren campaign, and the 12th, who were once again on invasion watch, received orders for Portugal. They were to form part of a wider reinforcement for the Army of the Peninsula as the British Government finally decided to put its principal military effort into a single campaign in Spain and Portugal. Embarking six troops each and leaving four behind to form a depot, they arrived in Lisbon on 17th and 25th July 1811 to join Wellington's army which, although successful in the defence of Portugal against French invasion since 1808, was still facing larger French forces operating in Spain.

THE HONOURABLE FREDERICK PONSONBY COMMANDED THE 12TH LIGHT DRAGOONS THROUGHOUT THE PENINSULA CAMPAIGN AND AT WATERLOO. AN OFFICER OF EXCEPTIONAL ABILITY, HE '*WAS THE BEAU IDEAL OF THE LIGHT CAVALRY SOLDIER. CHIVALROUS, MODEST, UNTOUCHED BY FEAR, HE COMBINED COOL JUDGEMENT WITH THE UTMOST RESOLUTION IN BATTLE.*'[1]

Over the course of the campaign to come both Regiments were to demonstrate most of the attributes that Wellington and others recognised in all of the British cavalry. Unbeatable in small numbers, they tended to lack self-restraint in large bodies, Wellington remarking that '*I considered our cavalry so inferior to the French from want of order, that although I considered one of our squadrons a match for two French, yet I did not care to see four British opposed by four French and still more so as the numbers increased and order (of course) became more necessary. They could gallop, but could not preserve their order.*'[2] Equally, General Excelmann, one of Napoleon's cavalry commanders, praised the British horses and riding but noted: '*The great deficiency is in your officers who seem to be impressed by the conviction that they can dash or ride after everything, as if the art of war were precisely the same as that of fox hunting.*'[3] More succinctly they were accused of '*galloping at everything, and.. galloping back as fast*'.[4] Despite these critical views, the cavalry gained – and never lost – its ascendancy over its French counterparts, as Wellington acknowledged by writing that '*on every occasion their superiority has been so great that the enemy does not use his cavalry except when supported and protected by the infantry*'.[5]

If there were concerns about his cavalry, Wellington's more immediate problems were an army in the south of Spain under Marshal Soult and a second in the north commanded by Marshal Marmont, each threatening Portugal along the invasion routes from Spain that were guarded by the enemy-held border fortresses at Ciudad Rodrigo and Badajoz. Other long-term difficulties continued to influence Wellington's planning throughout the campaign, foremost of which was the need not only to keep his coalition partners fighting, but also to prevent the French armies combining at a time or place where they might overwhelm his smaller British forces, a reflection of his limited numbers and particularly his shortages of cavalry and artillery.

From the moment of their arrival, the two Regiments' parts in the campaign diverged. The 9th were initially instructed not to disembark at all, but rather to hand over their horses to other in-country cavalry regiments who were short of them and then to proceed to Sicily, where they would act as part of the island's garrison as infantry. Although this order was quickly countermanded, many of their horses had already been handed over when, two days after landing, they were ordered to join Lieutenant General Sir Rowland Hill's Allied army

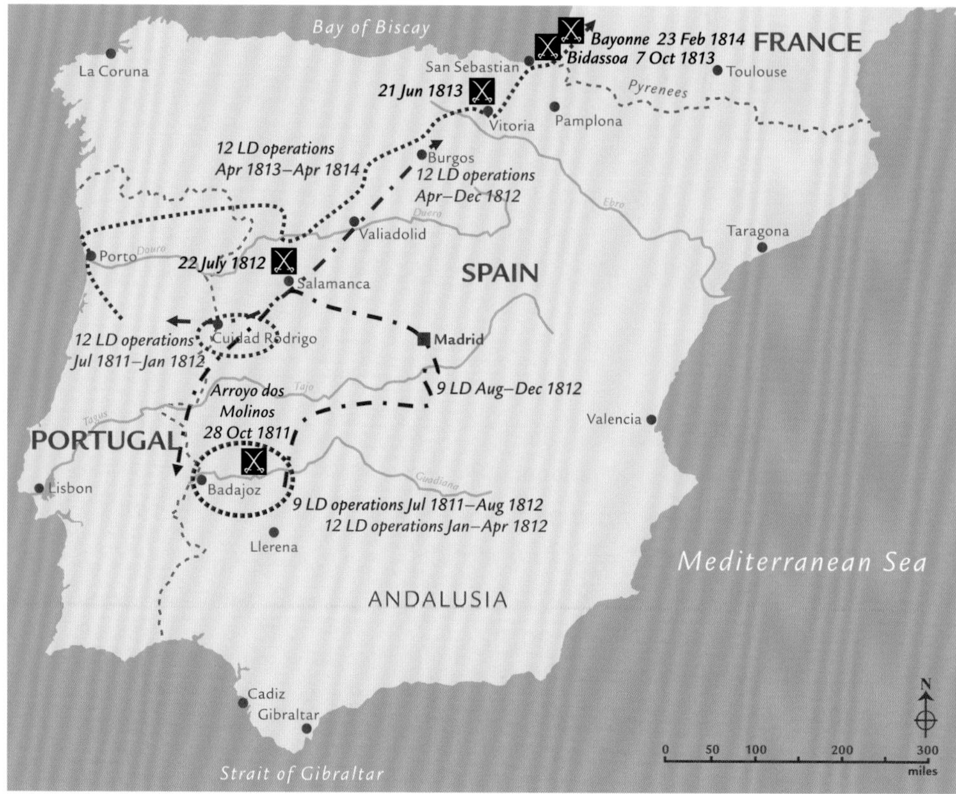

THE PRINCIPAL AREAS OF OPERATION OF THE 9TH AND 12TH LIGHT DRAGOONS DURING THE PENINSULA CAMPAIGN.

of 16,500 men, which was screening Badajoz and guarding the southern route into Portugal while Wellington and the main army moved north to besiege Ciudad Rodrigo.

The 9th were to join the 13th Light Dragoons and 2nd King's German Hussars in General Long's Cavalry Brigade, one of two British and one Portuguese brigades with Hill. By the time they arrived, however, the effects of Walcheren fever had reduced their strength to just over 100 men capable of making muster, while horses were in equally short supply, with only two of the three squadrons properly mounted until the end of the year.

Facing General Hill's army across the border was a weak and poorly supported French force of 6,000 men at Cáceres which, having strayed too close, had allowed itself to become isolated only three days' march from the Allies. On 22nd October, the Allies moved to take advantage of their exposed position. In appalling weather, by the night of 27th October, General Hill had approached to within five miles of the enemy. To maintain surprise, his army passed the night in driving rain with no fires to warm them or cook their food before moving at 2.30am to get within half a mile of the French billets at Arroyo dos Molinos. Here the lack of enemy outposts combined with the fog and rain to prevent detection and, with steep-sided hills to the rear of the village and routes out only to the south and east, General Hill pushed half his infantry into the settlement while the other half moved around to cut off the two lines of escape. Spanish cavalry took up position between the two infantry groups, with Long's Brigade formed in three lines of support, the King's German Hussars leading, with the two squadrons of the 9th and then the 13th Light Dragoons in the rear. The French, preparing for a day's march, were thrown into confusion and raced out of the village towards the cut-off group that was hurrying to block their escape, but soon formed two squares while their cavalry was checked by Hill's Spanish horsemen. General Long's brigade now moved across a flooded ravine before charging at the gallop. Although the initial onslaught by the King's German Hussars was held by the French Dragoons, the second line formed by the 9th caused them to break, starting a pursuit across the plain for over two miles until a detachment of fresh enemy horse was encountered. The pursuit began again as the second squadron of the 9th, which had been held in reserve, joined the fight. Elsewhere, the infantry had been successful too, the raid securing three guns and 1,400 prisoners for the loss of only 70 British dead. Its mission successful, the Allied force returned to its original billets in early November.

An attempt to repeat a similar expedition just before Christmas resulted in only a few skirmishes in dire weather as a reward for its efforts.

Following their disembarkation in July 1811, the 12th Light Dragoons had marched north-east to join Wellington's army at the siege of Ciudad Rodrigo, forming a cavalry brigade with the 1st Royal Dragoons in August under a Major General Slade, '*an officer almost universally unfortunate as a cavalry leader and a by-word for inefficiency throughout the army*'[6], while also suffering from a Colonel of the Regiment who was reluctant to meet demands for replacement kit, as he would have to pay for most of it. These disadvantages were at least partly compensated for by the arrival of a new commanding officer, Lieutenant Colonel the Hon Frederick Ponsonby, who was to prove exceptionally able. Deployed into a cavalry screen west and north of the town in order to allow Wellington's siege train to be brought forward unmolested, a series of strong probes by the French was dealt with in September, the 12th taking part in a notable action on the 26th when, as part of a small force placed and commanded by Wellington himself at El Bodón, the cavalry were called upon to make between 30 and 40 squadron charges, the strong French force of three columns being driven back as it tried to make for Wellington's headquarters.

The siege that year proved unsuccessful. Faced by superior French numbers and unwilling to become decisively engaged, Wellington withdrew again to Portugal, satisfied that the French, in launching their spoiling action, had further reduced their limited supplies. Content to watch Ciudad Rodrigo

OFFICERS OF THE 9TH AND 12TH LIGHT DRAGOONS. THE 9TH RETURNED TO THEIR BILLETS IN JANUARY 1812 TO HEAR OF THE INTRODUCTION *'OF THE NEW LIGHT DRAGOON UNIFORM, WITH ITS BELL-TOPPED SHAKO, SO RIDICULOUSLY LIKE THAT WORN BY THE FRENCH AS TO BE INDISTINGUISHABLE FROM IT AT A DISTANCE.'*[9] ANOTHER REGIMENT DESCRIBED IT AS *'QUITE SHOCKING'*.[10]

for the winter, the light cavalry began outpost duties as a screen well forward of the main position, with each brigade required to do the duty for a month at a time. For the horses, these duties were especially demanding due to a shortage of decent forage and veterinary treatment. An officer from another regiment commented that '*The horses get nothing by way of long forage but the long grass which the men cut themselves from out of the woods, for which they daily went a league. We were frequently eight or nine days without corn and in consequence lost many horses… we met them [the 12th Light Dragoons] on their march to the rear, and never were horses in such a state.*'[7] With logistics for a regiment of about 500 horses and mules requiring 300 additional mules to carry forage, a decision was soon taken to reduce the outposts to regimental strength in order to try to reduce the demand.

Wellington's opportunity for a general assault into Spain came early in January 1812, the French preparation for their invasion of Russia that year having depleted their armies in Spain of 27,000 men. First it required the routes guarded by Ciudad Rodrigo and Badajoz to be freed, the former falling on the 19th January 1812 after a 10-day siege, before Wellington turned south to begin the siege of the latter on 16th March. Joining General Hill's army, which had remained in the area, orders were given for a light cavalry division, including the 9th and the 12th Light Dragoons, to screen to the south to prevent any interference with the siege. Pushing the French screen far away from Badajoz, a charge by Long's Brigade at Mérida on 17th March succeeded in routing the enemy rearguard and led to Sergeant Major Dunwoody of the 9th capturing an enemy Commanding Officer. The cavalry reached Llerena on 12th April before, in its turn, being forced back by the advance of Soult's army from Andalucía.

The threat from Soult, together with concern over his Spanish allies' ability to hold onto Ciudad Rodrigo, caused Wellington to rush the siege of Badajoz, which eventually fell on 6th April, but with massive casualties as a result. The fall of the fortress caused Soult's withdrawal to Llerena in the belief that he was about to be pursued by Wellington and an army of 40,000. In reality, only three cavalry brigades, including both 9th and 12th Light Dragoons, came after him, the latter taking part in an action near Villagarcía in which a combined attack by two brigades succeeded in defeating the French rearguard. Described by one officer as the '*finest charge I ever had in my life*'[8], it was an unusually co-ordinated action by the British cavalry, several charges being successfully delivered by different regiments who all, uncharacteristically for the time, showed the ability to rally and reform when required, the pursuit of the broken French only halting on their arrival at their gun-line.

THE CHARGE OF THE 12TH LIGHT DRAGOONS AT SALAMANCA, 22ND JULY 1812.

SALAMANCA

Wellington was now able to move north, leaving General Hill's army of 18,000 to screen Soult and continue to guard the southern approaches to Portugal, once again condemning the 9th to long periods in the saddle on outpost duty while the 12th, as part of Wellington's army of 48,000, crossed into Spain near Ciudad Rodrigo. While Marmont's army was the immediate target for Wellington, his advance also threatened to split the French forces in the north and south, endanger Madrid and possibly take Burgos, a key point on the French line of communications. Arriving outside Salamanca on 17th June, a series of moves and counter-moves began in order to secure an advantage. The cavalry pushed forward to observe the withdrawal of Marmont's army north across the Douro, before in their turn being pushed back in a series of skirmishes as a stand-off developed. Lieutenant Colonel Ponsonby, commanding the 12th, assessed the situation in a letter to his mother: '*For two or three days we have been looking at each other without our being able to get at them or their wishing to get at us.*'[11]

In mid-July, news of possible French reinforcements reached Wellington, bringing an urgency to end the stately dance and force a battle. As was the norm, the light cavalry provided the picquet to screen the main body of infantry. One skirmish on the 17th July involved the 12th almost ended in disaster as they were forced back by a large body of enemy onto a squadron of the 11th Light Dragoons and the two guns in support of them. With Wellington and his staff in their midst, one of the latter gave the order '*Threes about!*' – the signal to withdraw – to the staff, which was understood to apply to everyone. The result was an unseemly retreat by staff, the two squadrons of light dragoons and the guns. Wellington apparently drew '*his sword and galloped for safety, laughing as he went*'[12], before the French were checked and the 12th reformed.

Minor engagements continued as the armies marched on parallel courses until, on 22nd July, Wellington seized the opportunity presented by Marmont's forces having become strung out. He launched an attack into the French left flank, delivering a crushing defeat and inflicting 14,000 casualties at a cost of 5,000 suffered. For the 12th, on the left of the British line where they had been acting as a rearguard, their opportunity to contribute materially to the Battle of Salamanca came at the end of the day when two charges were delivered in support of an attack into the only unbroken French division. Ponsonby broke his sword at the hilt as he led a squadron against 450 infantry who cunningly lay down when charged, to rise and fire when the 12th had passed.

Despite the comprehensive Allied victory, the success of Salamanca was not followed by a rapid pursuit, the Spanish failure to cut off the French line of retreat having allowed the enemy to withdraw north to Valladolid, harried on their way by Ponsonby and 40 of his best riders in the lead of Wellington's army. The city was entered on the 2nd August as the French left, Wellington's escort being provided by two squadrons of the 12th, the only troops to enter the town, and in the enviable position of being feted as heroes: '*We were met at every turn by bands of music, people of all descriptions, high and low, especially ladies, bearing streamers and trophies….women of all ranks bringing refreshments, even to the privates, walking by the side of our horses….whilst on every side were heard acclamations of "Viva el gran Capitán, viva los Heros Ingleses los Salvadores".*'[13]

The victory at Salamanca and the entry into Valladolid spelt the end of several months of frustration for the 9th Light Dragoons in the south, most of which had been spent on picquet duty or dealing with French raids before Soult, reacting to the news, left Andalucía and thereby freed General Hill in his turn to move north. For their part, the 12th Light Dragoons had been left in a screen on the Douro to watch the French to the north of the river while Wellington and a large proportion of his army entered Madrid on 12th August. The relative weakness of those left behind was soon capitalised on by the French, who immediately launched a limited counter-attack across the Douro, forcing the British force back in bitter fighting. At one time this required every second man in the cavalry brigade to dismount to hold the village of Tudela. Despite this setback, and with Wellington back from the adulation of Madrid, the advance north recommenced, the 12th distinguishing themselves in several skirmishes, so that by 19th September Burgos was besieged, the Regiment spending the next month on outpost duties to the north-east, occasionally skirmishing with the enemy to enliven an otherwise wet, tiring routine.

Burgos proved impossible to take. With Wellington's army operating on extended lines of communication, that were insufficiently equipped with heavy guns or siege equipment, and with French armies of 60,000 approaching, the task was abandoned on 21st October and a withdrawal to Portugal began. While Napoleon's retreat from Moscow, which was also beginning, was to prove a far more cataclysmic event in the war, the rigours suffered during the march cost Wellington 10 per cent of his force, brought on by poor weather, lost supplies and ill-discipline. It was, he said, *'the worst scrape I was ever in'*. General Anson's Brigade, of which the 12th formed a part, was ordered to form the rearguard and was almost immediately in action at Villadrigo on the second day of the march, as it defended a series of streams against large numbers of enemy cavalry, at one stage charging to try to save a bridge before being pushed back with Wellington himself amongst their number: *'I twice thought that Anson's brigade (which is weak in numbers and exhausted by constant service) would have been annihilated,…it had only four hundred and sixty sabres in the field…the French had sixteen hundred to two thousand swords against them. We had literally to fight our way for four miles.'*[14]

To the south, General Hill's force, guarding the central route into Portugal and providing flank security along the Tagus, had also come under pressure from a large French army. The cavalry screen felt much of its weight, magnified by the abandonment of the siege at Burgos. Overlapped on both sides, General Hill managed to avoid a decisive engagement, but had to abandon Madrid as he moved north to assist Wellington, the two meeting near Salamanca where the withdrawal to Portugal began again. Both 9th and 12th Light Dragoons furnished rearguards with their respective brigades in appalling weather on roads clogged with refugees and with little or no forage to sustain their horses, which rapidly lost condition. Colonel Vandeleur later recalled: *'We were all wet to the skin and had to skirmish with those fellows all day long, and the same thing for five successive days – out the whole of every night in the most severe, cold, rainy weather and often without a morsel of wood to cook our ration of meal, which we were as often without as with; and entirely without bread, or corn for our horses.'*[15] The rearguard provided by the light cavalry screen, coupled with an element of French timidity, prevented the withdrawal turning into a rout, before a halt finally came on 20th November when the army reached the comparative safety of Ciudad Rodrigo. By this time the French had also exhausted themselves and both Regiments could disperse gratefully to winter quarters.

Winter brought an opportunity to make up losses in both men and horses. The 9th had lost 75 men killed, wounded, captured or sick during the retreat, while the 12th required 212 fresh horses as well as the chance to enjoy Christmas. Vandeleur remembered: *'We have a Turkey, which cost three dollars, a sucking pig, rice pudding and potatoes, which I call a good blow-out!'* Wine was cheap *'but not very strong; one can drink three bottles and feel not the least effect as we have tried'*.[16] At about the same time Light Dragoons were issued new, foreign-looking uniforms that met with universal unpopularity from Wellington downwards, while, aside from the military's customary fascination with uniform, other diversions included shooting and hunting hounds.

For the 9th the pleasures of the time were overshadowed by a breakdown in order and discipline. This eventually resulted in a General Order being issued which singled out the Regiment and two others for wasting much of the forage provided for the army. *'Remonstrances and pointing out to officers the results of their inattention to duty having failed'*,[17] the commanding officers were ordered to be arrested for disobedience to orders. While there is no record of the outcome or a court martial it is clear that their stock was low. More evidence came from the pen of the new Regimental Commissary and well-known commentator, Captain Schaumann, who joined them at the end of December, the previous incumbent of the job having been sacked for neglecting his duties. Most of his reports appear to have been soured by a self-confessed dislike of British cavalry due to what he called their *'ridiculous pretensions'*, an inadequacy felt from having spent the summer in Lisbon away from the front line, and, perhaps, more than a hint of envy. He described the officers as: *'mostly young men of noble birth and well*

THE BATTLE OF VITORIA 21ST, JUNE 1813. THE DECISIVE BATTLE OF THE PENINSULA CAMPAIGN, THE FRENCH WERE COMPREHENSIVELY DEFEATED WITH THE 12TH INVOLVED IN A CHARGE THAT, WHILE INITIALLY CHAOTIC, SUCCEEDED IN DRIVING THE FRENCH CAVALRY ONTO THEIR INFANTRY DURING THE PURSUIT.

versed in all the dissolute pastimes of London, who did not trouble themselves much about their regimental duties ..[who]..spent their time riding or loafing about in the village, and in all kinds of tours de force in fine weather, and in drinking heavily and telling obscene and salacious stories in the mess when it was wet.'[18]

Whatever the truth, the attractions of London were soon to be available for the 9th who now heard that they were to return to England as the result of the arrival in Portugal of two new cavalry brigades and a shortage of mounts. Against the protests of Wellington, who wished to keep his veterans, the Duke of York ordered the four cavalry regiments that had suffered the heaviest losses to give up their horses. The 9th, who had over 370 men dismounted, surrendered their remaining 234 horses on 24th February 1813 and with Wellington remarking that he regretted '*that he should be deprived of the assistance of these brave troops*', the Regiment moved to Lisbon and from there to England. They had covered over 2,000 miles in their 22 months in theatre, their service, although not in any of the great battles of the campaign, being recognised in 1815 by the award of their first battle honour, 'Peninsula'.

Capitalising on the strategic advantage given by Napoleon's failure in Russia the previous year and his inability to provide reinforcements, Wellington began an attack into Spain in the spring of 1813 when the standing corn and young grass would help ease the problems of supply. The 12th, who had received an additional 20 soldiers and 40 horses, recommenced operations on the 26th April 1813 as part of a column under General Graham that was to move in a broad encircling movement north inside Portugal before swinging east to threaten the flank of the main French position on the Douro between Zamorra and Valladolid, there to link up with Wellington's main body advancing from Portugal. Elsewhere, partisan activity would be increased and an amphibious landing against Tarragona on the eastern coast of Spain would threaten the French rear and encourage their withdrawal to the north.

By 5th May, General Graham's column was at Oporto, though another month of hard marching in bad weather and on poor roads lay ahead. The routine, on entering Spain, returned to the familiar demands of patrolling, outpost duty and skirmishing. Vandeleur writing: '*I was ordered to feel where the enemy were, I found them to the amount of near two hundred and fifty with four guns on piquet at the north side of the bridge at Benevente. When I got within two miles of them I halted my two men and went on myself... until I got close up to their vedettes and saw all that I wished to know. Two of them... I allured away about a mile, but they got too cunning. If I could have got them as far as my two men we certainly should have taken them.*'[19] Across the front, the advance proved rapid, with General Graham taking Zamorra on 2nd June to link up with the main body a day later. The the French, meanwhile, who had been totally surprised and whose right flank continued to be threatened, fell back north-east to Burgos, short of supplies and harassed by the British cavalry as the pace of the advance increased. Horses now remained saddled through the night as they pressed on, Wellington bypassing Burgos and forcing the French to retire again to the Ebro. His outflanking manoeuvre continued until a halt was called on 12th June with the supply lines by now overstretched, the army having left the cornfields behind and a new supply route via Santander on the north coast not yet opened up.

VITORIA

Within six days, the army moved once more, General Graham's force again turning the French position on the River Ebro and forced them back to Vitoria where, on 19th June, the Emperor Joseph established his position. Two days later, with French reinforcements apparently imminent, Wellington attacked from the north, surprising the enemy who had expected a frontal assault and successfully taking both flanks and piercing the centre, while Graham's column advanced to the east to prevent escape. After involvement in the initial assault, the task of cutting off the enemy fell to General Anson's Light Brigade, but nearly ended badly when the leading squadrons failed to act in unison. First a squadron of the 16th Light Dragoons charged an enemy post and was held before being ridden into by a squadron of the 12th, the fault compounded by a further squadron of the 16th who repeated the mistake, the whole incident ending in a mêlée from which they were forced to move back and reform. With Ponsonby steadying them, the pursuit once again continued, the 12th and 16th this time driving back the French cavalry onto their infantry in a far more satisfactory manner. The French defeat at Vitoria was total and proved the decisive engagement of the campaign, the French losing all but one of their guns and most of their baggage train. Valued at an estimated £1 million the ensuing looting saw a complete loss of control as Wellington's infantry ran riot. Captain Schaumann wrote: '*In some cases, particularly over the plundering of the wagons carrying the war treasure, our men fought to the death. No officer dared to interfere. In short, more thorough and more scandalous plundering has never been.*'[20] Needless to say Schaumann's indignation did not stop him paying bargain prices for various items that caught his eye at the jumble sale that took place later.

Although the looting led to the pursuit not being prosecuted as forcibly as it should have been, Vitoria marked the end of Napoleon's dominance of

Europe, with news of the defeat leading Austria to join Prussia and Russia in once again declaring war on France. For the Spanish, the complete liberation of their country became only a matter of time as the advance once again continued. Pamplona and San Sebastian, the only towns still held by the French, were beseiged as the key passes over the Pyrenees were secured to prevent counter-attacks from France. The 12th Light Dragoons, still with General Graham's force as it attempted to cut off the retreating French, ended their chase on the borders of France as they drove the enemy over the River Bidassoa on 1st July. Held there, Captains Andrews and Vandeleur nevertheless took the opportunity to row across, thereby claiming to be the first of the army into France, if only briefly.

Despite the success overall, San Sebastian and Pamplona remained beseiged, a task for which the 12th was not required, while Soult's final attempt to break through the Pyrenees involved them only in patrol activity as they helped keep open the lines of communication between the left and centre of the army. With the sieges still continuing, life for the cavalry during the summer became more pleasant, with both horses and men in good condition, while other distractions presented both opportunities and threats. The young Vandeleur wrote: '*We frequently have balls and are constantly in the society of the most beautiful girls I ever saw…They say they will go home with us…I hope they will not insist upon it as it may be disagreeable.*'[21]

San Sebastian's capture on 31st August allowed preparations for the invasion of France to begin in earnest and on 7th October Wellington crossed the River Bidassoa with a thunderstorm fortuitously masking the preparations. Part of the westernmost column, the 12th crossed a ford at Fuenterrabia as Ponsonby once again ensured they were at the thick of the action: '*all the other cavalry are up to their bellies in fine hay and straw doing nothing…but Colonel Ponsonby is such a man he is never quiet unless we are in the middle of everything.*'[22] Pressing on against light opposition, Ponsonby wrote to his mother that '*he never saw the French troops behave so ill*'[23]. The 12th and some sharp-shooters reached Urrogne, where the main French reserve drove them back. The fall of Pamplona on 31st October ended any threat to the rear areas and spelt the end of an enforced halt during which Wellington, in a successful bid not to alienate the local population, had ordered the army in France to conduct minimal activity and to behave with consideration towards them, a job made easier by the groups of camp-followers who appeared to make life more pleasant. Vandeleur recalled: '*many were the bottles of stout which, night after night, were consumed at the sign of the Jolly Soldier.*'

Foul weather delayed the next stage of the advance until 10th November, when the 12th Light Dragoons were involved in a feint attack on Urrogne. A successful action further inland forced Soult back to the River Nive as General Hope's force, with which the 12th were grouped, reached the walls of Bayonne. Intent on encircling Bayonne, the advance began again on 9th December, though strong French counter-attacks pushed General Hope back in an action in which the 12th were only lightly engaged. Three days later General Hill's force to the east was also attacked. The Regiment marched 16 miles at night in treacherous weather to reinforce him, their arrival narrowly preventing what might have been serious defeat. Despite the need to do outpost duty, once again it appears that the 12th also used the chance to indulge in some unknown and unrecorded activity that may have given rise to one explanation of the origin of the Regimental Hymns. Vandeleur hints at some background – '*I am afraid your correspondent who told you a story about nuns is rather partial to drawing the long bow*' – but there is no history of the hymns being given as a punishment for whatever cause, though the gossip in Britain had clearly picked up on it. With the situation stabilised, the 12th again resumed outpost duties before being withdrawn to quarters to sit out the winter, the usual round of balls and other entertainments taking place with Wellington and his staff who were co-located in St Jean de Luz.

'We frequently have balls and are constantly in the society of the most beautiful girls I ever saw…'

Wellington's plan for the new year of 1814 aimed to split the French forces at Bayonne by manoeuvring around their flank and, in so doing, drawing strength away from the besieged city as it was assaulted by General Hope's force, of which the 12th continued to form a part. With the flanking actions successful in reducing the French garrison, on 23rd February General Hope's force began their assault, planning to cross the River Adour west of Bayonne among the sand dunes near the sea by using a bridge of boats. Initially unable to build the bridge, General Hope pressed on with an amphibious operation pushing eight companies of foot guards and 160 dismounted 12th Light Dragoons over in boats and rafts to create a bridgehead that successfully beat off a sortie from Bayonne. The following day, the lodgement was reinforced by a much larger force, including two squadrons of the 12th, boats carrying men and saddles while their horses swam alongside. By 26th February the bridge was finally completed and

BY THE END OF THE PENINSULAR CAMPAIGN THE 12TH LIGHT DRAGOONS HAD EARNED A FORMIDABLE REPUTATION UNDER PONSONBY, THEIR BRIGADE COMMANDER STATING *'THE 12TH CAN BOAST OF WHAT NO REGIMENT IN THE ARMY CAN, EXCEPT THE ONES THAT CAME OUT THE OTHER DAY, THAT THEY NEVER LOST A SINGLE MAN TAKEN BY SURPRISE, NOR A PIQUET OR PATROL HAS EVER BEEN TAKEN, NOR A MAN DESERTED OR EVEN TRIED BY COURT MARTIAL'.*[24]

15,000 troops encircled Bayonne, cutting it off from the other French forces as Wellington, to the east, drove Soult back towards Toulouse.

Although Bayonne would not capitulate until 26th April, some 20 days after Napoleon's abdication and the fall of Paris, its investment left the 12th free to rejoin Wellington's advance at the end of February. By now Napoleon's support was falling away and the Regiment entered Bordeaux unopposed on 12th March, before moving to patrol the area between the Dordogne and the Garonne as the war drew to a close in early April. News of a cessation of hostilities finally arrived and appropriately Ponsonby was chosen to carry the despatch the 150 miles from Bordeaux to Wellington in his headquarters at Toulouse; a task he completed, with characteristic verve, in 19 hours.

The end of the war with France brought the 12th back to Britain, where they were inspected by the Duke of York at Hounslow and heard the news that they too had been awarded the battle honour 'Peninsula'. Routine was quickly re-established, with the only incident of note the suppression of a food riot in Berkshire. Earlier, the 9th had moved in rapid succession between various towns in England until, in late 1814 and with the threat in Europe apparently gone, they embarked at Bristol for further duty in Ireland, their unhappy association with shipping continuing on this trip when bad weather extended the time spent on the transports from a few days to a month. With insufficient forage on board, the horses inevitably arrived in Dublin in bad condition and with sore feet, having to be led to their quarters in short stages while the baggage continued round by sea. Even this short trip ended in disaster when a storm blew it across the Irish sea to be completely wrecked on the Welsh coast.

WATERLOO

Napoleon's escape from imprisonment on Elba in February 1815 brought their newly established routines to an end for both Regiments, Wellington insisting that as many of his Peninsula veterans as possible were returned to him. This *'infamous army, very weak and ill-equipped'* as he described it, included six troops from 12th Light Dragoons, while the 9th, who had also been called upon, would only get as far as Manchester before Napoleon had been dealt with.

Returning to the Continent once again, the 12th's initial billets in Belgium proved excellent, with plenty to eat and, with champagne at only four shillings a bottle, a very far cry from the demands of Spain and Portugal. Brigaded with the 11th and 16th Light Dragoons under Major General Vandeleur, they were inspected by Wellington, who told them: *'he was happy at having again under his orders a corps which had always been distinguished for its gallantry and discipline, and he did not doubt, should occasion offer, but it would continue to deserve his good opinion; and he hoped every man would feel a pride in endeavouring to maintain the reputation of the Regiment.'* The 12th moved to the west of Brussels in late May while Wellington, biding his time, liaised with his Prussian allies and, with a defensive battle in mind, awaited Napoleon's move.

Napoleon intended to deal the resurgent Allied coalition a series of knock-out blows before they could fully mobilise against him. With France rallying to his cause, his immediate priority was to seize Brussels and defeat the threat from Britain, Prussia, Holland and Belgium before turning to deal with Austria and Russia in the east. Striking north from France into Belgium, he was faced by two armies – an Anglo-Dutch one of 90,000 men commanded by Wellington and a larger German one under Blücher – which he aimed to keep separate and defeat in turn. In executing this plan he proved only partially successful. The actions at Ligny and Quatre Bras on 16th June, although forcing both armies back, failed to knock them out completely and they were able to fight again at Waterloo two days later.

In these preliminary operations Wellington was forced to move at short notice from his concentration area guarding the route to Brussels from Mons, to come in on the Prussian right and help block the route from Charleroi some 20 miles to the east. As part of the move, the 12th, with the rest of General Vandeleur's brigade, set off towards

Nivelles at 5am on 16th June but arrived, with much of the rest of the army, as the action at Quatre Bras drew to an inconclusive close at 2pm. They were able to do little more than show themselves, suffering a slight bombardment as they helped cover the battered infantry's withdrawal, before spending the night behind the battlefield, with picquets placed in touch and the infantry to their rear.

Forced to comply with the Prussians' retreat from Ligny, the following day Wellington began a deliberate withdrawal north to Mont St Jean and the site chosen for the next day's battle, the cavalry being used to provide a rearguard for the move. Wellington remarked: *'Well there go the last of the infantry and I don't care now'*[25], either indicating his modest opinion of his cavalry or his belief that they were more than capable of looking after themselves. Followed by French cavalry and under some shellfire as they moved back, the 12th, in the most easterly of the rearguard's columns, withdrew with only a slight skirmish on the way, their chief enemy the appalling weather that continued throughout the day and night as horses sank deep in the mud. The Regiment finally took up its position for the next day's battle while torrential rain soaked everything and men tried to get what rest they could.

The morning of 18th June brought fine weather, though the ground remained sodden and muddy. Posted to the eastern flank of the British line with only one brigade beyond it, General Vandeleur's Brigade was provided with a grandstand view of the valley, across which much of the battle would be fought. Able to watch the early stages of the battle comparatively undisturbed, it was only in the afternoon, following the Household and Union Brigades' charges in the centre, that Vandeleur's brigade became intimately involved in the battle. While the Household Brigade had succeeded in checking their charge and reforming to withdraw, the Union Brigade swept on up the opposite side of the valley to charge the main enemy battery of 80 guns. Coming under attack from four regiments of enemy lancers and cuirassiers, who, with the advantage of fresh horses, began to wreak havoc among the Union Brigade, General Vandeleur ordered a charge by the 11th and 16th Light Dragoons to help extract it, while instructing Ponsonby, who was further to the left, to act on his own initiative to relieve pressure on them.

Colonel Ponsonby's immediate reaction was to attack a formation of infantry to his front. Keeping the Regiment's advance at a slow, steady pace despite the incoming artillery and musket fire he managed to maintain the cohesion and energy of the Regiment until, with the order to charge finally being given, the French broke under the hammer blow. In the subsequent fighting Ponsonby was seriously wounded and fell from his horse, his presence at this critical moment being sorely missed as, with the Regiment still not reformed, it was counter-attacked by an infantry reserve and a regiment of light horse lancers. Shattered by the onslaught, the 12th could only extract themselves from the desperate battle that followed with the assistance of the remainder of the Brigade, under whose cover they moved back to their original position where they reformed as two squadrons. The charge, though later described as *'beautiful'*[26] by Wellington, had cost the 12th a third of its strength in killed, wounded or missing.

For the rest of the battle General Vandeleur's Brigade remained on the flanks until the loss of the pivotal position at La Haye Sainte required it to move to support the centre of the line with the dual tasks of counter-attacking any breakthrough should it occur and of providing moral support to the Dutch-Belgian troops that it was feared might buckle, a task carried out by placing the Brigade directly behind them. The precaution proved unnecessary, the arrival of the Prussian army and the failure of the final assault by the French Imperial Guard signalling the end of the battle. With the enemy broken, a general advance began, General Vandeleur's Brigade launching an attack into 1,000 enemy infantry before ceding the pursuit to the Prussians.

THE 12TH LIGHT DRAGOONS AT WATERLOO. INITIALLY SUCCESSFUL IN BREAKING A BODY OF FRENCH INFANTRY IN A CHARGE IN WHICH PONSONBY WAS WOUNDED, THE 12TH WAS THEN COUNTER-ATTACKED AND LOST NEARLY A THIRD OF ITS STRENGTH IN CASUALTIES OR MISSING.

FREDERICK PONSONBY AT WATERLOO

Colonel, The Honourable Frederick Ponsonby survived the charge by the 12th and his story has passed into the folklore of Waterloo: 'In *the mêlée I was almost instantly disabled in both arms, losing first my sword and then my reins, and followed by a few men, who were presently cut down, no quarter being allowed, asked or given. I was carried along by my horse, till, receiving a blow from a sabre, I fell senseless on my face to the ground. Recovering, I raised myself a little to look round, being at that time, I believe, in a condition to get up and run away – when a lancer passing by cried out 'Tu n'es pas mort, coquina' and stuck his lance through my back. My head dropped, the blood gushed into my mouth, a difficulty of breathing came on, and I thought all was over.*' Surviving the blow however, he remained on the ground through the rest of the day, while being looted twice and used as a musket rest by a French infantryman '*loading and firing many times, and conversing with great gaiety all the while*', though a French officer took more care, giving him some brandy and making him comfortable before, to add insult to injury, he was ridden over by his allies: '*It was dusk when two squadrons of Prussian cavalry, both of them two deep, passed over me in full trot, lifting me from the ground and tumbling me about cruelly.*'[27] That night he was again robbed, this time by a Prussian, before he was guarded by a British infantryman who had lost his regiment. It was only the following morning that he was searched out and found, near death, by Captain Vandeleur and brought in to recover from his wounds. Ponsonby apparently later attributed his recovery to being bled by a surgeon.

INDIA, SOUTH AFRICA AND CRIMEA

1815–1857

Punniar | Sobraon | Chillianwallah | Goojerat | Punjaub | South Africa 1851–1853 | Sebastapol

THE VICTORY OVER NAPOLEON, while making heroes of every man at Waterloo, robbed Britain's armed forces of any credible threat and dictated its development – or lack of it – for most of the 19th century until its effects were finally felt in the Boer War. For both the 9th and 12th Light Dragoons immediate change would come with the adoption of a new weapon and name but, for the remainder of the century they, with the rest of the cavalry, would see little difference to their lives, besides the compulsion to tinker with dress, their employment and tactics remaining largely unaltered despite considerable advances in technology elsewhere.

OFFICERS OF THE 12TH LANCERS IN 1817 SHOWING THE EARLIEST FORM OF LANCER UNIFORM, INCLUDING THE CHAPZKA OR LANCE CAP. BOTH REGIMENTS HAD CONVERTED TO THE LANCE IN 1816 AS A RESULT OF THE EXPERIENCES OF THE NAPOLEONIC WARS.

Militarily, aside from the initial requirement for domestic security that kept them in the United Kingdom, the century saw activity in support of the Empire and its security, and in this they were fortunate, for the heavy cavalry regiments were initially prevented from duty in countries where the horses available were unsuitable for their weight. India features largest in their story and, aside from the bravery displayed there that earned the 9th its huge haul of Victoria Crosses, it also served as an arena in which the cavalry flame, from a military perspective, was kept burning brightest.

The most immediate and inevitable impact of the end of the war was a period of retrenchment as the government struggled to deal with a depression brought on by the shrinking of the wartime economy and mounting demands for reform across the country. This resulted in an abrupt decline in the army's budget from £43 million in 1815 to £10.7 million in 1820, and then to under £8 million in 1836, with a significant increase only coming in the 1850s as a result of the Crimea and the Indian Mutiny. A reduction in numbers was inevitable, the army shrinking from 230,000 men in 1815 to just over 100,000 in 1828, a further 15,000 being lost over the next 10 years.

The cuts hit the infantry particularly hard as there appeared little need for large numbers of slow-moving battalions, whereas the cavalry, although losing eight regiments, could employ their greater mobility and presence to act as agents of the law across the country to augment or replace the yeomanry, no regular police force having yet been established. Faced with crises ranging from unrest in Ireland to riots over the price of corn, electoral reform or the mechanisation of industry, the authorities (in this case the Duke of Wellington), argued that '*It is much more desirable to employ cavalry for the purposes of police than infantry; for this reason: cavalry inspires more terror at the same time that it does much less mischief. A body of 20 or 30 horse will disperse a mob with the utmost facility, whereas 400 or 500 infantry will not effect the same object without the use of their firearms, and a great deal of mischief may be done.*'[1] Despite

12TH LANCERS BILLETING. THE END OF THE NAPOLEONIC WARS SAW BOTH REGIMENTS IN A WIDE VARIETY OF POSTINGS ACROSS BRITAIN, USUALLY BILLETED IN TOWNS AND VILLAGES AND AS A READY SOURCE OF LAW AND ORDER. WELLINGTON WAS TO NOTE THAT *'IT IS MUCH MORE DESIRABLE TO EMPLOY CAVALRY FOR THE PURPOSES OF POLICE THAN INFANTRY; CAVALRY INSPIRES MORE TERROR AT THE SAME TIME THAT IT DOES MUCH LESS MISCHIEF'*.

avoiding the wholesale cuts that befell others, both Regiments' establishments shrank and by 1821 the 9th were down to 363 soldiers, while the policing role they were now required for meant that, as in the previous century, they were billeted in small detachments across a wide area with consequent damage to training and cohesion.

Although the reductions in the size of the army were inevitable, the victories won in the Peninsula and at Waterloo had brought an upsurge in its prestige and popularity. This might have been expected to signal an era of increased professionalism and an improvement in all areas of military life. Instead, financial stringency, complacency, innate military conservatism and the lack of a clearly defined threat would blight progress in most areas, including training, equipment and conditions of service.

Recruits continued to join largely as a result of economic necessity or through dubious recruiting methods, although the proportion of English and Welsh in the ranks increased steadily from 43 per cent in 1830 to 58 per cent in 1867, while the numbers of Irish dropped. Those who did join the cavalry (for a term of service of 24 years) found that the improving zeal of the Victorians seemed to have bypassed the army, particularly in terms of soldiers' conditions or administration. Barracks remained unhygienic, overcrowded and cramped, soldiers sleeping four in a wooden crib until 1827 with 200–300 cubic ft of air per man as opposed to the 600 that was considered the minimum essential in British prisons of the time. All activities, including cooking, cleaning and washing, were conducted in the barrack rooms while ablutions were largely non-existent, 'urine-tubs' forming a central feature of the room at night, the tub doubling up as a washing facility after it had been emptied in the morning. This can only have added to a thoroughly fetid atmosphere that in many cavalry barracks, where the men lived above the horses, must have been overpowering. Food was monotonous and unhealthy, with the junior soldiers responsible for its production: a probably not-unrelated statistic from 1857 shows that mortality amongst soldiers was double that of civilians.

Few diversions such as organized sport or games were made available to dispel the boredom, leading to a heavy reliance on drink, which was available in quantity, resulting in high rates of suicide and indiscipline: *'to be brief, the state offered every inducement in the way of monotonous diet, monotonous occupation, climatic discomfort, bad housing and abundant alcohol that could lure men to drink: and then deplored the drunkenness of the army.'*[2] Stoppages continued to erode a cavalryman's one shilling three pence/day (the infantry received only a shilling) and went to pay for everything from the riding master to laundry and even medical treatment. By 1847 regulations were required to ensure that a soldier received at least one penny per day, while as late as 1877 the average a soldier could expect to save was less than five pence per day. Against this backdrop, minor improvements such as the issue of medals for Egypt and the Peninsula and the institution of an award for good conduct in 1836 must have been seen as of limited tangible benefit.

Routine in barracks was unrelenting, harsh and demanding. There were rules for everything and a series of prescribed punishments for those who failed to achieve the standards required. The demands of looking after the horses set the pattern for the days and months, as did endless parades and repetitive weapons drill, including an ungenerous ammunition allowance of 40 rounds per man per year. Collective training, if it happened at all, was largely set-piece and rehearsed, the emphasis being on the glamour of the charge rather than the more mundane but challenging business of reconnaissance, patrolling and screening – an imbalance in emphasis that failed to acknowledge the improvements made in artillery and small arms throughout the century that would render the massed cavalry charge practically redundant. From time to time, standards of soldiering did rise, but this was largely due to the efforts of particular Commanding Officers. The 9th, commanded by Lieutenant Colonel Charles Morland from 1813–1828, managed to surprise an inspecting officer by the performance of the captains and subalterns which *'exceeded every expectation entertained of their efficiency'*, while the soldiers were praised as being *'orderly, attentive, silent and soldier like, steady in the ranks, obedient to the words of Command, and evidently possessed of good training and Discipline. Their conduct as men is equally commendable.'*

In an organisation that positively discouraged marriage, wives of those who had been granted permission to marry stayed in the same barrack rooms, their bedspaces separated at best by a curtain, and here they lived, gave birth and brought up their children, sharing the few facilities available with the unmarried men. Quarters were only widely provided from the 1850s, the Sanitary Commission of 1857 finding that only 20 of the 251 stations in Britain had any, while wives 'off the strength' had no resort to help at all. On foreign postings, a ballot would be taken to determine which wives could travel, the limit being set at six per 100 men, with the remainder given a fare to a chosen destination, support coming only from the money a soldier might send home. For those not married, the authorities seemed to accept that brothels and pubs were the natural outlet for soldiers' more fundamental demands, legislation in 1869 seeking to reduce the incidence of venereal diseases by regulating the supply, rather than the demand.

Punishment for crime, while harsh by today's standards, reflected the mores of wider society. The death penalty was available for a wide variety

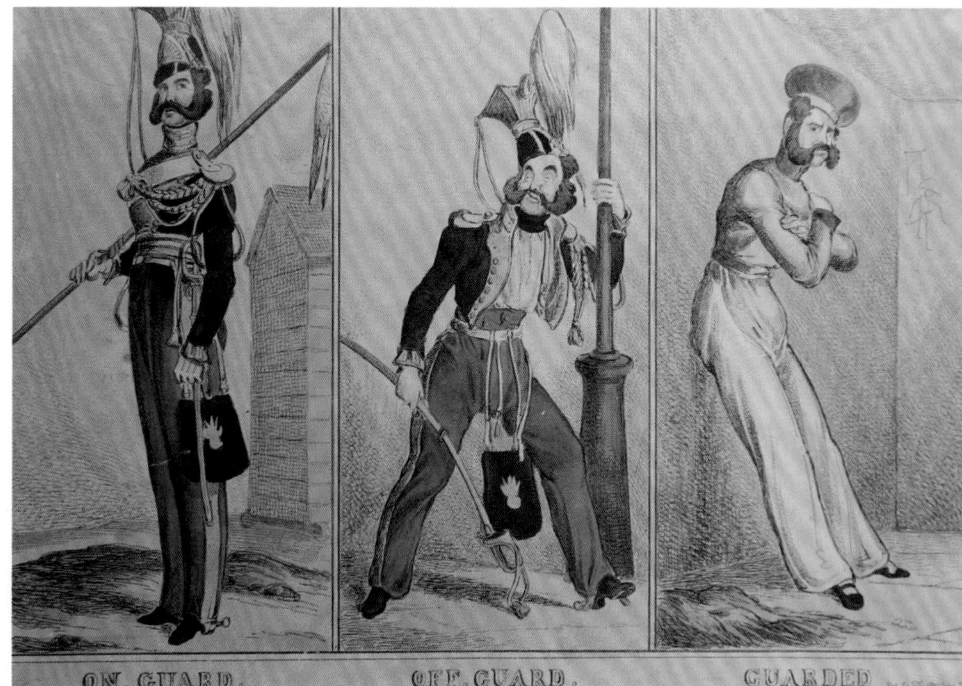

1 A SUMMARY OF THE LIFE FACED BY MANY SOLDIERS DURING MUCH OF THE 19TH CENTURY, FOR WHOM DRINK PROVIDED THE ONLY SOURCE OF ENTERTAINMENT.

2 THE 9TH LANCERS IN REVIEW ORDER. SUCH TRAINING AS TOOK PLACE CONTINUED TO FOCUS ON RIGID, SET DRILLS AND THE GLAMOUR OF THE CHARGE.

1 THE REFORM MOVEMENT WAS OFTEN CRITICAL OF THE ARMY, THE EXAMINER OF 1840 SINGLING OUT LANCERS AND HUSSARS FOR *'OFFENCES AGAINST THE PEACE AND DECENCY OF SOCIETY'*[6]. THIS SENTIMENT IS ECHOED IN THE HEATH CARTOON OF 1830: 'WOT ARE YOU GOING ARTER WE MY SWEETHEART?' 'SHE'S MY SWEETHEART, YOU BUMPKIN'.

2 MAJOR DE MONTMORENCY OF THE 9TH LIGHT DRAGOONS WAS TAKEN PRISONER DURING THE PENINSULAR CAMPAIGN AND HELD IN PARIS WHERE HE WATCHED POLISH LANCERS ON EXERCISE. BASED ON HIS OBSERVATIONS IN 1820 HE PUBLISHED THE FIRST MANUAL ON LANCE DRILL AND LAID THE FOUNDATION FOR ALL FUTURE LANCE TRAINING.

of sometimes bizarre misdemeanours and, while used as sparingly as possible in the cavalry, it was still employed: Lieutenant Colonel Hope Grant of the 9th, an outstandingly humane soldier, had a man shot in Meerut in 1847 for striking an officer in the hope of being sentenced to transportation to Australia. Colonel Hope Grant stated that *'the bad characters [two others had also committed the offence] arrived at the conclusion that there was little satisfaction in running the risk of being shot for the satisfaction of being transported.'*[3] If the death penalty remained the ultimate sanction, flogging seems to have been the only area of discipline that caught the wider public's eye. In this area, the powers of courts martial reduced throughout the century, with a regimental court martial (the most junior form) first limited to 300 lashes in 1829 and then 200 in 1833, though it could still order 50 lashes in 1846. Abolition only came in 1881, although by then the frequency of flogging had reduced dramatically, down from 246 cases across the Army in 1835 to 163 a year later.

More minor punishments tended to be less prescribed and their application varied widely so that, while some martinets existed, tolerance was also shown with the cavalry having less use for draconian measures and more leeway. A newly arrived officer of the 9th recalled in 1836 that *'the men were a wildish lot, and very often late for watch-setting, but as long as the duty was well done not much notice was taken. When the orderly sergeant reported men absent at watch-setting, "Give them half an hour" was the usual answer.'*[4] This rather gloomy picture of a soldier's life for much of the 19th century should not disguise the reality that there were also attractions, and that good regimental

PROPOSED RULES AND REGULATIONS

FOR THE

EXERCISE AND MANŒUVRES

OF

THE LANCE,

COMPILED ENTIRELY FROM THE POLISH SYSTEM, INSTITUTED BY MARSHAL PRINCE JOSEPH PONIATOWSKI, AND GENERAL COUNT CORVIN KRASINSKI,

AND ADAPTED TO

The Formations, Movements, and Exercise

OF THE

BRITISH CAVALRY.

TO WHICH IS AFFIXED,

AN HISTORICAL ACCOUNT OF THE MOST CELEBRATED BANNERS AND ORDERS OF CHIVALRY, BEING EMBLEMATIC AND DESCRIPTIVE OF THE ORIGIN AND HONOR FORMERLY ATTACHED TO BEARING GONFANONS, OR GONFALONS, CHIVALRIC BANNERS, AND LANCES.

BY LIEUT. COLONEL REYMOND HERVEY DE MONTMORENCY,

H. P. YORK HUSSARS,

LATE LIEUTENANT COLONEL AND MAJOR IN HIS MAJESTY'S 9TH LANCERS.

"By Jove, I am not covetous for gold;
Nor care I who doth feed upon my cost;
It yearns me not if men my garments wear;
Such outward things dwell not in my desires:
But, if it be a sin to covet honour,
I am the most offending soul alive."

SHAKESPEARE.

LONDON:

PRINTED FOR LONGMAN, HURST, REES, ORME, AND BROWNE, PATERNOSTER-ROW; T. EGERTON, MILITARY LIBRARY, WHITEHALL; AND JOHN CUMMING, NO. 16, LOWER ORMOND-QUAY, DUBLIN.

1820.

officers frequently did their best, at considerable personal expense, to offset the negligence of the government by investing in welfare for their soldiers. *'The evil dealing of the State and the counter-measures of the officers were all brought to light by a Commission [A Commission on Military Punishments 1836]; and at last in 1836 the State began from shame to learn from the officers.'*[5]

Ironically, the death of Wellington in 1852 allowed for greater reform, although initiatives remained largely piecemeal and un-coordinated. Some education and training for both officers and soldiers took place, while the purchase of land at Aldershot and the provision of a camp at Chobham allowed troops to exercise in large, formed bodies, though the role envisaged for the army remained one of home and imperial defence. The shortcomings revealed by the Crimea campaign and the Indian Mutiny also led to further reform. For the cavalry this included a government stud to breed horses, new saddles and more practical dress, although the tales of heroism from both theatres seemed to overshadow the problems and gave the illusion that all was fundamentally sound.

The best known reforms of the 19th century were those brought in by Edward Cardwell between 1868 and 1874 who, amongst other innovations reflecting a more widespread interest in the welfare of junior ranks, reduced colour service (initially to 12 years) and introduced proper career patterns and regularized pensions. For officers, Cardwell drove through the abolition of the purchase of commissions in 1871 after considerable protest, not least from the Treasury who faced a compensation bill of some £7 million. In the event, the headline-grabbing reform did little to change the make-up of the cavalry's officers, the main financial barrier to a commission coming not from the initial purchase price but rather from the extravagant lifestyle, with its outlay on uniforms, horses and mess bills. The make up of the Officers' Messes therefore continued to be the subject of adverse comment and followed the strictures of the earlier Reform movement that had criticised the Army for allowing wealth and birth to override consideration of military efficiency. An example in the Examiner of August 1840 singled out two groups of regiments for attack: *'We specify Hussars and Lancers because…we find that the greater number of offences against the peace and decency of society have been committed by individuals of those rich and generally aristocratic bodies.'*[7]

Despite the slow pace of change over the rest of the century, both the 9th and 12th Light Dragoons were immediately affected by one of the earliest lessons identified from the Napoleonic wars. The value of the lance had been proven by Napoleon's Polish Uhlans, who had used the extra reach provided by

THE LANCE

The first lances appear to have been used by Cyrus the Great of Persia in the 5th century BC when his cavalry, equipped with heavy spears and armour, was used as shock troops. Thereafter, the spear or lance was used by cavalry across the world, forming bodies using it to break the enemy's line and then following up with close quarter work using the sword. In Britain, individual knights continued to use and practise with it until the weapon disappeared from the British armoury during the Middle Ages. Other armies continued to use the weapon but its greatest exponents proved to be the Polish cavalry *husaria* who carried a 15ft lance. This was used to such effect at the Battle of Vienna in 1683 to rout the invading Turks that their reputation fascinated the West for a century.

Napoleon was the first to convert this fascination into action when he introduced Polish lancers into the French army before converting six of his own dragoon regiments to the weapon, their effect being most notable at Albuera where three British battalions were decimated, the worst taking 643 casualties from a strength of 755. Britain followed the French lead at the end of the wars with France with the 9th and 12th converted in 1816, although Lieutenant Colonel Frederick Ponsonby of the 12th Light Dragoons had already commissioned some lances of his own, taking them out to the Peninsula in December 1811 to show his men how to deal with the threat and accustom their horses to the pennants.

The first lances issued to the Regiments were 16ft long, though this was soon reduced to a more manageable length of 9ft. Over the following years several refinements were made to the tip and shaft until, by 1829, a final pattern was approved at 9ft 1in long and weighing 3lb 11oz with an ash shaft and a butt and tip of steel, the latter incorporating blood runnels to make extraction of the lance from its victim easier. Male (solid) bamboo replaced ash for service in Britain from 1864. Bamboo had to be of a particular size to fit directly into the butt and tip. Cutting to fit caused the bamboo to perish, leading to 90 per cent of bamboos sent for approval being discarded and a shortage of shafts. As late as 1896 questions in Parliament were being asked about the material, the Under Secretary of State for War replying that bamboo would be used in war and ash '*brittle, unreliable, and unfit for active service*'[25], would be kept for peace. The Germans, with no ready source of bamboo, used steel shafts and, perhaps unsurprisingly, even experimented with a folding shaft.

The pennant derived from the Polish nobility's personal banners (another reason for lancer regiments not carrying guidons) and were generally removed for battle in order to reduce the visible signature and to make it easier for the lance thrust to enter the body. Beyond their use as a weapon, the lance proved useful as a more general tool, an aspect approved of by Thomas Baines in the Kaffir War of 1852: '*the superiority of the lance over all other weapons was now evident for the men, striking two of them in the ground and with the another passed horizontally through the loops and a blanket stretched over it, formed most excellent and convenient tents, slightly varied where height was not an object by forming the uprights of a couple of swords and passing the lance which served as a ridge pole through the hilts.*'[26]

The lance required a high degree of accuracy and training in order to be properly used, with tent-pegging and pig-sticking used as practice, while the difficulty of mastering the weapon was equalled by the ferocity of the debate throughout the 19th century over how it should be used. The suggestion, never adopted, was that only the front rank of a charge should use the lance to deliver the initial impact, while the rear rank would carry the less unwieldy sword.

Not everyone was an admirer of the lance. Captain Nolan (who delivered the order for the charge of the Light Brigade) wrote in his '*Cavalry: Its History and Tactics*' in 1853: '*If lances be such good weapons, surely those who wield them ought to acquire great confidence in them, whereas it is well-known that, in battle, lancers generally throw them away; and take to their swords. I never spoke to an English lancer who had been engaged in the late Sikh wars that did not declare the lance to be a useless tool, and a great encumbrance in close conflict.*'[27] An infanteer, Lieutenant George Younghusband, provided a different view, having witnessed a cavalry action in which an Afghan lancer charged in 1878. '*Now some people are fond of deprecating the lance: they say it is heavy, unwieldy and hampers a man. Quite so, but if you ever happen to be situated as were the British officers at that moment with no weapon of offence or defence but a poky little sword, perhaps you might take a different view. Of course, theoretically the gallant swordsman with one turn of the wrist thrusts the lance aside, and with another deft turn spits the rash lancer through the waistcoat or other vulnerable part. In practice, however, if the lancer means business, he will have two feet of lance through you before your turn comes.*'[28] A Hussar officer in the Indian Mutiny thought it '*an admirable weapon.. They (mutineers) lie down on the ground and it is difficult to reach them with a sword, whereas a lance can touch them up anywhere.*'[29]

QUEEN ADELAIDE, THE WIFE OF KING WILLIAM IV, IN WHOSE HONOUR THE 9TH WERE RENAMED THE 9TH QUEEN'S ROYAL LANCERS IN 1830, AND WHOSE CIPHER IS STILL WORN ON THE 9TH/12TH LANCERS BUTTONS AND ACCOUTREMENTS.

their weapons to negate the infantry tactic of lying down to escape a sabre thrust and against some objections to this 'foreign' invention (the Colonel of the 12th remarked that *'good swordsmen have no occasion to fear the lance if they are equally good horsemen'*) the decision was taken to convert five regiments. With surprising rapidity a training cadre was established in London in February 1816, with 28th September 1816 set as the conversion date. Not for the last time, however, equipment procurement seemed unable to keep up and the lances did not appear until March of the following year. Leading the instructors was Major de Montmorency, an officer of the 9th who, captured in the Peninsula in 1811, had been allowed to live in Paris on parole, where he had studied the Polish lancers on exercise, his knowledge eventually forming a manual for lance drill which, published in 1820, remained the basis for all future lance training. The advent of the new weapon forced the Regiments to abandon their carbines and change their titles, the 9th becoming the 9th Light Dragoons (Lancers), a title they would keep until William IV's reign, while the 12th went for a more radical re-designation as the 12th or Prince of Wales's Royal Lancers as, for the first time, the crossed lances appeared behind the Prince of Wales's feathers in their badge.

The short period spent in France following the defeat of Napoleon proved an easy posting for the 12th, marked by good relations with their recent enemy, and improved by the news that everyone at Waterloo would receive a medal, the first to be issued to all ranks, as well as counting as the equivalent to two years' service towards their pension. Excesses were perhaps inevitable, one officer being dismissed in September 1816 for taking £8,000 from another while gambling, the latter having already lost £7,000 that night. The incident was made worse by the victim's age; he was only 16, and therefore *'ignorant of and unused to play, and affected by the wine he had been prevailed upon to take'*.

Frequent changes of location in England and Ireland became the norm for both Regiments for the next 20 years, London proving a regular posting where they took part in escorts, reviews and other ceremonial duties, including a Royal Review in 1819 in Hyde Park in which both Regiments, together with the 19th Lancers, took part and demonstrated their new skills with the lance. Chosen to form part of William IV's escort following his coronation, the 9th underwent a further name change on 23rd July 1830 to become 9th Queen's Royal Lancers, named after Queen Adelaide, the King's wife, whose monogram continues to be used on the modern Regiment's buttons and accoutrements.

Foreign travel in this period was limited to the 12th's despatch of four troops to Portugal in January 1827 as part of an ill-judged attempt to influence a revolution there from which they returned the following year. Otherwise the use of arms was limited to riot duty as popular demand for political change mounted. Whether in England or Ireland, the work was unrewarding and unexciting, a Lord Lieutenant for Ireland highlighting the difficulties that had been faced by the 9th in 1833: *'the calm bearing and the high intelligence evinced by the officers, the uniform attention and assiduity of the Non-commissioned officers, and the patient and exemplary forbearance of the men, insulted and even attacked as they have sometimes been, have called forth the approbation of all who have observed their conduct. In war great exertion and sufferings are generally requited by Honour and Glory, and this is ample reward to a high mind, but in the unhappy domestic strifes the Army is now daily called upon to quell less stimulating inducements to exertions are in view. The greater then is the merit of those who act thus virtuously under very aggravating circumstances.'*

Relations with the populace were not all bad. The city of Norwich gave a squadron of the 9th a barrel of beer *'as a small testimony to their uniform good conduct during their residence in this city'*, though the more prim people of Brighton reprimanded the 12th for frivolity in 1838, a paper reporting that *'we understand that in consequence of the 12th Lancers having marched to church headed by the band playing Rory O'More and other lively tunes, they will not be allowed to attend St. Peter's, Brighton, any more, and that services will be performed every Sunday within the Barracks'*. In spite of such levity, the same year also saw Prince George of Cambridge attached to the 12th, although without a commission.

INDIA

After a lengthy period spent at home, both Regiments were about to start a series of more exotic postings including a relationship with India that would span nearly 100 years. The Honourable East India Company's presence and power in India had, almost since its foundation in 1600, entangled the British government. Since 1757, Parliament had stationed British regiments in India not only to provide additional troops to supplement the Company's armies, but more importantly to produce a reliable core for operations and a visible marker of British intent. The first British cavalry regiments in the country had been raised specifically for service there and had arrived in 1782. These were soon followed by regular regiments of the standing army, known as King's or Queen's (as opposed to native) regiments. The inflow of these regiments produced a ratio of one British soldier for every three native ones, though crucially the ratio had reduced one in six by the time of the Mutiny. Of the British cavalry regiments, only the light cavalry were considered suitable for service in India, and these, like their infantry counterparts would be brigaded with native regiments, normally in a ratio of one to two.

For many, service in the British or Royal army in India was not a highly prized jewel. Officers often transferred to another regiment to remain in Britain, a 9th Lancer captain paying £1,500 to exchange elsewhere in 1841, while many of those who went out there did so because they could not afford to do otherwise. As a consequence, a general decline had set in, the *Naval and Military Gazette* of February 1837 stating that *'at the present moment such is the degraded state of the army in India, and the feeling against serving in that country, that none but needy adventurers and seedy boys can be procured for the King's regiments there'*.[8]

Others saw advantage in service in India: it offered variety from endless time in Britain and it was easier to save money, while, with native labour in such cheap supply, even the most junior soldier could lord it over someone, a troop sergeant normally having a servant whose relatives would act as batmen for the rest of the troop. Officers were almost swamped by staff and could also indulge in a range of sports from wildfowling and quail shooting, to polo and racing before moving on to the more exotic tent-pegging, pig-sticking and tiger and big-game hunting.

1 THE 9TH LANCERS IN ABOUT 1842. WILLIAM IV BELIEVED THAT 'SAILORS SHOULD WEAR BLUE AND SOLDIERS SHOULD WEAR RED', THOUGH THIS ORDER WAS RESCINDED WHEN QUEEN VICTORIA CAME TO THE THRONE. ALTHOUGH THE CAVALRY REVERTED TO BLUE, THE 9TH LANCERS WERE ALLOWED TO CONTINUE TO WEAR SCARLET AS THEY HAD JUST BEEN ISSUED NEW UNIFORMS.

2 CAMPAIGNING IN INDIA INVOLVED A HUGE AMOUNT OF CAMP FOLLOWERS – AN OFFICER TYPICALLY REQUIRED SIX CAMELS, THREE CARTS AND A DOZEN SERVANTS TO KEEP HIM ON THE ROAD.

1	2

9TH LANCER OPERATIONS IN INDIA 1843–1849.

Despite these benefits, soldiering in India remained, for many, an unpleasant affair, with life in the cantonments based outside the cities monotonous, squalid and prone to disease. Private Gillings of the 9th wrote that *'the soldier who goes out to India often curses his own folly in entering the service'*, with its constant heat, insects and irritations. By the middle of the century, transportation to the penal colonies of Australia, one of the more common punishments for serious offences, was often actively sought by soldiers who were tired of life in the service of the Raj, leading the authorities increasingly to use the death penalty as a disincentive.

Life while campaigning was equally different. The column that the 9th Lancers formed a part of in the Punjab War of 1845 included 3,000 fighting men and two 12-pounder elephant gun batteries. To keep them on the road required about 11,000 camp followers and a menagerie of elephants, bullocks, horses and other animals, with an officer's personal equipment carried on half a dozen camels and two or three bullock carts, whilst he himself might be surrounded by a dozen servants and grooms. Young women, euphemistically called dancing girls, would also form part of the retinue, so that *'an Indian Army taking the field in these spacious days resembled rather a tribal migration than a fighting force, and was to an incredible degree cumbersome, troublesome and uncontrollable'.*[9]

Although the 12th would remain in England and Ireland until 1851, for the 9th a long association with India began when, in 1842, 45 officers, 80 warrant officers and NCOs and 621 private soldiers left England, accompanied by 74 women and 65 children. Conditions in India had already affected them by their arrival in Cawnpore in February 1843, the journey from Calcutta claiming one officer, 71 soldiers, 14 women and 18 children, mostly the victims of cholera. The posting that awaited the survivors was regarded as one of the least attractive in India, with a long, miserable summer of hot, fierce winds by day and ravenous insects by night. Medicine and ventilation was almost non-existent while drink, mainly local spirits such as arrak, was in plentiful supply and frequently provided the only source of relief. By June 1843, the Regiment was 104 under strength and by the end of the month up to eight men a day were dying from heat apoplexy with listlessness and apathy omnipresent.

PUNNIAR

Britain had by now a considerable degree of control over many of the previously independent states in the south and centre of India, though to the north the process of annexation was less advanced with tension the inevitable result. The 9th's first operations in India began soon after their arrival, when, at the end of 1843, the tension once again erupted into conflict as the Governor-General despatched forces to the state of Gwalior some 80 miles south of Agra. Designed as a show of strength, the campaign intended to eliminate a potential trouble spot that might interfere in the increasingly likely war with the Punjab to the north by intimidating Gwalior's army that had recently ejected the pro-British administration. Part of the smaller of two columns of troops, the 9th despatched two squadrons and a headquarters as part of a cavalry brigade to participate in a campaign that was settled by two simultaneous actions on 29th December 1843 in which the enemy sent out from Gwalior were defeated. For the 9th Lancers, the Battle of Punniar was limited to providing escorts for the guns while the day was fought and won in a rapid series of attacks by the infantry across ground unsuited to cavalry. Despite this limited involvement, the Regiment was rewarded for its efforts with the battle honour Punniar, six months' field allowance, a bronze medal made from the enemy's guns and, more immediately attractive, enjoyment of a three-week party held by the re-instated head of Gwalior.

SOBRAON

Returning to Cawnpore in February 1844, the Regiment gradually built up its strength until, at the end of 1845, Britain's relations with the Sikh

kingdom of Punjab, the last great independent state in India, caught them up. The Punjab's army, a powerful, well equipped and modern force with a well-deserved reputation, had recently secured political power and was spoiling for a fight, for which British Indian forces had been preparing for some time. The initial incursion by the Sikh army was dealt with in late December 1845, forcing them back to Sobraon on the River Sutlej, the border between the Punjab and British India, where both sides awaited reinforcements. Among them was the 9th Lancers, who had already travelled to Meerut in November and arrived at Sobraon on 5th January 1846 as part of a combined arms column.

Faced with the strong Sikh position on both banks of the Sutlej, the British waited as the siege train and more ammunition was brought up. Meanwhile the enemy continued to improve its position, simultaneously sending another force to threaten British lines of communication, a manoeuvre stopped by a British victory at Aliwal some 60 miles to the east. The 9th, now grouped in a cavalry brigade with two regiments of native cavalry and some horse artillery, remained at Sobraon, where it was occupied by minor skirmishes with Sikhs sent across the river until, by 10th February, preparations for an assault were complete. Faced by the Sikh's extensively fortified positions, the Battle of Sobraon turned into a brutal slugging match initially conducted by the artillery and then the infantry, with the cavalry little used beyond initial reconnaissance of the enemy positions before escorting the guns and acting as a mobile reserve. For their part, the 9th Lancers were deployed in support of the attacks on the right, a single squadron being sent to draw the enemy's fire and allow their guns to be pinpointed before rejoining the Brigade as the main attack got under way. Private Gillings of the 9th described the situation. As the enemies guns became effective, their fire *'flew over the heads of the advancing infantry into our ranks, and came fizzing and whizzing about our ears most unpleasantly, and rattled amongst the horses' legs, and in less than five minutes upward of twenty horses were disabled. To render it difficult for the Sikhs to get our range, we kept changing ground alternately to the right and left. By this means we fortunately lost but two men. As the infantry forced themselves into the [enemy] trenches, the 'long balls' decreased; at the same time we moved up to their support at a trot, and as we approached the trenches the last expiring shot the Sikhs fired on this side [of the River Sutlej] fell scattering – for it was grape – at our horses' feet. The day was lost to them, and the British troops were now in possession of their camp and guns.'*[10]

The British victory at Sobraon was complete, costing the feared Sikh army all its artillery and leaving Lahore wide open for occupation. The subsequent peace treaty brought the First Sikh War to a close with the State of Punjab becoming a British Protectorate, the army limited in size and an indemnity, including the Koh-I-Noor diamond, which was given to Queen Victoria, exacted. The 9th were free to return to Meerut where, three months later, a less glittering but equally welcome gratuity was awarded, a trooper's share coming to 76 rupees which was all spent in a few 'glorious' days in which *'bottles of liquor were dispatched as fast as the Sikhs at Sobraon'*[11], the effects requiring nine to be treated in hospital, while one man drowned in a tank of water.

The return to peacetime routine saw more senior officers of the Regiment return to Britain on leave and allowed an exceptional talent to emerge. Major Hope Grant, who had only recently avoided court martial for seeking the removal of his Commanding Officer for drunkenness at Sobraon, assumed temporary command of the 9th Lancers and immediately acted with characteristic authority, instituting an hour's early morning drill before sunrise – *'to shake the listlessness out of them does all the good in the world'* – and rapidly reducing the sick list as a result.

…their fire 'flew over the heads of the advancing infantry into our ranks, and came fizzing and whizzing about our ears most unpleasantly…'

CHILLIANWALLAH

The resentment felt by the Sikhs of the Punjab after their recent defeat was not long in coming to a head and, following a short period in barracks, the 9th Lancers were once again part of a war with them. Faced with a wider rebellion against British influence that, by the summer of 1848, encompassed Kashmir, other north-western provinces and parts of Afghanistan, all of which sent contingents to fight with Punjabi rebels, the British decided to gather a single large army that would smash the Sikh army and finally end trouble in the area. The 9th arrived at the concentration area at Ferozepore on 21st October after a series of long marches conducted at night to reduce the effect of the heat. They were now brigaded with the 14th Light Dragoons and two native cavalry regiments under a commander, Brigadier Pope, who, despite his reputation for bravery, did little to boost confidence by being too old to get into the saddle unaided.

On 8th November the army advanced to engage the enemy that was believed to be on the line of the River Chenab, the 9th taking part in a small skirmish on 22nd November before

settling down to outpost duty as the two armies sized each other up. On 1st December, General Gough, the Commander-in-Chief, manoeuvred to attack the flank, a strategy foiled by an orderly Sikh withdrawal that the follow up force was unable to take advantage of. The 9th's brigade found that the Sikhs had gone too far, too fast and, after two days in which they became ensnared in almost impassable jungle, they returned to the Chenab *'harassed, tattered and torn by the jungle and almost dying of thirst'*. Once more they took up picquet duty in difficult country while the lines of communication to the rear were secured.

When the advance began again, the British force of 12,000 faced 30,000 Sikhs who were understood to have occupied a fortified position on the banks of the River Jhelum, for which General Gough now headed. Within days, the jungle had reduced progress to a crawl, though by midday on 13th January, the army had nearly reached the enemy position, with an enemy outpost being evicted from the village of Chillianwallah as General Gough, who had decided to attack the following morning, began to give orders for the camp that night. The Sikhs now forced the issue, bringing their artillery to bear and revealing that they had advanced from their prepared position on the Jhelum to the edge of the jungle with the intention of ejecting the British from the village which had the only water supply available. With no alternative but to fight immediately, and with no time to mount a proper defence, Gough gave orders to counter-attack. Both infantry divisions were in the centre, while the two cavalry brigades protected their flanks from the overlapping Sikh line which more than doubled the British in number. Pope's brigade was posted on the right of the British line, with the 9th, less two squadrons, at the farthest end, while inside came the two Indian regiments (each less one and a half

CAMPAIGN DISCIPLINE

When the 9th Lancers were marching to the attack on Sobraon, they were ordered to escort a number of heavy 24-pounder guns, each of which weighed over a ton, which were to be dragged by elephants into their firing positions.

Elephants were frequently used in India as pack animals, as well as the more usual horses, mules, donkeys and camels, and mostly proved an excellent way of conveying heavy loads over difficult ground.

There were hazards, however, arising from the occasional propensity of male elephants to run amok when in season, a condition known as 'musth'.

On this occasion, the 9th Lancers were dismayed when one of the gun elephants, said to have 'turned rusty', refused to pull his gun.

The head man in charge of the elephants, known as a Mahout, seems to have ordered 'the refractory brute' to be brought before a court comprising the other Mahouts, under the guard of two other elephants who were presumably more reliable, to be tried by a court martial.

The sentence, almost unbelievable in these gentler times, was 25 lashes and was carried out by one of the other elephants, to whom a large double chain had been given for the purpose. The elephant took it in his trunk and, at the word of command, inflicted a most tremendous lash on the culprit, repeated 24 times, after which the rebel elephant was taken away and reportedly 'no longer refused to draw the gun'...

squadrons), the 14th Light Dragoons and 10 guns of horse artillery, the whole formation in a single line with no reserves or support. The detached squadrons, with a battery of guns, formed a flank guard on the extreme right, protecting the army from enemy Goorchurra horsemen who were threatening from the north.

The advance into the jungle broke down all command and control, the infantry and cavalry soon losing contact with each other, the enemy, according to Trooper Pearman, having chosen *'a rare place for us to work. We could not combine one [infantry] regiment to the other, so close was the jungle in places.'*[12] On the order to advance, the cavalry had moved off at the trot on both flanks but soon found the jungle breaking their speed as they advanced on the cavalry that threatened the flanks. After initial difficulty, the left-hand brigade pushed the enemy horse back, while on the right Pope's brigade came to a line of cover that brought the centre of the line, where Pope was positioned, to a halt. Urged to attack by his subordinates on the flanks who could see and in some cases were engaged with the enemy, Pope vacillated while, at this critical moment, Sikh horsemen charged the native cavalry and from somewhere unknown the order was given *'Three's about!'* to turn about and withdraw. The instruction spread up and down the line of the Brigade in the confusion of the jungle. With no one able to see what was happening, the 9th and the 14th quickly followed in what soon turned into a disorderly and speedy retreat which, when the Brigade was finally reformed in a clearing on the edge of the jungle by Hope Grant and others, revealed the loss of all the Brigade's guns. The infantry in the centre, who they were supposed

THE VICTORY AT THE BATTLE OF CHILLIANWALLAH ON 13TH JANUARY 1849 WAS OVERSHADOWED BY THE INEPT HANDLING OF THE CAVALRY BRIGADE IN WHICH THE 9TH LANCERS WERE SERVING. MAJOR JAMES HOPE GRANT, THEN A SQUADRON LEADER, DISTINGUISHED HIMSELF BOTH ON THE BATTLEFIELD AND AFTERWARDS WHEN HE DEMANDED THE RESIGNATION OF THE COMMANDING OFFICER FOR BEING DRUNK.

THE 9TH LANCERS IN THE PURSUIT DURING THE CLOSING STAGES OF THE BATTLE OF GUJERAT ON 21ST OCTOBER 1849. THE BATTLE ENDED THE SECOND SIKH WAR AND BROUGHT THE LAST MAJOR INDEPENDENT KINGDOM IN NORTHERN INDIA UNDER BRITISH RULE.

to have been protecting, had been attacked from behind, while the cavalry brigade's losses were only light.

Elsewhere in the battle the detached squadrons and artillery on the extreme right flank had met with more success, repulsing several waves of cavalry as they attempted to come round the side but finding that *'the enemy were almost impervious, from the shields, armour and wadded clothes they wore – the men of the 9th Lancers often failed to pierce them,'* though the officer also says *'our men ran their lances so far thro' the Sikhs, they could not pull them out again, and they were obliged to leave them'.*[13]

The blame for the débâcle in the centre has been laid squarely, and it would appear rightly, on the shoulders of Pope, who was mortally wounded in the retreat and so was unable to defend himself. His lack of experience was shown in the formation adopted which, in difficult country, not only lacked a reserve but rendered command and control impossible, while his advance managed to mask the guns, depriving both his own forces and the supported infantry of vital fire support. Who gave the order to turn about will never be known, but the battle

'...the enemy were almost impervious, from the shields, armour and wadded clothes they wore – the men of the 9th Lancers often failed to pierce them...'

brought little credit to either British regiment or to the native cavalry, upon which the Governor-General wished to inflict some *'petty indignity'* until dissuaded from it by Gough. The final verdict of the court of inquiry into the conduct of the brigade was that *'their retrograde movement originated more from mistake than a fear of encountering an insignificant enemy'*[14], it later being held that *'to place good regiments, and both the 9th Lancers and the 14th Light Dragoons were good regiments, under the command of such a man [Pope] was like placing valuable porcelain in the hands of a child'.*[15]

GUJERAT

Despite the withdrawal, Chillianwallah had been held and the Sikhs driven back to their positions, but at a price both in casualties and British pride. Torrential rain prevented further immediate advance and a period of stalemate ensued while both sides awaited reinforcements. General Gough refused to be drawn into battle until sufficient troops and superiority in artillery arrived some five weeks later and this allowed him to be certain of conquering the Punjab entirely. On 21st February he was ready and, with an army of 20,000 men and 88 guns, attacked the Sikh force of between two and three times that number, but with only 59 guns, in

their unprepared position on the plain at Gujerat near the River Chenab.

The 9th Lancers were now in Brigadier White's brigade which, together with an infantry division, formed the left wing of the army from which it was separated by a deep dry river bed or *nullah*. As was the custom, a three-hour artillery duel began the battle until, at midday, the British advance began with the main effort against the left-centre of the enemy's line, initially stiff resistance eventually being overcome as the enemy gave ground along the front. Throughout the day, both flanks remained threatened by enemy cavalry that on the left totalled 4,000 men, including artillery and 1,500 Afghan horsemen, their numbers threatening to overlap and turn the British line. Rapid changes of ground and other manoeuvres prevented significant casualties until eventually the enemy horse decided to attack, advancing towards White's brigade as Lieutenant Colonel Hope Grant was ordered to meet the threat by taking the Scinde Horse and the 9th charging.

Colonel Hope Grant summed up the charge in a few modest words: *'our men drove at this force and routed it, killing about forty men,'* while General Gough was more generous: *'the whole of the right of the Sikh line was turned, and the day decided. The victory was ours, and the hostile army rapidly dissolved into flying fragments, before a relentless pursuit'.* Trooper Gilling provided more dramatic detail: *'We did not move out of a walk until within about a hundred and fifty yards from their front, they all the time peppering away at us most fearfully. The two left squadrons fired their carbines, and the ominous words 'Trot', 'Charge!' followed in quick succession afterwards. And now followed a clashing of swords and lances, accompanied with a loud 'Hurrah!' mixed with the Afghan curse of 'Feringhee dog!' and the Sikh 'Feringhee brian!' followed by*

other imprecations and the groans of the wounded; and in about the space of two minutes our foes turned their backs upon us and fled like chaff before the wind. We pursued them until, coming up with a gun they had abandoned, we were ordered to halt for the remainder of our artillery to come up. Two of their colours had fallen into our hands at the first onset, and now we captured a nine-pounder gun which, strange to say, turned out to be one that was taken from us at Chillianwallah.'[16]

The closing hours of the Battle of Gujerat saw a relentless pursuit of the disintegrating Sikh army back through the village and the enemy camp with, at its height, all the cavalry formed in a line a mile long as they completed the destruction, leaving the Afghan contingent the only part of the army still in one piece, to be chased back over the border in the ensuing days as the rebels sued for peace. The terms of the subsequent treaty incorporated Punjab into British India and freed General Gough's army to disperse, though the 9th and others remained behind on garrison duty, spending a dry, hot and miserable summer at Wazirabad in the Punjab where the only gloss was the award of the customary *batta* or prize money.

SOUTH AFRICA 1851–1853

Within two years of the 9th's engagements in India, the 12th Lancers' long period of home service came to an end. Although British involvement in South Africa had been formalised with the establishment of the Cape Colony following its enforced purchase from the Dutch in 1813, the British presence had already been the cause of friction both with the earlier European settlers and the indigenous population with whom the various clashes became known as the Kaffir, Cape Frontier or Xhosa Wars, the numbering of which largely defies convention.

AN INSPECTION OF THE 12TH LANCERS AT GRAHAMSTOWN SHORTLY AFTER THEIR ARRIVAL IN SOUTH AFRICA IN 1851 TO FIGHT THE KAFFIR OR XHOSA WARS. THE PARADE GROUND UNIFORMS WERE SOON FOUND TO BE A MENACE – WITH ONE SOLDIER UNABLE TO REMOUNT WHEN HIS HORSE HAD BEEN SHOT UNDER HIM AS HIS OVERALLS WERE TOO TIGHT.

Regular British army involvement in the country had remained limited and, at the time of the 12th's deployment in 1851, only two other British cavalry regiments had ever served there, and these for limited periods, the authorities preferring to rely on local forces to maintain security. By 1850 these troops had proved incapable of dealing with the disaffected tribes of the Eastern Cape region (known at the time as kaffirs, a term that did not then carry the overtly racist connotations of today but appears to have been used to designate the Xhosa people), and the raids by the Basuto into the Colony itself, forcing the authorities, with considerable reluctance, to seek reinforcements from Britain.

Arriving in East London in October 1851, the 12th immediately found themselves committed against the rebel tribes in the Colony. In a campaign that was designed to give the rebels no chance to rest, a series of large sweeps was made through the Transkei, an area to the north of the Kei River, to seize the livestock on which the tribes depended, while a small detachment from the Regiment was temporarily detached to ensure the safety of the threatened town of Butterworth. Although successful in depriving the enemy of 30,000 cattle and hundreds of horses and goats in the period between November 1851 and January 1852, the British, operating in miserable conditions, could never bring the rebels to battle. The latter chose instead to move into the Kroome range of hills in which, despite efforts by the 12th and others to hunt them down using scorched-earth tactics, they remained undefeated in a small area known as the Waterkloof.

As so often, the nature of the conflict suited a crafty, elusive enemy and their basic weapons. Knobkerries, or throwing sticks, could be hurled great distances, while the seven assegai spears they carried (six for throwing and one for stabbing), were complemented by basic musketry skills and their exploitation of the familiar country to launch ambushes and raids. The British regular troops found the country quite unsuited to their large-

WRECK OF THE BIRKENHEAD

On 26th February 1852, the Birkenhead, a ship carrying reinforcements, including two officers, one sergeant and five soldiers destined to join the 12th, sank off Danger Point on its way to Port Elizabeth. The stories of the wreck of the ship and the heroism displayed, in particular the attempts to get women, children and horses off, are many and include that of Cornet Bond of the 12th whose act of saving two young girls who had been left below decks is recorded in TMH Kenny's picture of the wreck. The final moments of the ship, as the men waited in column on the aft deck prior to finally going down were held up as examples to the world of courage and discipline, with the King of Prussia ordering that all his regiments should be read the story. *'The behaviour of all ranks, far exceeded anything that I thought could be effected by the most perfect discipline. All received and carried out orders as if embarking for a world's port instead of for Eternity. There was only this difference. I never saw an embarkation conducted with so little confusion'* stated a survivor.[30] Of the troops on board, only five officers and 109 soldiers survived, with 14 officers and 394 soldiers drowning. Cornet Bond himself made it to shore two miles away: *'by careful negotiation I finally got to land. What was my astonishment on looking round to find my own charger standing near! Of my draft of the 12th Lancers only one man survived – and he was killed in the first engagement with the enemy.'*

WRECK OF HM STEAMSHIP 'BIRKENHEAD', WHICH SANK OFF DANGER POINT SOUTH AFRICA ON 26TH FEBRUARY 1852. ON BOARD WAS A DRAFT OF REINFORCEMENTS FOR THE 12TH LANCERS, INCLUDING CORNET BOND WHO MADE THE SKETCH ON WHICH THIS PRINT IS BASED. 23 OFFICERS AND 468 SOLDIERS AND SAILORS DROWNED OR WERE EATEN BY SHARKS, ALTHOUGH ALL WOMEN AND CHILDREN ON BOARD WERE SAVED. THE DISCIPLINE SHOWN BY THOSE ON BOARD CAUSED THE KING OF PRUSSIA TO HAVE THE STORY READ TO ALL HIS TROOPS AS AN EXAMPLE. CORNET BOND SWAM TO THE SHORE WHERE HE FOUND HIS CHARGER WAITING FOR HIM.

scale charges, the weather atrocious and their weaponry not necessarily appropriate (the flintlock pistol was still in use), the 12th's Commanding Officer insisting that all officers carry a carbine and that the advance guard carry a double-barrel version as used by the Cape Mounted Rifles. Of the lance itself, not all were enthusiastic: '*I was glad to observe that a large proportion of the men were armed instead of lances with double-barrelled carbines and that the officers patronised long-range rifles rather than funny little spikes upon the end of fairy wands which a kaffir would consider but a poor equivalent for an assegai.*'[17] Not for the last time in South Africa, the horses, despite being Cape mounts, suffered too in the endless marches and counter-marches, the 12th losing 40 dead by the end of their first expedition.

A fresh attempt to clear the enemy from the Waterkloof feature in March 1852 proved more successful. Initially tasked with providing a cut-off group, the 12th Lancers then joined the pursuit of the rebel army in which 6,000 enemy were reported to have died and 80,000 cattle captured. Despite the impact of these losses, which brought a temporary halt to the campaign, re-infiltration into the area required the operation to be repeated in August.

The conclusion of the second sweep gave the British commander, Sir George Cathcart, sufficient confidence that his lines were secure in order to allow him to move north to deal with the Basuto, whose raiding parties attacked from outside the Cape Colony to steal the Boer farmers' cattle. The Basuto were at least as formidable an enemy as the rebels of the Eastern Cape. Heavily armed with knobkerries, assegais and battle-axes, they also had muskets and a formidable 7,000-strong force mounted on tough horses. Facing them, Cathcart assembled 2,500 men, including two squadrons from each of the 12th and the Cape Mounted Rifles, two weak infantry brigades, two guns and four rocket tubes. Equipped for three months in the desert, the column moved off from Burghersdorp on 27th November and marched north for a fortnight, resting at the Orange and Caledon Rivers *en route* before entering Basuto country on 10th December to come in sight of Thaba Bosia, the Basuto leader's base, three days later. With the British camped at Platberg, the Basuto sued for peace, but found the fine of 10,000 cattle imposed too harsh. War becoming inevitable when their offer of 3,500 cattle was rejected and Cathcart decided to collect the balance.

From a forward base on the River Caledon, Cathcart despatched three columns on 20th December to make for Thaba Bosia then sweep the Berea, a table-top plateau stretching away to the north onto which the Basuto had driven their cattle. Detailing troops for the two groups that would move to the west of the plateau and then sweep across the top, the 12th further provided half of a cavalry column totalling a little under 250 men and commanded by Lieutenant Colonel Napier of the Cape Mounted Rifles whose task was to screen to the north and east of the plateau and prevent the escape of the Basuto and their cattle.

In the event the wholly inaccurate mapping, which had not revealed the full extent of the 25 mile long plateau, forced Napier's command to cut across the top to effect the cut-off. Using a long wide valley to climb the 600ft to the top, they began to collect cattle and were descending with 4,000 head when the rearguard, formed by the 12th, was attacked by 700 dismounted and mounted Basuto troops. Turning to face the enemy they charged three times but were then surrounded, just managing to break out and join

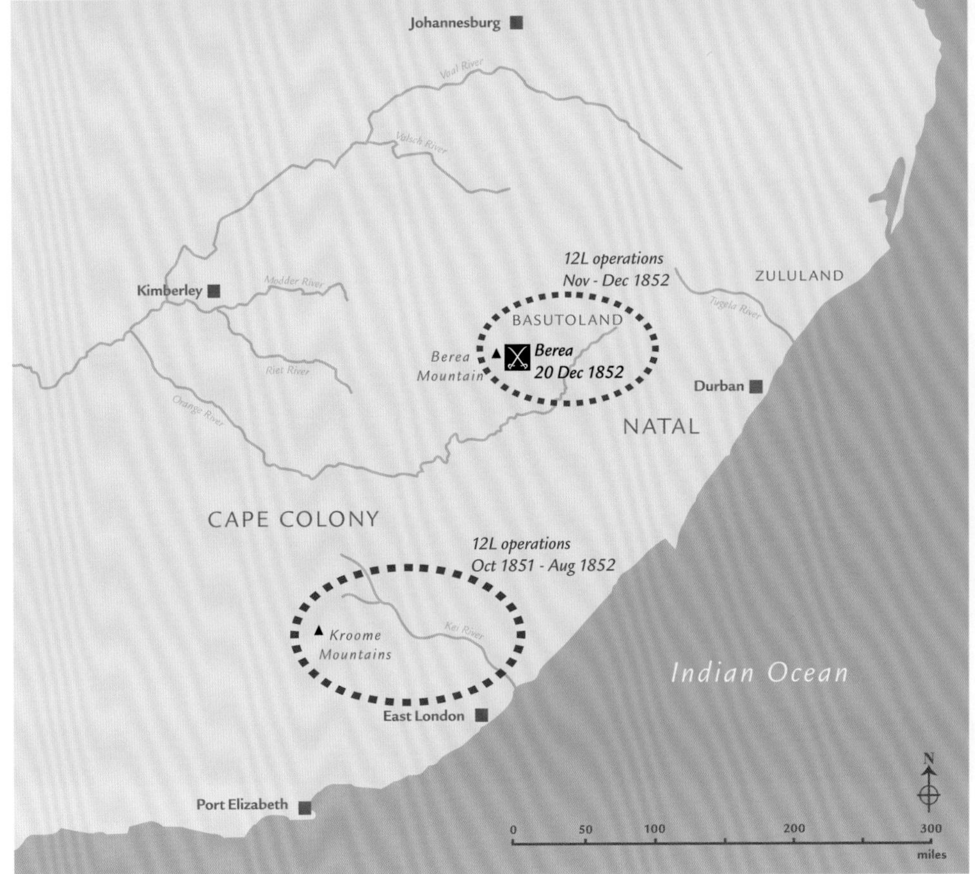

1 THE COLUMN CONSISTING OF THE 12TH LANCERS, THE CAPE MOUNTED RIFLES AND ARTILLERY CROSSING THE GREAT ORANGE RIVER IN DECEMBER 1852 TO ATTACK THE BASUTO HOMELAND FROM WHERE RAIDS INTO CAPE COLONY WERE BEING MADE.

2 THE KAFFIR WARS - OPERATIONS AGAINST THE XHOSA AND THE BASUTO.

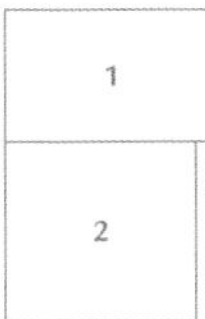

THE 12TH LANCERS ROUNDING UP CATTLE WHILE IN SOUTH AFRICA, A FAVOURED WAY OF PUNISHING THE BASUTO OR DEPRIVING THEM OF THEIR LIVELIHOOD.

the rest of Napier's force which was itself now under attack. After fierce fighting, the column managed to break clean and return to the British lines but not before the Regiment had lost 27 dead. An officer of the rearguard described their part in the action: '*We did our best, we drove one squadron in, and then another at our best pace, and then confronted their main body… we now re-dressed our line at 300 yards from their centre, which was three deep, their flanks advanced in an attitude to surround us. We charged, and received at 70 yards' distance a concentric fire from the whole line, afterwhich the semi-circle closed its horns upon us, and we were surrounded and cut off. We were therefore compelled to dash back and re-form close to them, but their regular and overwhelming advance pushed us on and we were obliged at last to gallop for our lives. Our retreat was headlong, for the enemy had headed us and pursued us with good speed.. Tottenham [12th Lancers, commanding the rearguard] behaved like a hero; the last to turn, he remained almost the last in the retreat, and by cool courage and good riding managed to save a sergeant major by shooting a Basuto while just about to stab him. After a mile we were pulled up by a stone wall and here many fell..*'[18]

The groups sweeping the top of the plateau had met with greater success. Having rounded up cattle at little cost, however, they, too, were surprised as they withdrew, this time by Basuto soldiers equipped with lances captured from Napier's column, the troops managing to get away only after a stiff fight. The day's actions had been sufficient to cause the Basuto to negotiate that evening and agree to pay the fine in cattle which, apart from a couple of calves that found their way into the officers' and sergeants' mess tents, were then distributed to the Boer farmers.

In the aftermath Napier was criticised for collecting cattle when he had other orders, but the action also demonstrated other, unforeseen, weaknesses. For many, the lance and sword proved unwieldy in close combat, while the issue flintlock pistols proved useless, especially when compared to the axes carried by the Basuto or the double-barrelled carbines of the Cape Mounted Rifles. There are also reports of at least one man, who had lost his horse under him, dying because the fashionable close fit of his issue uniform overalls prevented him remounting.

The period of calm that, at least temporarily, settled on the Cape released the 12th Lancers, the last British cavalry regiment to serve in the country for 15 years, to sail for India at the end of 1853, where they rapidly settled in, their skills learnt on active service in South Africa earning early praise from Captain Henderson who had recently transferred into the Regiment: *'their smartness and soldier-like bearing could not be excelled, or their riding. The latter I have never seen equalled; their long service at the Cape had brought them, as we say of a race-horse, 'as fine as a star and as fit as a fiddle' for roughing it in any part of the world.'* Other opportunities were also exploited, the extra allowances that married men could get from the East India Company appearing to increase the frequency of weddings, though Henderson felt that had *'seen better looking men as regards countenance'*.[19] After barely a year in the country they found themselves once more on the move, this time as part of the reinforcements that Britain and France required for their ill-fated campaign in the Crimea.

CRIMEA

When the 12th Lancers received orders for the Crimea the campaign had been dragging on for over a year. Sebastapol remained in Russian hands and reinforcements were badly needed to make good the losses both from combat (including the charge of the Light Brigade) and from sickness brought on by the terrible weather, poor sanitation and disastrous logistics. While the grim reality of the campaign was yet to be revealed to them, the Regiment's move to the Crimea via Aden and Suez in early 1855 provided at least one distraction when the Pasha of Egypt laid on a feast for the officers but mistook the Sergeants' Mess for the intended guests, a mistake that went uncorrected as they made themselves at home: *'Champagne corks were continually flying, bitter beer flowed copiously; roast capons and delicate hams, splendid roast beef and delicious mutton… disappeared like magic.. One stuffed a capon into his haversack, another 'boned' a lot of splendid cigars out of a glass on the table; a sergeant major, pretending to be in a violent passion, threw an entire ham at a private who appeared at the door of the pavilion, and who straightway picked it up and walked off with it.'* The party continued until the officer of the day walked in, the awkward silence that followed finally being broken by the Mess coming to attention and reporting *'Sergeants' Mess all right, Sir!'* the officer sensibly replying: *'All right, you did the duty, and the Pasha pays for the dinner, so it is all right.'*

Balaclava harbour was reached on 7th May 1855 and the 12th Lancers immediately joined the army besieging Sebastopol. Together with the 10th Hussars, who had also just arrived, one of their first duties was the Queen's Birthday Review on 24th May. Here the effects of the previous year were starkly revealed, the two new regiments producing 800 of the 1,400 men of the Cavalry

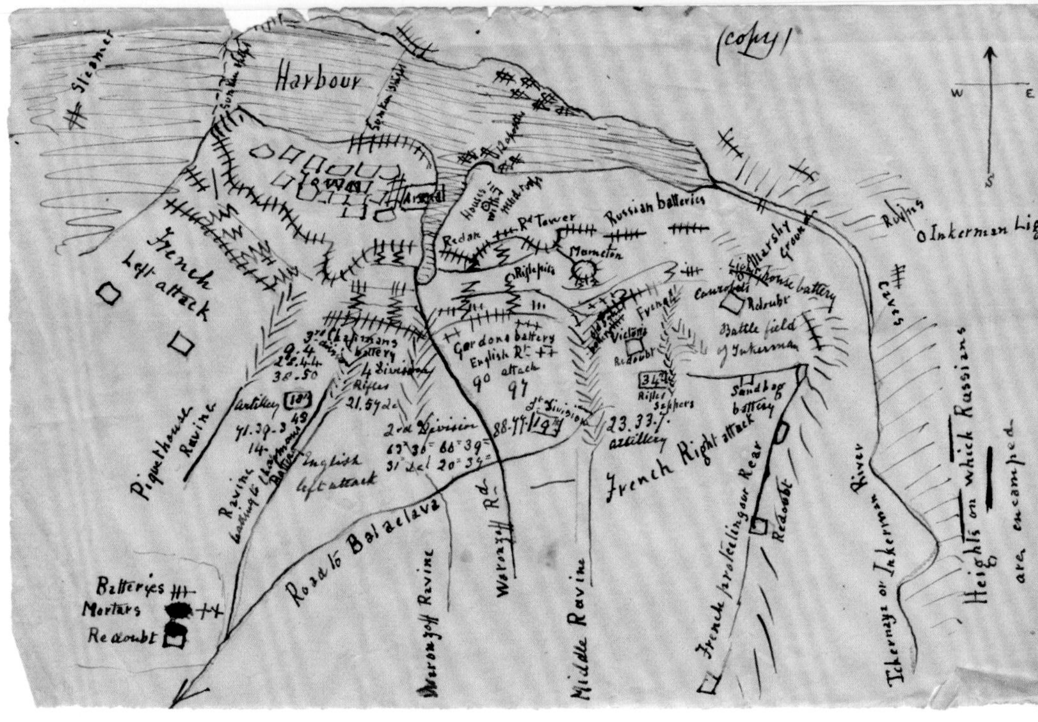

A SKETCH OF THE CAMP AT INKERMAN AND THE POSITIONS SURROUNDING IT. THE 12TH DEPLOYED TO THE CRIMEA IN 1855 TO REINFORCE THE DECIMATED RANKS OF THE LIGHT BRIGADE AND SPENT MUCH OF ITS TIME ON OUTPOST DUTY DURING THE SIEGE OF SEBASTOPOL.

Division on parade, while the remainder of the Light Brigade, less the 8th Hussars, could only produce 100 men between them. The routine of the siege, piquet duty and patrolling, preceded orders for the 18th June, when the next attempt on Sebastopol was to be launched, with the cavalry expected to follow up infantry gains. However, in a manner typical of the incompetence of the campaign, the bombardment that should have initiated the attack failed to materialise and condemned the French and British assaults to costly failure, leaving the 12th to resume their familiar tasks.

The death of Lord Raglan, for whom the 12th provided an escort for the funeral cortège, was followed by a reorganisation of the cavalry in the Crimea. Of limited effect, it did little to address the disastrous logistic situation that rapidly began to wear down the Regiment, an officer of the 12th writing *'The cavalry were almost entirely dependant upon themselves for bringing up their own forage and this was effected by slinging sacks over the men's saddles, the horses being led. In my own regiment alone, sixty men and horses were continually employed upon this duty, and thus rendered non-effective for other purposes; whilst the men were fatigued by marching, loading and leading their horses under a burning sun. Saddlery was constantly broken, and there was a great difficulty in getting it repaired.'*[20]

If the Allies had no intention of altering their plan and so interrupting the routine of piquets and patrols, the Russians did with an attack on 16 August on the French and Sardinian positions along the upper Tchernaya River. Alerted to the impending attack, the Light Brigade had already been moved behind the French position to assist them should they need support, a precaution that proved unnecessary, but which now led to near disaster, as the Brigade received orders to advance *'in full view of the enemy and, from the moment they moved, under the fire of his guns, the squadrons were to advance in open column to the small plank bridge which crossed the aqueduct supplying Sebastopol, and across which they could only defile in threes; re-forming on the far side, they were to advance half-right to a dangerous ford across the Tchernaya, defile across this, re-form, turn left, and advance up the far bank of the river – all within easy range of the enemy guns. It seemed madness, a second Balaclava.'*[21] General Paget, commanding the Brigade, remarked that *'if ever the troops were doomed to certain destruction here was a case in point'*[22] and it was therefore fortunate that, just as the earlier Light Brigade disaster was about to be repeated, a French staff officer arrived with new orders to halt and withdraw.

> '...if ever the troops were doomed to certain destruction here was a case in point.'

The failure of the Russian effort passed the initiative back to the French and British who, on 9 September, launched a successful assault, the Regiment screening the heights around the city to prevent enemy interference. Despite the long-awaited capture of Sebastopol, no clear idea existed of what to do next. In order to speed the Russian withdrawal from the peninsula, it was then decided to harass their lines of communication by sending the Light Brigade to reinforce the French and Turkish army, which had for some time been at Eupatoria on the western shore of the Crimea.

Arriving by ship on 18th and 19th October, the reality of the task soon threw its utility into question. The Russian lines of communication were two days' march inland across a waterless desert in which a forward operating base had already been established, while the minor harassing operations envisaged were more than capable of being done by the troops already in the area without inducing the greater logistic burden brought about by the Light Brigade's arrival. Despite concerns over their intended role inland, the Brigade were soon employed over the perfect cavalry country that lay in the immediate vicinity of Eupatoria, at times with up to 100 squadrons manoeuvring to try to bring the enemy to a fight. While these proved unsuccessful, other operations achieved better results including, on 2nd November, the capture by two squadrons of the 12th of a Russian supply dump along with *'a Russian Commissariat office, a Cossack, about forty Arabs and three thousand head of horses, camels, oxen and sheep. Three Russian carriages were brought in, and a considerable number of inhabitants of the village.'*[23]

Winter had now set in, bringing with it delay to operations and lower temperatures (the Regiment was still in much of the clothing brought from India) as well as testing the commissariat. Although food was still sufficient, Major Tottenham would have been concerned by the sight of a French soldier swinging a dead cat by its tail and declaring that *'Eh, le manger pour sur: avec des oignons ca va assez bien.'*[24] Perhaps with these sort of privations in prospect, the minimal benefit being gained by the presence in Eupatoria was balanced and found wanting. Evacuation was ordered and on 8th December 1855, the 12th Lancers were the last of the Light Brigade to depart the Crimea, travelling to Scutari on the Black Sea where they were to spend the next few months before the campaign petered out and the Treaty of Paris of 30th March 1856 formally brought the conflict to a close.

THE INDIAN MUTINY AND THE SECOND AFGHAN WAR

1857–1880

Delhi 1857 | Central India | Lucknow | Charasiah | Kabul 1879 | Kandahar 1880 | Afghanistan 1878–1880

WAZIRABAD, where the 9th Lancers had been stationed since the end of the 2nd Sikh War, happily proved a short posting. With its boiling summers and freezing winter winds that combined to induce high levels of sickness it was with some relief that, after two years there, the Regiment moved to Ambala in February 1851. Here, in 1854, one of the most able soldiers of the 19th century, James Hope Grant, assumed command, the next couple of years passing calmly until, just as the Regiment was due to return to England in the summer of 1857, the established order was turned upside down and the Indian Mutiny embroiled them in a campaign marked by horrific levels of violence and recrimination and which earned them a huge haul of Victoria Crosses.

Though the causes of the Indian Mutiny were complex and deep-rooted, the spark that ignited the initial rebellion by the native Indian regiments garrisoned at Meerut on 9th May 1857 was the public disgrace and imprisonment of sepoys (native infantrymen) who had refused to use cartridges greased with animal fat. The revolt spread rapidly across large portions of the Bengal Army, fuelled by recent violations of religious sensibilities and military privileges. Although 24 infantry regiments were quickly disarmed or disbanded, 45 more mutinied, leading almost instantaneously to the fall of Delhi amid scenes of immense brutality, and the beginning of the sieges of the garrisons at Lucknow and Cawnpore. To make matters worse, the revolt turned into a more general uprising among the civilian population and then took on a wider aspect as the recently annexed northern provinces seized the opportunity to regain their lost power and independence. With only 45,000 European troops out of a total of 270,000 regular forces in the country, most of the north of India was quickly lost and the situation that the 9th, along with the rest of the European establishment in that area, now found itself in was extremely precarious. Fortunately other areas of India remained largely unaffected, the Bombay command having only two regiments in revolt and the Madras Presidency, where the 12th had arrived in late 1856, none. Both these armies and the Punjab Irregular Forces that had remained loyal would help to suppress the mutineers in the future while, most importantly, the majority of the Indian camp followers, so essential for keeping the army on the road, remained loyal. Indeed, men of the 9th Lancers apparently named the Regiment's head *bhisti* or water carrier as the person they thought most worthy of receiving the Victoria Cross after the siege of Delhi.

In Ambala, some anticipation of the revolt had led to the 9th Lancers, together with two troops of artillery, to patrol at

OPERATIONS OF THE 9TH AND 12TH LANCERS DURING THE INDIAN MUTINY 1857–1860.

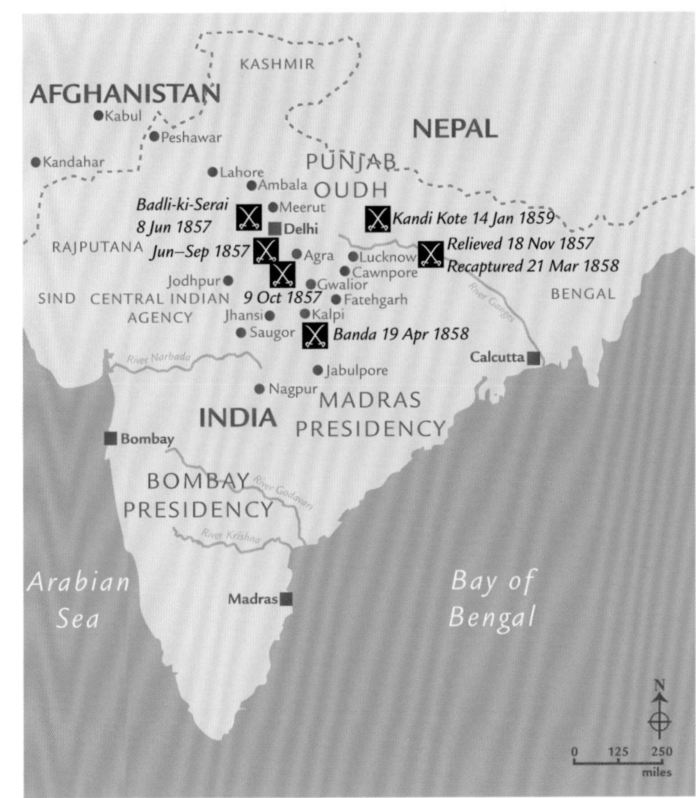

SIR JAMES HOPE GRANT

Sir James Hope Grant was one of the finest cavalry officers of the mid-19th century. Born in 1808, he had joined the 9th Lancers at the age of 18 and, having paid £5,000 for his rank up to captaincy and spent the rest of his £10,000 wealth in living expenses in what was considered a very expensive regiment, was about to leave in 1841 when his musical ability on the cello caught the eye of a senior officer. He made him his brigade major for the war in China in 1841–2, for which he gained a CB. A talented and passionate sportsman, he was also a skilful and daring horseman. He had both physical and moral courage, the latter founded on his religious beliefs, manifested by his tenet: 'Act according to your conscience and defy the consequences.'[30]

His strong opinions were demonstrated after the Battle of Sobraon in 1846, where he sought to remove the 9th's Commanding Officer. On the morning after the battle, Hope Grant, by then a Major, went to see the Commanding Officer and demanded that he either leave the 9th Lancers for having been drunk and clearly incapable on the previous day or Hope Grant would personally arrest him. The Commanding Officer replied: '"Will you, indeed. Very well, I will be beforehand with you, and I now place you in arrest for bringing a false and insulting accusation against your commanding officer," and I went to my tent in arrest.'[31] After the subsequent inquiry, Hope Grant was returned to duty, having apologised not for the substance of the accusation, which was never in doubt, but rather for the way that he had brought it. Campbell kept command, though he was not mentioned in the report of the battle. The high moral tone continued when Hope Grant took over command, forcing seven officers who were gambling addicts to retire having earlier removed the billiard table on which they played.

Despite having little money, he acquired his lieutenant colonelcy without purchase as a result of a 'death-vacancy'. Courageous, strict but fair, he assumed command in 1854 and he may have passed into relative obscurity had the Indian Mutiny not intervened. From then on he could do little wrong. He commanded the Regiment and other elements of the cavalry in the early part of the mutiny. He was promoted to Brigadier during the siege of Delhi, before commanding the cavalry brigade at the relief of Lucknow and a division when it was finally captured and held. Unskilled in the technical business of soldiering, he struggled to read a map and was unable to express himself on paper or verbally, though these shortcomings were more than compensated for by his instinctive skill when fighting battles.

Promoted to Major-General in 1858, he fought in the China War of 1860, was Commander-in-Chief of the Madras Army, Quartermaster-General and in 1870 commander of Aldershot Camp where, in the face of considerable opposition, he introduced autumn exercises and military study. He died in 1875, by which time his far-reaching reforms of outpost duties, based on his Mutiny experiences, had considerably improved the performance of the British cavalry.

SIR JAMES HOPE GRANT AS A LIEUTENANT COLONEL. HOPE GRANT COMMANDED THE 9TH LANCERS DURING THE EARLY STAGES OF THE INDIAN MUTINY BEFORE ASSUMING COMMAND OF THE CAVALRY DIVISION AND WAS ONE OF THE GREATEST COMMANDERS OF THE 19TH CENTURY (NATIONAL GALLERIES OF SCOTLAND).

HOPE GRANT AT THE CELLO – A TALENT WHICH HE SAID SECURED HIM THE POSITION OF BRIGADE MAJOR ON THE EXPEDITION TO CHINA IN 1841.

THE SILVER COMPASS CARRIED BY HOPE GRANT IN INDIA.

night for two weeks beforehand. The limited disturbances were therefore quickly dealt with and it was here that it was decided to gather together the troops loyal to the Crown. As forces from other garrisons arrived, cholera spread in the increasingly cramped quarters at Ambala, the 9th losing 20 dead before they moved out, while 95 had to be left behind in the hills in outstations, further exacerbating the deficit caused by the absence of 24 officers on detachment or leave and leaving only 16 officers, 493 men and 652 horses to begin operations to deal with the rebellion.

The recapture of Delhi and the removal of the native king had been decided upon as the highest priority and, although lacking logistic support or a siege train to take the fortified city, four columns set out from Ambala between 17th and 27th May, each accompanied by a squadron of the 9th Lancers. Travelling by night to avoid the intense heat, the columns from Ambala and Meerut, where other loyal forces had concentrated, joined at Alipur on 7th June but between them still only produced a force of 3,500 men with 22 field and 24 siege guns. These were divided into three brigades, two of infantry and one of cavalry, under Brigadier Hope Grant, consisting of the 9th Lancers, the 6th Dragoon Guards and Hodson's Native Horse.

The advance to Delhi began the next day, intelligence indicating that a large rebel force at Badli-ki-Serai held the road five miles outside the city, with a strongly held centre resting on a river to the right and a canal to the left, though with insufficient troops to cover the whole gap in strength. Concentrating on this weakness, the British launched a dawn attack in the centre, while the 9th, with two troops of horse artillery, made their way around the flank during the night to attack, simultaneously, from the side and rear. Cornet AS Jones later described the events: *'There was a beautiful full moon shining when we quietly left our camp on Sunday night at 12pm and crossed the canal by a bridge and over ploughed fields which deadened the sound of our guns, and the double plantations on the banks of the canal effectively concealed the movement from the enemy, so that all should have turned out perfectly had we not been impeded a good deal by the ditches and cuts forming the canal, the banks of which had to be cut down for our guns. About daybreak we heard the guns on our left flank and began to quicken our pace, and re-crossing the canal astonished the enemy by appearing precisely in their rear when they were all engaged with our main column advancing on the road to Delhi. The enemy were taken completely by surprise, but bore it well and turned some of the heavy guns they had in position upon us and poured in a good shower of grape. We were half an hour late, but we did well enough, and I believe we none of us disgraced ourselves, though I was in great fear sometimes that the small numbers and inexperience of the officers we had would bring us to grief.'*[1] Modesty clearly prevented Cornet Jones mentioning his own part in the affair for which he was awarded the Regiment's first Victoria Cross for his part in capturing a fleeing enemy horse artillery piece, although he later recorded more detail: *'I caught sight of an actual field gun with six horses taking a line of its own to the extreme left front of our line and quite close to our flank. On the spur of the moment I felt that the bird in hand must not allowed to escape, pulled up short, and as soon as I was clear of the rear rank men made straight for my prey and managed to point it out to RSM Thonger, as I passed him where he happened to be riding in serrefile rank near the left flank of our squadron. Of course, my Arab charger had the pull over horses with a 9-pounder field gun behind them, but the six drivers were very plucky little fellows, plying their whips as they looked at me over their right shoulders until my last stride brought my sword within striking distance as I ranged up alongside of the off-wheeler. He crouched from my blow and fell between the*

1 MUTINEERS WITH PLUNDER SURROUNDED BY THE 9TH LANCERS.

2 THE ACTION AT BADI-KI-SERAI ON 8TH JUNE 1857 DURING THE ADVANCE FROM AMBALA TO RELIEVE DELHI. CORNET ALFRED JONES WON THE 9TH LANCERS' FIRST VICTORIA CROSS FOR CAPTURING AN ENEMY GUN.

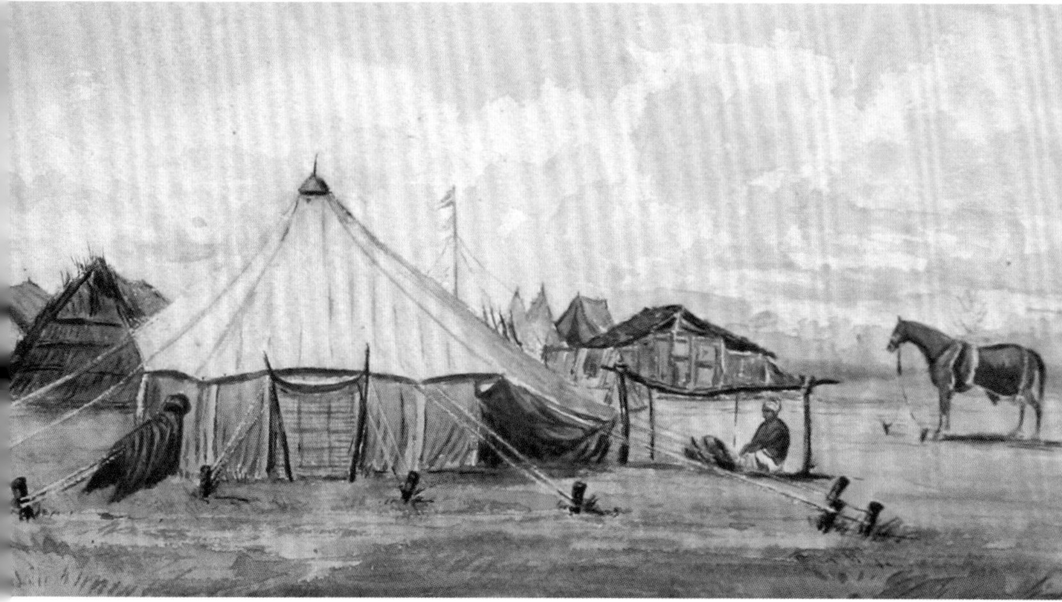

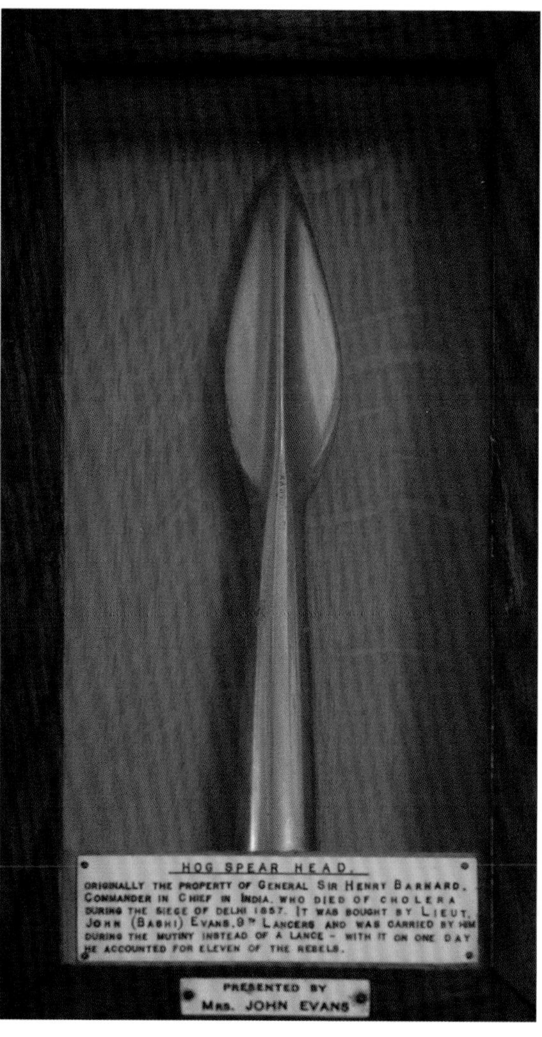

1 A VIEW PAINTED BY CAPT OGER UPTON ON 7TH JUNE 1857 DURING THE SIEGE OF DELHI. ALTHOUGH THE CAMP LOOKS TIDY ENOUGH THE BRITISH FORCES OUTSIDE DELHI MORE CLOSELY RESEMBLED THE BESIEGED. FOR MOST OF THE THREE-MONTH SIEGE CONDITIONS WERE TERRIBLE WITH DISEASE, PARTICULARLY CHOLERA, ENDEMIC.

2 A HOG-SPEAR ORIGINALLY BELONGING TO GENERAL SIR HENRY BARNARD, WHO DIED OF CHOLERA WHILE COMMANDING THE FORCES BESIEGING DELHI. IT WAS BOUGHT BY LIEUTENANT JOHN EVANS WHO CARRIED IT THROUGHOUT THE REST OF THE MUTINY. THE INSCRIPTION RECORDS THAT 'ON ONE DAY HE ACCOUNTED FOR ELEVEN OF THE REBELS' WITH THE WEAPON.

horses, and I suppose convulsively clinging to his bridle reins, stopped the gun. Instantly the sergeant major and two or three men he had brought tackled the other drivers, while I sat on my horse trying to realise my position in the middle of a wide bare plain……Presently the rest of the regiment turned up and we unlimbered the gun and fired a few rounds at a village which was still occupied by the enemy.'[2]

THE SIEGE OF DELHI

Victory opened the route to nearby Delhi but, with their small numbers, the force was in no position to do anything more than capture and hold the old cantonments on the Ridge, an area of high ground to the north-west of the city where they began to establish the early stages of a siege. The Ridge would be their home for the next three months, a period in which they more closely resembled the besieged force as they sheltered amongst the ruined buildings on a reverse slope from the city while subjected to continuous bombardment and raids. Unable to do much more than cover the exits from the city that they could see from their position, the 9th Lancers guarded the perimeter and endeavoured to keep open the lines of communication to Alipur, providing convoy escorts to bring in vital ammunition. It had became so short in supply that on occasion they had to pay camp-followers to pick up the shot the enemy fired at them.[3] Enemy raids and attacks continued throughout, while the heat spiralled and the cramped conditions, insects and rains produced the ideal conditions for disease, particularly cholera, to spread. The sick list climbed steadily, so that of the 2,040 cavalrymen who were on the muster at the time of the assault, 618 were unfit for duty through illness.

Throughout the three-month siege, repeated attacks were made from the city to dislodge the British position. Having repulsed several frontal assaults, news was brought on 19th June that the rebels planned to assault from the rear. To clarify the situation Brigadier Hope Grant took a squadron of the 9th and six guns to the Ochterlony Gardens, where he found that the rebels had already arrived and that they were able to use the walls and hedges to dominate the area and gain a vital foothold in the British perimeter. With light fading, a charge was ordered with illumination given by the flash of flintlock and gun, Captain Anson wrote to his wife that '*it was all we could do to repulse the enemy after dark, when we could not see what we were about.*'[4] Cornet Jones was more graphic: '*My squadron came down the highroad in a column of dust in rear of a troop of Horse Artillery, who were nearly overpowered by a fire of musketry from two gardens and the road in front. The officer commanding the troop of Horse Artillery cried out as we came up: 'Get along to the front, you cavalry; I can't stand this!' and poor Colonel Yule [who had only succeeded Hope Grant in command twelve days earlier], thus excited, brought us to the front, and before I had time to form the squadron on the road cried out 'Charge!'… poor Yule was here shot, fell from his horse, and was seen by none of us*

till next morning, when his body was found, horribly mutilated. Twenty or thirty yards after we got into the swing of our pace the road became contracted to pass over a bridge, so that the squadron could only pass in column of threes or six abreast, and beyond this the road was bordered by gardens with hedges, which were lined by infantry, who should coolly have potted the whole squadron, but by God's providence they fired wildly at the head of the column, and the bullets whistled thick about and above our heads....This gallop lasted half or three-quarters of a mile... It was getting quite dark then, as I formed and told off the squadron in a ploughed field. We were then in a very awkward predicament, but I knew that our only chance was to keep good order and get out of it as well as I could, so we moved off at a steady trot and, making a good circuit, steered for the flashes of some guns which we hoped might prove our own. This turned out the case, and there we fell in with another squadron of ours.'[5] In the attack, Hope Grant nearly suffered the same fate as Yule when he too came off his horse and was saved by his native orderly, Rooper Khan and Troopers Purcell and Hancock. The latter two were both awarded the Victoria Cross for their actions, though Rooper Khan, a *sowar* of the 4th Irregular Cavalry, despite being highly written up, proved ineligible for the medal.

The siege train finally arrived on the 4th September and immediately needed 60 officers and men from the Regiment to be detached to serve the guns where manpower was particularly short. Several of those sent, including Trooper Potiphar, had already grown used to the demands of the work in the batteries: *'all our men working at the guns are to receive double pay and an extra portion of Grog and Beer, which is quite needful, as I can speak from experience by working in the batteries since June last'*. Potiphar went on to describe the scene in the gun line just before the assault in which most of his crew, working through both day and night, were wounded before he was able to hand over to another troop, in order *'to be in the saddle again by 3a.m...By the time I reached my tent I was pretty tired.'*[6]

The artillery bombardment forced two breaches in the northern wall and, on 14th September, an assault commenced by four columns, two attacking the breaches, another the Kashmir Gate while the last cleared the suburbs to the west before entering via the Kabul Gate. Originally planned to support this last assaulting column, Hope Grant's cavalry brigade soon received fresh orders to move closer to the city in order to guard the siege batteries which, as the infantry columns moved away, would become exposed. The threat soon became a reality when the failure to dislodge the rebels in the western suburbs allowed them clear sight of the guns, the flanks of the other three columns that were by now at the walls and the camp itself.

THE 9TH LANCERS CHARGING TO REPULSE A RAID ON 19TH JUNE 1857 IN WHICH THEIR COMMANDING OFFICER, LIEUTENANT COLONEL ROBERT YULE WAS KILLED. PRIVATES PURCELL AND HANCOCK WERE AWARDED THE VICTORIA CROSS FOR RESCUING BRIGADIER JAMES HOPE GRANT, WHO BY NOW COMMANDED THE CAVALRY, AND HAD BEEN UNHORSED.

'it was all we could do to repulse the enemy after dark, when we could not see what we were about.'

TRUMPETER KELLS WON THE VICTORIA CROSS DURING AN ACTION AT BULANDSHAHR ON 24TH SEPTEMBER 1857 IN WHICH THE ENEMY REARGUARD WAS ROUTED. LIEUTENANT ROBERT BLAIR AND PRIVATES DONOHOE AND ROBERTS WERE SIMILARLY HONOURED.

To combat the rebel attack, the brigade charged through the batteries and then formed into line. Hope Grant wrote: '*It was necessary to retain our position to prevent the enemy from taking our batteries...Not a man flinched from his post...and when a poor fellow got knocked over it seemed to put the men in good spirits.*'[7] Standing for over two hours under fire, the 9th lost six men killed and 40 wounded with 61 horses dead, a historian of the campaign, Sir John Kaye, commenting that '*for two long hours the brigade stood firm as a rock, and as one after another fell riddled with grape or canister, there was no wavering in the ranks.....There was nothing else in their demeanour to distinguish this grand scene of defiance and endurance from an ordinary cavalry parade.....The presence of the cavalry brigade alone prevented the enemy, who had driven back the fourth column, from advancing along the open ground between the Ridge and the city, and taking the whole of our left attack in flank.*'[8]

After six days of bitter street fighting, the city eventually fell on 20th September, the brigade moving to the south of the city to cut off the rebel retreat before new orders followed for parts of the brigade to be grouped into a 'Moveable Column' with four infantry battalions to clear the area south-east of the city of rebels and then begin the advance to relieve Lucknow. Setting off on the 24th September, the cavalry vanguard met with a well-prepared enemy force in the village of Bulandshahr, against which the brigade's artillery was employed while the infantry for once showed a reluctance to advance, '*they could not be got to look round a corner or to advance in any way*'. This prompted Major Ouvry of the 9th, who was commanding the cavalry element, to attack the position using his cavalry alone – an acknowledged departure from conventional wisdom: '*Forming the 9th Lancers into threes, I ordered them to charge through the main street. I went through with them myself. We passed through a shower of musketry from both sides of the houses. We met with no loss till we got to the other side of the city. There the enemy made a stand for the moment, but the head squadron charging, the rebels took to flight. We had no business to charge into the town, but I know that unless we did so they would have held the town against us.*' In this single action the 9th Lancers increased by five their remarkable accumulation of Victoria Crosses, the medal being awarded to Lieutenant Blair, Trumpeter Kells and Privates Donohoe, Roberts and Jordan.

RELIEF OF LUCKNOW

The advance to Lucknow continued, with a number of enemy positions overcome on the way. A poorly equipped force was defeated at Aligarh on 3rd October, with the mutineers pursued in the crops outside the town in a manner compared to beating turnip fields for game, while later a request for help from the garrison at Agra, which was expecting an attack from a large rebel force from Gwalior, diverted them there. Reaching the outskirts of Agra on the morning of 9th October, the column found nothing untoward and settled down to make camp, unaware that its actions had been observed by rebels who now approached through the cover of the standing crops and, with the officers having breakfast with the permanent garrison in the city, attacked.

The rebel assault was initiated by four mutineers who had entered the camp posing as native conjurors and, surprising the 9th Lancer piquet, killed the duty sergeant before Sergeant Hartigan set about them, killing all four and earning himself the Victoria Cross. Simultaneously, the waiting rebels had assaulted from the crops, catching the 9th by surprise. Recovering rapidly, the Regiment stood to, the first men mounted racing to protect the gun lines (a result of '*a sort of free-masonry that existed between the 9th Lancers and the artillery*', wrote a gunner of the time) while the rest of the camp formed itself up in line. With the return of the officers from their disturbed breakfast the order was given to charge, an action carried out with devastating effect as the rebels fled with despairing cries of '*Delhi bhala-wallah*' (the local tongue for 'The Delhi Spearmen') before being pursued for 10 miles with the loss of 13 guns and 400 carriages until tiredness brought a halt.

Hope Grant now assumed command of the whole column, reaching Cawnpore on 26th October after a skirmish at Kanuj, to link up with the rest of the The Lucknow Relief Force. This managed to reach the Residency on 18th November, the 9th's involvement largely limited to a number of minor skirmishes, or as guards and escorts as the infantry battled through the city in intense street fighting. With no chance of holding Lucknow, the evacuation of the 500 women and children and 1,500 sick and wounded who had survived the siege from its start in June began immediately, the Regiment providing part of the flank protection to the long, slow-moving column on its journey back to Cawnpore, which was by now itself under attack.

The returning column now had to break through the enemy cordon, cross the bridge into Cawnpore and then, having freed itself of the encumbrance of the Lucknow survivors, turn to deal with the enemy army outside the city. On 6th December, with the enemy fixed in the north and centre, a turning movement to the south using four brigades of infantry and one of cavalry (including the 9th) managed to offset the enemy's numerical advantage (6,000 men faced 25,000) with few casualties, the dispirited rebels fleeing '*as soon as they saw us striking our tents*'[9], said Lieutenant Colonel Ouvry. The only serious opposition came from the rear of the position, though this was rapidly overwhelmed by combined attacks of infantry, cavalry and artillery before a pursuit over 15 miles began, 16 guns being captured in the process.

1 SERGEANT HARTIGAN IN THE ACTION AT AGRA ON 9TH OCTOBER 1857 IN WHICH HE WON THE VICTORIA CROSS. REACTING TO THE SURPRISE ATTACK ON THE COLUMN THAT HAD JUST REACHED AGRA, THE 9TH LANCERS CAPTURED 13 GUNS AS THE REBELS FLED WITH DESPAIRING CRIES OF 'DELHI BHALA-WALLAH' – 'THE DELHI SPEARMEN'.

2 THE RELIEF OF LUCKNOW ON THE 18TH NOVEMBER 1857. THE 9TH WERE THE ONLY REGIMENT PRESENT DURING THE THREE MAJOR ACTIONS OF THE CAMPAIGN AT DELHI AND LUCKNOW.

3 LANCE-CORPORAL WILLIAM GOAT WAS AWARDED THE VICTORIA CROSS DURING THE CAPTURE OF LUCKNOW FOR RECOVERING THE BODY OF MAJOR SMYTH OF THE 2ND DRAGOON GUARDS ON 6TH MARCH 1858.

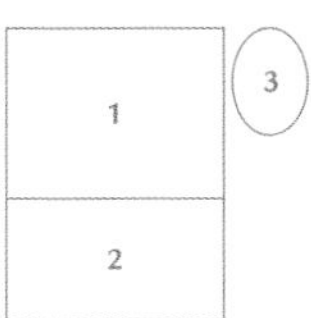

The defeat of this last large enemy army in the area now allowed attention to be turned to securing of the lines of communication between Calcutta and the North West provinces, a task undertaken throughout December as the fragmented enemy forces were dealt with in detail. Sergeant Forbes Mitchell, of the 93rd Regiment of Foot recalled one engagement by Hope Grant's infantry and cavalry brigades: '*My company was in the centre, and I could see the tips of the lances of the Ninth wheeling into line for a charge right in the enemy's rear. He was completely out-generalled and his retreat cut off. The 41st Native Infantry was the principal regiment of the enemy's line. Directly they saw the Lancers in their rear they formed square. The Lancers came down on the square, who stood their ground and opened fire. The Lancers charged well up to within about thirty yards, when the horses turned off right and left from the solid square. We were just preparing to charge it with the bayonet, when at that moment the squadrons were brought round again, just as a hawk takes a circle from a swoop on its prey, and we saw Sergeant Major May,*

LANCERS CAPTURING MUTINEERS IN MOPPING UP OPERATIONS.

who was mounted on a powerful, untrained horse, dash on the square and leap right into it, followed by the squadron on that side. The square being thus broken, the other troops of the Ninth rode into the flying mass, and in less than five minutes the 41st Regiment of Native Infantry was wiped out of the ranks of the mutineers. The enemy's line of retreat became a total rout, and the plain for miles was strewn with corpses speared down by the Lancers or hewn down by the keen-edged sabres of Hodson's Horse. Just before sunset we saw the Lancers and Sikhs returning with the captured standards and every gun which the enemy had brought into the field in the morning. The infantry formed up along the road to cheer the cavalry as they returned.'[10] On the next day Fatehgarh was occupied, the Regiment remaining in the area throughout January 1858 with the principal engagement the defeat of rebels at Shamsabad on the 17th in which two squadrons were involved, Regimental Sergeant Major Spence earning a Victoria Cross for his rescue of the wounded Private Kidd.

The 9th returned once again to Cawnpore in early February 1858 to join the 30,000 men who had been assembled to recapture and then hold Lucknow. Hope Grant commanded the cavalry division of two brigades that had by now been reinforced by the arrival of the Bays and 7th Hussars from Britain. After a preliminary operation in early March to clear the enemy to the west of the Lucknow to Cawnpore road, the division rejoined the rest of the army to advance to the outskirts of the city and established itself in Dilkusha Park where the 9th, as part of the advance guard, cleared the enemy outposts to the east of the city. On 6th March, two columns began the assault on the city, the 9th joining 12,000 men as they moved around to the north via a pontoon bridge constructed over the River Gumti, and their brigade dislodged a strong enemy picquet. Following up too far, the Bays found themselves engaged by enemy infantry in broken country from which the 9th had to extract them, Private Goat earning a Victoria Cross for his bravery in attempting to save the body of the Bay's Major Smith from mutilation by the mutineers. Kept busy by reconnaissance and patrolling as the siege progressed, the 9th were next heavily engaged in the closing stages when the strongpoint at Musa Bagh to the west of the city was attacked, a squadron of the 9th pursuing the retreating rebels, capturing 12 guns and earning Troop Sergeant Major Rushe and Private Newell Victoria Crosses as a reward for their conspicuous gallantry.

The fall of Lucknow on 21st March 1858 with its reprisal and looting, then heralded the equally familiar task of rounding up the remaining mutineers and sweeping the local area. The 9th Lancers played their part in the various pursuits or the more mundane duty of escorts until, with the rebels confined to the state of Oudh, the Regiment returned to their quarters at Ambala to sit out the hot season until their final defeat could be brought about.

CENTRAL INDIA

An immediate return to India had been fully expected by the 12th Lancers following their participation in the campaign in the Crimea. However, the once-generous Pasha of Egypt had decided to bar British troops from crossing his country and forced them to return to England in June 1856. The pleasure no doubt felt by the 12th was to be short-lived, for within weeks new orders arrived: they were to complete their posting in Bangalore, and were to be there by the end of the year.

The loyalty of the native troops in the Madras Presidency allowed the 12th Lancers to escape the savagery of the early stages of the mutiny but only in early 1858, when Madras was deemed secure, could they be released to help further to the north. They were to join a force tasked with securing the lines of communication between Bombay and Central India and relieving pressure on Lucknow, though first they would have to complete a 600-mile march to Nagpur in the centre of India.

The British plan for the area of operations involved two columns, the Central India Field Force and the Saugor Field Force, moving on parallel

routes through the mutinous areas, the former via Jhansi to Kalpi and the latter to its south-east from Jabulpore to Banda, with the intention of the two co-operating where possible. The Saugor Field Force, consisting of a brigade of cavalry (including the 12th), a brigade of artillery and two brigades of infantry, began operations on 10th January 1858. Its cautious commander, General Whitlock (likened to *'a bad revolver, always going round but never going off'*[11]), was immediately made to look pedestrian when he finally left Jabulpore on 17th February, the day that Saugor, its target, had been captured by the other column. Increasingly frustrated by the slow progress, the members of the Saugor Field Force eventually moved north to assist the Rajah of Pannah in combating the rebels there, although it soon became apparent that no such help was required. By now the Central India Field Force needed help at Jhansi and General Whitlock finally took decisive action on 10th April by attacking the enemy at Jhigan after a difficult night march on atrocious roads. Two squadrons of the 12th and a detachment of the 2nd Hyderabad Cavalry, supported by artillery, successfully charged a rebel position and killed over 100 enemy, including one rebel who, pierced by a lance, clung on and would not let go: *'doubling his fist, [the 12th Lancer trooper] leant over the dying man and shook it energetically in his face, with the words, 'G-d d-m your eyes, if you don't let that there go I'll get off my horse and punch your b-y head.'*[12]

Pressing on towards Banda, whose Rajah and his army forces presented the main threat to the region, the Saugor Field Force was unsuccessfully ambushed as they moved past Kubrai just before dawn on 17th April forcing the Rajah, if he was to hold onto his capital, to stand and fight. The position chosen was formidable and covered the road to the south and west of Banda with its flanks protected by rough ground carved with deep nullahs and watercourses that would prevent outflanking manoeuvres. Holding it were 6,000 troops on the position and 3,000 more in reserve supported by carefully sited artillery.

At 4am on 19th April, General Whitlock attacked with his usual caution, though the advance guard, including a troop of the 12th, soon became involved in a bitter struggle in a nullah from which it had to be rescued, though not before the troop had taken an enemy gun. Trying to work around the enemy's left, the main body of the artillery and cavalry had also been checked by the rough ground and the attack appeared to be stalling until Major Oakes of the 12th Lancers, who was in command of the force's cavalry, led the rest of the Regiment across the deep nullahs in single file before forming up and charging into the enemy on the far side. The sight proved enough to break the enemy who ran, pursued for four miles and leaving 300 dead, until Oakes reformed.

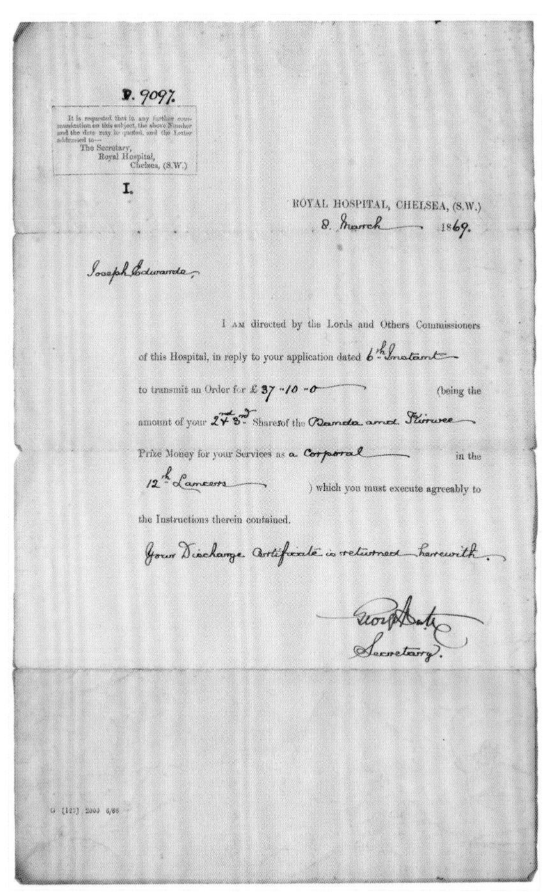

D. 9097.

It is requested that in any further communication on this subject, the above Number and the date may be quoted, and the Letter addressed to—
The Secretary,
Royal Hospital,
Chelsea, (S.W.)

I.

ROYAL HOSPITAL, CHELSEA, (S.W.)
8. March 1869.

Joseph Edwardes,

I am directed by the Lords and Others Commissioners of this Hospital, in reply to your application dated 6th Instant to transmit an Order for £ 37 - 10 - 0 (being the amount of your 2nd & 3rd Shares of the Banda and Kirwee Prize Money for your Services as a Corporal in the 12th Lancers) which you must execute agreeably to the Instructions therein contained.

Your Discharge Certificate is returned herewith.

[signature]
Secretary.

1 PRIZE MONEY CONTINUED TO BE A MAJOR ATTRACTION OF SOLDIERING. CORPORAL EDWARDES, 12TH LANCERS, WAS GRANTED £37 AND 10 SHILLINGS (ABOUT £1,700 AT TODAY'S PRICES) AS HIS SHARE OF THE PROCEEDS FROM THE ACTION AT BANDA. THE SPOILS FROM THIS ACTION, WHERE A LARGE TREASURY WAS CAPTURED, LED TO CONSIDERABLE ILL-FEELING AMONGST THE OTHER TROOPS IN CENTRAL INDIA WHO HAD FOUGHT AS HARD BUT FOR FAR LESS REWARD.

2 TROOP SERGEANT-MAJOR SPENCE WAS AWARDED THE VICTORIA CROSS FOR SAVING PRIVATE KIDD WHO HAD BEEN WOUNDED AT SHAMSABAD ON 17TH JANUARY 1858.

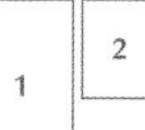

The enemy's secondary position was soon dealt with by the infantry and another cavalry charge, in which the Regiment captured a large brass gun, leaving Whitlock free to occupy the city where he remained for a month while awaiting reinforcements.

Whitlock now marched on Kirwi, which surrendered before engagement. In doing so, the young rulers of Kirwi had saved their lives but not their vast treasury and, with financial reward one of the greatest lures of soldiering, the booty acquired in the Central India campaign soon became a matter of dispute and considerable, enduring, ill-feeling amongst the men of the two columns. In total, Whitlock's force netted 4.5 million rupees and countless jewels, dwarfing those of Rose's men who had worked harder and suffered more but were only to share 465,000 rupees.

The recommencement of the campaigning season at the end of 1858 saw both Regiments engaged in mopping-up operations against bands of thugs and the personal followers of local rulers who presented neither a cohesive nor effective opposition. While the 12th Lancers continued to operate in Central India until April 1860, the 9th swept the north of the country to pin the rebels against the Himalayas, the Regiment's last action

The Calcutta Gazette, EXTRAORDINARY.

WEDNESDAY APRIL 13, 1859.

No. 502 OF 1859.

NOTIFICATION.

Fort William, Military Department.

THE 13TH APRIL 1859.

AFTER a long and brilliant Career in India the 9th, "Queen's Royal," Lancers are on the eve of leaving Calcutta for England.

From the beginning of the Hostilities in which the British Army in India has recently been engaged, this Regiment has held a foremost place in the Contest.

Its name is inseparably connected with the Siege of Delhi, during which the Services rendered by its Officers and Men were various and most important: and in the later Campaigns in Rohilcund and Oude it has closed its term with much Honor.

In taking leave of the 9th Lancers, the Viceroy and Governor General in Council desires to offer to this distinguished Regiment his hearty Thanks, not only for its good Service before the Enemy, but for the admirable Example which it has presented to the young Soldiers of the Indian Army by its perfection of Discipline, Conduct, and Efficiency.

The Regiment will be saluted by the Guns of Fort William on its departure.

By Order of His Excellency the Viceroy and Governor General of India in Council,

R. J. H. BIRCH, MAJOR-GENERAL,
Secretary to the Government of India.

PRINTED BY THOMAS JONES, AT THE BENGAL SECRETARIAT OFFICE.

1 ON LEAVING INDIA AFTER THE MUTINY THE 9TH LANCERS WERE HONOURED WITH A SALUTE FROM THE GUNS OF FORT WILLIAM AS THEY SAILED FROM CALCUTTA. THEY HAD WON 13 VICTORIA CROSSES IN THE CAMPAIGN.

2 MEMORIAL TO THOSE 9TH LANCERS WHO DIED IN THE INDIAN MUTINY IN EXETER CATHEDRAL.

taking place at Kandi Kote on 14th January 1859 where 14 guns were captured.

This final victory set the seal on a remarkable campaign for the 9th during which they had covered 3,000 miles and been the only regiment present at its three most famous engagements: the siege of Delhi and both the relief and final capture of Lucknow. They had been awarded 13 Victoria Crosses and earned the title 'The Delhi Spearmen' from their enemies and the honour of a 21 gun salute from the Governor General as they sailed from Calcutta on 1st May 1859.

Peacetime soldiering of a sort awaited both regiments on their return to Britain, the period until their next overseas postings spent in a variety of locations from which they moved every couple of years. The only operational duties occurred in Ireland where the 9th spent from 1864–1869 and the 12th from 1865–1869. Although largely peaceful, calls to help the police deal with the threat from nationalists occasionally gave rise to brutal and bloody encounters which added to the ever-increasing store of ill feeling on both sides. The 12th earned the unfortunate nickname of the Dungarvan Butchers after one incident in which, having been attacked by a nationalist mob, they charged, killing and injuring many rioters, including some women.

Less dramatic activities included the presentation of five of the 9th's Victoria Crosses by the Queen at Windsor in 1859 and, reflecting the amount of time available for sport and other activities, the introduction of polo to Britain, saw the 9th playing the first inter-regimental match on British soil at Hounslow Heath in 1870. In a match lasting an hour and a half and involving eight players on each side, they were beaten by the 10th Hussars by three goals to two, a newspaper report headlining the event as 'Hockey on Horseback'.

In terms of military development, the jolts caused by the Crimea and the Mutiny failed to alter the army in any radical manner. Cardwell's reforms addressed some of the more obvious failings and a gradual improvement to soldiers' conditions was becoming perceptible but, in terms of doctrine and training, there remained a rigid adherence to set-piece tactics through a centralised system of control. The wars of the later part of the century remained, as earlier, essentially limited in nature, conducted against unsophisticated opposition for which the tactics remained perfectly satisfactory, while the introduction of modern weaponry such as machine-guns seemingly made little difference to British military thought, particularly in regard to cavalry.

Limited service had been introduced in 1847, reducing the 21-year engagement to 12 years, with an option for a further 12 when a pension would become available. 1862 saw the first gymnasiums built, to be followed shortly afterwards by the first set of orders on physical training. Such improvements did not reduce the absentee rate, which was running at about 14 per cent in the cavalry in 1859 and caused corporal punishment to be re-introduced for that crime in the Mutiny Act of that year. It was finally abandoned in 1868. The following year fines for drunkenness, as opposed to imprisonment, were introduced, reducing considerably the numbers of men away from their post, though habitual drunkenness (taken as a fourth offence) still resulted in a court martial. Colonel Oakes of the 12th attributed the higher rates he saw in India to the fact that '*the men had nothing to do*'.[13]

Pay remained poor, with stoppages still accounting for large amounts of it. Other abuses were addressed, the Colonels of Regiments having responsibility for the supply of uniform removed from them in the early 1860s. The Sanitary Commission of 1858, with Florence Nightingale as its instigator and unseen prompt, began to have an impact on the health of the army. By the 1870s, it appears that food had been improved, the report having noted that previously soldiers had '*the prospect of dining on boiled meat every day for 21 years*'[14], while improvements to barrack accommodation gradually reduced the mortality rate, although a report in 1861 found most cavalry barracks '*saturated throughout with ammonia and organic matter*'.[15] Family quarters had by now begun to be provided for Warrant Officers, NCOs and privates who were 'officially' married:

THE FIRST POLO MATCH PLAYED IN BRITAIN TOOK PLACE ON 1ST JUNE 1870 AT HOUNSLOW BETWEEN THE 9TH LANCERS AND THE 10TH HUSSARS. DESCRIBED BY ONE NEWSPAPER AS 'HOCKEY ON HORSEBACK' THE 10TH HUSSARS WON BY THREE GOALS TO TWO.

BERESFORD VC

Captain Lord William Beresford served with the 9th Lancers in the Afghan war in 1879 and then went on to serve on the staff in the Zulu war. He was awarded the Victoria Cross for returning to rescue a sergeant of the 24th Regiment of Foot who was surrounded by Zulu warriors. Beresford pulled the sergeant onto his horse and, with the aid of another soldier, Sergeant O'Toole, they made their escape. When he was awarded with his VC, he is said to have told Queen Victoria that he would refuse the medal unless it was also given to Sergeant O'Toole. She agreed and they both received the Victoria Cross.

After the battle of Ulundi he was said to have been the first man to get into the Zulu King's kraal by jumping the thorn fence that surrounded it. His nickname in the Army was 'Fighting Bill Beresford'.

OPERATIONS OF THE 9TH LANCERS DURING THE SECOND AFGHAN WAR 1878–1880.

by the mid-1890s a married private got just one big room and a kitchen and Warrant Officers considerably more.

The abolition of the purchase of commissions should also have altered the make up of the Officers' Mess but failed to do so; the 'Tribe Scandal' catching the public eye when in 1872 a new officer, Mr EGR Tribe, joined the 9th Lancers – one of the first to do so without purchasing his commission. Apparently disliked as well as incompetent – he could not ride and appeared unwilling to learn – his case was brought to a court of inquiry. Using his political connections (the case was brought up in the Parliament) he managed to get the unfavourable report overturned and the 9th were ordered to take him back and the *'officers to make themselves agreeable to him.'*[16] His conduct remained poor and not only did the boycott that had been in place continue but he was eventually arrested, the Regiment's application for a court martial being refused, although the Commander-in-Chief severely reprimanded him before returning him to the 9th. Throughout the case supporters of Cardwell's reforms in both Parliament and the press cited this case as an example of the reactionary forces in the Army, even though two non-purchase officers had joined before him and been fully accepted. The support for Tribe was only silenced when, shortly after rejoining the Regiment, he went permanently absent, having pawned all the military equipment on his charge, borrowed money from an NCO and left behind a significant number of bad cheques, including one complete forgery.

Other routes into the Officers' Mess came from those commissioned from the ranks, the forerunners of today's Late Entry officers. Few chose this path and those that did went exclusively into the four posts of adjutant, pay-master, riding master and quartermaster, the lack of interest stemming from the poor overall pay when the expenses of living in the Mess and the demanding nature of the posts were taken into account. For direct-entry officers an exam on entry had been introduced in 1849, though the Duke of Wellington gave away its purpose as not so as to ensure competence as *'to have some certainty that the applicants for commissions... have been educated as gentlemen'*. The 1850s saw promotion exams introduced and the Staff College established, though the numbers attending were few, the cavalry sending only 38 officers for this voluntary course between 1858 and 1881.

AFGHANISTAN 1878–1880

For the 9th, the end of their time in England came in early 1875, when they proceeded once again for India, where they were joined by the 12th two years later. The army in India to which both regiments returned had changed considerably, the Crown having taken over the army of the East India Company, while stipulations over the ratio of European to native troops added to the prohibitions on native soldiers having control of artillery or arsenals. Sialkot provided the 9th's home for the next three-and-a-half years, where they once again adapted to the routine of soldiering in India. Little of significance occurred, apart from the establishment of the Regimental Institute (today's PRI) *'to supply to the men of the regiment the best articles that can be procured at low prices, and to provide a place where every man can at any time in the day procure a good and comfortable meal'*.

The peaceful routine was ended by the next phase of the Great Game, the struggle between the British and Russian empires that had been in progress for much of the 19th century as both powers sought influence along their borders and the domination of India. This latest round had been brought on by the decision, made under duress, of the Emir of Afghanistan, Shere Ali, to allow the Russians to establish a diplomatic mission in Kabul, having earlier turned down a similar request by the British. The Governor-General of India had predictably despatched a British mission that was equally predictably stopped on the border in November 1878, giving Britain its excuse to invade Afghanistan and begin the Second Afghan War.

British military strategy for an invasion of Afghanistan was by now well developed, with simultaneous attacks planned through the Khyber Pass and the Kurram Valley into the east of the country towards Kabul while, to the south, an attack

through the Bolan Pass near Quetta was aimed at Kandahar, the intent being to put pressure on the Afghans rather than to occupy their country. The 9th, with a strength of 350 men, made up part of the 16,000-strong Peshawar Valley Field Force, which would cross the Khyber Pass. Reaching Nowshera, just short of the Pass on 18th November 1878, they exchanged their flintlock pistols for Martini Henry carbines and waited, Lieutenant Hunter writing that *'life here is healthy, but very dull, as there is nothing whatever to do, and there is no prospect as yet of our moving'.*[17] The wait continued, with a short move forward in December as the rest of the Force began operations around its base at Jalalabad before the 9th crossed the Khyber Pass in March 1879 to reach Basawal. The Regiment spent the next few months guarding the lines of communication back to India until, in June, following the death of Shere Ali and the installation of his son as Emir, a conclusion was reached. The Treaty of Gandamak ostensibly ended hostilities and brought with it the withdrawal of all British forces in the country apart from those in the Kurram district.

While the rest of the 9th Lancers joined the wider withdrawal to India, two troops from the Regiment totalling a little over 100 men remained in the country, having been detached in January to Major General Roberts' force in the Kurram Valley. After a couple of months in the cantonment at Kohat, *'a very pretty little station, with a library, racquet courts, swimming bath, and all sorts of luxuries....They have lawn-tennis parties and dances every week',*[18] the troops then joined the rest of the Kurram Valley Field Force shortly before the fragile peace deal was agreed. The next few months clearly hung heavily on Lieutenant Hunter as *'there is no drink to be had here; no beer of any sort'*, with *'no amusement except what is got up amongst ourselves'.*[19] Their boredom was soon dispelled by the news of September 1879 that the newly installed Emir had been overthrown and the British envoy and his staff in Kabul murdered, as a result of which General Roberts' force was immediately despatched to occupy Kabul, while the recently broken-up columns reassembled to cross, once again, the Khyber and Bolan Passes to join them.

> ...Kohat, 'a very pretty little station, with a library, racquet courts, swimming bath, and all sorts of luxuries...'

CHARASIAH AND KABUL

General Roberts' force by now consisted of two infantry brigades and a brigade of cavalry (still with two troops from the 9th), totalling 7,500 fighting troops and 6,000 camp followers. Facing the usual

1 SEVENTY-FIVE GUNS WERE CAPTURED WHEN THE CAVALRY BRIGADE CONFIRMED THAT KABUL HAD BEEN ABANDONED IN OCTOBER 1879.

2 A RUSSIAN CUP DATED 1876 WITH INSCRIPTIONS INDICATING THAT IT WAS A GIFT FROM A RUSSIAN GENERAL TO AN AFGHAN. IT IS SAID TO HAVE BEEN LIBERATED FROM KABUL BY CAPTAIN LORD WILLIAM BERESFORD, 9TH LANCERS, WHO LATER WON A VICTORIA CROSS IN THE ZULU WAR.

SHERE ALI'S PALACE IN KABUL.

logistic difficulties of a campaign in the country, 3,500 transport animals were taken, though Private Crane of the 9th noted that each soldier was limited to 25lb of baggage, while the squadron was forced to surrender 60 of its 80 regimental camels for general transport. By early October, General Roberts had advanced against light opposition to the plains south of Kabul, but now faced a strong enemy position on the ridges either side of the River Logar just north of the village of Charasiah which blocked the road and the route to the capital.

On 6th October he attacked, sending his cavalry to conduct a detailed reconnaissance before fixing the left side of the enemy position in a heavy engagement in which the 9th Lancers present expended all their ammunition. Elsewhere, the infantry cleared the enemy from the ridges while the cavalry retired to guard the British camp and rear areas from the Afghan troops in the surrounding hills until, with the main position cleared, the cavalry brigade reformed for a hastily organised pursuit over 20 miles which succeeded in verifying that Kabul had been abandoned, together with the cantonment at Sherpur in which 75 enemy guns were captured. With the surrounding area secure, General Roberts entered the city on 12th October, quartering the whole of his garrison in the Sherpur cantonment, a vast camp with a four-and-a-half mile circumference to the north of the city. Reinforcements from India, including the main body of the 9th, arrived shortly afterwards, an onlooker '*being rather staggered by the amount of their baggage (they even had their full-dress uniforms with them), and still more when I saw camels in the rear toiling along with machinery which turned out to be the regimental soda-water factory*'.[20]

As preparations for the winter began and huts were constructed in the Sherpur cantonment to provide the first proper shelter for many in 13 months, the Afghans, for once acting in unison, advanced on the capital, with upwards of 100,000 troops coming from several directions. To stand any chance of his 8,000 men surviving, General Roberts realised that he must deal with each group individually and prevent them concentrating. He therefore he sent two columns to act in unison and defeat the enemy to the north and west of the city. To guard the approach to Kabul from Ghazni, on 11th December, Roberts dropped off a small force in the Chardeh Valley just to the west of the city with orders to co-operate with a larger formation to the north, though not to become decisively engaged until ordered to. Commanded by Brigadier Massy, the blocking force of about 250 men found by

Rough Sketch of action of 11th Dec 1879

9th Lancers
"Killa Kazi" Kabul
Dec 11th 1879

A SKETCH BY CAPTAIN JAMES STEWART-MACKENZIE, 9TH LANCERS, OF THE BATTLE AT KILA KAZI TO THE WEST OF KABUL ON 11TH DECEMBER 1879. ALTHOUGH THE REGIMENT'S FORCE OF 250 MEN WAS VASTLY OUTNUMBERED AND FORCED BACK, THE ACTION BOUGHT ENOUGH TIME TO ALLOW OTHER FORCES TO MOVE INTO POSITION AND SAVE KABUL. THE 9TH LANCERS' CHAPLAIN, THE REVEREND JAMES ADAMS, WAS AWARDED THE VICTORIA CROSS FOR RESCUING THREE MEN.

two squadrons of the 9th, one squadron of the 14th Bengal Lancers and four guns from the Royal Horse Artillery, moved to Kila Kazi.

Faulty intelligence would mean that the instructions proved impossible to follow. Within three miles, the advance guard formed by a troop of the 9th suddenly saw the enemy, according to Private Crane, *'advancing over the hills in dense masses like a swarm of bees'.*[21] Estimates put their numbers at around 9,000, of which 3,000 formed a crescent of about two miles *'developing two horns, quite à la Zulu'*, with the remaining 6,000 behind. Lancers and artillery began to engage, the men dismounting to cover the withdrawal of the guns as they fell back. With the enemy dispersed, both carbine and artillery fire proved ineffective in checking their advance as the situation, only seven-and-a-half miles from Kabul and with no other British forces in striking distance, became critical if the capital and Sherpur was to be held. Captain Stewart-Mackenzie of the 9th relates the next phase: *'General Massy, who was in command, now ordered Cleland [Commanding 9th Lancers] to charge and to use his own discretion as to how far he should go. I heard Cleland say, 'How far am I to go?' and Massy said, 'Use your own discretion.' We were now about 500 yards from the enemy, who were advancing in skirmishing order, the ground intersected with nullahs and watercourses. The Colonel gave the order to charge in extended order. Off we went, opening up as we went, the Colonel right ahead of us. It did not take us long to open out, and before we knew where we were we were among them. The ground we had to get over was awful ground for cavalry, deep watercourses and nullahs, but not withstanding the pace was good; the enemy were scattered all over the place in small bodies, some behind hillocks, some on horses, but all firing like the devil into us, dropping men and horses all over the place. I must tell you that we were only 126 in the ranks, so you may imagine that when we got among them, that it was all we could do to hold our own; they were all round us, and the ones in rear of them coming up firing as they came. In the melee I found myself next the Colonel, who was on his horse supported by two men. I saw that he was badly wounded, so I told them to take him to the rear. I then as senior assumed command, and finding that the men were falling fast and that we were getting surrounded on all sides, I ordered the retirement… The enemy, those that were mounted, kept following us, riding round and firing, and then cutting at us with their swords, shouting at the top of their voices, 'Allah, Allah.'*[22]

Picking up the wounded as they retired, the 9th moved back to the line of the guns where, in order to provide more time for the withdrawal of the artillery, another charge was made from the left, which again was beaten back by fierce fire, by which time Roberts and his staff had rushed from Sherpur to the action: *'the engagement had now become a question of time. If Mahomed Jan [the enemy commander] could close with and overwhelm our small force, Kabul would be his.'*[23] With one gun lost and then spiked in a water course, Roberts now ordered the remaining three back to a village but these were soon forced to move back again, though on the far side they too became stuck and had to be abandoned. Stewart-Mackenzie again takes up the 9th's tale: *'We retired on the village where the*

ROBERTS' FORCE IN KABUL WAS EFFECTIVELY BESIEGED IN THE SHERPUR CANTONMENT FOR MUCH OF DECEMBER 1879 WITH THE CAVALRY JOINING THE INFANTRY ON THE RAMPARTS.

'Thousands of fellows advanced with great yelling and shouting on our front, but this, I think, was meant for a feint, as their chief attack was on our left.'

guns were gone, and on arriving there found them in the act of being abandoned; they had fallen into a deep ditch, and the horses were unable to pull them out. After this it was 'sauve qui peut' and you never saw such a scene of confusion. We were all jammed into a corner of a field at the side of a village, only one place that we could get over, the enemy close behind pouring volleys into us. At last we all got over somehow, and on clearing the village I dismounted some men to cover the retreat, which they kept on doing till the 72nd [Regiment of Foot from Sherpur] took up the fighting.'

The action of Massy's force had clearly bought time, although the precarious situation was only saved by the intervention of the larger column from the north that had marched to the sound of the gunfire and now attacked the Afghan rear, forcing them to abandon their advance. This attack was joined by 50 of the 9th Lancers who had been reformed by Brigadier MacGregor, General Roberts' Chief of Staff who, with infantry in support, managed to recapture the guns lost earlier in the day. In this confused battle the 9th lost two officers and 16 men, including Lieutenant Colonel Cleland who later died of his wounds, as well 34 horses killed and slightly more injured while the Regimental Chaplain, the Reverend JW Adams, earned the Victoria Cross for rescuing three men who had been unhorsed.

Given the odds that they faced in the early part of the battle, Brigadier MacGregor was to prove uncharitable in his opinions of the performance of the Regiment, stating of an early part of the battle that '*the 9th Lancers did make a sort of charge, but not a good one, then retired…9th Lancers were quite out of hand, would not face them, and went back*'.[24] His views are at odds with those of General Roberts, who wrote of the same incident: '*the effort was worthy of the best traditions of our British and Indian Cavalry*', though Roberts did note that once unhorsed their weapons proved an encumbrance rather than a help: '*it was a sorry spectacle to behold these men, with their swords dangling between their legs and impeding their movements while they vainly endeavoured to defend themselves with their lances.*'[25] No doubt this would have shaped his views of the lance

THE SERGEANTS' MESS OF THE 9TH LANCERS IN KABUL, 1880.

as a weapon while, with 40 carbines lost by the Regiment (the cavalry insisted on the carbine being attached to the horse, while the sword was attached to the man), a new sling, devised by the new Commanding Officer, Lieutenant Colonel Bushman, was adopted by the 9th which allowed the carbine to be carried across their backs when the enemy were in sight, while the sword was attached to the saddle, a pattern finally adopted by the rest of the army in an order of 1891.

General Roberts' plan to defeat each column in turn was now untenable and over the next two days a defensive battle based on the Sherpur cantonment began, with the infantry dislodging the enemy on the heights overlooking the camp, while the cavalry were engaged in breaking up the large bodies of troops as they pressed in from the north and east. On 13th December, General Roberts withdrew all forces into the cantonment's fortifications and a siege commenced. The 9th, together with the rest of the cavalry, joined the infantry lining the walls and vedettes, while at night producing mounted picquets outside. On the morning of 23rd December, the enemy made a final assault, described by Lieutenant Little: '*Thousands of fellows advanced with great yelling and shouting on our front, but this, I think, was meant for a feint, as their chief attack was on our left. Independent firing continued for about three minutes; a hotter or quicker fire one could not imagine. Needless to say they were driven off. The firing now slackened and the enemy made off. About twelve o'clock the main body of the cavalry were sent out, but too late to get at them on the hop. We however, did a little dismounted work and blazed into the brown of them bolting back to the Bala Hissar.*'[26]

Reinforcements arrived on the same day and the fragile enemy coalition dissolved, allowing Roberts to secure the immediate area over the winter and spring of 1880 until the summer's heat prevented further operations.

The strategic situation had by now altered, diplomatic activity securing an uneasy peace and a new Emir who was, in principle, acceptable to all sides. This would allow the British to evacuate Afghanistan with some face though. Before the plan could be implemented, there was to be one more twist. A new claimant to the throne, Ayub Khan, had marched on Kandahar, defeating a British force at the battle of Maiwand on 24th July 1880 and besieging the remaining garrison in the city. To relieve them, on 9th August, General Roberts set out with the Kabul-Kandahar Field Force of 10,000 soldiers, including a cavalry brigade of three Indian Army regiments and the 9th Lancers. This relief force including 7,000 camp followers and 8,500 animals, reached the city in 22 days after an epic march over

THE 9TH LANCERS WERE THE ONLY BRITISH CAVALRY REGIMENT TO JOIN GENERAL ROBERTS' EPIC MARCH FROM KABUL TO KANDAHAR IN WHICH THEY ALTERNATED AS ADVANCE, FLANK AND REAR-GUARD. THE SIEGE OF KANDAHAR WAS RAISED AS A RESULT AND AYUB KHAN DEFEATED AT THE BATTLE OF KANDAHAR ON 1ST SEPTEMBER 1880.

340 miles. Throughout the march, the four cavalry regiments rotated among their tasks, two producing the advance guard, some five miles ahead of the main body while two others flanked it, with a final squadron forming the rearguard. Although this involved little fighting, the appalling heat, frequent sand storms and scarcity of water called for the highest standards of battlefield discipline: '*halt and inspect the transport and troop stores, getting rid of some of the latter. Sir F. [Roberts] is angry at our losses [of horses], and won't hear of any Government property being abandoned*'.[27]

The approach of the relieving force was enough to make Ayub Khan raise the siege and withdraw to a position in the hills, possibly expecting the British to collect those in the city before retiring to India. Roberts had other ideas and on the day after his arrival he attacked, the infantry closing with the enemy while the cavalry moved behind the position to cut off their retreat. It was not quick enough to deal with the enemy who fled rapidly, Lieutenant Hunter of the 9th recording: '*we arrived as usual just an hour too late*', leaving only a few stragglers to be taken during the subsequent pursuit.

Kandahar's recapture represented the end of the last serious opposition to the new regime and allowed the British withdrawal to continue with some sense of pride having been salvaged. While others returned to India immediately, the 9th spent a couple of months in the city which Lieutenant Hunter described in less than flattering terms as '*Not a very lively spot…the flies are something frightful; they go into one's tea, and to eat jam is almost impossible without swallowing at the same time about a dozen flies.*'[28] At the end of November 1880 the Regiment finally left, crossing into India via the Bolan Pass before entraining for Ambala where it arrived in mid-December after nearly two years away, '*dressed in thick Guthrie coats, helmets covered, everything thickly begrimed with dust, not having been able to get a wash or a shave, and pretty nearly done up for want of sleep, looking, as we were, old warriors returning from an arduous campaign.*'[29]

THE BOER WAR AND REFORM

1880–1914

Modder River | Relief of Kimberley | Paardeberg | South Africa 1899–1902

WHETHER IN INDIA OR AT HOME, the experiences of the Afghan War did little to accelerate improvement in the army or prepare it for the shock it would receive 20 years later. The annual inspection at the end of the training season continued to form the pinnacle of military activity, with detailed instructions dominating life in barracks and in the field. Orders, many remarkably familiar today, covered subjects as diverse as getting married without permission, the ownership of dogs, crockery damages in the cookhouse and the wearing of mixed dress. Training continued to be unimaginative and almost exclusively based on rigidly applied drills centred around the massed charge, while small-arms practice was regarded with some suspicion, smacking, as it did, of the mounted infantry units that were now being formed. It was limited to 150 rounds of ammunition per man per year.

THE 12TH LANCERS ON EXERCISE IN INDIA BEFORE DEPARTING FOR SOUTH AFRICA.

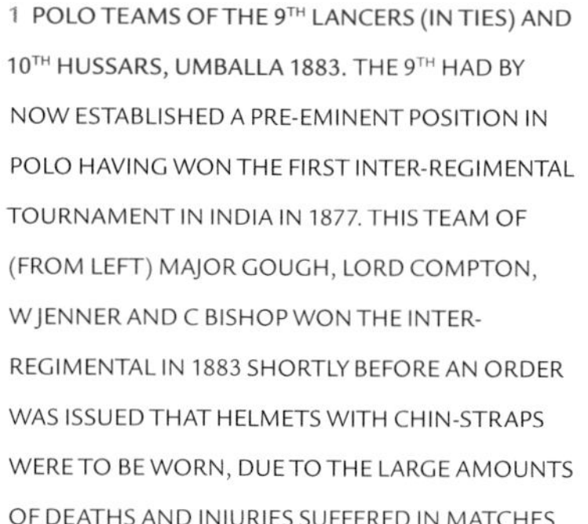

1 POLO TEAMS OF THE 9TH LANCERS (IN TIES) AND 10TH HUSSARS, UMBALLA 1883. THE 9TH HAD BY NOW ESTABLISHED A PRE-EMINENT POSITION IN POLO HAVING WON THE FIRST INTER-REGIMENTAL TOURNAMENT IN INDIA IN 1877. THIS TEAM OF (FROM LEFT) MAJOR GOUGH, LORD COMPTON, W JENNER AND C BISHOP WON THE INTER-REGIMENTAL IN 1883 SHORTLY BEFORE AN ORDER WAS ISSUED THAT HELMETS WITH CHIN-STRAPS WERE TO BE WORN, DUE TO THE LARGE AMOUNTS OF DEATHS AND INJURIES SUFFERED IN MATCHES.

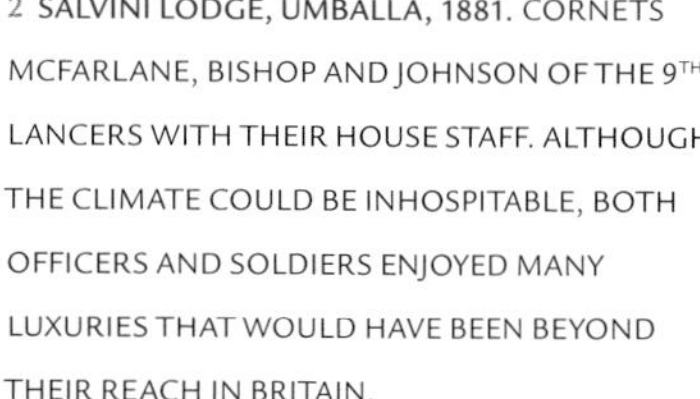

2 SALVINI LODGE, UMBALLA, 1881. CORNETS MCFARLANE, BISHOP AND JOHNSON OF THE 9TH LANCERS WITH THEIR HOUSE STAFF. ALTHOUGH THE CLIMATE COULD BE INHOSPITABLE, BOTH OFFICERS AND SOLDIERS ENJOYED MANY LUXURIES THAT WOULD HAVE BEEN BEYOND THEIR REACH IN BRITAIN.

3 FIELD MARSHAL LORD BIRDWOOD OF ANZAC. ALTHOUGH COMMISSIONED INTO THE 12TH LANCERS IN 1885, BIRDWOOD LEFT TWO YEARS LATER TO JOIN AN INDIAN ARMY REGIMENT. HE ACHIEVED DISTINCTION WHEN COMMANDING THE EVACUATION FROM GALLIPOLI, AND WAS THEN COLONEL OF THE 12TH FROM 1920–1951. HE STATES IN HIS AUTOBIOGRAPHY, WITHOUT ANY BITTERNESS, THAT HE LEFT BECAUSE HE KNEW HE COULD NOT AFFORD THE EXPENSE OF LIFE IN THE 12TH, THIS DESPITE THE ABOLITION OF THE PURCHASE SYSTEM NEARLY 15 YEARS EARLIER.

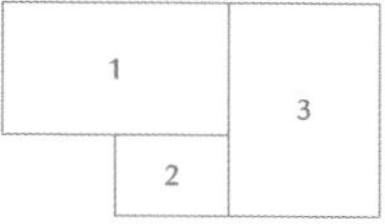

Standards of military horsemanship remained mixed so that, although innovations such as endurance rides that aimed to improve the stamina of both horses and men (a troop of the 12th rode from Bangalore to Mysore and back, a distance of 171 miles, in 51 hours), little was done to reduce the weight of nearly 20 stone that a horse had to carry when a man and all his specified equipment was mounted. Sport probably prepared many, particularly the officers, for war better than their military training. Polo, hunting, shooting and racing formed the main activities, with distinguished owners and riders in both regiments. For added spice, India offered new diversions such as pig-sticking by moonlight, mounted on bullocks.

The make up of the Regiments remained static. The majority of the soldiers came from the urban, unskilled workforce, which was generally neither fit nor well educated, while the officers' background remained wealthy and privileged. Although Cardwell had abolished the purchase of commissions in 1871 in the face of considerable protest – including from the Treasury as the cost to the State in compensation was some £7 million – it had done little to change the background of the majority of officers. The main financial barrier to a commission remained not the initial purchase price but the subsequent lifestyle with its outlay on uniforms, horses and mess bills, for which a private income of about £500 a year was required to top up a subaltern's pay of £95. Few joined with any idea of making a profession of soldiering and even fewer had aspirations beyond command of their own Regiment. For them soldiering provided a club-like existence that gave structure to a lifestyle based around field sports and polo, though the newly arrived officer would not have found it instantly welcoming. He would find himself '*in a Mess where he was practically ignored, told, if he spoke, to speak when he was spoken to, sent to riding school as if he had never been on a horse, and generally made to understand that he was of no account*'.[1]

While not materially altering either attitudes or standards, some changes to the Regiments were implemented. The establishment leapt by over 200

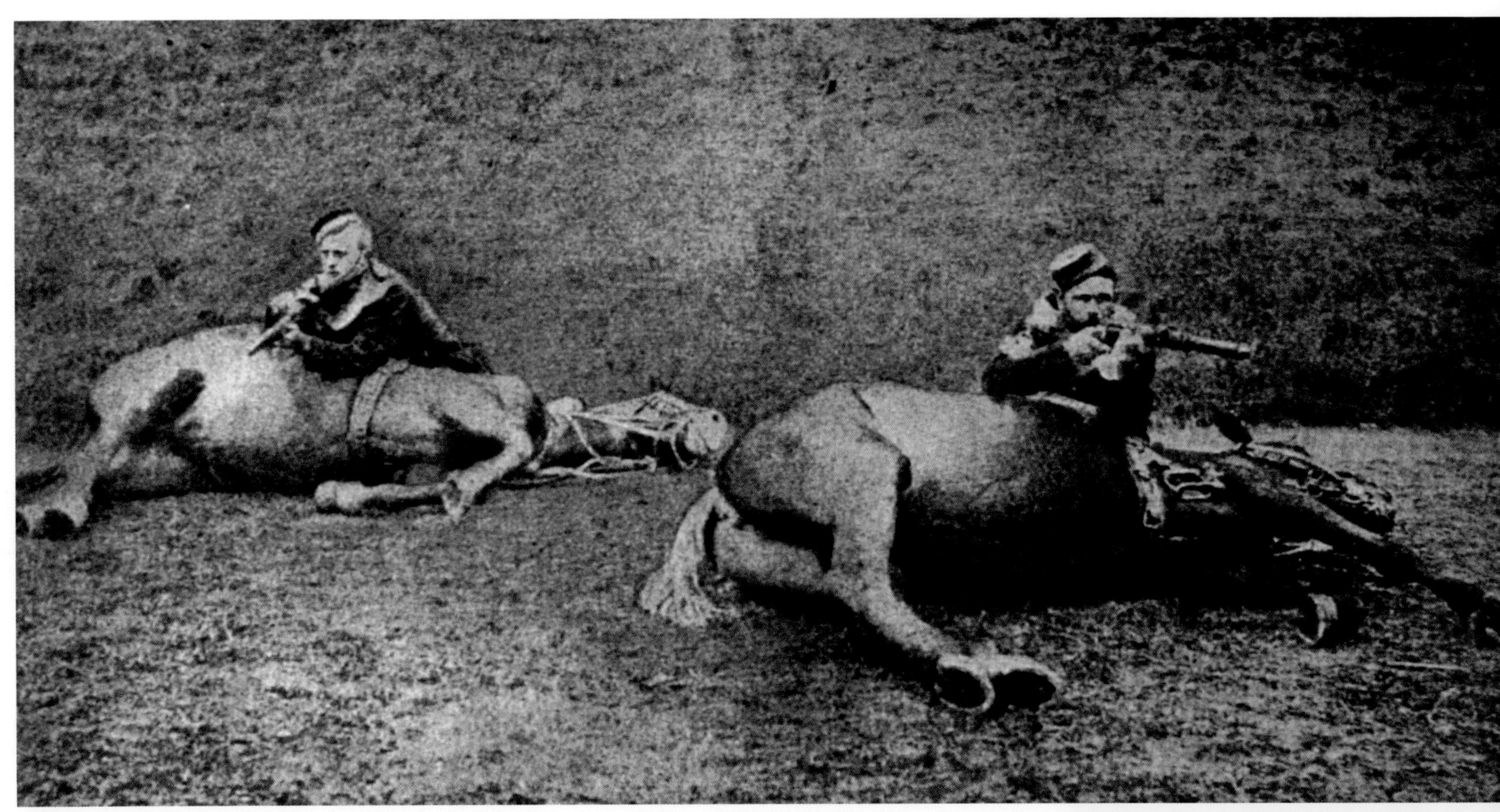

'the 12th Lancers, with their fluttering pennons, went by like a wall... the gallop past was a thing to be seen and remembered...'

personnel to 706 all ranks and 424 horses in 1890 and the squadron system of two large troops was adopted, thereby introducing a degree of delegated command. New carbines, swords and pistols came in the following year while over the rest of the decade the regiments received khaki uniforms, smokeless powder and a machine-gun section. More widely, the army improved artillery and communications, introducing telephones, printers and typewriters, as well as food in cans.

Forming the backdrop to these activities, the two Regiments continued to serve in Britain and overseas. The 9th left India in 1885 and the 12th followed two years later to begin a series of postings in various parts of England, Scotland and Ireland. The movement between postings was still carried out by route marches. The SQMSs rode a day in advance to secure billets, the majority of which were somewhat dangerously in pubs. Foreign service began again in August 1896, when the 9th embarked for a short posting to Pietermaritzburg and then Ladysmith in South Africa, before moving back to India in March 1898.

The 12th remained in Britain for a few more years and were taken in hand in 1897 by a new Commanding Officer, Lord Airlie, who was appointed after the removal of his predecessor who, even by the standards of the day, was deemed to be insufficiently attentive to his duties, managing to fit in all his work and make the morning train to London. Airlie, in contrast, was a fanatical soldier, a keen sportsman and a man of high moral principles who involved himself in every facet of regimental life, paying particular attention to officers' education and turning the poor report that had led to Hill's removal into a glittering testimony a year later when a spectator of the Cavalry Manoeuvres wrote, *'the 12th Lancers, with their fluttering pennons, went by like a wall...the gallop past was a thing to be seen and remembered...This Regiment showed itself the best Cavalry Regiment in the two Army Corps. The men walked, trotted, and galloped past to perfection.'*

INITIAL ACTIONS OF THE BOER WAR

Airlie's intervention was timed to perfection. The combination of British imperialism, Boer intransigence and, above all, the lure of gold had for years been fuelling tension between the two independent Boer republics of the Transvaal and the Orange Free State and the British-controlled

FRENCH NEWSPAPER PHOTOGRAPH OF 12TH LANCERS ON EXERCISE AT ALDERSHOT, PROBABLY IN 1899. LORD AIRLIE (ABOVE) HAD BY NOW TAKEN THE REGIMENT IN HAND, A COMMENTATOR DESCRIBING THEM AS 'THE BEST CAVALRY REGIMENT IN THE TWO ARMY CORPS'.

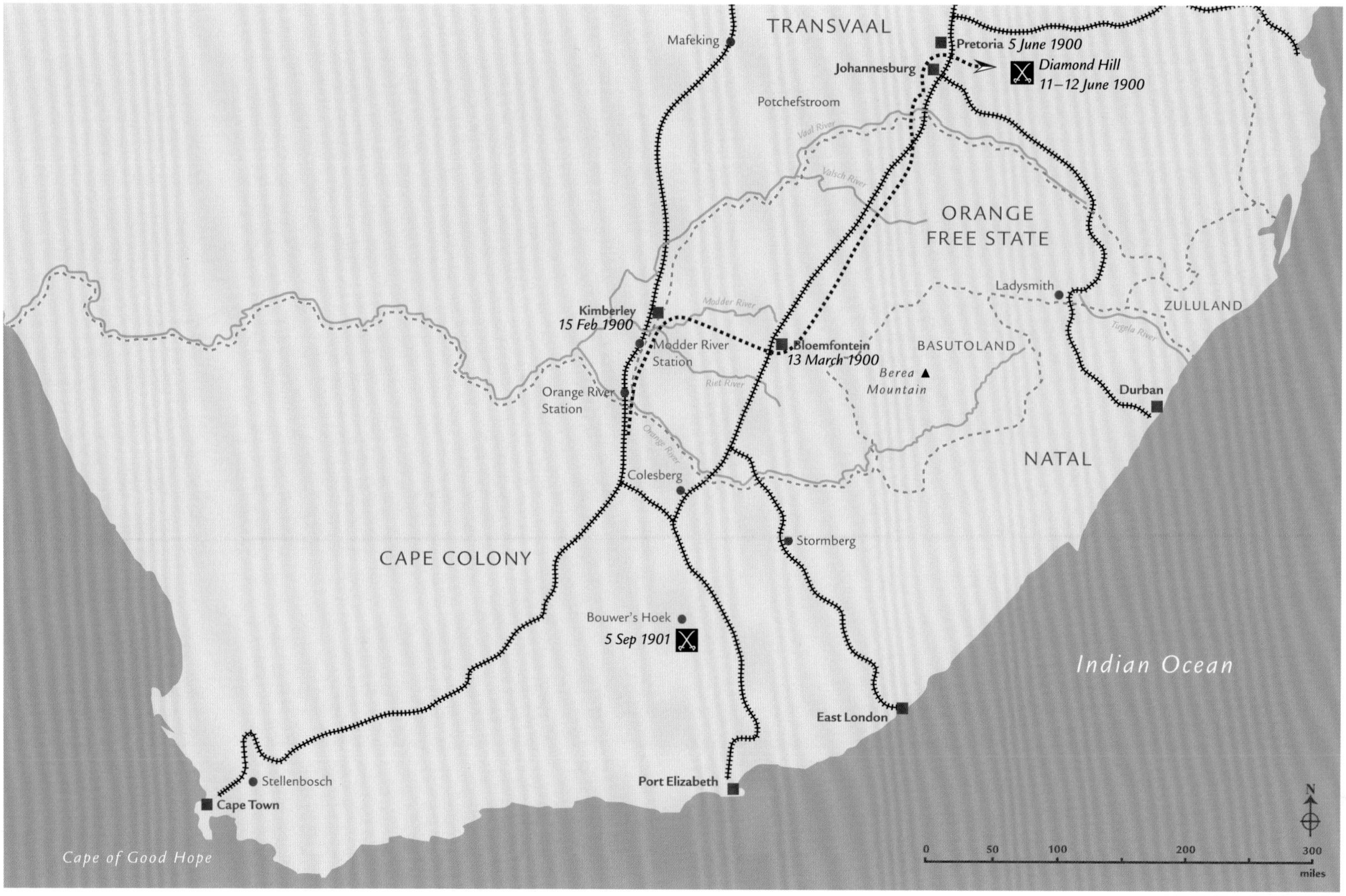

SOUTH AFRICA, SHOWING THE CAPE COLONY AND THE BOER REPUBLICS OF THE ORANGE FREE STATE AND THE TRANSVAAL. THE MARKED ROUTE IS THAT TAKEN BY BOTH REGIMENTS FROM OCTOBER 1899 TO JUNE 1900 WHEN THE CONVENTIONAL PHASE OF THE BOER WAR ENDED.

Cape Colony to their south. On 12th October 1899 the tension led to a war for which both regiments were already preparing, the 9th leaving Bombay on 25th September and the 12th sailing from Britain on 22nd October to provide reinforcements to the 22,000 British troops who faced 60,000 Boers along the border.

The two armies could not have been less alike. Although well equipped and disciplined, the British Army had grown used to dealing with an unsophisticated enemy in colonial conflicts. The infantry was highly regulated, slow and geared to fight pitched battles, while the heavily laden cavalry was ill-prepared for the demands that long marches over rough terrain with insufficient forage or water would make on their horses. Boer forces, by contrast, consisted of a small regular element, principally a well-equipped and trained artillery corps augmented by a paramilitary police, while the bulk of their troops comprised volunteer 'commandos' of sharp-shooting farmers mounted on tough ponies. Operating in small, highly mobile groups, after the arrival of British reinforcements they used the ground to overcome their numerical disadvantage and avoided being sucked into pitched battles after the early stages of the war. Unlike many of Britain's recent enemies, who had often attacked bravely but foolishly in near-suicidal charges, the Boers fought to live and presented a different challenge to which the army facing them was slow to adapt.

Realising that their numerical advantage would be short-lived, the Boers had struck the first blows of the war, launching a pre-emptive attack of three columns into Natal and the Cape, each achieving tactical success but crucially failing to strike a knock-out blow. More importantly, although they reached Colesberg and Stormberg in the centre, they fixed the bulk of their forces in strategically disastrous sieges at Ladysmith in the east and Mafeking and Kimberley in the west. This removed their own freedom to manoeuvre and allowed the initiative, however bungled, to pass to rapidly expanding British forces.

The 600 men and 500 horses of the 12th Lancers arrived without mishap in Cape Town on 19th November. As so often in the past, sea travel and the 9th had not gone well together. One of their three ships was caught in a storm that caused the horses to smash through the wooden stables, either to be

RACING

Horses and racing have played a large part in the lives of Regimental officers, even after mechanisation. Each Regiment has produced notable horsemen, many making national headlines.

Lord Beresford of the 9th Lancers (later to win the VC in the Zulu Wars) was one of the best riders of the 1870s while, in 1890, Eustace Crawley of the 12th Lancers won the Regimental Point-to-Point with neither reins or stirrups, having fallen and remounted early in the race. Crawley went on to win the Grand Military twice on horses belonging to Eustace Loder, a brother officer.

Eustace Loder owned the 1906 Derby winner Spearmint, while still serving, and was a man of considerable wealth. The silver centre piece in the Officers' Mess was presented by him. While stationed in Egypt, the standard of food in the Officers' Mess was deemed unsatisfactory so he fed the officers at his own expense for a month. He owned many horses, including the incomparable filly Pretty Polly, which won the 1000 Guineas, the Oaks, the Coronation Stakes, the Nassau and the St Leger in 1904.

LIEUTENANT EUSTACE CRAWLEY ON EUSTACE LODER'S SIR ROLAND WINNING THE 12TH LANCER REGIMENTAL RACE WITHOUT REINS OR STIRRUPS IN 1890. A VERY SHORT OFFICER, WHEN IN FULL MARCHING ORDER HE HAD TO HAVE A SECOND STIRRUP HOOKED TO HIS STIRRUP IN ORDER TO MOUNT HIS CHARGER. A BRILLIANT SPORTSMAN HE WAS KILLED WHEN SECOND IN COMMAND OF THE 12TH IN THE TRENCHES IN 1914.

MAJOR EUSTACE LODER OF THE 12TH, BELIEVED TO BE THE ONLY MEMBER OF EITHER REGIMENT TO HAVE OWNED A DERBY WINNER, SPEARMINT, WHILE SERVING. AFTER RETIRING HE WENT ON TO OWN OTHER CLASSIC WINNERS AND RUN THE JOCKEY CLUB.

Many successful military leaders were also excellent jockeys. David Campbell, who was to lead the 9th Lancers in the early part of the Great War, won the 1896 Grand National on The Soarer. He rode his last winner, aged 61, as a full General, when he won the Military Drag Hunt Cup at Aldershot in 1930.

Between the wars, both General Dick McCreery and General Herbert Lumsden were outstandingly successful riders while with the 12th Lancers, before showing themselves equally fine commanders, of the Eighth Army and X Corps respectively, in the Second War.

Frank Furlong of the 9th Lancers rode his own horse, Reynoldstown, to win the National in 1935 the year after he left the Army. The following year, the same horse won again, ridden by his former brother officer Fulke Walwyn, who went on to become perhaps the finest National Hunt Trainer since the war, training such horses as Mont Tremblant, Mill House and Mandarin. He also trained in later years for Queen Elizabeth while she was Colonel in Chief of the 9th/12th Lancers.

In 1967, Queen Elizabeth gave the regiment a steeple chaser called Bel Ambre. Ridden by Nigel Wright, he won six races while the Regiment was in Catterick. Nigel was the son of Stephen Wright who had served with the 9th Lancers in 1940, been captured and imprisoned in Colditz for trying to escape.

Fulke Walwyn also trained Special Cargo, which won three consecutive Grand Military Gold Cups in 1984, 1985 and 1986. It was a great honour for the Regiment that Queen Elizabeth ran Special Cargo as being for the 9th/12th Lancers.

Officers have won the Grand Military twice in recent years: Charles Perry in 1967 on Willow King and Algy Smith-Maxwell on Brother Geoffrey in 1989. Both were sons of former officers in the Regiment.

OFFICIAL PHOTOGRAPHS TAKEN OF A 12TH LANCER WHICH ILLUSTRATES THE PLETHORA OF DIFFERENT EQUIPMENT HE HAD TO CARRY AND MASTER. THE PHOTOGRAPHS WERE DESIGNED TO SHOW THE WIDE UTILITY OF THE CAVALRY IN BOTH THE MOUNTED AND DISMOUNTED ROLE, A TOPIC THAT BECAME THE CENTRE OF CONSIDERABLE DEBATE IN THE YEARS FOLLOWING THE BOER WAR.

swept overboard or seriously injured. Lieutenant Lord Blackwood recalled: *'Now came the most horrible scene I have ever witnessed. The deck was covered with one struggling mass of horse and mules mixed up with the broken woodwork of the stables, the whole being hurled first to one side of the deck and then the other. Out of fifty horses and mules on my deck only three were saved.'*[2] In total, 92 of the 150 on board had been lost. Despite these losses, the Regiment was hurried to Modder River Station.

Expecting an easy fight, the British had decided to deal with all three Boer incursions simultaneously. In the west, the 9th Lancers, together with Rimington's Guides and two companies of mounted infantry, formed the mounted contingent of fewer than 1,000 men within Lord Methuen's force of 8,000, which was tasked with the relief of Kimberley. Assembling at the Orange River Station, they moved off on 21st November and, within two days, they had met their first Boer opposition on the high ground east of Belmont. The engagement set a pattern that was to become familiar, the Boers moving back from one delaying position to another along the railway line, while British tactics invariably involved frontal attacks by the infantry, with the cavalry probing the flanks to try to cut off the enemy's retreat or attack him in the rear. Almost as inevitably, the carefully sited Boer artillery and sharpshooters inflicted heavy casualties on the British before they could engage at close quarters, while the speed with which they withdrew frustrated the cavalry's efforts, and left them meeting, at best, a small rearguard.

At the sequential battles at Belmont (23rd November), Graspan (25th November) and Modder River (28th November) the story was the same. Lieutenant Allhusen recalled: *'We were advancing on the flank of the infantry farthest away from the enemy, the whole force moving around the enemy's position. No sooner were we within easy artillery range than they began shelling us.. We had very few moments peace that day on account of those beastly shells. Their shooting was splendid, and if we got under cover they moved the gun and fired at us from a fresh position.'*[3] In these engagements the 9th Lancers provided reconnaissance and screens but already more than half their horses were unfit. To compound their problems, the slow progress made against the Boer's delaying positions caused Lord Methuen to fix on Lieutenant Colonel Gough of the 9th and relieve him of command. It was an act that failed to recognise the wholly inadequate numbers of mounted troops present or the limited preparations that had been made for the advance. It would have been small consolation that Methuen was himself soon to be removed when Lord Roberts took over, the latter remarking, *'I am resolved that he should not be given any independent command'.*[4]

Methuen held at the Modder River with both sides using the opportunity to build up strength, the Boer force increasing to 8,000 as it prepared a strong

defensive position at Magersfontein a couple of miles to the north. The British forces now totalled 15,000, including the 12th Lancers who had joined it on 3rd December, having spent the latter part of November with the central column at Colesburg carrying out reconnaissance tasks. One of these, imaginatively written up by the press, still carried the jingoistic note characteristic of the early part of the war: *'The reported retirement of the Boers from Arundel is confirmed by a patrol of the 12th Lancers whose Colonel [Lord Airlie] with reckless bravery ordered his men under cover and himself advanced to the post supposed to be occupied by the enemy, which, however, he fortunately found unoccupied.'* Lord Airlie was somewhat less dramatic: *'At last I made up my mind that we must clear up the situation which we did by riding pretty wide round the nullah.'*[5]

Methuen's force, although just a tantalising three days' march from Kimberley, now faced a Boer position entrenched north of the Modder River along the Magersfontein Ridge, where carefully

concealed trenches and fire positions dominated the river, the railway line and the open ground on the British side. Reconnaissance by the cavalry found the ground well-prepared and crossed by wire, a patrol by the 12th ending in disaster with two dead and three captured, though a Boer newspaper paid the compliment of announcing in its headline: '*Capture of the bravest officer and the best horse yet seen in the present war.*' Elsewhere, Boer forces continued to raid British lines, the 12th racing 20 miles south to Enslin to relieve two infantry companies that were surrounded by the enemy.

The assault on Magersfontein ridge began on 11th December, with the infantry moving up under cover of darkness for a dawn attack, the cavalry providing flank protection and the artillery delivering a lengthy preliminary bombardment. In expectation of these tactics, the Boer commander, Koos de la Rey, '*with an originality which, if it had been displayed by a young British officer in an examination for promotion, would probably have injured that officer's prospects,*'[6] had sited his positions at the foot of the hill, catching the Highland Brigade as they moved into position. Lieutenant Allhusen again described the scene: '*Monday. Moved off at dawn, and before it was light we heard a most awful fusillade. This was the Boers firing at the unfortunate Highland Brigade, who had been led up in column of quarter columns, a very close formation, the troops being more or less massed like a church parade. I don't know what the casualties were at this point, and one shrinks almost from inquiring. It was too cruel. The Brigade as a fighting unit ceased to exist for the day and, I am afraid, for many days to come.*'[7]

For the first time since their formation, the two Regiments were now working side-by-side as, with G Battery RHA in support, they tried to relieve the pressure by working their way around the left flank of Boer position, only to be held by fire from a low ridge to their front. The 9th moved to the flank from

THE 9TH LANCERS AT BELMONT 23RD NOVEMBER 1899. BELMONT WAS THEIR FIRST ENGAGEMENT OF THE BOER WAR WHEN, AS PART OF THE FORCE TRYING TO RELIEVE KIMBERLEY, THEY DISCOVERED THE EFFECTIVENESS OF THE BOER DELAYING TACTICS.

13/12/99.

My dear Airlie

I have had much pleasure in bringing to notice the good work done by your dismounted Sqn on the 11th under yourself. I would also like to add that Pte Symes one of the men you sent back with a message at one time impressed me as being a useful man

Signature [illegible]

No. Date
From To
Place Place
Despatch h. m. M Receipt h. m. M

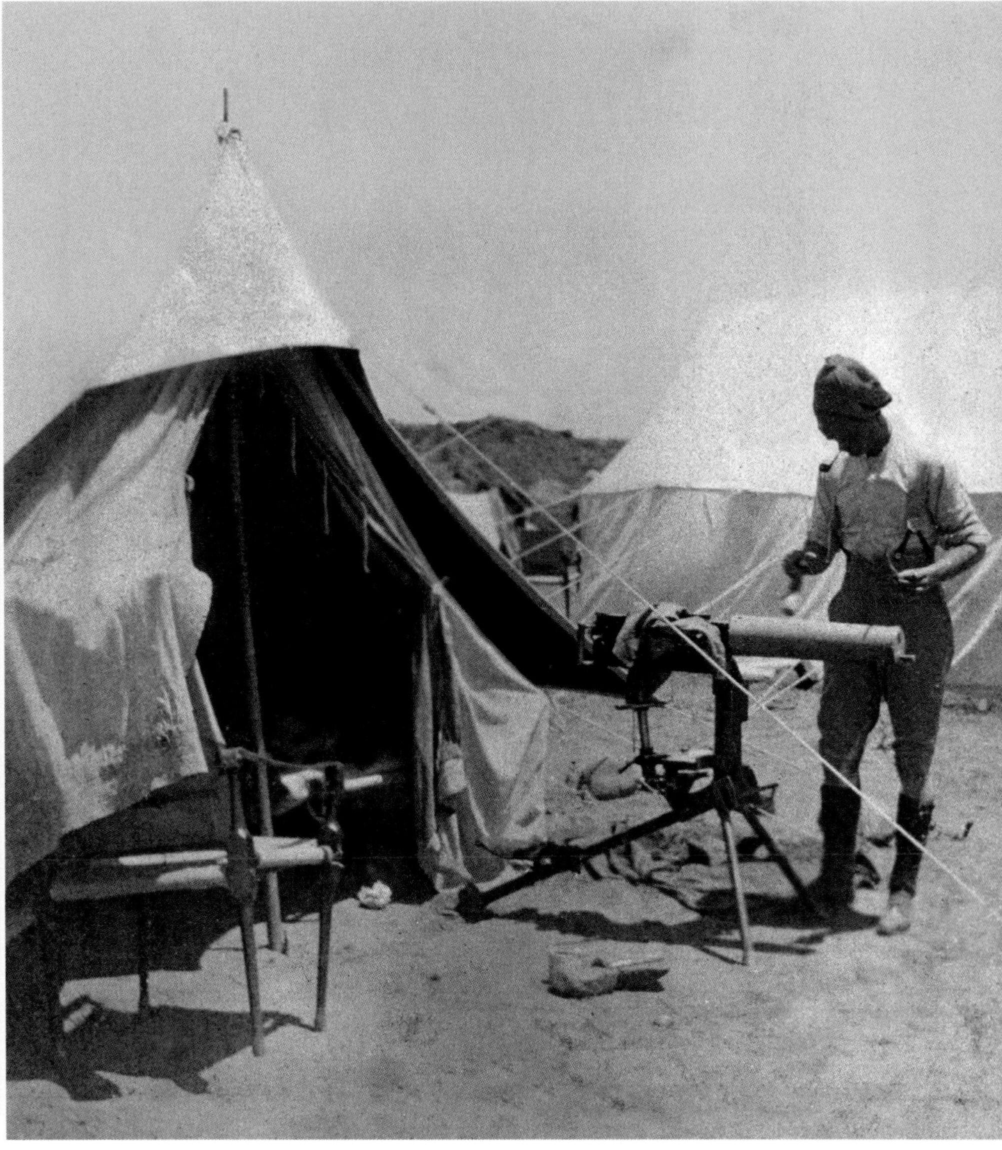

THE BATTLE OF MAGERSFONTEIN IS THE FIRST DOCUMENTED OCCASION OF BOTH REGIMENTS ACTING IN DIRECT SUPPORT OF EACH OTHER. LIEUTENANT ALLHUSEN OF THE 9TH LANCERS (PICTURED) KEPT HIS MACHINE-GUNS GOING THROUGHOUT THE DAY, WHILE HIS COMMANDING OFFICER SENT THIS NOTE TO LORD AIRLIE OF THE 12TH AFTER THE BATTLE PRAISING THE WORK OF HIS DISMOUNTED SQUADRON.

where their machine guns kept up sustained fire throughout the day, staying in position long after the withdrawal of the rest of the Regiment, while simultaneously B Squadron of the 12th escorted the artillery forward to a small knoll, coming in behind the Highland Brigade who were pinned down in dead ground to their front. With the guns soon in action, Lord Airlie took the other two squadrons and some mounted infantry, dismounted and moved forward to join them, laying down fire with both machine guns and carbines in a duel that lasted until well into the afternoon. The combined efforts of both Regiments and the guns repelled several Boer counter-attacks and provided cover for the infantry withdrawal until finally relieved by the Coldstream Guards. With no hope of progress, Methuen's entire force withdrew that night to leave the Boers firmly in control of the approaches to Kimberley. In assessing the action, Sir Arthur Conan Doyle, not an enthusiast for cavalry, highlights the 'unconventional' (ie dismounted) role of the 12th Lancers: '*Lord Airlie deserves all praise for his unconventional use of his men, and for the gallantry with which he threw both himself and them into the most critical corner of the fight*,'[8] while the official historian credits them with preventing '*the reverse becoming a disaster for the whole division*'.[9]

The defeat at Magersfontein combined with the other British debacles along the front at Stormberg and Colenso to create the 'Black Week' of December. All offensive operations across South Africa were checked, with limited patrolling by the cavalry the only relief to the listlessness and signs of sickness that began to set in, while already critics claimed that the mounted arm was insufficient in numbers and that their horses were unfit for service, a result of too much weight being carried and, in many cases, poor horsemanship.

THE RELIEF OF KIMBERLEY

The appearance of Lord Roberts of Kandahar as the new commander in South Africa resulted in a change to the previous strategy of simultaneous attacks on all fronts. British forces would concentrate in the west to relieve Kimberley before swinging east along the River Modder to take Bloemfontein, the capital of the Orange Free State, whose capture was expected to knock that part of the Boer coalition out of the war.

In preparation, and to conceal the build up of forces that were arriving with the new commander, both Regiments were involved in a series of feints in January and February 1900 against the Modder River Station and the position at Magersfontein, reinforcing the Boer view that '*the English do not make turning movements; they never leave the railway, because they cannot march*'.[10] Both Regiments were further affected by a wider reorganisation of the mounted arm into a single division under Sir John French, comprising three cavalry and two mounted infantry brigades, supported by six batteries of guns, the whole totalling nearly 5,000 men. The 12th Lancers, together with a composite regiment of the Household Cavalry and the 10th Hussars, formed the 2nd Cavalry Brigade, while the 9th and 16th Lancers made up the 3rd. At the same time, training and reduced equipment aimed to keep horses fitter produced better reconnaissance and faster movement.

Roberts' detailed tactical plan to relieve Kimberley abandoned the advance straight up the railway line in favour of a wide sweep by the Cavalry Division to the east of the Boer position at Magersfontein before striking north towards the town.

Roberts' detailed tactical plan to relieve Kimberley abandoned the advance straight up the railway line in favour of a wide sweep by the Cavalry Division to the east of the Boer position at Magersfontein, before striking north towards the town. Threatened with being cut off from Bloemfontein, the Boers would be forced to abandon their position, but would be prevented from moving east along the River Modder by the infantry who, following more slowly along the route taken by the cavalry, would take over and hold the crossings, freeing the mounted troops to push on.

On 11th February, the Cavalry Division moved out with six days' rations and five days' forage. With the Boers still convinced that the move, involving several deception measures, was only a feint, a crossing over the River Riet was seized before the Division moved on to the Modder. On 14th February at Klip Drift, the 12th managed to capture two Boer leaguers and a convoy, including 13 wagons and much-needed forage and water while further along, at Rondeval Drift, the 9th Lancers achieved a similar result. The pace now slowed as the Cavalry Division paused for a day while the infantry caught up, their arrival at 6am on 15th February allowing the cavalry to move again shortly afterwards. Despite the rest, the effect of the harsh, arid country was already proving a major factor, the 12th Lancers' horses reduced by 21 dead, 25 missing (presumably abandoned) and 37 unfit for immediate service.

The available Boer forces had used the day of respite to prepare for the advance with characteristic thoroughness, taking up a position on two low flat ridges forming a natural amphitheatre

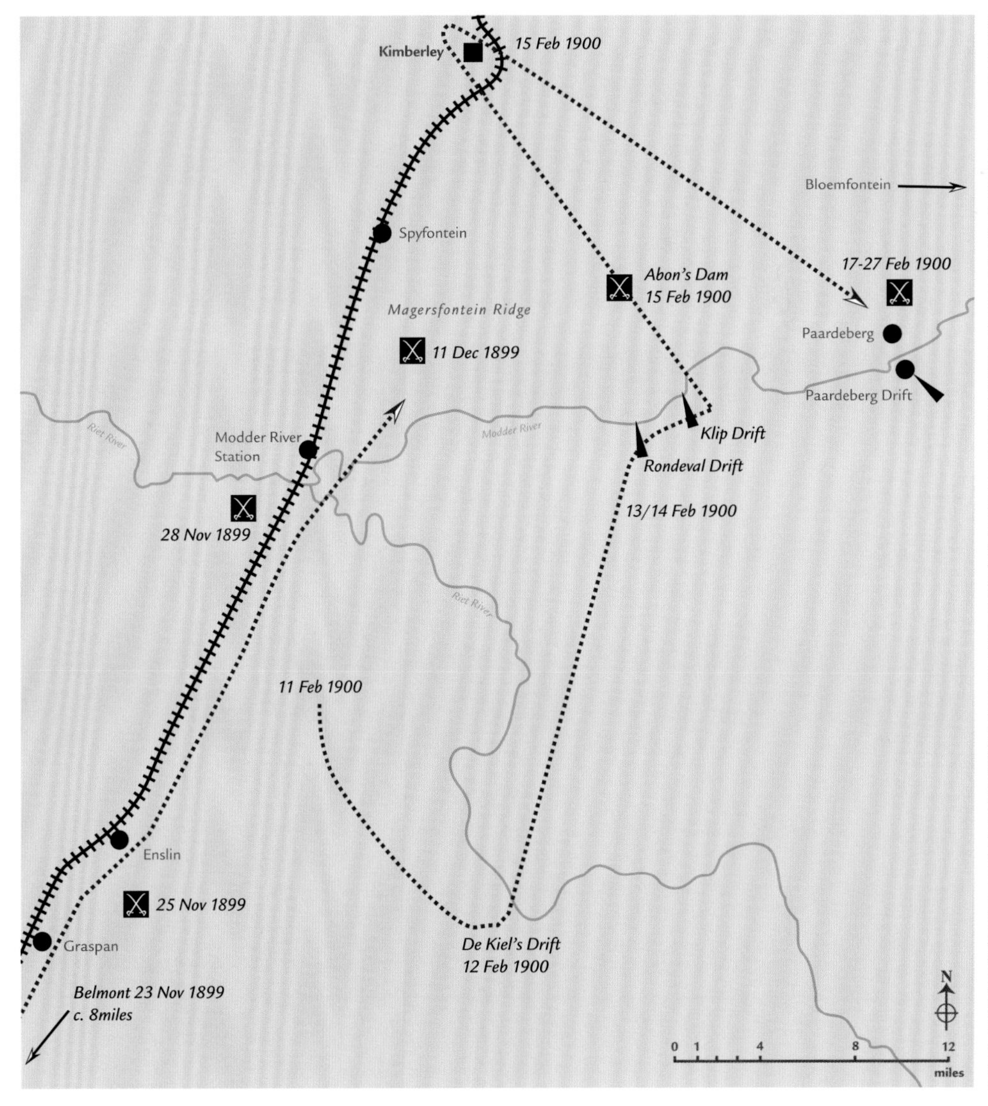

THE RELIEF OF KIMBERLEY AND THE CAPTURE OF THE BOER FORCES AT PAARDEBERG.

SPEARMEN

KLIP DRIFT, 15TH FEBRUARY 1900. THE ACTION AT KLIP DRIFT, WHICH INVOLVED BOTH REGIMENTS, OPENED THE WAY TO KIMBERLEY AND WAS ONE OF THE RARE OCCASIONS IN THE BOER WAR WHEN CAVALRY CHARGED IN ANY GREAT NUMBERS.

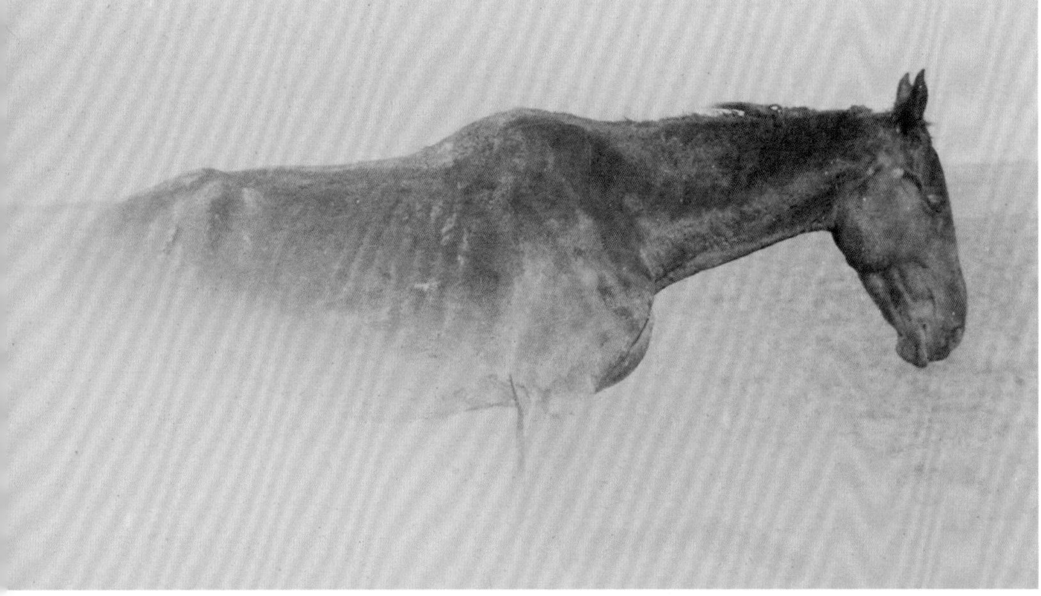

HORSES, SUCH AS THIS ONE OF THE 9TH LANCERS, RAPIDLY LOST CONDITION DUE TO POOR LOGISTICS AND THE DEMANDING CONDITIONS WITH MANY HAVING TO BE CAST. EVERY OPPORTUNITY TO WATER BOTH MEN AND HORSES WOULD HAVE BEEN TAKEN AND ALTHOUGH THIS PICTURE OF THE 12TH DURING THE RELIEF OF KIMBERLEY SHOWS A SUCCESSFUL STOP, ON A LATER OCCASION TWO OFFICERS DIED AFTER DRINKING BAD WATER – THE WHISKY THEY ADDED ALTERING THE TASTE BUT NOT REDUCING THE LETHALITY.

with a small gap or nek at its northern end, through which the Cavalry Division must pass on the only route to Kimberley from Klip Drift. The 9th Lancers, at the head of the Division, had barely moved out from the cover of the river bed and into the open when they were engaged with rifle and artillery fire. Despite five batteries of British guns returning fire, General French faced either delay – and the prospect of the Boers reinforcing their position as he waited for an infantry assault – or possible disaster if he rushed the gap, potentially leading to another Balaclava.

Thinking the ridge to be lightly held, French took the second option. He ordered the 3rd Brigade to charge the gap, with the 2nd in a second line 800 yards behind, while all available guns would provide support. The Official History records the action: '*These four squadrons* [the 9th and 16th Lancers had only two squadrons available each] *he deployed in extended order, eight yards between files…the rear ranks formed a second line twenty yards behind. Placing himself at the head of his brigade, Gordon* [commanding 3rd Brigade] *led it forward at a pace of about fourteen miles an hour, which he judged to be the fastest that the horses in their enfeebled condition could keep up; the nek was about two miles off, the ground was good, and fortunately free from wire. The squadrons came at once under a shower of bullets both from the front and flanks, yet few fell. The extended formation, the pace of the charge, and the thick clouds of dust puzzled the burghers, while the supporting fire of the batteries shook their aim. Though bullets knocked up jets of dust all round the extended files, the casualties of the main body of the leading brigade were slight. As the lines of the Lancers approached, at a steadily increasing pace, the crest of the nek, the burghers manning it became nervous, shot worse and worse, and then mounted their ponies and galloped off in headlong flight. The few staunch men who stayed to the end were struck down or made prisoners. It was the most brilliant stroke of the whole war, alike in both the prompt decision with which it was ordered and the consequences which followed from it.*'[11] The Daily News reported: '*Such a sight has not before been witnessed by this generation… there was no faltering, regiment after regiment swept by at an easy gallop, the 9th and 16th Lancers, Householders, 12th Lancers, 10th Hussars, and a squadron of Inniskillings followed each other in open formation.*'

Although the hyperbole of the press gives the action the feel of a full-blown charge, and was used as justification for maintaining this tradition after the war, the nature of the action was more of a rapid movement by mounted troops to bypass an enemy position, with very little shock and awe about it. Notwithstanding this, the success of the events at Klip Drift were measured in the relief of Kimberley that followed and the astonishingly light human casualties, the whole division having only 12 wounded of which one later died. The damage to horses, for many of whom this charge represented their last breath, was far more severe, the 9th alone losing five killed, 15 wounded and 10 dead from exhaustion. Sir Arthur Conan Doyle wrote of them: '*The horses, which had come a hundred miles in four days with insufficient food and water, were so done in that it was no uncommon sight to the trooper not only walking to ease his horse, but carrying part of his monstrous weight of saddle gear. But in spite of fatigue the force pressed on until in the afternoon a distant view was seen, across the reddish plain, of the brick houses and corrugated roofs of Kimberley. The Boer besiegers cleared off and that night the relieving column camped on the plain two miles away, while French and his staff rode into the rescued city.*'[12]

The action at Klip Drift (or Abon's Dam) opened the path to Kimberley, which the exhausted men and horses reached that evening. The 12th Lancers led the way, to find that the beseiging Boers had gone. With little time to reflect on their successes, a pursuit of sorts was begun the next day by the 1st and 3rd Brigades, though, with their horses so

done in, they met with little success. Similar results met the 2nd Brigade, who patrolled to the south but were unable to locate the Boer forces that had finally abandoned the position at Magersfontein and were moving rapidly east along the Modder River towards Bloemfontein to escape the British net closing around them.

PAARDEBERG

To trap the fleeing Boer army, General French received orders late on the evening of 16th February to move south-east to cut off their route to Bloemfontein. His problem lay in how to execute the directive, for by now the Cavalry Division was severely depleted in horsepower, a typical example being the figures for the 9th Lancers. Of the 422 horses that had left the Modder River Station five days earlier, only 105 were fit, while across the whole Division mounts for only two regiments were immediately available. French gave these to the 2nd Brigade, bolstered by some of the Carbiniers and 12 guns, with orders to prepare to move immediately, with the 3rd Brigade to follow 24 hours later.

At 2am on 17th February, French and the 2nd Cavalry Brigade left Kimberley with the usual prospect of more difficult country ahead as they sought to catch Cronje and his army which was, by now, well to the east of the route from Klip Drift. What followed was, according to Viscount Anglesey in his definitive history of the British cavalry, *'an astonishing feat with starved, leg-weary horses. An average pace of 5mph for seven successive hours, most of them in excessive heat, places this march high among the achievements of cavalry.'*[13] By 11am, the advance guard from the 12th spotted the Modder River in the distance with the enemy nearby, the intelligence being confirmed by the capture, by B Squadron, of a Boer signalling station at Kameelfontein Farm, at which the Brigade then concentrated and watered their horses.

Six miles to the south, at Vendutie Drift, Cronje and his escaping army could be observed crossing the Modder and yet, despite having surprise on their side and with the enemy not expecting any more interference, the British were in no position to launch a full-blooded attack. Their horses were worn out, and the 1,300 men of the Brigade faced four or five times that number of an enemy whose flanks rested securely on the river. General French therefore elected to fix the Boers in position and await the arrival of greater forces, ordering the artillery onto a ridge 2,000 yards from the enemy from where they began to shell them as they began to cross the river. Inevitably, the Boers responded quickly, sending out two assaults, the first of which, coming in on the flank of the guns, was stopped by dismounted fire from A Squadron of the 10th Hussars and C Squadron of the 12th. The second, an attempt to move to the left and shell General French's headquarters at Kameelfontein Farm, was checked by B Squadron and two of the guns, the fire being kept up from dismounted positions throughout the day. With daylight fading, the pursuing British infantry were at last seen approaching, though contact with them was impossible, leaving the Brigade to continue in its task throughout the night. The official history noted that this opening event of the Battle of Paardeberg (so called because the only other settlement nearby, Stinkfontein, was deemed an inappropriate name for a battle), *'having regard both to the skill and audacity displayed by General French and to the immediate strategic results thereby obtained, must be reckoned amongst the great achievements of the British cavalry in war'.*[14]

The Boers were now fixed at Paardeberg as the main British forces arrived. Kitchener, temporarily in charge of the Army, mounted a poorly co-ordinated assault with heavy losses on the following day while the 12th, who had continued patrolling, were finally able to get some rest for their horses, Airlie recording, *'No forage, horses dead beat, lying down and dying'.*[15] At the same time, one of the Boer heroes of the war, Christian de Wet, had attempted to relieve the trapped army by seizing a commanding hill to the south of the river and preventing its complete encirclement. The 2nd Brigade's immediate attempts to dislodge him amounted to little more than shelling until two days later an attack, including the 9th Lancers and infantry, succeeded in evicting the force. With de Wet gone, the Boer position was now hopeless. Unable to manoeuvre due to the large baggage train and the numbers of camp-followers in the leaguer, and subjected to continual shelling with little hope of relief, the Boer commander Cronje and his entire force of just over 4,000 capitulated on 27th February, a devastating blow to the Boer cause that effectively ended the conventional war in the western area.

Refurbishment was now essential to make good the losses in horses across the Cavalry Division. It precluded a dash for Bloemfontein, the army finally moving off on 6th March, with both regiments taking part in the action at Poplar Grove on the following day where Christian de Wet again delayed the British advance. The British momentum was however unstoppable and Lord Roberts entered Bloemfontein unopposed on 13th March, with the 9th Lancers providing his escort into the city.

The capture of their capital failed to remove the Orange Free State from the war, and Roberts now looked north to advance towards the Transvaal capital of Pretoria, though before he moved both sides took stock of their experiences. For the Boers, the use of large wagon leaguers and supply

THE EMPTY SADDLE. A PATROL OF THE 9TH LANCERS RETURNING FROM AN ACTION.

trains was abandoned to improve their mobility and enable them to elude their slower-moving opponents. Among other changes, the British reorganised and trained the cavalry, making the carriage of four days of supply the norm in a bid to overcome the problems of supply. Reinforcements and remounts arrived, together with wounded and released prisoners, while administration included the issue of new boots and uniforms, the 12th wisely burning all their underclothes, which had been worn continuously for the last five weeks. As they waited, both Regiments continued to provide patrols and quick-reaction forces, with frequent skirmishes the result as the small, mobile Boer commandos continued to harass British outposts and supply lines, preventing complete recuperation of either men or horses.

Despite the lack of absolute security in the conquered area, Lord Roberts was anxious not to give the Transvaal Boers too much time to prepare and began the move north towards Pretoria on 3rd May, splitting the mobile elements into two columns either side of the line of the railway along which the main body moved. The series of flanking movements, while preventing the Boers from delaying the advance, once again never succeeded

in bringing them to a pitched battle while, once again, the lack of forage and poor condition of the horses reduced the speed of the cavalry. Orders could also contain an unrealistic expectation, such as those given a 9th Lancer force instructing them to seize a railway bridge in the Boer rear north of Johannesburg. Captain Campbell noted: '*The undertaking was of a somewhat stupendous character, as not only was the country full of Boers, but also the horses were in poor condition, and the journey of over sixty miles to the bridge was about as much as most of them would have been able to perform, and the return would still have to be done.*'[16] Additional risks lay in the unsanitary conditions in which everyone operated, with hygiene and disease a perennial concern, illustrated by two 12th Lancer officers who, failing to boil water from the only source available (a pool with a dead horse in it) and using whisky to hide the taste, contracted enteric and died.

Despite these setbacks, Lord Roberts was in Johannesberg by 30th May, with Pretoria falling six days later. While the lack of a major battle on the march from Bloemfontein to Pretoria gives the impression that this was a routine affair, the physical endurance demanded was noteworthy and executed over what the Official History described as, '*apparently endless prairies, in blazing sun and bitter cold, swept now by hot and choking dust storms, now by rushes of icy hail, fording rivers and floundering through sand, with scanty food and shelterless bivouacs*'.[17] The demands on the cavalry on the flanks, where both Regiments were posted, were even more severe, with distances increased from the 300 miles faced by the main body as it followed the railway line, and the lack of rest days caused by the requirement for constant patrolling.

DIAMOND HILL

The fall of Pretoria on 5th June 1900 was expected to spell the end of the war, but de Wet's continuing successes against the British lines of communication in the Orange Free State had put fresh heart into the Boers of the Transvaal. Their army, largely still intact and numbering about 5,000, took up a position on a chain of hills straddling the railway line running east from Pretoria. On 11th June, Roberts attacked the Boer flanks with two columns of cavalry in the hope of avoiding an expensive frontal assault. Neither column was to prove successful in breaking through but, on the southern end of Diamond Hill where the enemy position lay, the 2nd Cavalry Brigade, supported by the 3rd and some mounted infantry, appeared to make progress, leading to two guns being pushed too far forward with insufficient support. To rescue them, the Household Cavalry and the 12th were ordered to make separate charges but, with most of the Regiment scattered about patrolling, Lord Airlie could only muster 50 or 60 men, including several from the 10th Hussars, who now charged, causing the Boers to withdraw and saving the guns. Almost immediately, Boer sharpshooters began to engage the withdrawing troops, concentrating their highly accurate fire on Lord Airlie and his white horse (he had earlier had another shot under him) and killing him with a shot to the heart.

Winston Churchill, a war correspondent at the time, commented that it '*was a fine, gallant manoeuvre, executed with a spring and elasticity wonderful and admirable in any troops, still more in troops who had been engaged for eight months in continuous fighting with an elusive enemy*'.[18] More than simply saving the guns, which had been the strictly limited objective of the charge, a conversation held some years later revealed a possible further and unexpected benefit of Airlie's action at Diamond Hill. At a dinner held at Sandringham hosted by King George V and Queen Mary on 18th November 1931, Lady Airlie was said to have been told by Field Marshal Smuts who had been with the Boers at Diamond Hill: '*Do you realise… that your husband's charge destroyed the master scheme we had planned? We were bringing in our Commandos so as to encircle the whole British Army, with General French and the whole GHQ. I stood on the heights with the others, and we watched the gaps closing, closing. Do you understand that we should have had your CinC and all his staff prisoners? And just as we thought we had succeeded I…saw a movement – a break- and said 'Good God! There is a break! a charge!' and knew the movement we had planned had failed.*'[19] Whether such ambitions were ever likely to be realised, or were just a polite and comforting thought for a widow, the battle of Diamond Hill, which continued into the next day when the Boers were finally forced from their positions, secured Pretoria for the British and marked the end of the conventional phase of the war.

GUERRILLA WARFARE

British claims to control the two Boer republics, which had been formally annexed as Colonies, ignored the reality that the Boer commandos still retained their freedom of movement beyond the garrison towns and their immediate environs and could reassert their authority when opportunity arose. What came next was not to be a gentle mopping-up operation but two years of guerrilla warfare that would bring the total of casualties inflicted on the 9th Lancers during the war to 55 per cent for officers and 22 per cent for soldiers. Both Regiments now became caught up in a series of arduous treks chasing a dangerous and elusive enemy better suited to this type of warfare. A detailed description of their marches and engagements would be near impossible and confusing, and perhaps unjustly has not been attempted here.

The treks began almost immediately after the capture of Pretoria, with both Regiments involved

12th LANCERS, POTCHESTROOM, 1901. BY NOW THE WAR HAD TURNED INTO A DISPIRITING AND EXHAUSTING SERIES OF MARCHES AIMED AT DEPRIVING THE ROVING BOER COMMANDOES OF THE MEANS TO FIGHT ON. *'THE BRITISH TROOPS EXPENDED THEIR UTMOST STRENGTH UPON OBJECTS APPARENTLY SO INSIGNIFICANT, YET SO DIFFICULT TO ATTAIN.'*

in the first 'de Wet hunt' as part of several large columns sent to trap the Boer commander and his men who, despite some British successes, managed to stay one step ahead of his increasingly tired pursuers. The debilitating effect on the horses in particular was again acute, while the increasing frustration of the chase led to more draconian measures being adopted by the high command in a bid to separate the commandos from their supporting bases. Lord Kitchener, assuming command from Lord Roberts in December 1900, based his strategy on scorched earth, internment and containment. This was unattractive soldiering, with farms, crops and cattle either being taken or destroyed, seemingly with little impression being made on the enemy, while the task was made even less appealing when the population, mainly women and children who had been deprived of their homes, were forced into the newly established concentration camps, the aim being both humanitarian (the camps were intended to provide food and shelter to the dispossessed families, though proved a breeding ground for disease) and military, as the measure deprived the Boer forces of local support.

At the end of May 1901, the 9th moved to the Cape Colony, with the 12th following in July, as both Regiments returned to the pursuit of Boer commandos who had entered the colony to try to whip up support there. Once again the Official War History observed that '*the British troops.. [expended] their utmost strength upon objects apparently so insignificant, yet so difficult to attain*'.[20] One rare success was the capture of Lotter's commando in which the 9th, operating in the Cape Colony in September 1901 as part of a small column commanded by General Scobell, surrounded a farmhouse and kraals where the Boers were resting. In the ensuing fire-fight 13 enemy were killed and 120 captured, including 46 wounded, along with 200 ponies and 30,000 rounds of ammunition. On the British side nine were killed and a similar number wounded, of which seven of the dead and five of the wounded came from A Squadron as they fought through the kraals to get to their position in order to prevent the withdrawal of the enemy. Lotter and seven of his commando were subsequently court martialled and executed as Cape rebels.

Such victories were, however, few and far between, with the campaign continuing to be characterised by long marches, worn-out horses and an enemy that was only gradually being overcome. Against this backdrop, Lord Kitchener's strategy, despite opposition at home and abroad which increased as details of conditions in the concentration camps became known, was now coupled with sweeps against the lines of wire and blockhouses that were constructed across the country. The cavalry were employed as 'beaters' in the drives conducted over vast distances. In the face of the changing nature of the conflict, the cavalry assumed the features of mounted infantry, the lance and sword being withdrawn from October 1900, while the carbine was replaced by the infantry pattern .303 Lee-Enfield rifle and bayonet, which at least gave them parity with the enemy, the relevant order stating that the *'rifle will henceforth be considered the cavalry soldier's principal weapon'*.[21]

Faced by the apparently unlimited resources of the British Empire, the Boers appeared in a hopeless position and as the war ground on, divisions appeared in the enemy high command until, after protracted negotiations, a ceasefire was agreed. The Boer leaders surrendered on 31st May 1902, leading to the incorporation of the two republics into the British colony of South Africa. By this time the 9th Lancers had already left South Africa, while the 12th continued with a final series of sweeps across the veldt before peace allowed them to join the 9th in India. Both would no doubt have agreed with Sir Arthur Conan Doyle's assessment of their experiences of the campaign: *'The war has been a cruel one for the cavalry, who have been handicapped throughout by the nature of the country, and by the tactics of the enemy. They are certainly the branch of the service which has had least opportunity for distinction. The work of scouting and screening and patrolling is the most dangerous which a soldier can undertake, and yet from its very nature it can find no chronicler. The war correspondent, like Providence, is always with the big battalions, and there never was a campaign in which there was more unrecorded heroes…'*[22]

The embarrassment and difficulty of defeating two small states in South Africa triggered a root-and-branch review of the army at all levels. For both Regiments, a major element of the debate was, unlike so many others in the military, of immediate relevance, for it concerned the role and employment of the mounted elements of the army. The Boer War had proved the immense utility of skilled, armed, horsemen, though not of the large bodies of massed cavalry that the army retained on its establishment.

THE CAPTURE OF LOTTER'S COMMANDO AT BOUWER'S HOEK IN CAPE COLONY ON 5TH SEPTEMBER 1901 BY A SQUADRON OF THE 9TH LANCERS WAS ONE OF THE RARE OCCASIONS DURING THE GUERRILLA CAMPAIGN THAT A CONCRETE VICTORY COULD BE CLAIMED. THIRTEEN BOERS WERE KILLED AND 120 CAPTURED, ALONG WITH 200 PONIES AND 30,000 ROUNDS OF AMMUNITION.

TRICK-RIDERS OF THE 12TH LANCERS. BOTH REGIMENTS PRODUCED A VARIETY OF DIFFERENT RIDING DISPLAYS AND APPEARED AT THE ROYAL TOURNAMENT. MORE IMPORTANTLY, THE PERIOD SAW A CONSIDERABLE IMPROVEMENT IN THE STANDARD OF HORSEMANSHIP ACROSS THE CAVALRY.

Two opposing schools of thought emerged: the first, 'the Old School', favoured the retention of a cavalry arm whose almost exclusive role was the shock action of the charge. Their opponents, 'the New School', held that such tactics were redundant and that the future of horses on the battlefield lay with the mounted infantryman. Sir Arthur Conan Doyle, writing on some lessons from the war said, '*let a man be a fine rider, a trained horsemaster, a good skirmisher, and a dead shot, and he becomes more valuable than any mere cavalryman can be*'.[23] Lord Roberts, by now Commander-in-Chief of the whole army, sided with the reformers: '*in future wars shock tactics will be few and far between. Since Napoleon's time there has very seldom been much done by shock tactics, and cavalry will have to fight more frequently on foot than they have ever thought of doing before,*' General Knox added: '*We do not want any cavalry; we want men mounted who can shoot.*' On the other side, Generals French and Haig said: '*cavalry can do everything that mounted infantry can do and other duties in addition.*' They commented that removing swords and lances would be '*to take away from cavalry its power of assuming the active offensive by mounted action by depriving it of the arme blanche* [literally the 'White Arm' – a French term for cavalry armed with sword or lance], *is to withhold from it a very considerable advantage without any compensating gain.*'

Both sides cited examples from the Boer War to advance their views, the Old School arguing that it had not been a typical war as the enemy did not have formed cavalry with which to engage, while the opposing party countered that it had proved the potency of modern artillery, smokeless ammunition and a flat trajectory bullet able to render massed cavalry charges impossible. The reformers gained the upper hand early in the debate, Roberts issuing Army Order 39 in March 1903, which abolished the lance '*on guard, in the field, at manoeuvres and on active service*', reissuing the guidance he had given in the war that the rifle would '*henceforth be considered as the cavalry soldier's principal weapon.*' This order did not apply in India, where both Regiments were at the time stationed, for one of the few areas that both sides could agree on was that the lance remained particularly effective in dealing with civil unrest, particularly in India, where the use of firearms might not only be disproportionate but also less effective. Roberts himself acknowledged in 1903 that '*occasions may arise, particularly in campaigns against savages, who are ill-armed, or who may have an innate fear of horsemen, when the lance may be the surest and speediest means of demoralizing the enemy*'.[24]

Though neither 9th nor 12th Lancers was therefore affected by the decision to discard the lance in Britain, it was clear that change was approaching. *The Cavalry Training Manual* issued in

1904, although written under Haig's guidance, was prefaced by Roberts, who appealed not only to common sense but also hinted at the underlying snobbery attached to some of the Old School views: *'I would beg of cavalry officers not to be led away by the feeling that there is something unsuitable to the mounted arm and detrimental to its prestige in employing dismounted men when cavalry is opposed to cavalry… I confidently predict that the commander who makes use of his rifle fire in an intelligent manner will beat the commander who despises, or does not know how profitably to avail himself of, the deadly weapon about to be placed in the hands of our cavalry soldiers.'*[25]

Lord Roberts' retirement as Commander-in-Chief shortly afterwards gave the Old School the upper hand. The 1907 edition of *Cavalry Tactics* showed a change of emphasis: *'the rifle, effective as it is, cannot replace the effect produced by the speed of the horse, the magnetism of the charge and the terror of cold steel.'* The rifle would be carried *'to supplement the sword or lance'*. As a result, Army Order 158 of June 1909 reinstated the weapon: *'regiments of Lancers will in future carry the lance not only on escort duty…but also on guard, during training, at manoeuvres and when so ordered on field service,'* an order that remained in service until 1927, when Army Order 392 finally decreed it should only be retained for ceremonial purposes.

A MOUNTED PARADE OF THE 9TH LANCERS IN AMBALA 1903. DESPITE THE DEBATE SURROUNDING THE FUTURE ROLE OF THE CAVALRY, LIFE IN INDIA CONTINUED LARGELY UNCHANGED. THE DECISION TO REMOVE THE LANCE AS A WEAPON OF WAR DID NOT AFFECT THOSE POSTED TO INDIA, WHERE IT WAS FELT IT WAS PARTICULARLY EFFECTIVE FOR INTERNAL SECURITY.

'let a man be a fine rider, a trained horsemaster, a good skirmisher, and a dead shot, and he becomes more valuable than any mere cavalryman can be.'

SUSAN MEGGS, SHAGGER AND OTHER ANIMALS

Aside from the obvious attachment to horses and dogs for hunting (packs were established in the Peninsula and in each World War) both Regiments have always had a strong affection for keeping pets both in peacetime and on operations. One of the best-known dogs kept by either Regiment was Susan Meggs, a mongrel terrier owned by Captain Burrell of the 12th Lancers, who accompanied him throughout the Boer War from 1900 and who was eventually buried in India. Besides having a portrait of her painted in oils, depicting her wearing her owner's medals (the Queen's Medal and the King's Medal for the Boer War) she was also given a handsome gravestone when she died in Ambala in 1907.

Other dogs have achieved similar degrees of affection, particularly on operations where they have added a degree of normality to day-to-day life. In the Second World War the 9th Lancers were accompanied by 'Shagger' for over six years, the relationship ending only when the Regiment was due to sail back to Britain from Egypt in 1947 and the effects of his dope wore off during the captain's inspection. In the 12th Lancers detachment on escort duty to the Royal Family and the Cabinet from 1940–42, Lance Corporal Cobly (who specialised in driving the Prime Minister) owned a black Scottie dog that had a love-hate relationship with Churchill. The tradition has been kept going on recent operations with dogs seeming to inveigle themselves into every camp. One dog, 'Mutley', showed considerable stamina in trying to accompany virtually every foot-patrol out of camp in North Belfast in the early 1990s. The Balkans and the Middle East have more recently seen canine companions appear as camp dogs fawned upon by doting soldiers, though here the risk of rabies and other diseases have resulted in a less tolerant attitude being shown to them by the authorities.

While dogs have been the usual companions, more exotic pets have made frequent appearances, typically while on foreign postings. Captain Mansell-Pleydell of the 12th in 1880 had a tame panther chained up at the end of his house in India, while more recently in Malaya '*the Commanding Officer [Lt Col Horsburgh-Porter] had an otter, Capt Hudson a pig, Capt Lowther a gibbon or Wa-Wa, Maj Abraham an enormous and most destructive cockatoo and Capt Brockbank was always surrounded by birds until he got married at Ipoh*'.[38] Inevitably, any sort of pond or lake has inevitably led to attempts to breed a wide variety of fish. More mundane introductions have included pet rats and a pair of rabbits that ranged freely on the subalterns' corridor in Wolfenbuttel in the mid-1980s, their happy existence cut short by the protests of the long-suffering cleaners.

While their presence both in peacetime and on operations has almost universally been seen as benign, there seems always to have been an irresistible urge to try to regulate them and, more importantly, their owners. As early as 1881 the instructions for the 9th at Ambala restricted the number of dogs '*to what is intended by the regulations*', though usefully without saying what these were. At various times it has been felt necessary to point out that they were to be kept tied up until after morning parade, that they were not to go on the rifle range and that they were not allowed to roam the parade ground while a parade was in progress.

One other animal, a chicken, deserves a particular mention if only because, at the height of hostilities in the desert in 1943, she merited an obituary in the War Diary of the 12th Lancers: '*Sarah (chicken), killed on Active Service by falling off the Officers' Mess lorry. This remarkable bird has seen continuous service with the Regiment for over a year, and has some 300 eggs to her credit. Her loss is mourned by all and particularly her stable companion, Emma.*'

SUSAN MEGGS AND HER GRAVESTONE.

BARRACK ROOM IN 1908. ALTHOUGH SPARSE AND CRAMPED, SOLDIERS' CONDITIONS OF SERVICE WERE FINALLY BEGINNING TO IMPROVE.

Although this victory seemed a triumph for the Old School and the reactionary element in the army, it represented their high-water mark. Sir John French and others remained in positions of authority and influence but, by the publication of the 1912 edition, a more balanced tone had been struck: *'The rifle endows cavalry with great independence in war, and numerous situations will occur when it can be used with greater effect than the sword or lance; but a bold leader will find frequent opportunities for mounted attack which will produce more rapid and decisive results than can be gained by even the most skilful use of the rifle. It is, however, by no means necessary when an attack is made that only one of the two methods should be employed, for fire action can create favourable opportunities for shock action, and a well executed combination of the two methods will often present the greatest chances of success.'*

Such views, and those of Royal Commission, which had as early as 1903 recommended that: *'Cavalry should still be armed with the sword, if not the lance, and trained in shock tactics, but should also be more carefully trained than heretofore to fight on foot and use the rifle'*, may appear undecided but masked a huge change of attitude and character amongst the cavalry. Despite its reputation for being resistant to change, the years that followed the Boer War produced a mounted force that would consistently outperform both its allies and opponents in the First World War.

Even if the exact role of the cavalry had not been decided, there was clearly a need to improve their horsemanship. The Boer War had involved long distances, the 9th Lancers calculating that they had covered 8,530 miles during the campaign, but Sir John French told the Royal Commission that the cavalry *'understood stable management better than care of horses in the field'*[26], while a more cynical view held that *'the British cavalry officer talked more and knew less about horses than anyone else on earth'*.

Regiments did much to improve matters themselves and responsibility for achieving high standards passed from the instructors in the riding school to the chain of command that would be affected by them, thereby developing the squadron system begun at the end of the 19th century and devolving greater responsibility to the squadron leaders. Major General Baden-Powell (the Inspector-General of Cavalry for Great Britain and Ireland) exhorted in 1906: *'Our training now has to be effected by instruction rather than mere drill.. the useless NCO who was formerly considered efficient if he was able to throw up his chin and to spout, parrotwise, a string of aids to a squad of men, no longer passes muster where "instruction" to each recruit is required in his own words and by his own demonstration.'*[27]

Collective training was also made more relevant, with a common approach to operations and administration laid out in the newly issued *Field Service Regulations*, with tactics emphasising scouting, dismounted work and small-arms training at the expense of charges. All this reflected General Baden-Powell's view of the cavalry's role, *'to cover the front of the army, and, by gaining full information on the enemy's main force and concealing their own, to give their Commander-in-Chief complete liberty of action; also to prevent the enemy's cavalry doing the same on their part. To threaten the enemy's communications,'* before going to describe its task as *'to destroy the enemy's cavalry; to keep the infantry informed and protected; to cut off and hold the enemy; to chip*

2LT CHARRINGTON'S TROOP, 12TH LANCERS, AMBALA 1908. ALL THE SERGEANTS WOULD HAVE HAD INDIAN SERVANTS WHOSE FRIENDS WOULD HAVE ACTED AS BATMEN FOR THE REMAINDER OF THE TROOP. 'IT WAS GOOD TO SEND FOR THE BEARER AND SAY "I AM FOR GUARD TO-NIGHT, I WANT A GOOD TURNOUT", ALL THAT YOU HAD TO DO PERSONALLY WAS TO ATTEND TO YOUR RIFLE'.

in where required on the battlefield; to smash up the enemy in pursuit or to protect one's own side from pursuit.'[28] Inevitably the degree to which each Regiment entered into these new occupations depended on location and the particular phase of the debate, but the familiar round of troop, squadron and regimental training became established – with much more of it being done in the field. The result led Trooper Hanlon, who joined the 12th in 1909, to comment that '*we come back from these shows [exercises] sun-burned, ragged and rough, but fit, efficient, happy and ready for the next show*'.[29]

The introduction of the short Lee-Enfield rifle, the same as that used by the infantry, but five inches shorter and a pound lighter, did at last give the regiments a realistic prospect of making a significant contribution at distance, one commentator noting that '*the British cavalry was the only cavalry that could shoot…and was prepared to get off its horses in order to do so*'.[30] These improvements were not only restricted to Britain. In India, where both Regiments were stationed for much of the period up to 1914, the cavalry gained a reputation for producing excellent shooting, with both Regiments winning a number of competitions in all their stations. While seemingly anachronistic, July 1908 saw the introduction of a new pattern of cavalry sword exclusively designed for thrusting, as opposed to slashing or cutting or a combination of the two, and which has remained in use, admittedly largely for ceremonial, ever since. Other new introductions to the army were staff cars and some motorcycle despatch riders, a retired 9th Lancer officer providing the newly formed Army Motor Reserve's first Permanent Staff Officer in 1906. More practical uniform of a standard pattern and with a peaked hat was also introduced early in the century, alongside a bandolier for 90 rounds to be carried over the shoulder.

More widespread reforms improved pay and conditions of service, with a real, but largely unsuccessful attempt to reduce the degree to which an officer would have to rely on a private income, not only to join a regiment but then to survive. For soldiers, the length of service required was reduced to make recruitment more attractive, while there were also determined efforts to improve the standing of soldiers in society and to improve their employment chances on discharge. Recruiting nevertheless remained difficult while pay for soldiers continued to be uncompetitive with civilian labour rates, though the quality of life in barracks was by now increasing significantly. Less draconian punishments were administered and reduced rates of drunkenness reported, while good conduct badges bringing higher rates of pay encouraged higher standards.

Despite these improvements, a cavalry soldier's day was long, an ex-trooper of the 12th writing in 1906, '*life for a recruit was one long continual grind, and we never had a forty hour week*',[31] though, again, the situation in India was ameliorated by the plentiful supply of help for all ranks. As Trooper Hanlon of the 12th commented: '*It was good to send for the bearer and say "I'm for guard tonight, I want a good turn-out", the result being that lance, sword, boots, brasses, buttons and spurs would all be at your bedside ready to put on at the appointed time. All that you had to do personally was to attend to your rifle… all this went to make life tolerable during the great heat of the summer when, after early morning parades and stables, and possibly a lecture, all one had to do during the long afternoons was to lie and sweat under the punkahs.*'[32]

An increasing sense of pride and esprit de corps manifested itself in both Regiments. The 1st January 1911 witnessed the birth of the 12th Lancers' Regimental Association to promote *'fellowship and association between past and present members of the Regiment; promote the welfare of discharged soldiers; to assist the wives and families of members who are in distressed circumstances'*[33], the last aim an indication of a more understanding attitude towards families, with the number of wives allowed on postings beginning to increase. This increased sense of belonging was to pay dividends in the next war, generating a desire to serve typified by Corporal Davies of the 12th who, invalided home after injury at Mons in September 1914, reappeared with no kit of any sort in France in December, having stowed away in Dublin.

At a higher level, various Secretaries of State for War, most notably Lord Haldane, successfully reorganised the War Office, introduced a General Staff and improved the utility of the reserves by creating the Territorial Army. While these may have appeared to be merely changes at the top, for both the 9th and the 12th Lancers the decision to create an expeditionary, all-arms force capable of rapid deployment was to have an immediate effect, as they found themselves on their return from their last pre-war posting to India caught up in the permanent divisional and brigade structure of the cavalry. Integrated with other arms, better training could now take place, while the speed of mobilization was significantly improved, the army of 1906 taking two months to put 80,000 men in the field, while that of 1914 could, and did, cross the channel with double that number in 15 days.

Throughout these reforms, both Regiments resumed a familiar pattern of soldiering, the 9th returning to India in 1902 to be followed by the 12th soon afterwards. One of the principal and earliest incidents of the 9th's tour, remembered for all the wrong reasons, was the 'Atu case', in which an Indian cook of that name was almost certainly beaten by soldiers from the Regiment and subsequently died. Although the incident was serious enough in its own right, the manner in which it was dealt with by the Regiment and the army became a *cause célèbre* and says much about society in India at the time. It reinforced the view of the Viceroy, Lord Curzon, which had been formed by several earlier cases that *'You can scarcely credit the sympathy with wrongdoing that there is here... provided that the malefactor is an Englishman'*.[44] In this instance, the 9th undertook a flawed and limited inquiry that proved nothing. A subsequent external inquiry a month later was unable to shed further light, with the Commander of the Punjab region deciding to close ranks, seeming, in his report, not only to blame Atu himself but, in Lord Curzon's words *'anybody in fact but the parties to whom all the evidence points'*.

Lord Curzon's wrath was palpable. He said of the report: *'can ineptitude go further?... [it was] animated by the spirit of a partisan'*.[35] Despite the inability to find the actual culprits, Lord Curzon and the Commander-in-Chief in India decided to punish the 9th by recalling all those on leave and blocking future leave for the next six months. The Regiment was also to be given a privately

THE BOER WAR BROUGHT WITH IT REFORM AND A GREATER EMPHASIS ON ALL ASPECTS OF SOLDIERING, INCLUDING MILITARY SKILLS AND SPORT. BY THE OUTBREAK OF THE FIRST WORLD WAR CAPTAIN FRANCIS GRENFELL, 9TH LANCERS, COULD DECLARE 'MY REGIMENT WAS NEVER BETTER AND MORE PREPARED IN ITS HISTORY'

THE MACHINE GUN DETACHMENT OF THE 9TH LANCERS AT LEWES IN 1911. THE REGIMENT HAD RECENTLY JOINED THE 2ND CAVALRY BRIGADE, WITH WHOM THEY WOULD SERVE THROUGHOUT THE FIRST WORLD WAR.

delivered reprimand of the strongest sort, and consideration was given to their exclusion from the Coronation Durbar in 1903. None of this was made public, but such was the gossip both in India and Britain that eventually a statement to the press was issued, though this did little to dampen the indignation of those who did not know the full facts and who rallied round the 9th. Lord Curzon, the Commander-in-Chief and the Secretary of State were of one view however, that the military would be taught *'a most salutary lesson'* by Lord Curzon standing up *'even against the crack regiment of the British Army – packed though it be with Duke's sons, Earl's sons and so on... if we yield to military and aristocratic clamour no Viceroy will dare to go on with the work that I have begun.'*[36] These were not the views of the time or of the majority, particularly those in India who, as the 9th passed the saluting dais at the Durbar, rose to their feet with a huge roar of applause.

The 12th's return to India in high summer was less headline-grabbing, but for many it proved equally traumatic: heat-stroke killed nine between May and July, the first of some 73 lives that would be lost in India before the Regiment left in October 1910. For both Regiments, sport and military skills competitions were to the fore as reform began to take hold in India. The 9th were posted to Potchefstroom in South Africa in October 1906, returning to England in 1910 when they handed over their camp and horses to the 12th Lancers.

...a spirit of excellence and a desire to succeed appears to run through every aspect of Regimental life at the time.

The 9th joined the 2nd Cavalry Brigade in Canterbury, moving with it to Tidworth in December 1912, the same year that the 12th returned to England to be posted to Norwich as part of the 5th Cavalry Brigade. They were now part of the formations with which they would serve throughout the approaching war. Diversions from the routine of training came, in the 9th Lancers' case, when they were put on standby for riot control in Yorkshire in 1911, while more glamorous occupation fell to the 12th: they provided extras for the film of the Battle of Waterloo, one of the first epics of British cinema. Although a sergeant from the Regiment did little to help the production by liberating Wellington's boots at a critical moment, the Regimental fund benefited by £100 in fees, while an accommodating American made the rounds of all the pubs at night to pay for drinks.

Despite such distractions, a spirit of excellence and a desire to succeed appears to run through every aspect of Regimental life at the time. The Boer War had established a desire to do things better and *'not since the days of the Commonwealth had the British Army been so generally gripped with a sense of professional purpose in peacetime'*.[37] This mood was given substance by inter-regimental rivalry, particularly on the sports field and by regular, large-scale mobilization and training exercises. As a consequence, as he prepared for war in 1914, Captain Francis Grenfell of the 9th Lancers could confidently declare that *'my regiment was never better and more prepared in its history'*.

THE FIRST WORLD WAR
1914–1918

Mons, Le Cateau | **Retreat from Mons** | **Marne 1914** | **Aisne 1914** | La Bassée 1914 | **Messines 1914** Armentières 1914 | **Ypres 1914, 1915** | Neuve Chapelle | Gravenstafel | St Julien | Bellewaarde **Somme 1916, 1918** | Pozières | Flers-Courcelette | **Arras 1917** | Scarpe 1917 | **Cambrai 1917, 1918** St Quentin | **Rosières** | Avre | Lys | Hazebrouck | Amiens | Albert 1918 | Hindenburg Line St Quentin Canal | Beaurevoir | **Sambre** | **Pursuit to Mons** | France and Flanders 1914–1918

AMONG MANY INNOVATIONS, Lord Haldane had produced a British Expeditionary Force (BEF) of two Corps, totalling six infantry divisions with a separate cavalry division of four brigades and a fifth brigade acting as an independent formation. The total number of cavalry, not including the supporting artillery, engineer and medical units, was just over 9,000 men (about half the size of an infantry division), with 10,000 horses. For their parts, the 9th Lancers, together with the 4th Dragoon Guards and the 18th Hussars, formed the 2nd Cavalry Brigade, while the 12th made up the recently formed 5th (Independent) Cavalry Brigade, alongside the Scots Greys and the 20th Hussars, groupings that would last throughout the conflict.

THE 12TH LANCERS ENTRAINING FOR FRANCE AT NORWICH STATION IN AUGUST 1914. BOTH REGIMENTS LEFT WITH ABOUT 630 MEN AND A SLIGHTLY LARGER NUMBER OF HORSES, THE SLICK MOBILISATION PROCESS GETTING THEM TO FRANCE WITHIN 12 DAYS OF THE DECLARATION OF WAR.

Mobilisation of both Regiments had already begun by the time of the war's declaration on 4th August 1914, the whole operation, including the recall of reservists, proceeding with remarkable efficiency although with some strange anomalies. The 12th Lancers, for instance, ended up with 14 farriers over their official war establishment. Leaving England between 10 and 12 days later, each Regiment took about 30 officers, nearly 600 men and a slightly greater number of horses, organised into three sabre squadrons and a regimental machine gun section comprising two Vickers guns.

For both Regiments, as for the rest of Britain's cavalry, the events of the next four years would define the future and set their courses in a manner unparalleled in any other arm. While the early months of the war, characterised by manoeuvre and mobility, gave an appearance of the enduring utility of a horse-borne combat arm willing and able to use 'cold

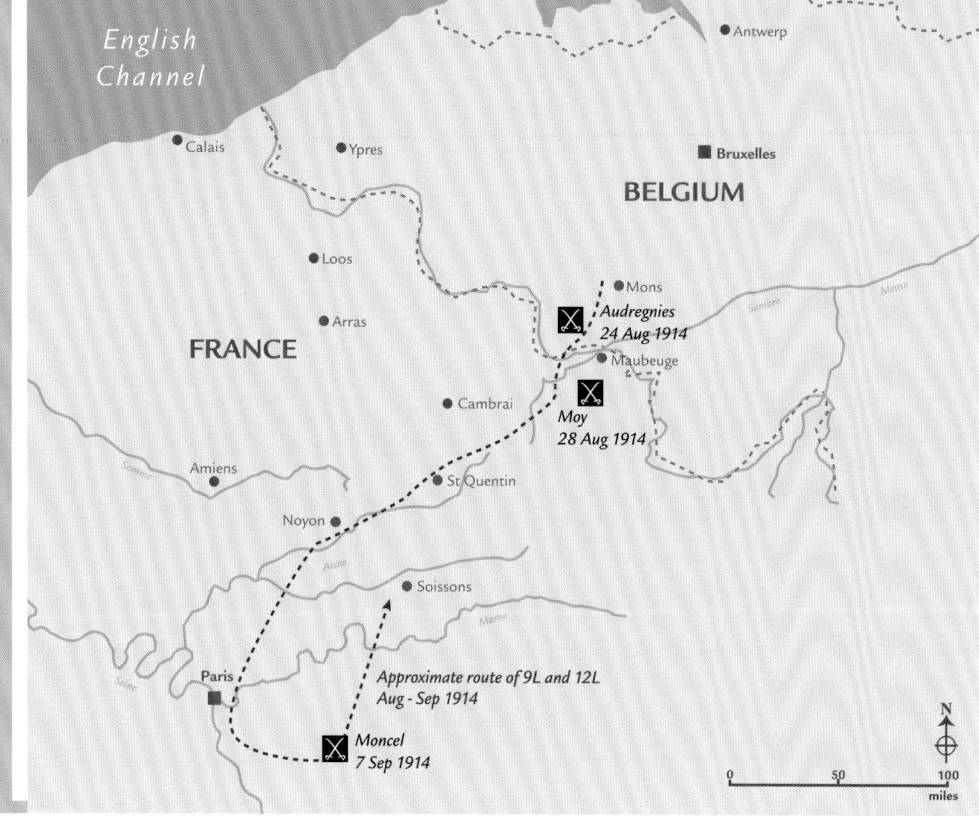

1 OFFICERS AND SERGEANTS (AND DOG) OF C SQUADRON, 12TH LANCERS, ON ARRIVAL IN FRANCE. ALTHOUGH NEVER OBLITERATED BY GOING 'OVER THE TOP', IN THE COURSE OF THE WAR CASUALTIES IN THE CAVALRY WOULD AMOUNT TO 23.3% DEAD, 66.3% WOUNDED AND 10.3% MISSING OR PRISONERS, FIGURES VERY SIMILAR TO THOSE OF THE INFANTRY.

2 AREA OF OPERATIONS OF BOTH REGIMENTS 1914-1918.

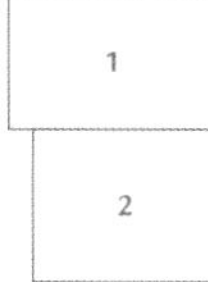

steel' in the attack or defence, the later years of the war proved this to be an aberration. 'The Gap' through which the cavalry were expected to pour never materialised, so that by the war's end, when there might have been a chance of turning the German withdrawal into a rout, the cavalry was such a small part of the Army that its effect could only be localised. If the Boer War had hinted at it, the First World War was to prove conclusively that machine guns, modern artillery and defence in depth had rendered the cavalry's traditional methods of warfare – and the lure of the *'arme blanche'* – utterly obsolete.

The death knell of massed, mounted action did not, however, mean that the cavalry would have an easy war after its frantic start, safely waiting in the rear areas for a breakthrough. Both the 9th and 12th Lancers were to spend significant periods of time in the front line on routine rotation in the trenches or as reserves, both mounted and dismounted, used to plug gaps in the line. Their adaptability was further tested by unglamorous roles such as pioneer work, road and trench construction and 'vulture' parties to clear the battlefields of the dead. As a result of the time spent on their feet, a dismounted contingent in 1916 was asked by a sentry, *'Is that the West Riding [Regiment]?'* to which Trooper Franks replied, *'No, it's the b.... Ninth walking'*. Although spared the horrific casualties of infantry battalions as they went over the top, in nearly all of these tasks the Regiments were subject to the close attention of the enemy, the casualty figures across all theatres for the cavalry being 23.3% killed and died, 66.3% wounded and 10.3% missing and prisoners. For the infantry the figures are 19.9%, 64.2% and 14.8% respectively.[1]

THE RETREAT FROM MONS

Within the Allied plan for a war against Germany, the BEF was to extend the French left flank along its frontier, part of the grand scheme to deal with the anticipated German hook through Belgium (the Schlieffen Plan), which sought to outflank French defences, bypass Paris and pin the French Army on the border against their own defences. The essence of the German plan was speed and crisply efficient staff work – and some determined marching. Envisaging victory in six weeks, it might well have succeeded but for their reducing the combat power in the hook and the BEF's success in delaying the enemy advance sufficiently to allow the Allies to cobble together sufficient forces to deal with the threat.

The 9th Lancers arrived in France on 16th August, the 12th landing a day later, before moving to the army's assembly area near Maubeuge. The Allied plan had by now been modified to take advantage of the greater than anticipated delay that the Belgian army had imposed on the Germans, allowing the Allies to go on the offensive rather than simply defend along the Franco-Belgian border. On 21st August the BEF advanced into Belgium armed with maps that would have taken them all the way to Berlin, but not the other way, and by the time the BEF reached Mons, it was clear that French attacks into Germany – in which they had placed so much doctrinal faith – had been repulsed. There was now a real danger that the French Fifth Army to the BEF's right would become enveloped. The BEF was therefore to hold the Germans for 24 hours to buy time for the French to withdraw, before falling back itself.

After a long march to the front, both Regiments deployed in a screen to the front of the army as it

moved to defend a line just north of Mons, the 9th Lancers, with 2nd Cavalry Brigade on the BEF's left flank, the 12th, with 5th Cavalry Brigade on its right. The cavalry's task was primarily to deal with the huge numbers of German cavalry in their vanguard. On 22nd August, the 4th Dragoons, in the same brigade as the 9th, fired the first British shots of the war as enemy patrols were engaged across the front. Ironically, neither Regiments' first casualties were the result of enemy action, one officer of the 9th dying of appendicitis, while another in the 12th accidentally shot himself in the leg with his revolver when running up the stairs to his billet. His evacuation to the hospital in Maubeuge allowed him to co-ordinate its defence as the German advance began.

Despite the successful defence of Mons on 23rd August, German pressure and the requirement to conform to the French Fifth Army's withdrawal to its right saw orders issued that night for the BEF to begin what turned into the Retreat from Mons, the cavalry screening the infantry as rearguard actions and ambushes added to the usual confusion of a withdrawal in contact. Subjected to frequent shellfire as they moved, often at night along slippery cobbled roads, the Regiments found themselves in difficult country, broken up by slag heaps, embankments, ditches and wire fences, and always handicapped by the lack of sufficient machine guns at regimental at level to mount a more effective defence. In the intense heat of the summer, and with little in terms of supply, the routine of the withdrawal was relentless, the Regiments moving out at dawn from behind the infantry outposts to provide the screen behind which the infantry moved, fighting a series of small-scale actions to delay the enemy, then coming back in after dark, still with their horses to be cared for before riders could think of food or sleep for themselves. Lieutenant Wernher of the 12th described the constant fatigue: '*It is not uncommon to see men riding along fast asleep. No one has had more than three hours sleep a night since we began retiring… The infantry were extraordinary to look at – all had beards; they had discarded a lot of their equipment, and cut their sleeves off at the elbow; very few were wearing puttees but all seemed in good heart…no one knew anything. Everyone was absolutely fagged out and men were falling off their horses with fatigue.*' Despite their tiredness the effect that was achieved was considerable, General Wavell later writing that '*it would be difficult to find any instance where cavalry have shown greater skill and endurance in retreat than the British cavalry did in the withdrawal from Mons to the Marne*'.[2]

BOTH REGIMENTS HELPED COVER THE RETREAT FROM MONS, MOVING OUT AT DAWN TO PROVIDE A SCREEN FOR THE REST OF THE BEF.

'We rejoined our troop just in time to hear Captain Grenfell say "Get mounted, lads, we're going to charge the guns."'

AUDREGNIES

Delaying actions were the most that could be achieved, and these were more on an opportunist basis, such as that involving the 9th on the first day of the retreat (24th August), when the 2nd Cavalry Brigade had been ordered to help cover the exposed left flank of the British line near the village of Quievrain. The Brigade's guns and the 18th Hussars were quickly posted to positions covering the exit from the village when large numbers of enemy were seen emerging. At this point both A and C squadrons of the 9th dismounted and began to engage, Corporal Easton recalling: '*The field had been cut and the sheaves of corn stoked and the first enemy line made a B-line for the stooks. We received the order "Rapid Fire Commence". They were such an easy target that I did not hear the order "Cease Fire Retire" but found myself alone with a trooper, "Farmer" Frond. We rejoined our troop just in time to hear Captain Grenfell say "Get mounted, lads, we're going to charge the guns"*.'[3] Although the exact sequence of who gave what orders remains confused, Lieutenant Colonel Campbell, commanding the 9th, is credited with the most likely account, recalling that the Brigade Commander had given him these specific instructions: '*I'm going to charge the enemy. I'll tell the 4th Dragoon Guards in the village [Audregnies] to make an attack on your left. As soon as you see them deploy, attack on the right with at least two squadrons.*'

CAPTAIN FRANCIS GRENFELL, 9TH LANCERS, WON THE FIRST VICTORIA CROSS OF THE FIRST WORLD WAR TO BE GAZETTED. THIS PICTURE, ENTITLED 'THE FIRST VC OF THE WAR' COMBINES TWO EVENTS ON THE 24TH AUGUST 1914 AT WHICH GRENFELL WAS PRESENT. THE FIRST WAS THE UNSUCCESSFUL CHARGE AT THE GERMAN GUNS AT AUDREGNIES IN WHICH HE WAS WOUNDED, THE SECOND, FOR WHICH HE WON HIS VICTORIA CROSS, HIS ASSISTANCE IN EXTRACTING BRITISH ARTILLERY THAT HAD BECOME STUCK.

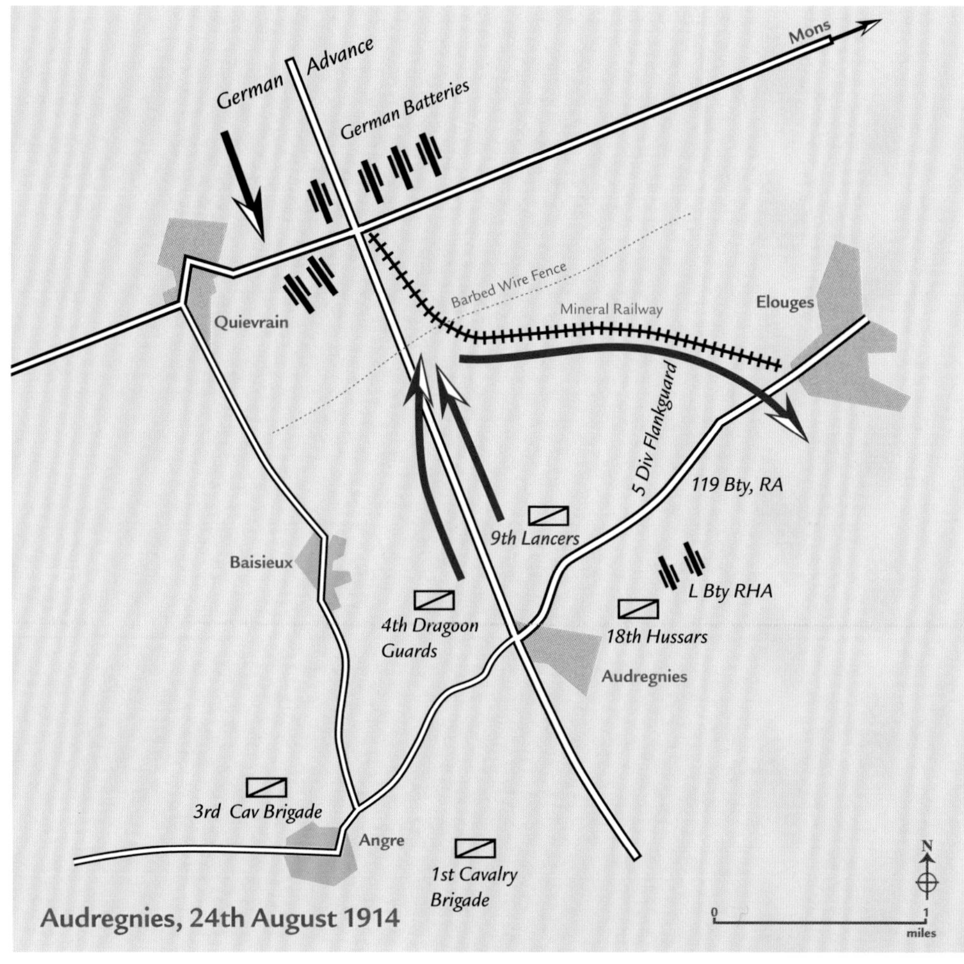

A and C Squadrons rapidly remounted and, with the 4th Dragoons, charged, Private Wells remembering the sequence: '*Move off at trot and ride knee to knee. "Carry Lances." See figures running about in the distance. "Lance engage." Gallop...*'[4] The ground, which had appeared to be made for just such an action, soon revealed itself to be criss-crossed by hidden lanes, cuttings and wire fences, while the enemy infantry hid themselves behind the corn stacks that were still in the field. Supported by a reported nine batteries of artillery towards which the charge was heading, the enemy began to break up the squadrons before they were finally brought to a halt by a wire fence running right across their line, Captain Francis Grenfell recording: '*We simply galloped about like rabbits in front of a line of guns, men and horses falling in all directions. Most of one's time was spent in dodging the horses.*'[5] From the chaos in which the now-mixed squadrons of the 4th Dragoons Guards and the 9th Lancers found themselves, many took cover and then, dismounted, engaged the enemy from the nearby slag heaps and a sugar beet factory. Others did the same from the position occupied by a squadron of the 18th Hussars, which rapidly became overcrowded, though the combined weight of fire and that of the gunners managed to hold up the advance of 12 German battalions for nearly three hours before the Brigade handed over to 1st and 3rd Cavalry Brigades to continue the delay.

1 THE 9TH LANCERS' ACTION AT AUDREGNIES, 24TH AUGUST 1914.

2 THE AFTERMATH OF THE CHARGE BY A AND C SQUADRONS 9TH LANCERS AND THE 4TH DRAGOONS AT AUDREGNIES ON 24TH AUGUST 1914 WHILE ACTING AS FLANK GUARD FOR THE BEF ON THE RETREAT FROM MONS. THE CHARGE NEVER REACHED THE NINE BATTERIES OF GERMAN ARTILLERY THAT WERE ITS TARGET AND SUSTAINED HEAVY CASUALTIES, A SUBALTERN IN THE 9TH RECKONING THAT THE BRIGADE COMMANDER *'LOST HALF HIS BRIGADE FOR NO REASON WHATEVER'*[7].

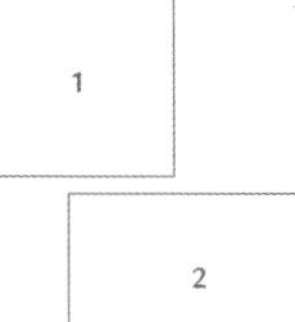

In the same engagement, 119 Field Battery, Royal Artillery had been supporting the 5th [Infantry] Division's flank guard immediately to the east of the charge from near Elouges when, faced by the German advance, it got its guns stuck and, with seriously depleted manpower, was unable to move them. Having survived the earlier charge but wounded by shrapnel in both leg and hand, Francis Grenfell, with a number of the Regiment who had also moved off to the flank, now found himself asked to help. *'We ran forward and started pushing the guns out, and Providence intervened for, though this was carried out under a very heavy fire and the guns had to be slowly turned round before we could guide them, we accomplished our task. We pushed out one over dead gunners, and I do not think we lost more than three or four men, though it required more than one journey to get everything out.'* For his action Grenfell was awarded the first Victoria Cross of the war to be gazetted. To his embarrassment, he became a national hero following his temporary invaliding home: *'I never felt such a fool in my life, after all I only did what every other man and officer did who was with me…The King came to see me in hospital and was extraordinarily nice…Lord Roberts came and asked rather direct questions as to why we charged and whom we charged, and who gave the order to charge.'*[6]

The last sentence is revealing for, while the action of the Brigade as a whole was successful in protecting the BEF's flank from being enveloped by a significant German attack, most of the effect had been achieved by fire from the dismounted squadrons and the artillery. The charge itself, despite the bravery shown, inflicted few casualties on the Germans, while causing the majority of the 2nd Cavalry Brigade's losses, which were initially thought to be much greater. There were 169 men killed, wounded or captured, and twice as many horses lost. It is highly likely that a more effective (and efficient) defence would probably have been made had the Brigade Commander simply left the 9th's two squadrons firing from the position they had already adopted, where they were already having a considerable impact. In the immediate aftermath of the action, the 2nd Brigade had become split up, a subaltern reckoning that the Brigade Commander *'lost half his brigade for no reason whatever'* and the divided Brigade, both halves of which contained large numbers of the 9th, only combined again four days later. Perhaps the final word belongs to the 9th's Commanding Officer, Lieutenant Colonel Campbell, who, when told that he was being recommended for the Victoria Cross, replied, *'I want my squadrons back, not VCs or medals'.*[8]

MOY

A more successful use of the lance to provide shock action occurred a few days later on 28th August. While known in every other account as the action at Cerisy, the 12th Lancers, for obvious reasons, remembered and commemorate it as the Battle of Moy, the last time that the 12th charged in large numbers with the lance. The day started, typically early, with the 5th Cavalry Brigade acting as 1 Corps' rearguard. The 20th Hussars were near Cerisy, with the Greys to their right and the 12th in reserve around the chateau of Moy. At around midday, the Greys began to engage German cavalry patrols to their front with machine gun and rifle fire until a larger enemy force of two squadrons advanced over the crest of a hill and into a valley, where they were also engaged by two guns of the brigade artillery. Their German riders having dismounted to return fire, the horses stampeded, leaving the squadrons to retire on foot to the top of hill over which they had come, to take cover amongst stooks of corn. The 12th meanwhile had been enjoying some rest in the grounds of the chateau, swimming, sleeping and eating *'lunch off some of the finest pears, white wine, bread and cheese. Then we wandered about…Rolly busied himself writing to his wife that there were no Germans near and all was quiet.'* On hearing the firing to their front, the Commanding Officer, Lieutenant Colonel Wormald,

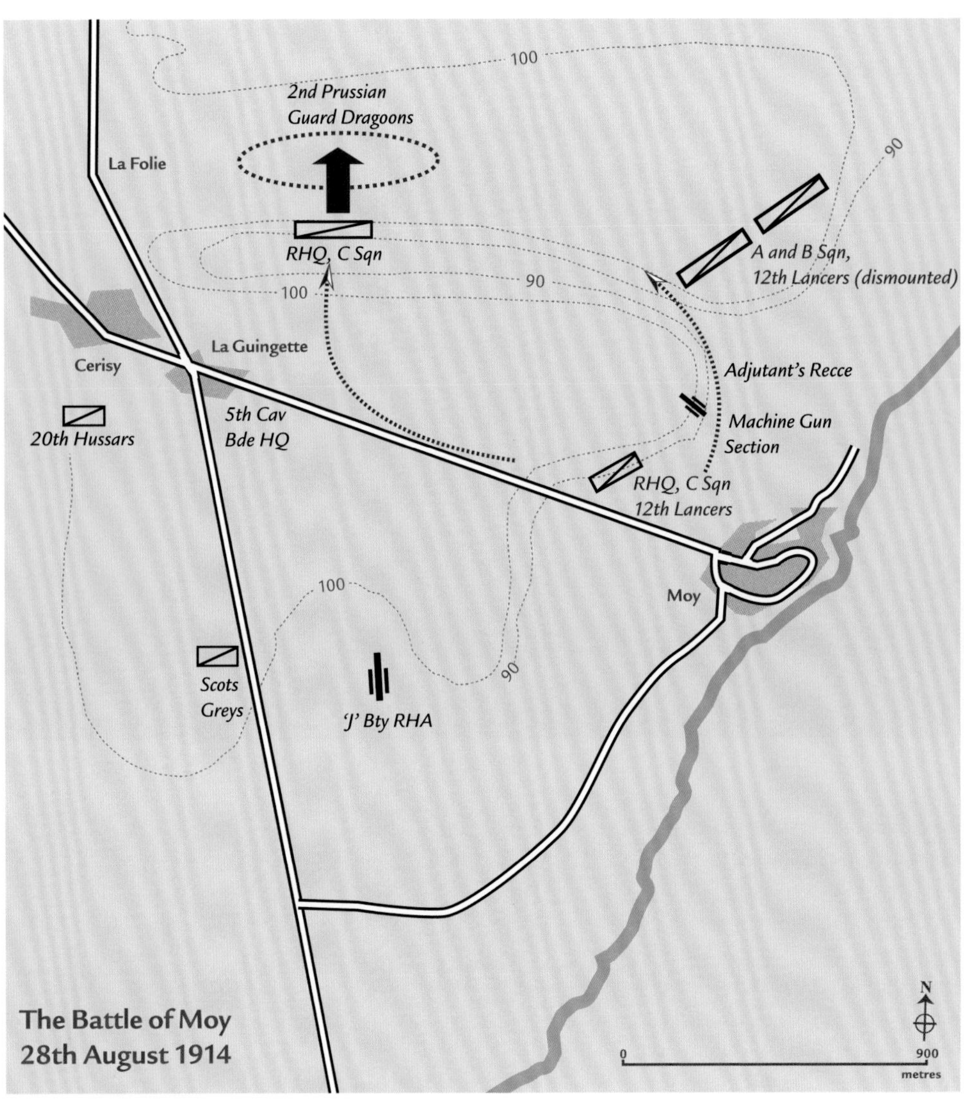

THE CHARGE OF THE 12TH LANCERS AT MOY, 28TH AUGUST 1914.

THE CHARGE OF LIEUTENANT COLONEL FRANK WORMALD AND C SQUADRON, 12TH LANCERS, AT MOY ON 28TH AUGUST 1914 DURING THE BEF'S RETREAT FROM MONS. THE ATTACK, SUPPORTED BY DISMOUNTED FIRE FROM THE OTHER SQUADRONS, WAS A COMPLETE SUCCESS AND RENDERED A GERMAN CAVALRY BRIGADE INEFFECTIVE, DELAYING ITS ADVANCE FOR FOUR HOURS. IT HELPED CONFIRM THE ASCENDANCY THAT THE BRITISH CAVALRY HAD ACHIEVED AND WOULD MAINTAIN OVER THEIR OPPONENTS.

and the Adjutant set off, ordering everyone else to saddle up and prepare to move, quickly followed by C Squadron and the machine gun section. The recce party, moving north-west, had seen the enemy as they moved down the forward slope of the hill, so C Squadron and the machine guns took up positions and joined the other troops in bringing down fire, assisting in the panic of the horses and the pedestrian withdrawal by the enemy.

A and B Squadrons had by now used dead ground out of sight of the Germans to take up their own position to the east of the enemy, from where they engaged them in the flank with rifle fire. Meanwhile the Brigade Commander brought the remaining guns up behind the C Squadron position and ordered two squadrons of the 20th Hussars to advance from the left. Colonel Wormald, sensing that the enemy, although still producing effective fire, was distracted, saw an opportunity to move C Squadron further forward to a better fire position if the Adjutant, who had been despatched on a recce, could find one. Fortuitously, his report suggested greater things were possible: *'the ground immediately in front of the German position was so dead that it was possible to approach within fifty yards of them without being seen, [the Adjutant] actually rode almost on top of the Germans in making*

certain of the fact, galloped back, and catching the Commanding Officer moving forward at the head of C Squadron, pointed out the wonderful opportunity for a charge. Realising that by this time the whole of the enemy's attention was concentrated upon the threat to their flank by A and B Squadrons, the Commanding Officer immediately decided to profit by the occasion. He moved C Squadron, which was now in dead ground, just under the ridge the enemy were lining, and then advanced at a walk up the steep ridge in line of troop columns, so as to keep the horses fresh till the last moment. Just before reaching the crest, line was formed, and as the squadron topped the rise 'Gallop' and 'Charge' were sounded in quick succession by the Regimental Trumpet Major and taken up by the C Squadron Trumpeter. With a ringing cheer the squadron swept forward in perfect line across the fifty yards which now separated them from the enemy, with the Commanding Officer, his Adjutant, the Trumpet Major, and two orderlies some twenty yards ahead of them.'[9]

The surprise achieved was complete. While some of the enemy lay down to try to avoid the lances' points, others stood their ground to try and fight it out. The leading group with the Commanding Officer was singled out and he was wounded, though not before successfully despatching one man with his sword. Trumpet Major Mowlam, too, was wounded, as was one of the orderlies, the other having his horse shot from under him. Despite this, the attack was pressed home. Even after Captain Mitchell, commanding C Squadron, was killed the squadron continued, rallying under Captain Bryant who reformed them after the charge, turned them about and took them back across the field two more times. Several more casualties were inflicted by Germans who, having apparently surrendered, fired treacherously into their backs before the Regiment collected their casualties and withdrew, covered by the fire from the rest of the Brigade, having lost four killed and six wounded. The Official War History assesses that the enemy suffered 300 casualties, 70 of which had been inflicted by the charge, which had destroyed one squadron and most of the headquarters of the 2nd (Queen Victoria's) Prussian Guard Dragoons and rendered ineffective the brigade to which they belonged. It confirmed the complete ascendancy that the British cavalry had by now achieved over its German opponents. A summary of the action came from Sir Hugh Gough: *'on my right, General Chetwode [commanding 5th Cavalry Brigade] brought off what has always seemed to me a model action, illustrating the combination of fire and shock, use of ground, and surprise.'*[10] More crucially for those they were covering, it brought four hours' respite from the German advance.

The retreat meanwhile continued with both Regiments continually engaged, until they crossed the Marne; the 9th at Gournay on 3rd September, the 12th on a parallel course to their east, crossing the Aisne at Soissons and then heading south. Once across the Marne, the Allied retreat finally halted and a respite could be taken, some officers even managing to make it to Paris, which was by now nearby. Although they were not aware of it, the days of endless withdrawals were now over while, most importantly, their will to fight had not been shattered. The Official History recorded: *'The Retreat from Mons was in every way honourable to the Army. The troops suffered under every disadvantage… They were short of food and sleep when they began their retreat, they continued it, always short of food and sleep, for thirteen days; and at the end of the retreat they were still an army, and a formidable army. They were never demoralised for they rightly judged that they had never been beaten.'*[11] More particularly of the cavalry's role, Field Marshal Robertson later wrote that it is *'no exaggeration to say that, but for the splendid work of our own small force of cavalry (five brigades) and the want of enterprise on the part of the cavalry masses of the enemy, our retreat from Mons might have been converted into a rout, in which case the subsequent course of the war might have been greatly changed to our disadvantage'.*[12]

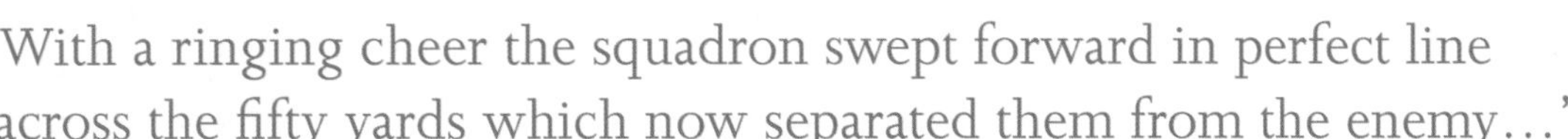

The relief of pressure on the BEF once it crossed the Marne had been caused by the decision by the German High Command to switch the direction of its most westerly First Army, causing it to pivot by 90 degrees to move east towards its neighbouring Second Army, thereby presenting its flank to the rapidly formed French Sixth Army and to its east, to the BEF. By 5th September, the Allies were in a position to counter-attack north from the Marne, with the BEF taking its place between the French Fifth and Sixth Armies as they punched into the thinly-held gap between the German First and Second Armies, with the cavalry leading the advance. All that the officers of the 9th heard of this higher-level planning as they set off on 6th September, after a brief respite following the retreat, was *'we are coming in on the Germans' right'.* By now, the cavalry force had been reinforced and divided into two divisions. Remaining with the Brigade they had begun the war with, the 9th Lancers joined the 1st Cavalry Division, while the 12th formed part of the 2nd Cavalry Division.

The BEF's advance from the Marne began cautiously, the result of a certain hesitancy at the top, but also of fatigue and difficult going caused

THE 9TH LANCERS' ACTION AT MONCEL DURING THE ADVANCE FROM THE MARNE, 7TH SEPTEMBER 1914. THE BATTLE GIVES IT NAME TO THE 'MONS' OF MONSMOY DAY.

by the number of rivers to be crossed. The pace increased as only light opposition was met and morale was boosted by early success as the gap between the German First and Second Army opened up, eventually reaching to over 30 miles as, over the next 12 days, the German screen and flank guards were pushed back.

MONCEL

One of the earliest engagements of the advance is commemorated by the 'Mons' of MonsMoy Day when, in the early morning of 7th September, the 9th formed the advance guard for the 2nd Cavalry Brigade as it moved to cross the River Aubetin and screen the BEF's right flank. German cavalry patrols were already being engaged by the Regiment as it approached the village of Moncel, where Lieutenant Colonel Campbell noticed that the high ground to the north of the village dominated the line of the advance and, were the Germans to hold it, they would seriously check the Brigade. With only two troops from B Squadron and a machine gun (a total of about 30 men under the Adjutant) available to him for immediate action, Campbell crossed the river and pushed up the slope, reaching the crest without sighting any enemy. Leaving the troops in cover behind a haystack, Campbell now took himself and his trumpeter off to investigate firing that he had heard coming from the eastern edge of the village. The rest of the story is best told by Campbell himself:

'At the north end [of the village] I saw some Lancers firing towards a wood to the east, but owing to the heat haze it was impossible to make out exactly what they were firing at. I left my trumpeter and went out towards the wood, and when about four hundred yards from it I saw one hundred to one hundred and twenty German cavalry beginning to mount. They advanced in my direction, but being very well mounted I had no difficulty in leaving them well behind. When I arrived at the haystack the Germans were still seven to eight hundred yards away. I brought the troops out from behind the haystack and gave the order, 'Left wheel into line gallop.' I forgot that I was riding a fresh horse and that the men's horses must be very tired, and did not perceive until I was about one hundred yards from the German lines, that I was at least one hundred yards ahead. It was, however, too late to wait, so I rode straight on, hoping for the best! As I approached the Germans, they closed in on their troop leader, and their long iron lances presented a very disagreeable looking wall. I directed my horse towards the troop leader, and when I got level with him I shot him as he was in the act of cutting at me with his sword. The next thing I remember was being carried very slowly over the tail of my horse to fall in a sainfoin [grown as a forage crop] field. Both the Germans and our own men passed right over the top of me, but marvellous to relate, not a single horse trod on my body. I got up on to my knees and saw the German cavalry galloping away in the utmost confusion in the direction of the wood to the west, all the men shouting at the top of their voices, and our own troops north of Moncel beginning to rally… There is now very little doubt in my mind that if we had not seized the plateau in the way that we did, the Germans would have been able to occupy Moncel and make it extremely difficult for the brigade to have crossed the Aubetin.'

Campbell's story is corroborated by Frederic Coleman who had driven his car, used for moving senior officers about, to the scene and who reported not only the speed of the 9th's charge compared to the Germans' but also the relative size of the two charging groups. The Commanding Officer of the 18th Hussars adds further detail: *'the 9th went through their opponents knocking a large hole in the squadron, unhorsing a good many riders and bringing the remainder to a standstill, but their small numbers prevented them completing their task and, after a short hand to hand fight, Major Beale-Browne [the second-in-command] rallied what was left of the troops and galloped for the village, pursued by a troop of the enemy…It was unfortunate that the 9th Lancers' machine gun jammed just at the critical moment, and could not fire a round in support of the mounted attack.'*[13]

The role of the machine gun in the action is of note, if only because many recent members of the Regiment have been told that it caused most of the German casualties, the story being further embellished to recount that it had been bought by the officers at the outbreak of the war. In fact neither is true, although there is an imaginative oil painting of the charge that might indicate it had a greater part in proceedings. The 9th Lancer history agrees with that of the 18th Hussars, stating that

THE CHARGE OF LIEUTENANT COLONEL DAVID CAMPBELL AND TWO TROOPS OF THE 9TH LANCERS AT MONCEL ON 7TH SEPTEMBER 1914 DURING THE ADVANCE FROM THE MARNE. THE CHARGE WAS THE LAST LANCE AGAINST LANCE ACTION CONDUCTED BY THE BRITISH ARMY.

the wretched gun *'perversely jammed... fell into the hands of the enemy, who abandoned it, after damaging it'*.[14] This in turn gives some credence to the German account of the action, which claims that a sergeant and six men *'drove off the gun crew and damaged the mechanism with a stone'*.[15]

The casualties suffered by the 9th in this charge were remarkably light, with one officer and two soldiers killed and seven of all ranks wounded, while the German casualties are not known. The charge, remembered as the last lance against lance charge ever made by the British Army, was subsequently exploited by those who, even after the end of the war, clung to the vision of cavalry on horses delivering shock action. General French's son, writing as late as 1951, insisted that it remained *'a potent instance of the immense value of shock action and an unanswerable illustration of the efficacy of the arme blanche'*.[16]

Over on the left flank of the advance, the 12th, who had earlier demonstrated the effectiveness of combined arms operations at Pezarches in an action that left them the proud possessors of a fine Benz car, were able to put in a charge on the 10th September. This was near the village of Gandelu, where a large German concentration of cavalry, infantry and logistics had been shelled and machine gunned out of the village by their brigade: *'a truly wonderful sight – the little village below full of Germans, and many more of them streaming away through the woods... and making desperate efforts to get a large convoy out of the valley.'* The Regiment went through the village and, reaching the top of the hill, *'turned left, formed line and swept along the top of the ridge, which was covered with retreating German infantry...We captured over two hundred and several machine guns; also a standard which, unfortunately, the RSM placed against a haystack, continued the pursuit and was unable to find again when he returned for it later in the day... Very few of the Germans were actually stuck, as they practically all knelt down and put their hands up, but a few of the rear files misconstrued the COs order to spare them as being spear them – and acted accordingly.'*[17] The tale ends sadly for, having captured a further haul of Germans in another village, the field grey of the prisoners being brought back by the 12th was mistaken by Scots Greys for an enemy counter-attack, their fire inflicting more than half of the day's casualties of five men killed and 10 wounded.

THE RACE FOR THE SEA

The BEF's arrival at the River Aisne in the middle of September 1914 marked the end of the Regiments' advance. Strongly held defences along the ridgelines to the north of the river effectively signalled the end of the war of manoeuvre and the beginning of the stalemate of the trenches. Though withdrawn from the front line, both Regiments conducted reconnaissance tasks in the weeks that followed and, more importantly, acted as mobile reserves, rushing to the front either to shore up sectors that were threatened, or to provide additional support to stretched infantry units, particularly with machine guns, which were at a premium. In a sign of things to come, they were issued with bayonets for the first time.

1 THE 9TH LANCERS LEADING HORSES TO THE REAR WHILE TAKING UP HASTY DEFENSIVE POSITIONS ALONG THE AISNE IN THE MIDDLE OF SEPTEMBER 1914. THE END OF THIS FLUID PHASE OF THE WAR, IN WHICH THE MOBILITY OF THE CAVALRY HAD BEEN SO USEFUL, USHERED IN THE ERA OF TRENCH WARFARE.

2 FARRIERS OF THE 12TH LANCERS IN 1914. DURING THE 'RACE TO THE SEA' THE CAVALRY CORPS RODE 150 MILES TO TAKE UP THEIR SECTOR OF THE LINE JUST SOUTH OF YPRES NEAR MESSINES IN THE EARLY PART OF OCTOBER.

A reduction in the tempo of the previous weeks of fighting permitted a more measured view to be taken of the Allied dispositions, the BEF moving north-west into Flanders to take up position to the left of the French in the solidifying Allied line. The redeployment not only shortened the British lines of communication to the Channel ports but reflected the mobility of the BEF which, although possessing well regarded and highly mobile and effective cavalry, lacked heavy artillery. The move, carried out efficiently and in secret, required the cavalry to march the 150 miles, while the rest of the BEF went by train. The outflanking movement now developed into 'the race for the sea' as each side attempted to take advantage of the only undefended sector of a line that now formed a continuous front from Switzerland to the coast. The long marches offered little in terms of excitement, but succeeded in exhausting men and horses as the Regiments moved to their allotted positions during the first two weeks of October. With two British (infantry) corps to their south and another responsible for Ypres itself, the Cavalry Corps (formed on 9th October from the two much-expanded divisions) occupied the ridge of high ground just south-west of Ypres, including the villages of Wytschaete and Messines, with each brigade holding a sector of about 600 yards. Both Regiments now found themselves close to each other on the southern flank of the salient, near Messines.

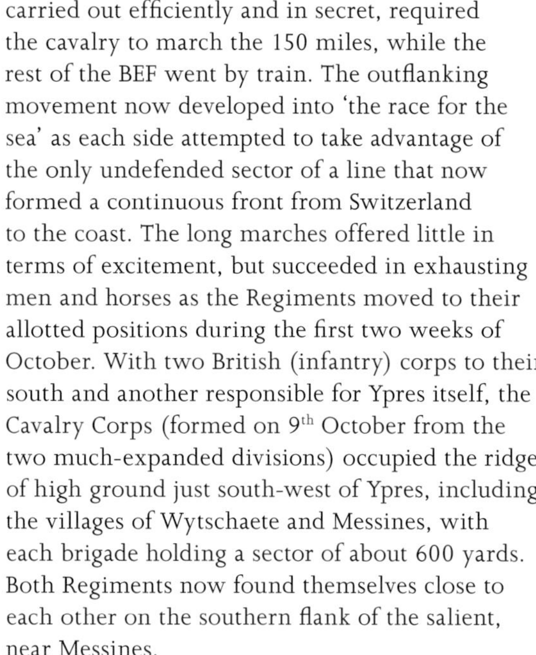

The Allied intention, having stabilised the front, had been for the British to break through the supposedly weak German defences between Ypres and the sea, though the arrival of four new German corps in the area ruled this out. More importantly it handed them the initiative and forced the British to prepare for their inevitable attack, an assault that would engulf the Cavalry Corps in some of its hardest fighting of the entire war. In the prelude to what would become the First Battle of Ypres, both Regiments began to dig in as best they could, making do with bayonets and bare hands, their equipment tables not providing them with the correct tools for this form of warfare. As a result,

they never succeeded in producing a continuous line of trenches, while the demands of looking after their horses, which were in lines to the rear, further reduced their numbers.

YPRES

On 20th October 1914 the German attack began along the whole of the Ypres front, the early fighting in their sector pushing the cavalry, who had until now occupied an outpost line, back on to the main position where they were once again attacked the next day. This time, the line held until the 3rd Cavalry Brigade, given incorrect orders, began to retire, leaving the left flank of the 12th Lancers exposed and forcing them to conform to the withdrawal.

Attempts to retake the lost ground failed and the whole of the 2nd Cavalry Division was now forced to move back to the next line of trenches under pressure from five German cavalry divisions. Strong German patrols prevented any rest while, during a typical 24 hour period, the lines held by the 12th Lancers were attacked on seven separate occasions, the periods in between being filled by continuous bombardment.

Further south, on 21st October, Le Gheer, a village that gave access to the Wytschaete ridge, had been captured, requiring the 9th and two battalions from the 4th Division to launch a successful counter-attack to retake the village, capturing over 100 prisoners in the process. Such dismounted work was rapidly becoming the norm, causing Captain Grenfell to write: *'We have had five of the hardest days of the war in trenches repelling German attacks. It has become such a recognized idea to use us for this work as soon as we get in touch with the enemy, that I am afraid all the cavalry traditions are for ever ended, and we have become mounted infantry pure and simple, with very little of the mounted about it…if you see a [mounted] man carrying a lance, sword, rifle, spade, and pick he looks just like a hedgehog. But it is a jolly hard life for them to have to fight their way up to the line, then hold it, all the time cleaning and trying to look after their horses.'*[18]

German pressure continued to build, focussing increasingly on the south-east of Ypres, which included the sector held by the Cavalry Corps, and reaching a crisis on 31st October when, against odds of up to six to one, they were swept off the Messines Ridge after fierce fighting. The 9th occupied a position near Messines and defended a large sector with only 150 men, the rest having been sent back to bring up remounts. They then found themselves engulfed in an attack by 12 enemy battalions launched against the 2nd Cavalry Brigade sector at 5am which soon exposed the 9th's flanks to enfilade fire. A second attack at 8am forced a withdrawal to secondary positions that formed a salient across the road just north of the village, before heavy shelling and continued pressure caused a further withdrawal, leaving three quarters of the officers and a third of the soldiers who had been in the line dead, wounded or missing. Amongst those wounded was Francis Grenfell VC, whose diary gives some indication of the fighting: *'At this moment [shortly after the first attack] heavy fire was directed on our trench not only from the rear but also from the right flank, where the Germans had brought up a machine gun… the officers reported that we were being shot at from front and rear. I ordered them to tell the odd numbers to fire to the front and the even numbers to the rear, and hang on…We were now being very heavily shelled by 'coal-boxes', and it seemed as hot as anyone could wish for. There seemed to be nothing in the air but shells. At this moment a shell pitched right into the middle of my squadron and blew it to the winds. I myself was hit through the leg, and could not move.'*[19]

The 12th had also suffered heavy casualties in this German assault, forcing them to withdraw, before taking part in a counter-attack to recapture the village of Wytschaete, which had finally fallen to the Germans on 1st November. With two infantry battalions attacking the south of the village, the 12th Lancers, with a squadron of 20th Hussars, assaulted the area of the chateau in the north-west corner at dawn, catching the enemy by surprise and driving them out with fixed bayonets. One subaltern describes his part in the action: *'I got my men out, fixed bayonets, gave a View Halloa, and charged. The hunting noise fairly set the men off. We dashed up the street shouting and bayoneting the enemy, and met another troop at the top. We hollered and ran down a bank to the left, and got into them again…'*[20] The time bought by this action was sufficient for French reinforcements to arrive and prevent a German breakthrough. Sir John French later stated that *'had the counter-attack of the 12th Lancers, the Lincolns and the Northumberlands not checked the Germans at the critical moment, just giving the French time to deploy… nothing could have prevented the Germans from occupying Mount Kemmel and driving a vital wedge in the very centre of our line'*, adding, to a different audience: *'One of the features of the campaign was how a weak cavalry division of less than three thousand rifles had held, without any reserves, over seven miles of trenches against a whole German Army Corps for forty-eight hours. The culminating point of British cavalry history was reached when a cavalry regiment, dismounted, attacked and took the village of Wytschaete at the point of the bayonet.'*[21]

Acting as a reserve for the French, both Regiments spent the next few weeks moving backwards and forwards between billets and trenches, moving rapidly from one threatened sector to another in improvised locations very close to the German front line. Lieutenant Benson of the 9th wrote of the time: *'We had one curious twenty-four hours in a little broken-down stable just in front of our line of trenches…it had sixteen dead bodies in it….The German trench was fifteen yards in front, and as it was too close to them to shell they were trying to sap up to it in order to blow it up. We kept on chucking hand-grenades into the trench – or rather were given hand grenades to throw – they were made by the Engineers, in jam-tins, and you lit the fuse at the top, preferably with a cigarette, and it exploded five seconds after lighting, which did not*

THE 12TH LANCERS PREPARING A DEFENSIVE POSITION. BOTH REGIMENTS LACKED THE CORRECT TOOLS AND THEIR MANPOWER WAS FURTHER REDUCED BY THE REQUIREMENT TO CONTINUE TO LOOK AFTER THEIR HORSES.

THE 12TH LANCERS DURING THE FIRST BATTLE OF YPRES, OCTOBER-NOVEMBER 1914. BOTH REGIMENTS EXPERIENCED SOME OF THEIR HARDEST FIGHTING OF THE WAR FROM HASTILY CONSTRUCTED TRENCHES THAT OFFERED LITTLE PROTECTION FROM FIRE AND NONE FROM THE ELEMENTS.

give you time for a very accurate shot, especially with a sniper potting at you at close range, so we gave it up.'[22]

Rest finally came on19th November for the 9th, though for the 12th in 5th Brigade, their order to move into general reserve was delayed. Major Charrington noted: '*We had by this time become pretty hardened to rapid disillusionments, but it was a disappointing moment when only a few hours later we got the order to move up and take over a portion of the trench in the French area…and the blinding snowstorm which set in just as we moved off did not add to our appreciation of the situation.*'[23] The trenches they found can have amused them even less: they were 40 yards from the enemy and the exhausted French had had no time to bury their dead or repair their defences. Lieutenant Leslie's trench was typical: '*My trench had from sixteen to eighteen inches of water in it, a clay bottom and no straw. The first thing I fell over was a dead man. There were three others, two still unburied, and one buried in the bottom of the trench. There was only one place where it was possible to stand upright, and owing to the water we could not lie down. As we cavalry do not have packs and blankets you can imagine our prospects for the next 24 hours were not exactly rosy… We did not allow the men to sleep. We should never have been able to wake them in time if they had been rushed, and moreover they would have been frost-bitten if they had slept… We stood most of the night marking time in the mud and water and with our backs bent to keep our heads down…*'[24] The following day they, too, were able to move into reserve as the snow brought to a close the First Battle of Ypres, which, while condemning the Germans to a prolonged war, had cost the BEF 58,000 casualties.

With the situation more stable, both sides spent the winter preparing for the following year and the offensives that would come, the conventional wisdom of the time still maintaining that an infantry and artillery breakthrough would create 'the Gap' that the cavalry could exploit. Reinforcements arrived, although, unlike the infantry of the BEF that had all but been destroyed, the cavalry, while suffering severe losses in their actions, had never been committed in battles where entire regiments had ceased to exist as fighting units. A consequence of this was that the cavalry continued to provide a reliable core of highly trained regular soldiers, largely still commanded by their own officers, which could be relied on to remain steady in any situation, a capability that would often be tested in the coming years.

Despite the changing of the conflict, horses still had to be cared for and the Regiments constructed improvised lines to provide some degree of shelter, while other activities provided some sense of normality, a staff officer writing in early December: '*what a funny nation we are; just because we are doing nothing for the moment the 9th Lancers are making a point-to-point course and have already begun schooling their horses – football is played daily…and so we make war.*'[25] Other lighter moments included leave, a pheasant shoot (for which the French Government rather ungraciously sent the Cavalry Corps a bill), following a harrier and greyhound pack and a travelling show by an improvised concert party from the 9th Lancers.

Although limited mounted training was conducted, orders for the cavalry to relieve the infantry in certain sectors in February 1915 required old skills such as shooting to be refreshed while new ones including trench construction, dismounted attacks, sniping and bombing were learnt. The most fundamental problem facing the cavalry as they went into the trenches, however, was that of numbers. A complete cavalry brigade produced far fewer troops than its infantry counterparts, yet was often required to take over a sector of the same size from them. Entering the trenches, brigades and regiments rotated between the front and billets to the rear for what was, by the standards of the war, an uneventful spell, the 9th taking *'only fifteen casualties (killed)… during the tour'*,[26] with shellfire and sniping a constant threat and their trenches a constant reminder of previous battles. While Lieutenant Wernher of the 12th noted that *'our parapets are made of dead men and we cannot dig down for fear of exhuming a corpse'*, he also points out the stoicism and black humour present: *'on one occasion three of us were sitting down on the floor awaiting a man to pour out some tea for us. A bullet came through the trench, hit two fellows in the head and passed three times through the man pouring out the tea, going through his arm and finishing up in his side. Cpl Hanlon went on eating his bread and cheese and said, "Anyone here not been hit?"'*[27]

Within a month both Regiments and their brigades were taken out of the line for what became a familiar activity during an offensive – they were held back as the exploitation force for the First Army attack at Neuve Chapelle on 10th March. They remained unused however, the German defences holding, despite an initially successful assault by infantry and a 'hurricane' artillery barrage. As was to prove the case so often in the future, careful planning might allow the forward positions to be broken into, but the challenges of moving up artillery and infantry reserves fast enough to complete the break out from them had not been resolved. After initially high hopes, stalemate set in and, within a few days from the start of the offensive, both Regiments had returned to their billets.

The German response occurred a few weeks later with the initiation on 23rd April of the Second Battle of Ypres on the northern side of the salient. Here gas was used for the first time, against which the Allies had no defence. Taken out of general reserve to support the French, the cavalry manned the reserve trenches as the Germans in their turn failed to achieve a breakthrough before the situation stabilised. In these actions both Regiments formed part of the mobile reserves that rushed to assist in checking German advances, counter-attacking or providing working parties and manning trenches as occasion demanded.

In relation to the overall scale of the fighting (the Allies suffered 58,000 casualties, the Germans 38,000 at Second Ypres), the actions fought by the Regiments were small, tactical, affairs, but they came at a price. An illustration of many such engagements occurred on 12th May 1915 when 300 men from the 9th Lancers moved up to take over a sector of the front line north-east of Wieltje as part of a cavalry force relieving two hard-fought infantry divisions. Torrential rain accompanied the incessant shellfire while the trenches they occupied were in a shattered state, with knee-deep mud and little protection. To the Regiment's flanks, both the 18th Hussars and 5th Dragoon Guards were shelled out of their flattened trenches and the enemy was only stopped by the combined fire of the rifles and machine guns of the 9th, who were able to sweep the area of the deserted trenches until they could be reoccupied. Relieved at 11 that night, the 9th could find no room in the second-line trenches and, after an uncomfortable night in the open, retired the following day having lost 18 dead and 52 wounded. In the words of one squadron leader from the 9th: *'It is quite impossible for any to get to England, or even to Hell, for the latter will be their starting point.'*[28]

Gas was increasingly used, in the worst cases lingering in trenches, dug-outs and shell-holes to saturate the newly issued gas-masks and render them ineffective. At the end of one defensive action by the 9th Lancer Group south-east of Ypres at Zouave Wood, where a sector had been held at considerable expense, the results of the gas and conventional firepower were graphically described: *'In the small hours of the 28th [May] a little party of some forty men stumbled in the half light along the Menin road through the crumbling streets of Ypres… Those who passed them saw figures like spectres, clothes all caked with dirt, and faces yellow from the poison gas. They were all that remained of the old 9th Lancers.'*[29] Of the 350 men of the Regiment who took part in the battle, a total of 208 were killed, wounded or gassed, including, amongst the 36 dead, Captain Francis Grenfell VC. The reward for these losses was that by the close of the battle at the end of May, the BEF had once again blocked a German drive on Ypres, the salient around the town

MEN OF THE 9TH LANCERS IN AN IMPROVISED BILLET. A DOG, AS EVER, IS PRESENT AS SOLDIERS OUT OF THE LINE FOUND TIME TO RELAX.

assuming a shape that would remain unaltered for the next two years, with the Germans holding three sides and the key ridges to the south and east from which to overlook the British positions.

Taken back with the rest of the cavalry to reconstitute in the rear areas in the early summer of 1915, the War Diary of the 12th records that *'much memo-writing was indulged in, to the delight of the Adjutant and the despair of the Squadron Commanders'.* June and July involved training and sending increasingly frequent work parties of about 200 officers and men to construct defences around the battlefield.

In the autumn, mounted training began again in preparation for the First Army attack at Loos where, together with the rest of the cavalry, both Regiments concentrated in September before returning once again to billets when the breakout failed to materialise, the problems of insufficient heavy artillery, poor communications and unrealistic expectations combining to thwart progress. From the 12th a 'vulture party' of two officers and 100 men was sent to clear the battlefield, the overall command of which fell to Brigadier Wormald, the 12th's Commanding Officer for the first part of the war, who was killed by a shell while supervising the work. '*If they will send up brigadiers to superintend 800 men burying dead what do they expect?*' wrote an officer

GRENFELLS

Always considered a family regiment, over the years there have been many cases of family members serving sequentially or at the same time. The most well known of these families is probably the Grenfells who, in one generation, provided four brothers who served in the 9th or 12th, including Captain Francis Grenfell, 9th Lancers, who won the first Victoria Cross of World War 1 to be gazetted.

Lieutenant Robert Septimus (the seventh brother of nine) Grenfell, 12th Lancers, was killed on 2nd September 1898 in the charge at Omdurman conducted by the 21st Lancers and alongside Winston Churchill. He had persuaded his uncle Field Marshal Lord Grenfell, who was Sirdar (Viceroy) in Cairo, to whom he was the Aide de Camp, to let him join the 21st Lancers for the Sudan Campaign. His field notebook containing sketches of the battlefield, and his personal account of the campaign up to his death is in the Regimental Museum in Derby.

ROBERT GRENFELL, 12TH LANCERS, DIED AT OMDURMAN IN 1898 WHILE ATTACHED TO THE 21ST LANCERS.

The First World War saw three other brothers serve with the 9th Lancers. Arthur Grenfell was a Captain in the Royal Buckinghamshire Imperial Yeomanry who joined the 9th Lancers as a Major in 1915. He was twice wounded, mentioned in despatches three times and awarded the DSO on the Somme in 1916. Because of his wounds he was transferred to the Royal Flying Corps in 1917 before leaving the Army and returning to business in 1918. Riversdale Nonus (the ninth brother) Grenfell was also in the Territorial Army but was able to join the 9th at the outbreak of war. His military career was tragically short. Just six weeks after the outbreak of war he was killed commanding his troop on 14th September 1914, near the hamlet of Chemin des Dames.

Riversdale's identical twin was Captain Francis Octavius Grenfell, who joined the 9th Lancers in May 1904 on transfer from the 60th Rifles. He won his Victoria Cross in the action near Audregnies on 24th August 1914 whilst commanding B Squadron. After treatment for his wounds he returned on 12th October, only to be wounded again on 31st October at Messines, remaining unfit for duty until April 1915 when, for the third time, he rejoined B Squadron. He was killed on 24th May 1915 near Hooge and is buried in the churchyard at Vlamertinghe. The lives of the twins are recorded in a book written by John Buchan and a stained-glass window in St George's English Church in Ypres commemorates their memory and all of the 9th Lancers who fell in the war.

Family links to the Regiment continued with Arthur Grenfell's grandson, Lieutenant Colonel P Lort-Phillips, and great grandson, Capt HPF Lort-Phillips, serving in the Regiment in an almost unbroken period from 1964–2003.

FRANCIS AND RIVERSDALE GRENFELL - BOTH WOULD DIE IN THE FIRST YEAR OF THE WAR.

bitterly.[30] Winter brought more work parties to build and repair trenches while the routine of stables and training continued.

Across the Army, manpower was, and remained, a critical issue. Although conscription was introduced in January 1916, on 30th December the 'Cavalry Division' was again sent into the line as infantry, each of the Cavalry Corps' divisions finding a brigade of three battalions, one of which came from each brigade. For each of the battalions every cavalry regiment provided a company, while the battalion headquarters was found in rotation. In the seven weeks the 8,200 men of the Division spent in the trenches, a total of 1,000 casualties were suffered, the 9th Lancers describing their casualties as 'minor' with 13 dead and 40 wounded in the five weeks they spent in the line. Another symptom of the shortage of manpower was the request for volunteers for commissions in the new infantry battalions then being formed, the 12th Lancers providing eight Non-Commissioned Officers in October 1915 (the total for the war was 46 permanent and 27 temporary commissions), including Sergeant Smeltzer who would, within two years, command his battalion and win the Distinguished Service Order and bar and the Military Cross.

THE SOMME 1916

The build up for the next major offensive involved training on the newly arrived Hotchkiss gun, while also improving logistic support to make the Regiments self-sufficient for the anticipated breakout across the Somme. Horses had to be got fit, the 9th swimming them in the sea on a day that the Royal Horse Guards were holding a ceremonial parade nearby, when a rider lost control and, naked, joined the rear rank of the Blue's squadron for the march past. *'What the numerous nursing contingents thought or said is not recorded.'*[31] Brought forward with the rest of the 1st and 3rd Cavalry Divisions to an assembly area near Albert, from where they were expecting to attack north towards Arras and assault the enemy's rear areas, the 9th waited in pouring rain, moving forward on the 1st July only to return when the breakthrough failed, a process repeated two weeks later until, in mid-August, they returned to the rear.

For the 12th Lancers, with the rest of the 2nd Cavalry Division, most of July and August was spent providing working parties around Ypres, but they now joined the rest of the cavalry for the next assault on 15th September. This was to be the first to use the newly invented tank but, despite the illusion of initial success in some areas, again no gap was made. The final phase of the battle finally ended in November 1916 and brought the year's campaigning to an end, the Regiments moving back to winter quarters where the horses began to suffer from the reduced allowance of feed, rationing having been introduced as a result of the U Boat campaign. Mounted training was further limited by the severe weather of the worst winter of the war and pioneer battalions were formed to build defensive lines and light railways to carry material to the front. Lieutenant Hunter of the 9th wrote home in January 1917: *'I am digging or rather… laying railways: it's wonderful what the Brit Cav can do when they really try. Our OC I believe is the [Great Western Railway] director, made a General for the job.'*[32]

In the spring of 1917 the strategic situation facing the Germans changed significantly, with the Russian Revolution in March potentially freeing them from one enemy, while the impending declaration of war by the United States (it came on 6th April) threatened another. On the Western Front they decided to remain on the defensive and from 16th–20th March a skilful withdrawal to the well-prepared defensive positions of the Hindenburg Line successfully reduced their frontage by 25 miles and freed up 14 divisions. Further benefit came from a ruthless scorched earth policy adopted during the withdrawal. This included the heavy mining and wholesale destruction of infrastructure and rendered a pursuit by the Allies impractical. For the Regiments, the severe winter combined with a reduced feed ration had caused their horses to lose condition rapidly and resulted in a high mortality rate in the months to come.

1 **MAJOR CHARLES BRYANT** WAS THE ADJUTANT OF THE 12TH LANCERS AT THE OUTBREAK OF THE WAR BUT WAS THEN ATTACHED TO THE ROYAL FLYING CORPS. VOLUNTEERS FOR COMMISSIONS WERE ALSO SOUGHT TO PROVIDE EXPERIENCED LEADERSHIP FOR NEWLY RAISED INFANTRY BATTALIONS. EIGHT NCOS FROM THE 12TH LANCERS COMMISSIONED INTO THE INFANTRY IN OCTOBER 1915, THE FIRST OF 46 PERMANENT AND 27 TEMPORARY COMMISSIONS GRANTED DURING THE WAR. THE MOST DISTINGUISHED OF THEM WAS SGT ARTHUR SMELTZER WHO COMMANDED A BATTALION OF THE EAST KENT REGIMENT AND WAS DECORATED WITH A DSO AND BAR AND AN MC.

2 **A TROOPER OF THE 9TH LANCERS IN 1916.** ALONG WITH HIS NORMAL ACCOUTREMENTS HE IS CARRYING A SMALL AXE AND MALLET TO DEAL WITH OBSTACLES.

THROUGHOUT THE WAR BOTH REGIMENTS FORMED COMPOSITE INFANTRY BATTALIONS WITH OTHER REGIMENTS FROM THE CAVALRY TO TAKE OVER SECTORS OF THE LINE. OTHER TASKS INCLUDED BUILDING DEFENCES AND 'VULTURE PARTIES' TO CLEAR BATTLEFIELDS AND BURY THE DEAD. LIEUTENANT HUNTER OF THE 9TH WROTE HOME IN JANUARY 1917: *'I AM LAYING RAILWAYS: IT IS WONDERFUL WHAT THE BRIT CAV CAN DO WHEN THEY TRY.'* BY THE TIME OF THIS PICTURE STEEL HELMETS WERE BOTH ISSUED AND WORN.

ARRAS 1917

Despite these difficulties, the Allies' plan for an offensive in the spring at Arras required the 9th and 12th Lancers to provide parties to build cavalry tracks across the shattered ground. *'Dismounted Lancers, Dragoons and Hussars, with rifles slung, spade in hand, filled sandbag or hurled debris and all the flotsam and jetsam of battle into the shell-holes in the track.'*[33] The attack began on 9th April with the increased emphasis on low-level infantry tactics and improved artillery co-operation leading to initial successes. Both Regiments once again moved forward with their brigades as a breakthrough appeared tantalisingly close, the 12th along its prepared tracks to Telegraph Hill, a strongpoint in the German second line, from where it had the privilege of a good view of the battle while they waited to break out. Yet again, lack of communications and the inability to gather more forces and artillery meant that the attack stalled on the German third line so that, by 8pm, in terrible conditions, the 12th were ordered back to Wailly. Major Charrington recalled: *'It was such an awful night, and so difficult and muddy our tracks over the trenches, and there was also such a lot of traffic on the road, that we took seven and a half hours to do five kilometres! – Halting every five yards for about ten minutes and not daring to dismount as the column might trot on at any moment. We got in about three-thirty, neither officers or men having fed, or more important drunk, since we left at 9am.'*[34]

As they prepared to move forward again the next morning, the 12th found several horses dead and many cases of frostbite and, under the cover of a blinding snowstorm that hid their movement, they arrived just short of the unbroken German third line at 6pm to discover that there was no chance of a further advance that day. The decision either to stay in place for the night, or return along the route that had just been travelled, was delegated to the commanders of the two cavalry brigades involved. The 3rd Brigade decided to move, while the 5th Brigade, with the 12th Lancers, remembering perhaps the previous night's withdrawal, chose to stay, a decision that would be regretted: *'The snow cleared a bit before dark, and the Germans spotted us and shelled us and we had a good many casualties, but they stopped after about twenty minutes. There we sat in the snow throughout the night, the men standing up to their horses all the time as they kept dropping odd crumps about. We were fairly lucky till about 3am when they dropped a big crump right into our headquarters staff, killing every horse and every man being killed or wounded... From that time on we were having casualties all the time and directly it got bright the shelling got very bad and we got machine gun fire as well.'*[35] Ordered to hold in their position to offer moral support to the infantry who were being counter-attacked, the brigade eventually moved back a mile, having been under constant shell fire: *'We were pretty badly shattered when the order came through to withdraw... but the men walked away as if nothing had been happening, although just as they began to move the head of the column was blown completely away.'*[36] Eventually moving back to Wailly, the Regiment rested, the horses were finally watered 33 hours after their last drink, and the cost of its involvement was counted at 56 killed or wounded and over 100 horses lost. Elsewhere, the 9th spent much of the battle waiting in freezing conditions while their dismounted party, acting as stretcher bearers and field-defence repairers, suffered 33 casualties from its start state of 73.

The cavalry again returned to the rear before, once again, taking on the dismounted role in the line for a month in May, with the rest of the summer of 1917 spent either as a mobile reserve or constructing trenches and emplacements in support of the Third Battle of Ypres (Passchendaele), which commenced in June. Training, inspections, sporting and social events broke the routine of life until the early part of November saw the whole of the Cavalry Corps head north-east to Peronne near

1 C SQUADRON, 12TH LANCERS, MOVE FORWARD FOR THE BATTLE OF ARRAS IN APRIL 1917.

2 FOR ALL THE MAJOR ALLIED ATTACKS THE CAVALRY WOULD BE BROUGHT FORWARD IN EXPECTATION OF EXPLOITING THE HOPED-FOR 'GAP'. AT ARRAS, THE 12TH WAITED IN FORWARD, EXPOSED, POSITIONS FOR 36 HOURS BEFORE BEING ORDERED BACK.

Cambrai, using night marches to complete the 100 move in secret.

CAMBRAI

Although originally conceived as a large-scale raid by the Tank Corps, the plan for the Battle of Cambrai, best known for the historic first use of massed tanks, had been expanded to emerge as a surprise combined, arms attack over a seven-mile front. With the familiar aim of securing an initial breakthrough, the cavalry were then expected to isolate Cambrai by cutting all the railways and then advance north. They were to be ready to launch any time after 10.50am, some four and a half hours after H Hour, and to be supported by a company of light Whippet tanks and 18 aircraft, the authority to advance being delegated to the cavalry commander.

Without the usual extensive preliminary barrage, the attack began on 20th November 1917 with the tanks moving forward behind a creeping screen of artillery. The effect was instantaneous, penetrating the Hindenburg Line with few British casualties. With the first line of trenches captured, the 1st Cavalry Division (with the 9th Lancers) was ordered to advance ahead of schedule, though hope quickly turned to frustration as the Division was ordered off one route onto another that turned out to be held by enemy, before returning to the original

THE GERMAN SPRING OFFENSIVE OF 1918 GAVE BOTH REGIMENTS SOME OF THEIR MOST DESPERATE FIGHTING OF THE WAR. DESPITE BEING PUSHED BACK, THEY REMAINED COHESIVE AND MOBILE.

track after a lengthy delay. Further brief progress was checked by depth positions near Bourlon Wood and Cantaing as the chance of exploitation faded with the light. A little to the east, the 2nd (12th Lancers) and 3rd Cavalry Divisions had been held at the two bridges at Masnières, one of which had collapsed under the weight of a tank. For both Regiments, there was nothing to do but remain saddled up throughout the night and wait. The next day proved equally frustrating. Checked again by the German defences, the 9th, which had dismounted two squadrons to join in the assault on Noyelles and had assisted in its defence, were unable to advance and eventually withdrew on 22nd November before sending 200 men forward as part of a dismounted cavalry battalion that remained in the reserve lines until 27th November.

The 12th Lancers, after their equally frustrating first day, spent the next four in the saddle moving to different parts of the line with increasingly slim chances of mounted action until, with Bourlon Wood finally captured but heavily counter-attacked, they too were ordered to form a dismounted company, sending 184 men into the wood on 27th November. Posted to its north-east corner, the company began to dig in overnight under shellfire, converting shell holes into a defensive line in order to create an improvised perimeter before the continuous attacks of the following day started at dawn. Trooper Espiner remembered: *'About mid-day the fun started properly. I don't know how many guns the Jerries had, but I think they were all being fired at us, and what with the shells and lumps of the trees that kept coming down it wasn't a pleasant afternoon.'*[37] Relieved that night, the remains of the company, their numbers reduced by five dead and 52 wounded, rejoined the rest of the Regiment, which remained in the area until early December. The company's efforts were recognised by the award of a Military Cross, a Distinguished Conduct Medal and six Military Medals.

Cambrai ended once again in stalemate, with the failure to exploit the initial gains blamed on an overly centralised system of command and control that took too long to react to success. More fundamentally, the lack of sufficient infantry and tanks required to punch through the depth lines indicated that the *'plan had outgrown the resources which the BEF possessed in late 1917'*.[38] The decision to double-hat the cavalry both as a reserve prepared to fight to get through and as an exploitation force further compounded the problem, and had they been launched *en masse* at the unbroken rear lines the result would have been massive casualties.

THE GERMAN SPRING OFFENSIVE 1918

After the disappointment at Cambrai, the front settled down with the Regiments withdrawn to billets. The winter of 1917–1918 was spent with several spells in the trenches as part of dismounted battalions, their last period ending in the middle of March 1918 when they were withdrawn in anticipation of the next German offensive. For this the Cavalry Corps, by now reduced from five divisions to three, would form the mobile reserve.

The German Spring Offensive of 1918, enabled by the transfer of 44 divisions from the Eastern Front after Russia's removal from the war, was timed to occur before the United States could make its presence felt and while the Germans had achieved a short-lived numerical advantage of 192 divisions against the Allies' 156. Aimed principally at the British sector, whose defeat, it was felt, would lead to an Allied collapse, the German high command envisaged a series of inter-related and relentless attacks, the first of which would hit the right of the British line and then swing north towards Arras. This sector, recently taken over from the French, was not only poorly prepared for defence but was thinly held, the Fifth Army holding a 42 mile front with all three cavalry and 12 (below-strength) infantry divisions, while the Third Army to its left held a 28 mile sector with 14 divisions.

For the cavalry the Fifth Army's contingency plans to meet the threat required reconnaissance of possible locations and training for short-notice moves followed, on 17th March, by orders to bolster the thinly spread front-line troops. For this both

Regiments contributed a large squadron to their brigade's dismounted battalion, leaving only about a third of the cavalry mounted and able to form a mobile reserve. In preparation, the 1st Cavalry Division (9th Lancers) moved north of St Quentin to the left centre of the Fifth Army, while the 2nd Division (12th Lancers) went to the south near Noyon.

The German attack exploded through their front lines on 21st March, its combination of a massive, sharp, artillery barrage, numerical superiority (43 divisions attacked the Fifth Army), improved tactics and thick fog caused confusion at a tactical level and near-paralysis higher up. Lieutenant General Monash later stated: '*It almost looked as if the whole of the British Army in this part of the world was in a state of rout.*'[39]

The role played by the two Regiments – and the rest of the cavalry – in helping to stem the German Spring Offensive was much the same. For both, a series of confused individual actions took place over the next few weeks, the 9th Lancers helping to plug the emerging gaps between the Third and Fifth Armies with their dismounted squadron heavily involved around Albert, while the 12th Lancers attempted to maintain the coherence of the southern flank around Noyon. The Regiments' dismounted companies of 200 men bolstered the other front-line troops, digging in with inadequate tools and sustaining considerable casualties in the fighting, with large numbers missing as a result of the chaos. For the remainder of the two Regiments, the value of the mounted arm was thoroughly vindicated by their actions. In the confusion of the British withdrawal, they were finally able to conduct themselves effectively in both the mounted and dismounted roles, providing reconnaissance and flank protection to various formations to try to fill in the yawning intelligence gaps. Equally importantly, they provided mobile units to inflict delay on an advancing enemy by fighting from hastily prepared defensive positions wherever the need arose.

After a week of fighting the Regiments found themselves in same area, the 12th having been ordered two days' march north to Compiègne to assist in the defence of Amiens, whose vital railway junction was threatened by German pressure. Supporting the few infantry units to the east of the town, the German attacks were checked as, across the front, the enemy began to run out of steam, though the costly local battles continued. One of the 12th Lancers' actions, on 30th March, while working with the 9th Australian Infantry Brigade near Hangard Wood, gives a picture of the state of demoralisation in many of the British forces and the nature of operations undertaken. '*The 12th Royal Lancers preceded the battalion and reached the wood east of Bois de Hangard at about 4.15p.m. This wood will in future be known as Lancer Wood... The Cavalry Commander also helped in this matter [the preventing of a general withdrawal by the garrison of the wood] by sending a squadron dismounted to re-establish their line... Their approach march instilled in the men the utmost confidence and enthusiasm and, I am glad to say, did much to counteract the effect of the straggling. They lost no time in effectively clearing Lancer Wood, and got there just in time, as the enemy had gained a footing in the southern and south-east edges of the wood. Their action now allowed us to move forward to the attack... On seeing the cavalry there, the enemy shelled Lancer Wood very heavily with 5.9s... The discipline shown during this shelling was an object lesson. During our attack the cavalry protected both our flanks, the left with Hotchkiss guns... The experience gained in this our first operation with cavalry was invaluable. One was able to judge of the splendid work they are doing for the army at the present time, and they cannot be too highly praised.*'[40]

With the threat from this first German offensive over, the cavalry could be withdrawn to reconstitute, the 12th Lancers receiving 110 reinforcements while the 9th counted their toll of 33% of their fighting strength made up of 33 dead, 85 wounded and 40 missing (only 16 of whom were found to be prisoners). Although they had not stopped the Germans on their own, the part played by the cavalry in helping to stem the enemy offensive did much to restore its battered pride, causing some of its critics to pause and consider the flexibility and usefulness of a well-drilled mobile force. Even allowing for the hyperbole of another Regimental historian, it is worth repeating his words '*..the 9th, in common with the whole of the reduced British cavalry, had played their part in this hard-contested and continuous series of fights. Time and time again had they been called upon at brief notice to fill a gap, to buttress a wavering segment of line, to serve as a rallying-point, or to hold on as a forlorn hope. They had not once failed, and more than once had saved a situation that already seemed lost irretrievably.*'[41]

The German offensives continued across the front, making gains but never the vital breakthrough, until the last in July revealed their state of complete exhaustion as a fighting force. Having raced to support the defenders of the next wave of attacks, both Regiments were able to use the late spring months to integrate reinforcements and to train, ready for the Allied counter-attacks of the summer that would be enabled by the build-up of US forces in France. Across the Army, the lessons from earlier assaults had been learnt, with close integration of air, tanks and artillery, better use of communications and more realistic aims being chief amongst them, while revised tactics would see the infantry seize initial objectives and the cavalry exploit the limited secondary ones, where they would wait, only pushing on if certain of success. To assist them, the Cavalry Corps would be supported by two battalions of Whippet tanks.

The final German offensive, stopped by a successful French–American counter-attack at the end of July, was rapidly followed by a counter-offensive

1 THE 9TH LANCERS MEMORIAL AT CANTERBURY CATHEDRAL.

2 A MENU CARD FROM A DINNER GIVEN BY THE TOWN OF PHILIPPEVILLE. THE 12TH LANCERS HAD BEEN ORDERED TO THE TOWN TO INVESTIGATE TALES OF LOOTING BY THE WITHDRAWING GERMANS BUT SOON FOUND THEMSELVES HELD UP BY A HUGE PARTY.

by the British Fourth Army and French First Army to the east of Amiens on 8th August 1918. Described by the German commander Field Marshal Ludendorff, as *'the black day of the German Army in the history of this war'*, a combined-arms assault using tanks, artillery, air, infantry and surprise began with a barrage of 2,000 guns, rapidly followed by an infantry assault which, within six hours, had achieved its first objectives. This allowed some exploitation by the cavalry, the 9th Lancers in their sector passing through the Canadians and, having cleared the limited enemy facing them, securing their objective. It was, according to the historian of the Fourth Army, *'The first occasion since the war began that the cavalry in France had been able to move rapidly across open country against a beaten enemy, and reap the fruits of a successful infantry and tank attack.'*[42] With the infantry catching up late in the day the advance was held before, the 9th advanced again the following morning having stayed close to the front line overnight. They were, once more, behind the Canadians who halted at Méharicourt and allowed the 9th to take the lead up to provide infantry divisions with their own cavalry regiments. The aim was not only to provide them with a capability to exploit success immediately, but also a reconnaissance and liaison capability at all levels, it being particularly difficult to establish friendly-force locations during the advance. This new role would keep the 12th busy for the rest of war with a succession of different affiliations.

Mounted formation training for both Regiments took place in earnest throughout September. A new confidence was felt by the participants that this time it might be used, before the assault on the Hindenburg Line began on the 26th with a general advance across the whole front, the rearmost German lines falling in early October. For the 9th Lancers, the 7th October saw their last casualties of the war, two men wounded in the area of Bellicourt. The Cavalry Corps was held in reserve from the middle of October until early November, when it was sent forward in readiness for a final, unrealised, chance to exploit.

Mounted formation training for both Regiments took place in earnest throughout September, with a new confidence being felt…

across difficult country that had not recovered from the fighting of the Somme in 1916. With resistance growing across the front, and in marked contrast to previous battles where more troops would have been flung at the problem, the Amiens battle was brought swiftly to a close. The 9th returned to Amiens, and attention focused elsewhere to keep the Germans off-balance.

The first day of the Battle of Amiens had cost the British 9,000 casualties against the Germans' 27,000, of which, perhaps more tellingly, 15,000 were prisoners, an indication of their increasingly fragile fighting spirit. The next blow came on 21st August, with the Third Army's successful attack in the Arras area, which continued to push the Germans back until the beginning of September. While the cavalry had been moved up to support the attack, once again the cut-up ground of old battlefields hampered movement. This limited their effective employment to reconnaissance patrols in support of the infantry formations to which squadrons had by now been attached. Regimental Headquarters acted as the collection and distribution centre for their reports.

The August battles forced the Germans to cede the gains made in the spring and withdraw to the Hindenburg Line on 2nd September, General Haig now sensing that a swift end to the conflict was finally achievable and that *'we ought to do our utmost to get a decision this autumn'*.[43] The August battles had once again proved the limited likelihood of cavalry being used *en masse* and, on 4th September, the 2nd Cavalry Division, of which the 12th formed a part, was split

For the 12th, reconnaissance and liaison duties with the infantry continued, although the enemy presence, supply situation and difficult going around Le Cateau meant that they were withdrawn at the end of October, to resume their duties as part of the next push on 4th November. Only on 9th November was anything like the cavalry role envisaged at the war's outbreak finally realised when a half squadron, *'pushing forward with the utmost dash captured Sais Poteries and pushed on to Solre le Chateau which they occupied, capturing a field gun, a machine gun, and an immense amount of rolling stock including one loaded ammunition train and a large shell dump, two lorries, three motor cars, and several hundreds of wagons and limbers.'*[44] Solre le Château marked the 12th Lancers' final position as, unable even with infantry support to dislodge an enemy force across the River Thure on 10th November, they returned to the town. Here throughout the last night of the war, shelling continued into the town, eventually finding the ammunition train and dump which detonated, the blast killing Sergeant Smith of C Squadron, the last man from the 12th to die in the war.

News of the armistice, to come into effect at 11am on 11th November, halted the 12th's participation in a planned attack over the river and standing patrols were mounted along the line held. To their north, the 9th Lancers, who had been detailed to lead the advance of the 2nd Cavalry Brigade that day, received the message as they moved along the Mons road near the village of Beloeil, within one hour's march of where it had first sighted the enemy over four years before.

MECHANISATION

1918–1939

THE END OF 'THE WAR TO END ALL WARS' led perhaps logically, if naively, to a government policy that Britain's armed forces need not anticipate a major conflict within the next 10 years, a policy refreshed every year until the mid-1930s. Allied to the intellectual argument, the post-war economic downturn led to inevitable reductions in defence expenditure and marked the beginning of a period of underinvestment that was to last for the next 20 years, the £43.5 million budget of 1923 having reduced to £36 million in 1932. The immediate consequence was a review of public spending that concluded in February 1922 and initiated a series of cuts, reducing the number of infantry battalions by 20 from their pre-war total, while amalgamations among the British cavalry regiments dropped their numbers from 31 to 22, the axe missing the 12th Lancers by a whisker.

THE 12TH LANCERS IMMEDIATELY FOLLOWING THE ARMISTICE.

1 ALTHOUGH DEMOBILISATION BEGAN IN DECEMBER 1918, BOTH REGIMENTS SPENT MUCH OF 1919 ON GARRISON DUTY IN THE RHINELAND.

2 A GROUP OF 12TH LANCERS READY TO RETURN TO BRITAIN AT THE END OF THEIR DUTY IN COLOGNE. THE WRITING ON THE WAGON READS XII ROYAL LANCERS, COLOGNE-BLIGHTY, AUG 1914-SEPT 1919.

In addition to the demands for economy, pacifism and then appeasement formed the backdrop against which much of the inter-war period was played out. Defence thinking tended to favour air and sea power, the idea of Britain contributing a land component to a war on continental Europe only being acknowledged in the late 1930s, by which time the Army was being described as the 'Cinderella of the Forces'[1] with a role only in the defence of overseas territories. Further difficulties included a poor public perception of the military and a military career, low manning levels (the 12th were 90 men short in 1937) and obsolescent weapons and equipment. Only in the late 1930s, as the threat from Germany was acknowledged, would a possible role on the Continent be seriously considered. This brought rearmament and investment in all areas, but left the BEF of 1939 far less well prepared than its counter-part in 1914 had been.

Given this depressing backdrop, it is surprising that there is no evidence that either the 9th or 12th Lancers suffered from poor morale or low standards as they endured a period of unusual uncertainty and change. In competitions, each regiment acquired a wide range of silverware, ranging from gardening through to pig-sticking, as well more conventional military activity such as shooting and skill at arms. Equally importantly, morale remained solid and a sense of pride fundamental. Sergeant Bryant of the 12th, on his return to Tidworth from Egypt in December 1934 remembered that, as he marched from the station, he felt *'a huge surge of pride in the Regiment, pride in my Squadron and pride in my mates'.*[2] Similarly, Bruce Shand, joining as a new officer for the 12th in 1937, recalls that, *'I suspect that standards of driving, gunnery and map-reading were very high; there was, for those days, a very sophisticated familiarity with the use of radio communication, then something of a novelty and even an object of suspicion in the British Army.'*[3]

Despite the changes, life for both officers and soldiers during this period was familiar. Accommodation in barrack blocks remained sparse, while Sergeant Bryant recalled his time as a recruit: *'"Bull" was the order of the day and well and truly was it carried out...one could see one's face in the polished wooden floor.. the table top and the two seats were scrubbed each night until they was snow white.. money was very scarce, pay was two shillings a day.. the bulk had to be spent at the Regimental Tailor's for such things as we had to have and had to be paid for by ourselves.. so there was not much left for wild nights in the canteen.'*[4]

For both Regiments the end of hostilities took them east towards Germany, the 12th delayed on the 15th November when, ordered to Philippeville to investigate talk of rioting and looting by the withdrawing Germans, they found nothing but a huge party in full swing, which held them back for a couple of days. As part of the force that would occupy a limited part of Germany, the 12th crossed the Rhine on 1st December, while the 9th arrived in Cologne five days later to begin duties that,

1 **THE BAND OF THE 9TH LANCERS ON THE KING'S BIRTHDAY PARADE AT ABASSIA, EGYPT IN 1923,** WHERE THE REGIMENT WAS GARRISONED FROM 1921 TO 1926.

2 **THE 12TH WERE RE-TITLED THE 12TH ROYAL LANCERS (PRINCE OF WALES'S) IN JANUARY 1921.** THIS PORTRAIT OF THE FUTURE EDWARD VII IS NOTABLE FOR THE PROPORTIONS OF THE PRINCE OF WALES'S HEAD. HE HAD ONLY POSED LONG ENOUGH FOR HIS HEAD TO BE PAINTED, THE ARTIST USING LIEUTENANT 'KATE' SAVILL TO MODEL THE BODY.

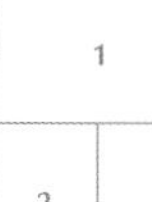

barring some minor public-order tasks, were largely peaceful. Demobilisation began almost immediately and progressed rapidly, the 9th sending back their first soldiers on Boxing Day 1918, leaving the remaining veterans to bring on the new recruits as they arrived. With the occupation over in September 1919, the 9th moved back to Tidworth and then onto Ireland in May 1920 where they joined the 12th who, as part of the garrison there, were now engaged in dealing with nationalist disturbances.

Patrols, raids and escorts formed the majority of the activity, with only the occasional action, the 9th mounting one successful ambush in which four terrorists were killed, but being caught by two enemy ones in which two officers died. Despite the risks, the thankless nature of the tasks and the limited success, enjoyment could still be had, the 12th's historian recording that *'although revolvers were the order of the day, and in spite of the threats of the IRA, the Regiment [12th Lancers] did manage to hold a point-to-point near the Curragh and it proved a very successful meeting...In the evening the troop who had been seated all day on a tarpaulin near the weighing tent took their loaded rifles from underneath it to the astonishment of the countrymen, by this time mellowed by racing and porter.'*[5]

From Ireland the 9th travelled to Egypt in September 1921 with a new order of battle that included, for the first time, Headquarters Squadron as well as three sabre squadrons. Part of a larger force whose role was to safeguard the Suez canal and ensure the country remained quiet, it also formed part of a wider Army strategy to maintain its primacy in the business of imperial policing in the face of growing claims by the Royal Air Force (frequently repeated in other spheres of military endeavour) that it could carry out such function more cheaply and efficiently. A familiar routine of training and inspections interspersed with internal security duties in Egypt and Palestine occupied the Regiment until in December 1926 they begin their final posting to India to begin an uneventful five-year tour, at the end of which they paraded with the lance for the last time, returning to Redford Barracks in Edinburgh in November 1931.

1&2 THE MUSICAL RIDE OF THE 12TH LANCERS, 1923, AND THE TRICK RIDERS OF THE 9TH LANCERS, 1925. BOTH REGIMENTS MADE REGULAR APPEARANCES AT THE ROYAL TOURNAMENT IN VARIOUS YEARS.

3 BOTH REGIMENTS' LONG ASSOCIATION WITH INDIA CAME TO AN END WHEN THE 9TH RETURNED FROM THEIR LAST POSTING THERE IN 1931.

The 12th, since January 1921 restyled from the 12th (Prince of Wales's Royal) Lancers to the 12th Royal Lancers (Prince of Wales's), left Ireland in March 1922 for Tidworth and then onto Hounslow but, stood down from possible involvement with the General Strike, the 12th moved to Egypt in 1926.

MECHANISATION

Despite the recent war providing stark proof that cavalry was outmoded as a method of allying firepower with mobility, only by the mid-1920s was anything done about it, the Prime Minister forcing the Secretary for War's hand in 1927 by writing that it would be difficult to justify training horsed cavalry if they were to be 'abolished in the near future'.[6] The question then remained of how to go about mechanisation, given that there was no money for such investment, resistance to change coming not just from a few reactionaries, but principally and predictably from the Treasury. Despite this, in 1926 and 1927 policy was introduced stating it was decided that no regiments would be abolished; that some regiments would begin to be converted to armoured cars and that no new Royal Tank Corps units would be raised. Additionally, a small reduction in the number of troops in horsed regiments would be offset by mechanising first-line transport and machine gun troops while also increasing the number of weapons in the latter to make them full squadrons. Simultaneously, the Army decided to form a trial 'mechanised division capable of covering at least 100 miles per day across country' which exercised from 1927–1929 and placed Britain, for a short period, at the lead of armoured warfare.

These decisions had an almost immediate impact on the 12th Lancers. In December 1927, B Squadron was absorbed into A and C Squadrons on the formation of the Machine Gun Squadron while, in December 1927, Army Order 392 abolished the lance as a weapon of war for regiments serving in the British Army, to be retained by lancer regiments for ceremonial duties only and when on the Indian Army establishment. By now it had been decided that the 11th Hussars and the 12th Lancers, the two most junior cavalry regiments not amalgamated in 1922, would convert to armoured cars from 4th April 1927, the first regular cavalry regiments in the world to mechanise. Confirmation came by a signal from the Colonel of the Regiment to Egypt. Despite fears that mechanisation would bring mass resignation, particularly among officers, none occurred, the Commanding Officer writing to the Old Comrades that year: *'Do not say 'It is all over' – do not say 'Ichabod', the glory is departed', but let us all get down to our new job just as well as we all got down to it on our feet during the greater part of our long hard years in France… remember…that we still remain part of the Cavalry Corps, retaining our old titles, traditions and privileges and retaining also…the old spirit.'*[7]

The first armoured cars, Rolls-Royce 1920 and 1924 pattern, arrived in January 1929 and went to B Squadron which had been reanimated and training since May of the previous year and now found itself with 11 vehicles, 10 in two sections of five with an 11th for the squadron leader. Armed with a .303 machine gun in the turret and with communication either by despatch rider or semaphore, the Rolls-Royces were considered fast and reliable, especially when compared with the Crossleys with which they were mixed as the rest the Regiment converted. Mechanisation was completed in September 1930, by which time B Squadron had already used them on active service

1 THE 12TH LANCERS AND THE 11TH HUSSARS WERE THE FIRST REGULAR CAVALRY REGIMENTS IN THE WORLD TO MECHANISE. THE NEWS WAS BROKEN IN 1927 AND, ALTHOUGH MASS RESIGNATIONS WERE EXPECTED, IT WAS FOUND THAT BOTH OFFICERS AND SOLDIERS TOOK TO THE NEW CHALLENGE WITH EASE, MOST ENJOYING THE REDUCED WORKLOAD BROUGHT ABOUT BY THE VEHICLES.

2 THE FIRST ARMOURED CARS WERE ROLLS-ROYCE 1920 AND 1924 PATTERN ARMED WITH A .303 MACHINE GUN. THEY ARRIVED IN EGYPT WHERE THE 12TH WERE STATIONED IN 1929 AND WERE SOON IN USE IN PALESTINE IN 1929 AND CYPRUS 1931.

3 CROSSLEY ARMOURED CARS WERE ALSO USED BY THE 12TH BUT PROVED SLOWER AND LESS RELIABLE THAN THE ROLLS ROYCES.

<table><tr><td rowspan="2">1</td><td>2</td></tr><tr><td>3</td></tr></table>

…in December 1927, Army Order 392 abolished the lance as a weapon of war for regiments serving in the British Army…

SOLDIERS QUICKLY ADAPTED TO THE DIFFERENT SKILLS REQUIRED BY MECHANISATION ALTHOUGH THE UNDERLYING STYLE AND ETHOS REMAINED THE SAME. DIFFERENT SQUADRONS OF THE 12TH LANCERS DEMONSTRATE OLD AND NEW SKILLS AT MOY DAY, NOVEMBER 1929.

in Palestine, moving there in August 1929 to carry out internal security duties, including patrols, raids and escorts over a two-month period. Initial difficulties with communications and a complete lack of transport were gradually overcome, five radio trucks arriving to provide communications to each squadron, a competency demonstrated by transmissions between the 11th Hussars in Tidworth and the 12th in Egypt in December 1932. Training included squadrons conducting long-range reconnaissance drives into the desert, C Squadron clocking up one of over 1,300 miles in 17 days in the Nile Valley, while others reached the Siwa Oasis to provide information that would later prove invaluable to the Long Range Desert Group.

The same squadron had also sent half its strength to Cyprus in October 1931 to help subdue rioting on the island, though returned five weeks later. They had seen nothing but produced a 'moral' effect. In 1934 the establishment changed to three squadrons, each of three troops of three vehicles, an orbat which neatly matched that of the 11th Hussars with whom they swapped stations in December, taking over their barracks in Tidworth and their Lanchester armoured cars. Although slower than the Rolls-Royce, they proved more solid and packed a greater punch with a .50 and .303 machine gun in the turret and a further .303 mounted in the hull.

The 12th's arrival back in Tidworth in early December 1934 was followed almost immediately

The essence of co-operation—Beer. Two hundred miles from anywhere.

1&2 A NUMBER OF LONG-RANGE RECONNAISSANCE EXPEDITIONS WERE UNDERTAKEN BY THE 12TH IN THE PERIOD IMMEDIATELY FOLLOWING MECHANISATION AND PROVIDED INFORMATION THAT WAS TO PROVE VITAL IN THE DESERT WAR THAT FOLLOWED. A RENDEZVOUS WITH THE RAF AT SIWA PROVIDED VITAL RESUPPLY.

3 THE 12TH WERE EQUIPPED WITH LANCHESTER ARMOURED CARS ON THEIR RETURN TO ENGLAND IN 1934. ARMED WITH A .50 AND .303 MACHINE GUN IN THE TURRET AND A .303 MACHINE GUN IN THE HULL, THEY PROVED SLOWER BUT MORE SOLID THAN THE ROLLS-ROYCES.

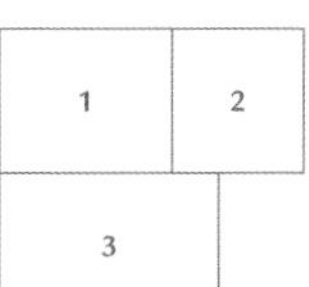

by the deployment of a force, formed as D Squadron and made up of eight armoured cars manned by five officers and 60 men, to travel to the Saarland on the French-German border. Their mission was to ensure a peaceful plebiscite that was being held to determine the future of the disputed area, which had been governed under a League of Nations mandate since 1920. Setting sail from Dover on 2nd January 1935, they drove across a welcoming France and then based themselves comfortably in Saarbrucken, patrolling the region in appalling weather until the vote passed uneventfully on 13th January. Their performance was reported by the British Commander to have been excellent: '*They have been grand…They were fairly bursting for work…and insisted on starting straight in. They had some difficult patrols on plebiscite night, on filthy roads, and I saw them at it – driving first class and no accidents.*'[8] Despite this apparent success the result of the plebiscite, in which those seeking unification with Germany took 90% of the vote, while those wishing to join France could manage less than 1%, probably explains the

THE 12TH LANCERS DROVE TO THE SAARLAND TO OVERSEE THE PLEBISCITE ON ITS FUTURE IN 1935 AS PART OF AN INTERNATIONAL FORCE UNDER A LEAGUE OF NATIONS MANDATE INCLUDING DUTCH MARINES. WELCOMED BY THE FRENCH ON THEIR WAY OUT, THEY RECEIVED A HOSTILE RECEPTION ON THE WAY HOME FOLLOWING THE OVERWHELMING VOTE TO SEEK UNIFICATION WITH GERMANY.

rather different feel of D Squadron's return back to Britain via France. Sergeant Bryant recalled that '*This proved to be a very different journey to the outward one. The crowds of people were still there but this time they were very antagonistic towards us, hissing, jeering and throwing the odd stick or stone at us. Typical frog!*'[9]

The Saar Plebiscite represented an early victory for fascism and, as its rise continued, the 12th were again called overseas to counter a further instance, this time from Italy, which was increasingly belligerent in Abyssinia and the Middle East.

Leaving A Squadron behind as a rear party stripped of manpower to make up for shortages elsewhere, the Regiment moved to Egypt in November 1935, by now with Lieutenant Colonel McCreery in command, as part of reinforcements to guard Egypt against Mussolini's forces in Libya. By the end of January 1936, 29 cars and their crews were once again back in their old camp at Helmieh, which was still occupied by the 11th Hussars, dealing with equipment shortages and preparing for operations in the desert. In March they moved west to spend six months based at Mersa Matruh joining the Mobile Force (inevitably known as the Immobile Farce), patrolling the frontier between Libya and Egypt and guarding the forward landing grounds near the border. Although several long forays into the desert were undertaken and the experience gained would prove invaluable in a few years' time, any large-scale training was hamstrung by lack of spare parts, which were a symptom of the lack of investment made in the preceding years. Despite this, the precautions proved sufficient to deter the Italians, the Regiment withdrawing from the Western Desert to Cairo in July before returning to England for Christmas to begin the first full year that the Regiment had had in England since 1926.

Mechanisation had already touched the 9th, who had relinquished their lances on leaving India at the end of 1931, though the slow speed of conversion continued to reflect the reluctance to invest in a capability deemed of use only in a major conflict,

RICHARD MCCREERY

Richard McCreery joined the 12th Lancers in the 1914-1918 war where he was badly wounded and was thereafter known as 'Hoppy' because of his limp. Despite this, he remained a distinguished race rider (winning the Grand Military twice) and polo player. Having commanded the 12th Lancers from 1935–1938 he went on to command the 2nd Armoured Brigade in which the 9th Lancers served in France 1940 and was then Chief of Staff of Middle East Command. In 1944 he took over command of the Eighth Army in Italy and was later Commander-in-Chief in Austria and the British Army of the Rhine. He was Colonel of the Regiment of the 12th Lancers from 1951-1960 and the 9th/12th from 1960–1961.

Major Bruce Shand remembered him as '*initially slightly frightening and austere, though probably as shy as I was; he also had quite a considerable temper. He walked with that very idiosyncratic gait (the result of a severe First War wound) which would become so familiar to thousands of soldiers in Italy by the end of the war.*' Others describe him as '*tall, lean, bright and highly experienced... had phlegm and cool-headedness*'[10] a quality he demonstrated when visiting Lieutenant John Robson in Italy in 1943. '*As he arrived, the Krauts decided to put an airburst over our heads, the first warlike bang I had seen or heard. All of us, except the General, hit the dirt. When we got to our feet the General asked me 'What was the name of the flower you laid down beside?' On replying that I didn't know, he responded 'You are going to be here for some time, so the least you can do is to learn the names of some of the flowers.*'[11]

THE 9TH LANCERS RELINQUISHED THEIR HORSES IN 1936 AND IN 1937 RECEIVED THEIR FIRST TANKS. IN THE FIRST DELIVERY WERE MARK V LIGHT TANKS EQUIPPED WITH A .303 AND .50 MACHINE GUN WHICH HAD RETURNED FROM EGYPT FULL OF SAND AND HAD BEEN WRITTEN OFF AS UNSERVICEABLE.

While eventually required to adopt an all-tank orbat, the 9th experimented with different organisations, squadrons at one point producing both tank troops and dismounted soldiers in carriers…

which policy stated would not happen. After three years in Scotland where the expense of travel and the lack of other units prevented any large-scale training, the 9th returned to Tidworth in 1934 where, in August, they conducted their last exercise on horses. Formally told at the end of 1935 that they were to convert to light tanks, 1936 saw the 9th surrender of all their horses, less the officers' chargers and 40 of the best troop horses, which were kept in order to participate in the Tidworth Horse Show and Tattoo that autumn. The remainder were sold or sent to other regiments that were still mounted. It was, for many, a *'depressing business, but the new work in hand left little time for sentiment'*,[12] with conversion courses and exercises taking place around Salisbury Plain and in Bovington.

Doctrine for the use of armour was, even at this stage, still the subject of considerable debate. While eventually required to adopt an all-tank orbat, the 9th experimented with different organisations, squadrons at one point producing both tank troops and dismounted soldiers in carriers, while the Commanding Officer, Lieutenant Colonel CW Norman, continued to emphasise the importance of ground weapons and dismounted action for periods when they might be 'unhorsed'. Conversion was carried out on Carden Lloyd carriers – a small, weaponless vehicle that proved highly unreliable and soon became scattered across Salisbury Plain – which were replaced for the 1937 training season by *'ancient'* Mark IIb light tanks and a few Mark Vs. Although equipped with radios and machine guns, these proved equally unreliable, having been returned from Egypt full of sand and condemned as unserviceable. The radios proved a novelty however, the Commanding Officer apparently audible at over half a mile despite nothing being broadcast over the ether, while the War Office distributed a letter warning that civilians were complaining about the language used on the net which they were picking up on their radios.

The full training season of 1937 was followed by a less satisfactory year during which the 9th, having had the benefit of most of the Army's training vehicles, saw them withdrawn for others to use and resorted to using trucks as surrogate tanks, with a resultant loss of gunnery and machine gun practice. The spring of 1938 brought organisational changes with the formation of the 1st Mobile (later Armoured) Division consisting of 1st and 2nd Armoured Brigades, the latter made up of the Queen's Bays, the 9th Lancers and the 10th Hussars, a grouping that remained unchanged throughout the Second World War. The new division, with its artillery, engineers and signals, added extra interest to training. A large exercise took place at the end of

1 THE DEDICATION OF THE 12TH LANCERS WAR MEMORIAL, MOOLTAN BARRACKS, TIDWORTH, 14TH OCTOBER 1922.

2 THE 9TH LANCERS COMMEMORATING MONS DAY AT REDFORD BARRACKS 1932, FRANCIS GRENFELL'S VICTORIA CROSS IS ON DISPLAY.

1938, though it fizzled out as the Munich crisis came and went, the 9th suddenly finding itself digging trenches and preparing for possible war while the 12th helped train the Yeomanry. The year saw new Commanding Officers in both Regiments, with Lieutenant Colonels CHM Peto and H Lumsden taking over the 9th and 12th respectively.

Throughout the inter-war period manpower remained scarce so that, when 2nd Lieutenant Tim Bishop joined the 12th Lancers in the late summer of 1938 with five fellow subalterns, he found that only four others had joined the Regiment in the previous five years. A year earlier, as rearmament began to pick up, the Commanding Officer of the 9th recalled being told by the Commander-in-Chief to brief the Secretary of State for War, Leslie Hore-Belisha, on the manning issue but to *'Be kind to him, because he doesn't know anything about the Army and asked me just now if there were eleven divisions in Tidworth. Mind you make his flesh creep.'* Even with extra recruiting, the deficiencies could not be made up and in the summer of 1939 reservists were recalled and Britain made its first use of peacetime conscription, their integration and training into both Regiments further complicated by the lack of mechanised experience and the deficiency of equipment on which to instruct.

The equipment deficiencies that faced the 9th were reflected in the 12th who, in the same period, took delivery of the Morris Armoured Car. In every way inferior to the vehicle it replaced, the Morris was the result of the sudden drive to re-arm and came with few spares, inadequate armament in the form of a Bren gun and a Boyes anti-tank rifle (a .50 rifle) and the thinnest armour to protect it, rapidly earning it the nickname 'The Suicide Box'. As war became inevitable and despite everyone's best efforts, after two decades of underinvestment only an echo of Grenfell's claim on the eve of the First World War could be made for either Regiment, the Colonel of the 9th stating later that his Regiment was only *'as fit and ready for war as was possible in the circumstances'.*[13]

ADAPTING TO THE CHANGE

At the highest levels reaction to mechanisation was generally favourable, with senior serving officers realising that, with the impotence of horsed cavalry against modern weapons, something had to be done to guarantee mobility on the battlefield. The Secretary of State for War wrote to the Prime Minister in 1927: *'so far from there being any opposition in the higher ranks of the army to mechanisation and new weapons, they are one and all thinking of nothing else'.*[14] At the Staff College in 1921, *'the students who were cavalrymen were very open-minded as a whole. In particular Rollie Charrington [who was to command the 12th through mechanisation] was quite ready to be convinced that the cavalry would use tanks in the future...The cavalry instructor, on the other hand, was a die-hard and determined to do all he could to retain horsed cavalry.'*[15] So much for the wisdom of the Directing Staff.

For both Regiments, mechanisation was greeted with mixed feelings. The older NCOs found the instructional requirement understandaly challenging, while the younger soldiers in particular appeared happy to adapt and learn new skills that might benefit them later, while also welcoming the reduced workload, particularly at weekends, that tending a mechanical object brought with it. Captain Fenton of the 12th wrote: *'before long the talk was all of differentials, carburettors and all the many parts which go to make up a car...In addition to the enthusiasm the next most favourable point was the youth and flexibility of mind of the majority of the men. They were able to absorb the new technical training with little difficulty.'*[16]

Mass resignations amongst the officer corps, though feared and the reason officers were allowed two government chargers until the war (they were even allowed to come with officers on courses), never materialised. Amongst the younger officers, many of whom had joined expecting that they would always ride, there may have been a feeling that they had been let down, although, certainly by the time of the 9th's conversion, many were already mechanically minded, owning their own cars and, for several, their own aeroplanes. The older generation might have been expected to be more reactionary. Most, however, had seen the effects of modern weaponry and welcomed the opportunity that the new equipment brought with it to make the Regiments relevant once again. CW Norman, who steered the 9th through mechanisation, wrote: *'In the twenties and thirties we continued to train on the old lines, though all of us who had seen war knew that we were acting in a farce. The armoured vehicle was to give back to us with interest our traditional role, and the 9th Lancers proved in battle after battle that they were masters of mounted warfare, whatever the mount.'*[17]

BOTH REGIMENTS ADAPTED QUICKLY TO MECHANISATION AND THE USE OF RADIO FOR COMMUNICATION WITH EARLY LINKS FROM EGYPT BACK TO ENGLAND BY THE 12TH LANCERS IN 1929. THE 9TH LANCERS USE OF RADIOS IN TANKS IN 1937 CAUSED THE WAR OFFICE TO ISSUE A LETTER WARNING ABOUT THE USE OF STRONG LANGUAGE AFTER LOCAL CIVILIANS COMPLAINED OF INTERFERENCE ON THEIR RADIOS.

ALTHOUGH LACKING THE ROMANCE OF THE HORSE, MECHANISATION REDUCED THE DAILY WORKLOAD FOR THOSE LOOKING AFTER THEIR NEW MOUNTS.

1&2 IN BOTH REGIMENTS MECHANISATION DID LITTLE TO DIMINISH THE LOVE OF THE HORSE, WHETHER FOR HUNTING, POLO OR RACING WITH BOTH REGIMENTS ENTERING A SECOND 'GOLDEN AGE'. THE 12TH APPEARED IN THE LAST FOUR FINALS OF THE INTER-REGIMENTAL POLO CUP BEFORE THE SECOND WORLD WAR WHILE IN RACING LIEUTENANT COLONELS RICHARD MCCREERY AND HERBERT LUMSDEN EACH WON THE GRAND MILITARY GOLD CUP TWICE. CAPTAIN PRIOR PALMER, 9TH LANCERS, WON THE FOXHUNTERS AT AINTREE ON O'DELL (PICTURED) IN 1936, A WIN REPEATED THE FOLLOWING YEAR BY HERBERT LUMSDEN. AT MUCH THE SAME TIME REYNOLDSTOWN WON THE 1935 GRAND NATIONAL WITH LIEUTENANT FRANK FURLONG AND IN 1936 WITH LIEUTENANT FULKE WALWYN (PICTURED WITH THE QUEEN MOTHER) – BOTH 9TH LANCERS WHO HAD RECENTLY LEFT THE REGIMENT.

3 RECRUITING POSTER FOR THE 12TH LANCERS FROM THE 1920S. THROUGHOUT THE INTER-WAR PERIOD RECRUITING WAS PARTICULARLY DIFFICULT AND AS WAR APPROACHED RESERVISTS WERE RECALLED AND PEACETIME CONSCRIPTION INTRODUCED.

1	3
2	

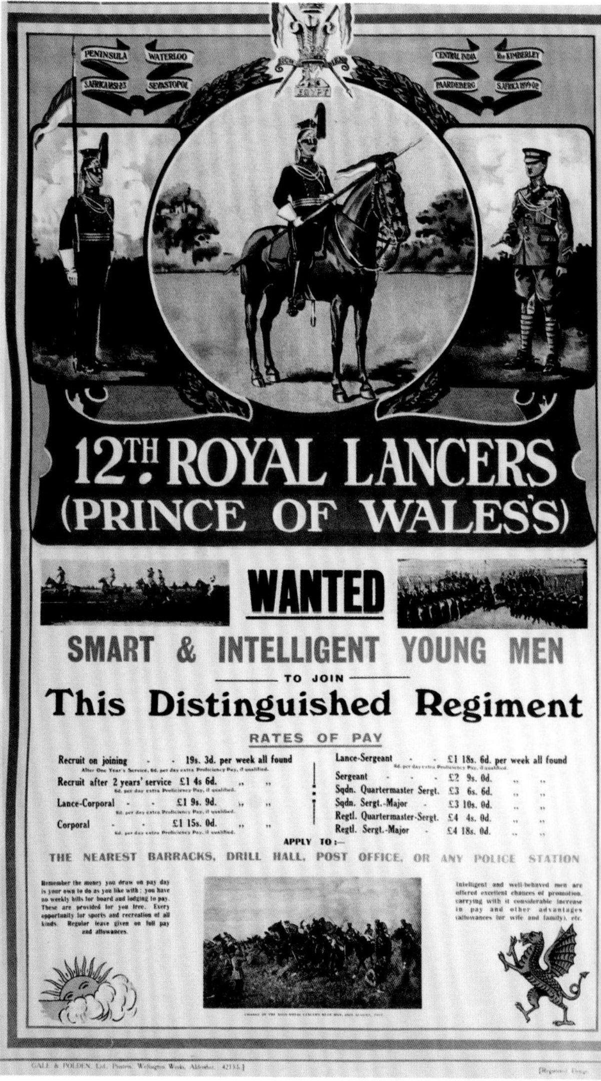

MAJOR MUNZL

In 1938 a Wermacht officer, Major Munzl, was attached to the 12th. His stay was noted in the Regimental histories of both the 9th and 12th Lancers. This *'agreeable young officer was permitted to see such training as was considered good for him'*, including a bridging exercise over the River Avon that was going less than well, due to a lack of manpower and modern bridging materiel. *'The young German arrived, very smart in his grey coat, went up to the Brigadier, clicked his heels and saluted smartly. The Brigadier acknowledged his salute and handed him a programme with the words: "Good morning, old boy; here's a piece of bumpf. Damn poor show, I'm afraid; don't tell Adolf!"'* His censored letters of the next few days revealed, *'Here in Tidworth there are few troops and still less modern material, and I am permitted to see such training as goes on during the week. But on Friday afternoons all ranks disappear. Practically no one is left except myself and the orderly officer, who looks after me. I can only conclude that there is some secret training areas where they spend their weekends doing up-to-date training with the latest equipment.'*[18] Despite this he appeared to have enjoyed his stay, presenting a silver salver engraved with a swastika to the 12th Lancers Officers' Mess. It remains in use.

THE SALVER PRESENTED TO THE OFFICERS' MESS BY MAJOR MUNZL OF THE WERMACHT AFTER HIS ATTACHMENT TO THE 12TH LANCERS IN 1938.

FRANCE

1939–1940

Dyle | Defence of Arras | Arras Counter Attack | Dunkirk 1940 | Somme 1940 Withdrawal to Seine | North-West Europe 1940

THE UNLIKELY SIGHT of the Bandmaster running broke the news of the declaration of war to the Commanding Officer and Regimental Sergeant Major of the 9th Lancers as they crossed the square at Tidworth on the morning of 3rd September 1939. In the ensuing days, Poland fell while Britain and France prepared for the fight, placing their faith in a coalition operation, including the British Expeditionary Force that was intended to move rapidly to France and then Belgium, and fill the gap between the end of the Maginot Line and the coast.

The forces that would face both Regiments in the coming campaign were, by comparison, far ahead in levels of preparedness and combat experience and consisted primarily of panzer divisions closely supported by the Luftwaffe. The Allies, in contrast, consisted of a French Army of varying quality and equipment organised in a haphazard way, while the BEF consisted of five regular divisions that had arrived in France by December 1939 and eight from the Territorial Army sent out between January and April 1940, the last three being so poorly equipped that they could only be counted as 'labour' formations. Within the regular British divisions, armour consisted of 'Infantry' tanks, their designation neatly capturing the pedestrian speed at which they moved in support of those on their feet.

For both Regiments, the declaration of war had been preceded by mobilisation of reservists who continued to arrive at the barracks while the main body dispersed from Tidworth to avoid the possibility of air raids. From there the 12th Lancers expected an early move to France but nearly found themselves left behind when the Morris Armoured Car with which they were equipped was recognised as obsolete. To add further injury, the Regiment was ordered not to travel but instead to hand in their vehicles and retrain for a new role in cruiser tanks. *'If it had not been so shocking this order would have been farcical, nobody but the blindest optimist believing that there would be any tanks available for months to come or that there was any point in reserving for their eventual arrival a unit which for eleven years, in Egypt, the Desert, and England had trained for an armoured car role. 'Lumsden [the Commanding Officer] judiciously procrastinated; and it was as well he did so. For without cancellation of the previous order the Regiment was ordered to move to France at a week's notice.'*[1]

Arriving in France on 16th October 1939, the 12th spent a short time providing local defence for General Headquarters (GHQ) before moving to billets near the Belgian border, where they spent the 'Phoney War' until spring of the following year. High-level planning anticipated an advance to the River Dyle east of Brussels which, while a

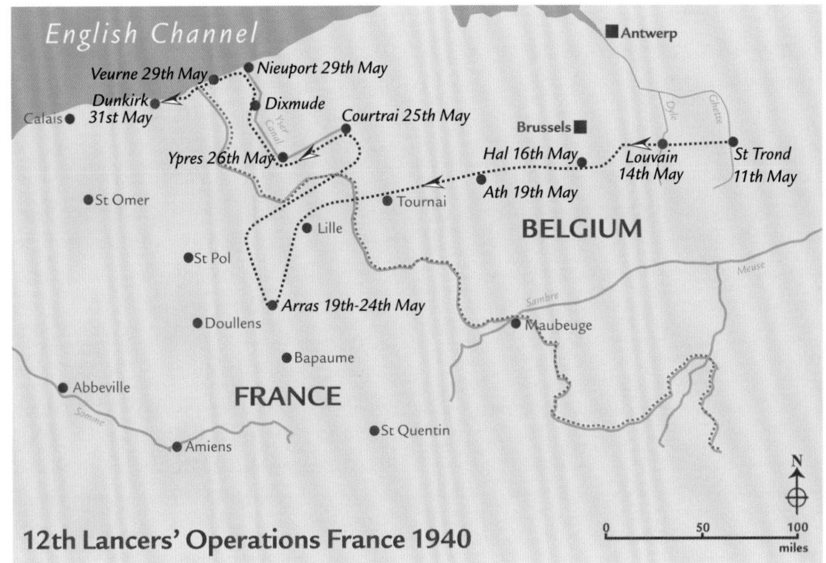

THE ROUTE OF THE 12TH LANCERS DURING OPERATIONS IN BELGIUM AND FRANCE, MAY 1940.

engl Ben: Armoured reconnaissance Car Morris **205** 21 (e)

Abk:

dtsch Ben: (wo nötig erläutern mit) **Panzerspähwagen Mo 205 (e)**

— engl Morris —

Abk: **Pz Sp Wg Mo 205 (e)**

Der Panzerspähwagen Mo 205 (e) stammt aus dem Jahre 1936 und ist für Fernaufklärung bestimmt. Der Turm ist oben offen.

Gewicht	etwa 6 t
Länge	4,76 m
Breite	2,04 m
Höhe	2,20 m
Panzerung	8—14 mm
Laufwerk	4 Räder
Aufbau	Panzerkasten und Turm Pz Blech genietet
Fahrbereich	etwa 200 km
Geschwindigkeit	„ 75 km/h
Bewaffnung	1 13,9 mm Pz Büchse 1 7,7 mm MG
Besatzung	4 Mann

1 A GERMAN RECOGNITION POSTER FOR THE MORRIS ARMOURED CAR.

2 A MORRIS ARMOURED CAR OF THE 12TH LANCERS IN VILLIERS ST SIMON, 25TH OCTOBER 1939. ARMED WITH A .303 BREN GUN AND A .50 BOYES ANTI-TANK RIFLE, THE VEHICLES WERE POORLY PROTECTED AND HAD ALREADY BEEN DECLARED OBSOLETE AT THE OUTBREAK OF THE WAR. THEY WERE NICK-NAMED THE 'SUICIDE BOX' BY THE REGIMENT.

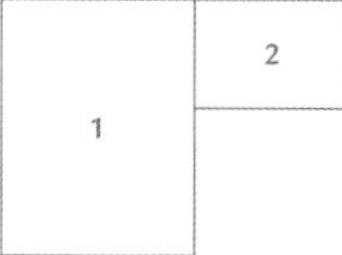

short observation line to cover, was a considerable distance to reach, a difficulty compounded by the Belgians who had not declared war and would not allow Allied reconnaissance across their frontier. The 12th were to act as the BEF's reconnaissance force and report to GHQ directly, while behind them the two corps would be provided with a further screen provided by the divisional cavalry regiments equipped with tanks.

As higher-level planning proceeded, Lumsden prepared the Regiment. '*To be bored is a sign of inefficiency and incompetence*'[2], he wrote, as they trained for their role and took under command a troop from the Royal Monmouthshire Royal Engineers, who were to prove invaluable. Throughout an exceptionally cold winter, spare time was filled with football, theatre trips and visits to Moy, while exercises often seemed to coincide with racing near Paris or golf at Le Touquet. Inevitably, a sense of frustration built up, especially as there were several false alarms that rushed the Regiment to the Belgian border. Freddie Hunn, a troop sergeant at the time, recalled: '*Our training was at its peak and all ranks were longing for something to happen; war had been declared some eight months before. We had not heard a shot fired in anger, or seen an enemy plane or heard a bomb fall. We were not prepared for the sight of bodies torn apart, friends dying of terrible wounds, the scream of bombs and shells, the fire and smoke and stench of war.*'[3]

At the moment the Germans launched their offensive into France and Belgium on 10th May 1940, the 12th Lancers were without a Commanding Officer, Lumsden having departed on promotion and without his successor yet in place. Despite this hindrance, the 12th were immediately ordered forward, but had to wait until 1pm before the barrier was lifted to cross the frontier. A troop leader, Lieutenant Bruce Shand, recalled that in the rather surreal situation of the moment he sat in a little garden while another officer '*produced a bottle of Moet & Chandon. With this and some bread and ham we made an excellent luncheon, while indulging in rather fantastic speculation about the future.*'[4] The Regiment crossed the border at the appointed hour with Corporal Sims sounding the 'Charge' on his trumpet as each troop passed, to find itself in Belgium where, 2nd Lieutenant Bishop remembered, it was '*feted all the way as "les saveurs".' It was "'ullo Tommy!" "Vive L'Angleterre!" and waving Union Jacks. When we had to slow down to pass through a town, the inhabitants swarmed onto the cars to push sprigs of lilac down the gun barrels.*'[5] Despite these distractions and more serious delays caused by the soon-to-be too familiar bombing and refugees, the 12th reached their positions 30 miles east of Brussels that evening. Here they were joined shortly before midnight by Lumsden, who had heard of the German attack in London that morning and flown straight back to France.

Communications with GHQ were now in place, with pigeons providing the back up and the following day, having handed over the bridges on the Dyle to the divisional cavalry regiments, the 12th moved further east to cover the rivers Ghette and Demer and take up positions that were as far to the east as any British troops would get for the next four years. Under heavy air attack, which took increasing toll of the refugees who thronged the roads, their progress not made any easier by the Flemish signposts that seemed to contradict their maps, which had the names in French. To their front lay the Belgian army, which it was intended would fight a withdrawal from the border to come in on the British left, while the French lay to the Regiment's right. Although contact had been made with the latter, faith in the former was already beginning to evaporate, Bruce Shand recalling that '*halfway to St Trond it became apparent that large numbers of Belgian troops were drifting westwards, in not much sort of order. None of them seemed anxious to stop or give any coherent information.*'[6]

German operational success would soon to render the Allied plan of little consequence. Holland's rapid capitulation had exposed the Belgian left flank while, to the south, the '*Sichelschnitt*' (sickle-cut) of the German operational plan had successfully infiltrated Panzer divisions through the Ardennes, which would soon punch through the French positions on the Meuse and race for the Channel ports. The effect was to leave the Allied armies fixed in Belgium and facing a double envelopment. The British had to turn to secure a shrinking pocket around the Channel ports and then to extricate themselves from it.

From their forward locations, the 12th began to engage the Germans along a series of river lines as they moved back from one position to another. Facing enemy recce patrols largely consisting of motor cycles and side cars, German horse cavalry was also engaged in the early stages, Sergeant Hunn recalling that '*a patrol of cavalry was encountered and destroyed. A beautiful black horse came into the possession of the Squadron. There was considerable discussion over the radio as to how the animal could be transported back for use in the Regimental Stables at the end of hostilities… at this stage of the war the full seriousness of the situation had not been grasped … shortly after this a troop saw a person uniform of a blue jacket and brightly coloured hat riding a bicycle down the road. The gunner got him in his sights and knocked him off the cycle. Unfortunately it turned out to be a Belgian postman.*'[7]

The rivers, although an obstacle to movement for the tanks of the day, were, by and large, little more than ditches while the Morris's and anti-tank rifles were not cut out for this sort of operation. Defences on the river-lines were strengthened by the engineers blowing bridges and by encouraging

HERBERT LUMSDEN

Herbert Lumsden was commissioned into the Royal Horse Artillery in the First World War where he won an MC, transferring to the 12th Lancers in 1925 before commanding the Regiment from 1938–1940. For his service in France while commanding the 12th he was awarded a DSO, his actions described as '*a classic example of how an armoured car should be handled*'.[24] In August 1941 he took command of 1st Armoured Division and took it to North Africa, winning a bar to his DSO during the Knightsbridge battles. The following year he took command of XXX Corps and then X Corps during El Alamein. Never one of Monty's men, who criticised him for not pursuing the Afrika Korps hard enough, he was posted back to the United Kingdom in January 1943. He was asked by John Robson, a potential officer who wished to join the 12th Lancers and was having lunch with him in the Cavalry Club, why he had left the Eighth Army. Lumsden's immediate reply was, '*you may think the Desert is a huge place but there wasn't room for two shits in it and, as I was junior, I had to go*'.[25] Thereafter Churchill appointed him as his Military Representative to General MacArthur in the Far East where he was killed in a kamikaze attack on the USS *New Mexico* in January 1945.

Described as ambitious, but blessed with humour and humanity, he was, even at 6ft tall, an outstanding jockey, riding several times in the Grand National and winning the Grand Military Gold Cup in 1926 on his own horse, Foxtrot. Bruce Shand, one of his troop leaders in France, recalled that he was '*a model of military leadership and clear thinking, giving enormous confidence to his overstretched Regiment. We were all to suffer from the lack of sleep but he seemed to survive on virtually none… One never saw him other than calm and unworried and immaculately dressed – a great inspiration.*'[26]

1 THE COMMANDING OFFICER AND ADJUTANT (LIEUTENANT COLONEL CHM PETO, IN THE TANK, AND CAPTAIN KJ PRICE)

2 THE SAME TANK LATER IN THE DAY

3 CROSSING THE PONT D L'ARCHE OVER THE RIVER SEINE ON 8TH JUNE 1940. THE FRENCH SENTRY IS GUARDING THE DEMOLITION CHARGE

the Belgians to do the same, though the impression given by the latter was that they were already a defeated army. Forced to conform to their Allies' movement on the flanks, on 14th May the 12th broke clean across the River Dyle as pressure on the bridges threatened to cut them off. Not for the last time in the campaign would the value of liaison officers be proved. They ensured that accurate information was give on the location of British forces. They also formed a local defence and counter-desant force for Lord Gort's headquarters to the west of Brussels, where rumours of Nazi sympathisers were rife. The day was spent in some degree of relaxation, vehicles were repaired, reinforcements integrated and sleep was taken, only two or three hours' worth having been had in the last 96, 2nd Lieutenant Bishop recalling that *'some of us were beginning to say things backwards and I found that people's outlines seemed to have white edges and misty haloes.'*[8]

French forces to the south had by now begun to fall back in the face of the German breakout across the Meuse, leaving the right flank of the BEF dangerously exposed. Placed under command of the 48th Division, and with the 4th Gloucesters (who were too tired to help initially), some infantry tanks and anti-tank guns under command, on 16th May the 12th formed a screen from just south of Brussels to the site of the Battle of Waterloo before turning west along the River Haine to Clabecq to assist in a delaying operation that would allow the BEF to move back to the River Escaut.

The Regiment remained in position throughout the day and night, with C Squadron imitating a larger force by continuously driving up and down their sector and the entire line subjected to increasing pressure from both the air and artillery bombardment line until, the following morning, they were withdrawn to regroup. It proved to be a short respite and later that day the Regiment moved forward to cover the approaches to Enghien to once again fight a series of engagements with infantry, motorcycles and dive bombers, though primarily against tanks, the only defence against which was movement. As the withdrawal continued, the 12th were ordered to cover 2nd Division's movement across the River Dendre, though by now the battle picture was utterly confused and the Regiment exhausted. Reduced to only three troops in each squadron, patrols were in constant use, checking that bridges were blown, barges sunk and locks covered by fire, while all around them the evidence of a retreat in full swing was visible. Despite this, assisted by artillery to disrupt enemy reconnaissance, sufficient time was bought for the Division to withdraw before a full-scale attack could be organised by the enemy, the 12th Lancers following them through Tournai before moving to the south-east of Lille.

Sleep on 19th May was broken by further orders from GHQ at 11pm. The German drive to the sea had broken through on the boundary between the French left flank and the British right, forcing the latter to bend back sharply to the west along the line of the River Scarpe from Arras north-west towards Douai.

There was little more information on the enemy and in particular on the German tank columns which were now making their way for the Channel. The 12th were therefore ordered to reconnoitre the box formed by the towns of Arras, Bapaume, Amiens and Doullens, with their main effort being the roads emanating from Arras. These were classic and familiar recce orders, but within minutes of setting off south from the line of the River Scarpe they ran into difficulties, with all of the squadrons meeting tank columns and coming under air attack, while streams of refugees blocked all the roads in the area, St Pol apparently '*impassable and resembled Tattenham corner on Derby Day*'.[9] With engagements occurring all day, by the evening the 12th had been forced back to the line of the Arras–St Pol road.

JOHN CLARK-KENNEDY'S ARMOURED CAR KNOCKED OUT BETWEEN ARRAS AND ST POL AFTER THE ACTION FOR WHICH HE WAS AWARDED THE MC IN MAY 1940.

ARRAS COUNTER-ATTACK

Encirclement of the BEF was by now a real possibility and an Allied decision was made to attempt to break through the thinly held walls of the Panzer corridor by a co-ordinated attack by the BEF from the north, who would link up with French and newly arriving British forces, principally 1st Armoured Division which (including the 9th Lancers), to the south. While the plan looked fine on paper the situation on the ground by now rendered it impossible, with neither element powerful enough for the task asked of it. In the north all that could be found were two tank battalions, supported by infantry with the 12th Lancers as flank protection, leading Bruce Shand to view his position with some trepidation: '*our role was suspiciously vague and amounted in fact to that of a suicide squad.*'[10]

Opposition to the Arras counter-attack on 21st May began from its outset and, despite advancing several miles with almost continuous engagements in which a battery of 5.9in guns were destroyed and some prisoners (an unwelcome burden) were taken, by evening the 12th were north of their original start line on the Arras–St. Pol road while elsewhere the tank battalions had also been stopped. The counter-attack had achieved only limited tactical success and certainly not cut the panzer corridor but the effect at the operational and strategic level was immense. General Rommel, who had personally stepped in to supervise its repulse, estimated that five divisions had attacked him, while Hitler ordered a temporary halt to the panzers' advance until infantry could be brought up to consolidate the corridor. The delay was to prove vital for the now inevitable evacuation of the Allies.

Arras was now in a salient and the 12th spent the next two days assisting in its defence by screening the north-west flank. A Squadron patrols further west confirmed the progress of the enemy near St Omer, which added to the threat that the BEF would be cut off from the sea. The remains of the squadron came close to annihilation when engaged by German infantry and armour, against which the Boyes anti-tank rifle was likened to '*a little girl trying to hurt a heavyweight boxer*'.[11] By now, the decision to evacuate the BEF from Dunkirk had been taken and the Regiment was withdrawn from the line with A Squadron reduced to five cars, B able to produce only two patrols and C Squadron three.

> The remains of the squadron came close to annihilation when engaged by German infantry and armour…

Rest was short lived and the Regiment redeployed almost immediately to the northern flank of the rapidly shrinking Allied perimeter around the Channel ports where, on 25th May, they began reconnaissance to Courtrai to confirm the presence of an enemy bridgehead on the flank of II Corps and to report on any gaps between it and the Belgian Army to its left. While the town was secure, the enemy were found north of the Courtrai to Menin road, where they had already crossed the canal and were increasing their numbers. Contact was also made with the Belgians on the left flank, but the outlook was not good. Major Horsburgh-Porter reported on a visit to the Belgian III Corps Headquarters that it was '*quite out of touch with the realities of the situation and was planning grandiose operations with non-existent troops; that it was unwilling to co-operate; and that it was in any case only offering a token resistance*'.[12] By nightfall, the Regiment had been forced west of the

THE DESTRUCTION OF THE BRIDGES ALONG THE YSER CANAL BY THE 12TH LANCERS AND THEIR ATTACHED SECTION OF ROYAL ENGINEERS SECURED THE LEFT FLANK OF THE BEF AND PREVENTED IT BEING CUT OFF FROM THE SEA FOLLOWING BELGIUM'S SURRENDER. 2ND LIEUTENANT NED MANN WAS AWARDED A DSO FOR HIS ACTIONS AT DIXMUDE WHICH HELD UP A GERMAN COLUMN OF OVER 250 VEHICLES FOR SEVEN HOURS.

Yser canal at Neuve Eglise, troop-level engagements failing to deal with the scale of opposition and resulting in mounting casualties throughout the day.

Evacuation from Dunkirk began in earnest on 26th May and efforts now switched to holding the perimeter long enough for the BEF to escape. The ground, dissected by canals and rivers, would assist but only if the perimeter remained intact at all points and the bridges over them could be destroyed or held, neither of which was a certainty. Adopting a position to the east of the Ypres–Comines canal, the 12th again found themselves pushed back, though not before the discovery that Ypres was held by a garrison of about 20 Belgian engineers and that the local bridges were intact, with the enemy nearby. B Squadron, with a few tanks of the 13th/18th Hussars and some anti-tank guns under command, were ordered to garrison the town and complete the demolitions, one car taking up position under the Menin Gate, while A Squadron moved to the north to make contact with the Belgians in the area.

The flank held by the Belgians between Ypres and the coast now became the most pressing concern. Reconnaissance to the north of Ypres revealed that the Belgians were withdrawing north rather than west and were thereby leaving a gap into which the Germans could now drive unopposed to get between the BEF and the sea. To fill it General Montgomery's 3rd Division was ordered into the line but until they could get there the 12th were to cover the gap using the Veunes canal as an obstacle. Lumsden, fully aware of the state of Belgian morale (they would surrender the same day) and their movement to the north, elected to adopt a position further forward than ordered, putting his line on the more easterly Yser Canal which, with fewer bridges to defend, allowed every crossing to the coast at Nieuport to be observed and bought time for the Veunes canal behind to be prepared for defence. As the Regiment took up its positions to defend the bridges Lieutenant Smith and his troop of engineers systematically worked northwards, blowing the bridges as they went.

The actions of the 12th in holding the line of the Yser Canal represent a model demonstration of the effect that a small force can have on well-chosen ground. One incident involved 2nd Lieutenant Mann's troop, which was guarding the bridge at Dixmude. He was joined by Lieutenant Smith, who had demolished all the bridges as far north as Dixmude. Before Smith could set off the charges left by the Belgians which, it turned out, had been tampered with, they were interrupted by someone who claimed to be a French major, saying his troops, which were following shortly, had been sent to guard the bridge. Mann moved up the road to check his story, saw no French soldiers and returned to find that the enemy agent had gone. The sappers now blew the bridge and within 10 minutes the first of the enemy forces of motorcycles and lorried infantry arrived.

Mann engaged them immediately and, assisted by the arrival of another patrol to swell his troop to four cars, held up the enemy advance, the citation for his DSO stating that '*by his skilful disposition and bold leadership he inflicted so many casualties on the head of the enemy column that he was able, when reinforced by another troop, to contain the enemy east of the Yser canal for over seven hours, by which time more than 250 vehicles had been counted entering Dixmude, and the road Dixmude-Roulers was a solid mass of transport*'. Across the length of the line, each crossing was probed and attacked by the enemy, while 2nd Lieutenant Bishop witnessed the practical effect of Belgium's capitulation: '*Their [two companies of infantry] commanding officer came across to ask us if we knew that the war was over before joining the tail of his column with evident satisfaction. It was a memorably revolting sight.*'[13] The destruction of the bridges further south had allowed what remained of the Regiment to concentrate on the defence of the many routes through Nieuport, which had by now become the focus for much of the enemy's attention.

Finally replaced by *ad hoc* forces, the 12th were ordered back inside the Dunkirk perimeter where they assembled south of Veunes on 29th May, having battled through the abandoned debris of the withdrawing army. Here they destroyed their surplus vehicles before marching towards the coast where at 4am on the following day the order was given to destroy all the remaining armoured cars. Sergeant Hunn recalled: '*we set about this task with heavy hearts. Each vehicle was drained of oil and water, the engines raced at full power until they exploded. The radio was dismantled and smashed completely with sledge-hammers. Guns and ammunition were set aside; these would be carried back to England. Tyres and wheels were made unserviceable, then, when all possible damage had been done, camouflage nets were soaked in petrol and oil, placed in the turrets and set alight. The vehicles were then pushed into the canal near Nieuport.*'[14]

Marched to the beach at La Panne at 11am, the men were ordered back to England though, like so many others, this order was soon countermanded. The 12th were now to help organise the evacuation and, by 1pm, three embarkation points, constructed of boats or of lorries driven into the sea, were ready with the troops mustered and the ships, which were to arrive at dusk, inbound. With all hands manning whatever craft could be found, the Regiment ferried men out to the waiting ships, 2nd Lieutenant Bishop recalling that, having delivered his cargo on his second trip to a destroyer he asked if a sailor or two could be spared to help: '*I was politely but reprovingly told: 'The ship's officers are at dinner, sir.' I thought that an admirably British reply… as we rowed an erratic course back to the khaki queues ashore, I hoped that the officers' port choked them.*'[15] Throughout the night the evacuation continued with up to 3,000 men moving off each hour, the pace only slackening as dawn came and the wind picked to make the use of collapsible boats all but impossible.

Although they had been told to embark themselves at 9am on 31st May, by 4pm the Regiment was still assisting others when their

1 THE FEW REMAINING ARMOURED CARS OF THE 12TH WERE FINALLY DESTROYED WHEN THE REGIMENT REACHED THE DUNKIRK PERIMETER. WEAPONS AND AMMUNITION WERE REMOVED BEFORE THE ENGINES WERE RUN AT FULL POWER WITH NO OIL OR WATER, THE RADIOS SMASHED AND THE VEHICLES SET ON FIRE AND PUSHED INTO DITCHES.

2 SERGEANT FREDDIE HUNN AT DUNKIRK. FREDDIE HUNN FOUGHT THROUGHOUT THE WAR WITH THE 12TH LANCERS AND WAS COMMISSIONED IN 1945 TO RETIRE 20 YEARS LATER AS A MAJOR. IN 2009 HE ACCOMPANIED THE COLONEL-IN-CHIEF TO THE EL ALAMEIN MEMORIAL SERVICE ON THE EVE OF HIS 90TH BIRTHDAY.

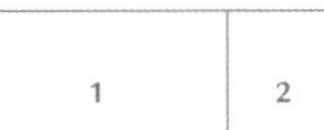

LORD GORT, COMMANDING THE BEF, WROTE THAT '*WITHOUT THE 12TH LANCERS THE BULK OF THE BRITISH EXPEDITIONARY FORCE WOULD NEVER HAVE ESCAPED FROM THE CONTINENT OF EUROPE*'. FORMAL RECOGNITION OF THEIR WORK CAME IN THE AWARDS RECEIVED BY THE REGIMENT.

orders to embark finally came. In a final twist however, the sea at La Panne was now too rough and the shellfire around the diminishing perimeter too close to permit evacuation there. They therefore marched, under bombing and shell-fire, eight miles to Malo les Bains near Dunkirk where they began embarkation at 9pm. Major Browne-Clayton, commanding B Squadron, remembered that they were by now '*rather a motley collection in what we were dressed in and what we carried*'[16] but they none the less retained all their weapons and collected more, including 30 Lewis guns abandoned by others on the march. Lumsden even ordered a man who had abandoned his Bren on the march to the beach to go back and get it, the soldier reappearing with the weapon four hours later.

There are a number of stories of the last moments in France, though that of Henry de la

DAILY SKETCH, FRIDAY, JUNE 14, 1940.—Page

Lieut.-Col. Herbert Lumsden, D.S.O.
Commanded the 12th Lancers with vigour, initiative, coolness and boldness. His regiment operated continuously and untiringly on the front and flanks.

Capt. Horsbrugh-Porter, D.S.O.
Although wounded, he continued in command when his services were indispensable. But for his action the enemy would have had a clear road to Hazebrouck.

Second-Lieut. Edward Charles Mann, D.S.O.
Demolished bridges over Yser Canal in spite of disguised enemy agents, and was able, when reinforced by another troop, to hold the road for seven hours. He is 22.

Second - Lieut. A. J. Clark-Kennedy, M.C.
By bold manœuvring of his troops inflicted heavy casualties. When his leading car was hit he silenced the enemy's fire and ensured the rescue of the crew.

Lieut. B. M. Hope Shand, M.C.
Repeatedly acquired valuable information on patrol. By fearless manœuvring of his troop covered the withdrawal of a column of our lorries and guns in face of fire.

THEY HELD THE ROAD TO DUNKIRK BEACH FOR THEIR COMRADES OF THE B.E.F.

Badge of the 12th Lancers. They are known as the "Supple Twelfth."

Of the thirty-one awards made by Lord Gort twelve went to the 12th Lancers for their gallantry in helping the B.E.F. to reach Dunkirk.

Here are hitherto unpublished pictures of eight of these heroes of the greate[…] rear-guard […] history.

R.Q.M.S. William S. James, D.C.M.
It was due to his excellent common sense, personal disregard for bombing and exceptional [..]forts that the regiment [...]ed ammuni-[...]

Sergt. Arthur Max Pearton, D.C.M.
The armoured car in front of him was stopped by fire and overturned. Although his gunner was killed beside him, he silenced enemy fire.

Sergt. James E. Watson, D.C.M.
Was always in the leading car of his troop, which inflicted heavy casualties. He showed the finest leadership and courage during all the actions in which his troop took part.

Falaise, a veteran of the First World War who acted as A Squadron's Liaison Officer and who was married first to Gloria Swanson and then Constance Bennett, shows typical Gallic flair. As he waded into the water, 2nd Lieutenant Bishop *'noticed a bundle on his head, some belongings wrapped in a gas cape. 'My divorce papers!' he explained with a laugh.'*[17] Climbing first into small boats that could get close to the beach, the Regiment transferred onto dredgers from Tilbury to carry them across the Channel to Margate, where they arrived the next day. They had been in action almost continuously for 21 days and covered a withdrawal of 250 miles from the opening shots of the German offensive, their contribution recognised by Lord Gort, the Commander of the BEF, who wrote in his despatches: *'Without the 12th Lancers, my reconnaissance regiment, the bulk of the British Expeditionary Force would never have escaped from the continent of Europe.'*[18]

The 9th Lancers' experiences of the opening campaigns of the Second World War were even more chaotic than the 12th's. At its outbreak, the 1st Armoured Division was still incomplete and therefore would not be deployed with the BEF, while at a regimental level it was felt that the reservists arrived, most of whom came from the days prior to mechanization, would have insufficient time to be trained on tanks. As a result only 50 could be retained, while the 9th were also forced to transfer large numbers of officers and men to the RAC depot at Catterick and the new 53rd Training Regiment in Tidworth to cope with the expanding numbers in the army.

Those left in the Regiment spent the first months of the war guarding the East Coast while based at Clare in Suffolk, before rejoining the 1st Armoured Division in Wimborne in Dorset in the winter of 1939. The establishment of the Division had continued to evolve, the arrival of cruiser tanks apparently rendering artillery support unnecessary at brigade level while, in April 1940 Brigadier McCreery (who had commanded the 12th Lancers in Tidworth from 1936–1938) took over the 2nd Armoured Brigade with the 9th Lancers in it. Early expectations were that the Division would go to Normandy in May to complete training, where it was promised that more new tanks would be delivered to add to the few that had already arrived.

The period of routine training that the Regiment was engaged in was broken on 6th May 1940 by orders putting them on 10 days' notice to move. Various Marks of cruiser tanks appeared in dribs and drabs, many of them in bad condition and of types unfamiliar to their crews who, it was supposed, would conduct training on them in France. With more still arriving but still with peacetime accounting measures in place, vehicles and drivers moved by road to Southampton on 17th May, seven days after the Blitzkrieg had begun in France. The remainder of the Regiment followed by rail on the 20th, one squadron leader driving to the port in his car laden with newly arrived machine guns and other indispensable parts for the tanks.

1 A9 ARMED WITH A 3.7IN HOWITZER AS A CLOSE SUPPORT TANK WERE GIVEN TO SQUADRON HEADQUARTERS.

2 A1 AND A9 TANKS OF THE 9TH LANCERS. WITH NO TANKS AT THE OUTSET OF THE WAR THE 1ST ARMOURED DIVISION WAS HURRIEDLY DESPATCHED TO FRANCE IN MAY 1940. EQUIPPED WITH A VARIETY OF UNFAMILIAR TANKS ON WHICH THEY WERE EXPECTED TO TRAIN IN FRANCE, IT WAS DISCOVERED THAT SOME HAD NO WEAPONS OR THE RIGHT SORT OF AMMUNITION WHILE ONE LIGHT TANK HAD A PLYWOOD TURRET.

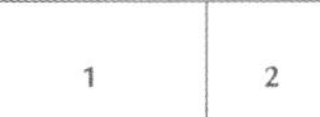

1 AN A10 OR CRUISER MARK 2 ARMED WITH A 2POUNDER GUN.

2 ROUTE OF THE 9TH LANCERS DURING OPERATIONS IN FRANCE, MAY–JUNE 1940.

Ahead of the main body, billeting parties had already arrived in Arras on 15th May to discover it full of refugees carrying news that the Germans were across the Meuse at Sedan. Despite the less than encouraging news, the 1st Armoured Division (in reality only 2nd Armoured Brigade – the 1st never crossed and the 3rd arrived later) arrived in France, the 9th landing at Cherbourg on the morning of 21st May where they dispersed to the outskirts, prepared their equipment and then left to join the advance party. Even now the Regiment was still far from ready in terms of equipment. A Squadron possessed tanks for only two of its four troops while its Squadron second-in-command, Captain Scott, although equipped with a new Cruiser Mark 1 with a 3.7in howitzer, had no ammunition. To make matters worse, his machine gun had no sight, though this hardly mattered as the armour had no hole for it anyway. Another new light tank came with a plywood turret.

The slow build up of the Divison, the deteriorating situation in France and the failure of the Arras counter-attack had, by 23rd May, made the original intention of joining the BEF impossible – especially if it involved a fight to get there. Isolated from GHQ a new scheme was devised to defend along the line of the Rivers Somme and Aisne to the (still intact) Maginot Line and prevent the Germans heading south. The line would be defended by 60 French divisions of mixed capability, of which only three were armoured, while two British divisions, the 1st Armoured and the 51st Highland, which were by now cut off from the rest of the BEF, completed the order of battle.

An accurate account of the actions of the 9th over the next month is difficult to reproduce and even their excellent Regimental history of the War, written by those on the scene at the time, concedes: '*the narrative which follows can only give an incoherent account of the part played by the 9th Lancers in the confusing events of the last few weeks of the Battle of France. It is difficult enough to follow the despatches of those in command; to give a clear picture of the actions of a regiment is well-nigh impossible.'*[19]

Ordered to defend the line of the Somme just to the west of Amiens, the 9th Lancers were to support the Bays and then be prepared to seize a crossing over the river – which the enemy by now had reached and, in places, crossed – with co-ordinating instructions that '*frequencies and code names as for the last brigade exercise in Wimborne*', which fortunately someone still had. Passing retreating elements of the French Ninth Army, the Regiment moved north to the area of Foret d'Ailly near Amiens as the enemy began to create bridgeheads south of the Somme. Troop-level contacts now began to occur and, in the confused fighting in the woods and on the outskirts of Amiens, several tanks were shot up as the Regiment suffered its first casualties and lost others as prisoners. That night they withdrew from the wood; it was by now partially in enemy hands and could not be held by the Brigade, which comprised exclusively of tanks.

Attempts to shore up the line of the Somme by supporting the French to their west occupied the 9th for the next two days and included a night march of 30 miles to the Abbeville area in order to support a planned French move to clear the south bank of the Somme prior to an attack north. Sadly, the French were clearly unaware of the weakness of 1st Armoured Division which still only

AN A13 OR CRUISER MARK 3 OF THE 9TH LANCERS IN FRANCE UNDERGOING REPAIRS FOLLOWING A GERMAN BOMBING RAID DURING THE RETREAT FROM THE SOMME DURING LATE MAY AND EARLY JUNE 1940.

BEFORE THE ONSLAUGHT: SERGEANT EDWARDS MM AND BAR ON HIS COVENANTER DURING PRE-DEPLOYMENT TRAINING.

consisted of the 2nd Armoured Brigade (the 3rd was still detraining and no supporting artillery of other equipment was present). Lieutenant Colonel CHM Peto described the whole plan as *'a "projet," an academic scheme which bore little relation to such practical details as lack of troops, guns and essential equipment'.*[20] A further attack north against the Abbeville bridgehead was launched on 27th May to relieve pressure on the BEF to the north, in which the 2nd Armoured Brigade, supported by French infantry and artillery, were ordered to capture an escarpment overlooking the Somme through heavily held German positions. With the supporting artillery delayed and then cancelled, the attack resulted in heavy losses for the two leading regiments, the Bays and 10th Hussars, leaving the 9th Lancers to adopt defensive positions while the others refitted, before acting as reserve to further, more successful, French attacks led by General de Gaulle over the next two days.

With the supporting artillery delayed and then cancelled, the attack resulted in heavy losses for the two leading regiments…

The Division had by now lost 120 tanks, while the remainder, particularly the newly arrived 3rd Armoured Brigade, was still missing equipment and already in need of reconstitution. British forces were increased by the arrival, on 30th May, of the 51st (Highland) Division, which had been on the Maginot line when the Germans invaded the Low Countries. Their combat power was increased when they were given a composite armoured regiment of RHQ, A and C Squadrons of the 9th Lancers, together with the B Squadrons of the Bays and 10th Hussars, the whole Regiment (the only 'runners' left in the Brigade) immediately becoming the Divisional mobile reserve based at St Léger aux Bois. The Dunkirk evacuation was by now nearing completion and the two divisions together with some lightly equipped logistic troops were the only remaining British forces in France. Together with the French, they were expected to hold the line of the Somme as the Germans now turned their full attention on them.

Attacking south-west of Abbeville on 5th June, the Germans met the Composite Regiment and the hard-pressed infantry brigades of 51st Division who defended along the River Bresle in the area of the Foret d'Eu. In a series of actions, the enemy were prevented from out-flanking the Division between the sea and the forest though anti-tank guns and infantry continued to wear down the Regiment including, in one engagement on the morning of 6th June, the loss of Lieutenant Colonel Peto when he led a troop attack by Regimental Headquarters in which a German officer and 43 men were captured. In the action, unable to depress his gun sufficiently to engage the German infantry at close quarters, Peto was severely wounded in the hand while firing his pistol from the turret, command passing to the Second-in-Command, Major JR Macdonell, who would lead the 9th for the next two years.

German pressure continued to build and, on 7th June, the 9th were ordered south-west to block the road down the coast from Eu in order to secure the Divisional left flank though, having only just taken up position, news arrived that German armoured columns had broken through the French lines near Amiens and were moving south-west towards Rouen. The Regiment was immediately moved east to Fresnoy to protect the Divisional right flank as patrols that evening confirmed the threat, before new orders were given that the Composite Regiment would revert to 1st Armoured Division. The Composite Regiment was to support 3rd Armoured Brigade in blocking the German thrust in their sector while a line from Dieppe to Fleury was prepared for defence. Moving rapidly and under air attack throughout, the Composite Regiment moved from Fresnoy to Les Hogues, north-west of Rouen, more detailed orders arriving in the chaos of a wider withdrawal to block the Germans between Pierreval and Critot, a position taken up at 4pm on 8th June. Refugees streamed past before the German armour ('snarlers' as the heavy tanks were called) appeared and began to be heavily engaged. In the fight one cruiser tank fired 42 rounds of 2-pounder in a long-running engagement that destroyed several of the enemy but left the Composite Regiment severely mauled. Second Lieutenant Steel described the end result: *'Thus the one and only tank in the squadron with a gun worth firing was now in a rather sorry state'.*[21] The Regiment withdrew south of the Seine that evening, to regroup north of Louviers, now seriously short of fuel.

The whole of the 1st Armoured Division was south of the Seine by the following morning, with 51st Division cut off on the coast with evacuation by sea their only (and unrealised) hope. Only a few, worn-out, tanks could be mustered across the Division (A Squadron was by now down to a single troop) and these lacked combined arms support, while there were few effective French troops in the area and no reserves. In such a situation, and despite the hope that the Seine might prove an effective obstacle, the only prospect was a long withdrawal, with the imperative to concentrate the working tanks to try to support the French where possible, while back-loading the remainder to the rear area for repair. German pressure continued to build as they crossed the Seine and then the Eure, bypassing Regimental positions among the forests of the area and threatening to cut them off despite several engagements until finally, on the evening of 10th June, withdrawal across the Eure was ordered, the exercise being made more difficult by fading light and the thick pall of smoke from the burning oil depot at Rouen.

At midnight an order came for all tanks, except 'strong runners' to withdraw to Le Mans to refit. The Composite Regiment folded and left only RHQ and one troop from each of B and C Squadrons to act, with a squadron of the Bays and Brigade Headquarters, as the rearguard for the Brigade withdrawal with orders to block the route to the south-west along which refugees were streaming. With little capacity to stop the German advance, the rearguard of 2nd Armoured Brigade was withdrawn from the line on the morning of 12th June, rejoining the remainder at Le Mans where the Regiment was able to rest and conduct maintenance, even being joined by reinforcements at this late stage.

Despite the apparent calm, the battle for France was over. At 1am of 15th June, orders ('code word "Blighty" ') were received for an immediate evacuation, the B vehicles and marching party leaving at 3.15am while the few remaining tanks were loaded for Cherbourg, the last that was seen of them as the train fell into enemy hands. While a small detachment in three armoured cars covered the evacuation and, having averaged 300 miles a

FOLLOWING THE LOSS OF ALL THEIR VEHICLES IN FRANCE, THE 12TH LANCERS WERE ISSUED WITH BEAVERETTE ARMOURED CARS WHEN ON INVASION WATCH IN SUFFOLK IN JULY 1940. CREWS (AT THE BACK OF THE PHOTOGRAPH) MAY APPEAR TO BE DELIGHTED WITH THEIR NEW EQUIPMENT BUT THE BEAVERETTE DID NOT INSPIRE CONFIDENCE - STEEL PLATES AUGMENTED BY WOOD PLANKING WERE BOLTED ONTO A STANDARD 12HP CHASSIS WITH MOLOTOV COCKTAILS AUGMENTING THE BREN GUN AS ARMAMENT.

BY THE MIDDLE OF 1941 BOTH REGIMENTS HAD BEGUN TO RECEIVE NEW EQUIPMENT, THE 9TH TAKING DELIVERY OF VARIOUS MODELS OF CRUISER TANKS AND AMERICAN M3 HONEYS OR STUARTS WHILE THE 12TH WERE RE-EQUIPPED WITH HUMBER ARMOURED CARS.

day, finally embarked from St Nazaire on 17th June, for the main body progress to Brest in the chaos of evacuation was slower. Only late on the night of 15th June was the Regiment embarked on the *Lady of Man* carrying weapons, equipment and ammunition, though it was not until 4.30pm of the following day that the ship sailed with over 2,000 men on board but only half that number of lifejackets.

Dunkirk may have been described by Churchill as a 'miracle of deliverance' but the danger was by no means past. Having arrived in Plymouth at dawn on 17th June (the day that France surrendered) and travelled to Warminster by train, to the cheers of crowds along the line, the 9th, like the 12th, were more than aware of the threat. Fear of an imminent invasion prevented either Regiment resting on their return *'to an England which was not the England we had left. It was an England standing alone in the front line'.*[22]

As the task of re-equipping the army began, the 12th Lancers, with 2nd Battalion the Middlesex Regiment under command, assumed responsibility for the defence of the Poole sub-area, before moving to Suffolk in July 1940 under the command of Lieutenant Colonel GB Clifton-Brown. Equipped with armoured cars in the purest sense of the word, the Beaverettes they manned were based on a Standard 12hp car chassis with steel plates bolted on and 2in of oak planking in vulnerable areas, their armament coming from a pintle-mounted Bren gun. To boost their firepower, Molotov cocktails were prepared and carried on each vehicle. The 9th had even less. Moving into a partially completed camp near Warminster, they

conducted basic training using salvaged weaponry from the ship home (A Squadron had collected 36 Brens to bolster the five on their establishment) while they awaited fresh equipment.

By the winter of 1940 and with the threat of immediate invasion over, both Regiments were able to concentrate on building up their strength through re-equipping, manning and training. Changes of locations took place, new recruits arrived and experienced soldiers were lost to form the nucleus for two new regiments that were being formed as a result of the rapid expansion of the Army. The 9th (with the 17th/21st Lancers) provided eight officers and 69 soldiers for the 24th Lancers, while the 12th found seven officers and 120 soldiers for the 27th Lancers. Equipment finally arrived, the 9th fielding a mixture of various models of cruiser and light tanks, with American M3 Honey or Stuart tanks appearing later on, while the 12th received Humber armoured cars in June 1941 which, although underpowered, were a considerable improvement on the Beaverette, the turret mounting a 0.5in gun, a .303 Besa machine gun and a pintle-mounted Bren.

The same month both regiments moved back to Tidworth. The 9th, still with 2nd Armoured Brigade, rejoined 1st Armoured Division where, in early August the new commander, Major General Lumsden, informed them that they would be going overseas in mid-September, the received wisdom being that Egypt was the destination. Similar news was broken to the 12th and for both Regiments the next few weeks were taken up by medicals, final training and the despatch of vehicles, before the 9th left Clydeside on 28th September and the 12th, with Lieutenant Colonel EO Burne in command, followed from Avonmouth two days later, both joining a huge convoy that would transport the 1st Armoured Division to Egypt. For once, sea travel and the 9th did not end in some sort of disaster, the people of South Africa showing generous hospitality en route, while Sergeant Hunn of the 12th Lancers, with admirable understatement, even reckoned that, *'apart from the blackout, the lurking danger of enemy submarines, the lack of female company, it could have been a wonderful cruise'*.[23]

CAP BADGES OR OTHER OF 24TH AND 27TH LANCERS.

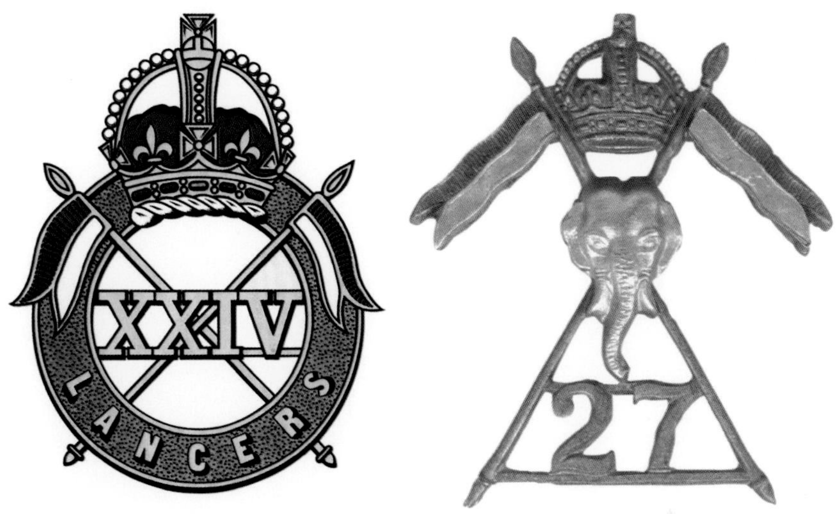

LANCERS IN MADAGSCAR 1942

In July 1941, the 2nd Armoured Brigade was ordered to form a composite squadron for which two troops of Mark VII light tanks from the 9th were required. The squadron, now designated 'C Special Service Squadron', departed for Scotland in August and immediately started training for combined arms amphibious operations, though with no clear idea of where it would be going. In March 1942 the two 9th Lancer troops were sent to B Special Service Squadron and sailed immediately for Durban in South Africa where orders were received that, as part of 29th Independent Brigade consisting of No 5 Commando and supporting arms, it would land at Courier Bay on the northern corner of Madagascar and seize the important Vichy French port of Diego Suarez and the town of Antisarane.

Despite the paucity of intelligence, the force made a successful landing on 5th May 1942 but, ordered to head straight for Diego Suarez, the tanks soon ran into a strong defensive position where four tanks were knocked out and their crews taken prisoner. Over the next 48 hours, the rate of casualties sustained continued to grow so that only three crews could be mustered, while all attempts to break through the enemy line failed. Only with a daring, frontal, assault by HMS *Anthony* directly into the port at Diego Suarez was the situation saved and the prisoners rescued, although another six months of fighting was to follow before the whole island surrendered on 6th November. Of the 9th Lancers, three soldiers were killed in the initial engagement, a similar number were wounded, with the remainder rejoining the Regiment in Tripoli in the summer of 1943.

9TH LANCERS IN MADAGASCAR

9TH LANCER CRUISER TANKS.

T15314

THE MORRIS DETACHMENT 1940–42

LIEUTENANT TIM MORRIS DESCRIBED THE NEW ARMOURED CARS AS *'A SNAPPY LITTLE VEHICLE BUT A LITTLE SHORT ON VISION'.*

Shortly after their evacuation from Dunkirk, the 12th Lancers detached a troop for 'escort duties' of an unspecified nature but which turned out to be a mobile guard for the Royal Family. Commanded by Lieutenant Morris with Sergeant Thurston, the troop initially rejected two antiquated Rolls-Royce armoured cars before they were finally equipped with four Guy armoured cars and an old Lanchester that had once belonged to the Regiment. Having converted them for passengers, the detachment was based at Wellington Barracks until October 1940, when they moved with the King and Queen to Windsor. Armoured, camouflaged saloon cars replaced the Lanchester and the troop's duties expanded to include movement of Churchill and other cabinet ministers around London, often at the height of some of the heaviest bombing raids. On learning of the 12th's deployment to Egypt in September 1941, the Regiment asked for them back though it was not until May 1942 that the Household Cavalry, who had by then converted to armoured cars from horses, could release them. Several members of the Morris Detachment received personal decorations from the Monarch and there are also tales of mixed relations between Churchill and a black Scottie dog owned by Lance Corporal Cobly, who specialised in driving the Prime Minister. Cobly was said to have been offered large sums by souvenir hunters who wanted a cigar stub.

THE 12TH LANCERS PROVIDED ARMOURED CARS TO MOVE THE ROYAL FAMILY AND MEMBERS OF THE CABINET FROM 1940–1942.

NORTH AFRICA

1941–1943

Chor es Sufan | **Saunnu** | **Gazala** | Bir el Aslagh | Sidi Rezegh 1942 | Defence of Alamein Line | **Ruweisat** Ruweisat Ridge | Alam el Halfa | **El Alamein** | Advance on Tripoli | Tebaga Gap | **El Hamma** | Akarit El Kourzia | Djebe Kournine | **Tunis** | Creteville Pass | **North Africa 1941–1943**

ITALY'S ENTRY INTO THE WAR after the removal of British forces from Continental Europe brought into play the only other theatre in which Allied forces could take on the Axis powers on land and, with the threat of invasion of Britain over, the campaign that would be fought in Egypt, Libya and Tunisia became Britain's main focus for operations for the next three years. The fight would be characterised by frequent, dramatic changes of fortune and long chases across the desert using the narrow coastal strip where the only routes lay, with success frequently dependent on secure supply lines and the quality and quantity of materiel that could be pushed along them. As both sides were to find out, unless the enemy ground forces could be completely annihilated, an advance over several hundred miles would serve to increase the winning side's re-supply difficulties while making the loser's easier until, like elastic reaching its limit, the victorious advance was inevitably reversed.

MAJOR NED MANN, CAPTAIN JOHN CLARK-KENNEDY AND SECOND LIEUTENANT PETER WILLES IN AUGUST 1942 IN THE IDIOSYNCRATIC DRESS THAT THE EIGHTH ARMY HAD ADOPTED OF '*SLACKS, SIDE HATS AND DESERT BOOTS*'.

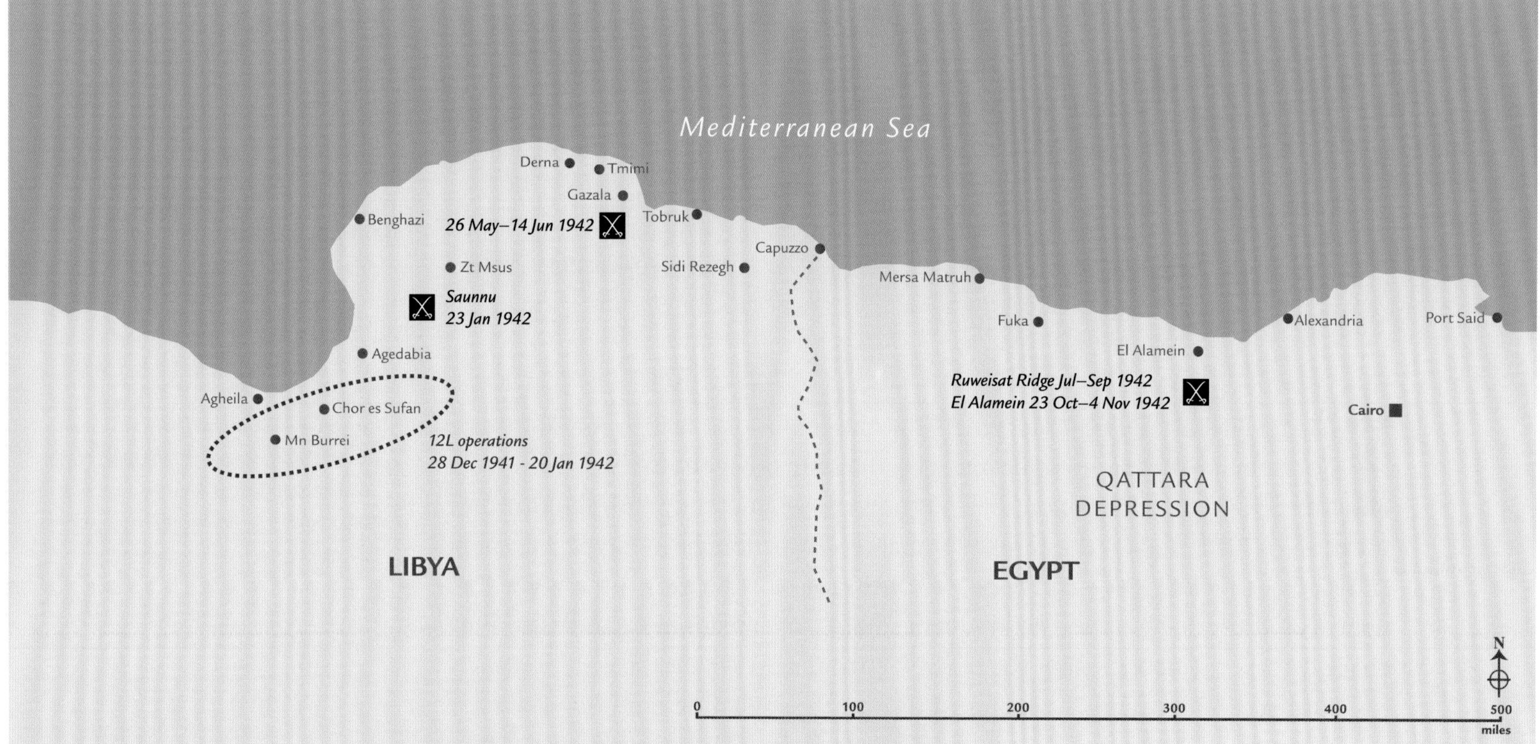

1 OPERATIONS FROM DECEMBER 1941 TO NOVEMBER 1942.

2 A SKETCH FROM THE 1942 CHRISTMAS MENU OF THE 12TH LANCERS REFLECTS THE EIGHTH ARMY'S VIEW OF ITSELF.

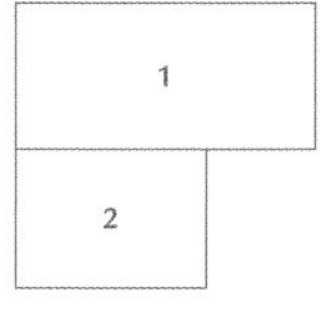

Despite its numerical disadvantage, the Allied army in Egypt at the end of 1940 and beginning of 1941 had largely succeeded in destroying the Italian Army and driven it back as far as El Agheila before Hitler intervened and sent the soon-to-be christened Afrika Korps under General Rommel to bale out the Italians. The Allies had in their turn been forced back behind the Egyptian frontier, leaving Tobruk besieged, before they launched the 'Crusader' offensive in the next round of the 'Benghazi Handicap' along the North African coastline. Begun on 18th November 1941, just as the 9th and 12th Lancers were nearing Suez, Crusader would force Rommel back to the bottleneck caused by the marshes near El Agheila by Christmas, though it crucially failed to destroy the Afrika Korps' armour.

The Army that the Regiments were about to join was already beginning to earn the fame that would lead Churchill to declare that, if a man were to be cross-examined as to his wartime doings, it would be enough for him to say that he had fought with the Eighth Army.[1] The North African campaign certainly produced a unique bond and esprit de corps among those who were part of it: *'I thought then'*, wrote Tim Bishop *'and know now that the Eighth Army had a unique esprit de corps. People liked each other; I never noticed any jealousy and one was often very thankful for the help of others.'*[2] Externally, this was manifested in eccentricities as far as language and dress were concerned, the former an assortment of local words and other phrases, the latter a mix of corduroys, faded shirts and pullovers that Sergeant Freddie Hunn described: *'The issue clothing consisted of a khaki drill shirt, those ridiculous looking shorts which were very wide and reached the knees…woollen stockings, gaiters, boots and a sun helmet completed the outfit giving the image of an actor in a comic opera. It was not long before this was discarded in favour of slacks, side hats and desert boots.'*[3]

For both Regiments, warfare in the desert posed new challenges and an adoption of new ways of operating and living. Fuel in particular was a constant concern, its delivery not helped by the flimsy British cans that proved unable to stand up to the rigours of the campaign in the same way that the eponymous 'jerrican' could. Rations, although supplemented by eggs from chickens that were often kept on the transport vehicles, were monotonous. *'Breakfast: Salt bacon or corned beef fried, tea; lunch: corned beef, hard biscuits, tea; supper: corned beef, mixed with biscuits (broken up by a hammer) mixed with a little water, cooked to make a stodgy stew.'*[4] Water was severely restricted, the allowance being half a gallon per man per day, and this might have to be shared with the vehicles' radiators as well. Despite this, Bruce Shand recalled that *'everyone was wonderfully well, living constantly in the open air on a rather spare diet. In such physical circumstances one's outlook changed and one felt, despite the immediate responsibilities, agreeably detached and free from the tiresome trammels of the world.'*[5]

Flies swarmed persistently and got everywhere, forming *'a thick black scum over the surface of one's tea and blackened any food; one could not keep them from one's face, bully beef and tea simultaneously. Dead or dying they had be scraped off everything in sight.'*[6] They brought 'gyppy tummy' along with other diseases and had a marked penchant for exposed desert sores on men's faces and hands, while the swirling desert sand-storm, or *khamsin*, managed to penetrate every defence and brought all activity to a standstill. Despite all the difficulties, the desert provided a 'clean' battlefield, free from the normalities of civilisation such as buildings and civilians that, in other theatres, brought the impact of war more starkly to life. It was also a theatre with a special code of conduct that bordered on chivalry. General Rommel's words *Krieg ohne Hass*, or 'war without hatred', summed it up. A graphic illustration was provided by Freddie Hunn: *'One of C Squadron's troops occupied an observation post in the Mekili area, close to a well, with an ample supply of fresh water, a great bonus for the Squadron and any nearby troops wishing to take advantage of such a treasure. This also applied to the German troops who once in a while, with a force of tanks, pushed our patrol back, then lorries would arrive, replenish water barrels and cans, then withdraw, leaving the well intact. No booby traps or mines would be set. It was a good gentleman's agreement.'*[7]

Learning the desert's ways clearly took time and the 9th's initial route march from disembarkation would have given them a taste of some of the difficulties as they set off with these instructions: *'Forty-seven miles on two hundred and seventy-seven degrees, then forty miles on two hundred and ninety degrees,'*[8] the fitters (The Black Gang) earning their pay as they managed to keep the Regiment on the road. Navigation continued to pose a problem throughout the campaign, the 9th's echelon making *The Times* with a story of how they had come across a minefield fence and a couple of Guardsmen on sentry duty by the Knightsbridge box: *'How very fortunate! Another few yards and we would have all been in the minefield'. 'On the contrary, sir' replied one of the Guardsmen, 'another few yards and you will be out of it.'*[9]

For the 12th much of the desert war was spent in troop positions with the Regiment typically

1 ALONGSIDE THE SHORTAGE OF WATER, BOTH REGIMENTS HAD TO EXIST ON A RELENTLESS DIET OF CORNED BEEF. FLIES PROVED A CONSTANT AND INVASIVE PRESENCE WHILE SANDSTORMS COULD BLOW UP SUDDENLY AND RENDER OPERATIONS IMPOSSIBLE.

2 9TH LANCER TANK COMMANDERS IN THE DESERT, INCLUDING SGT EDWARDS MM AND BAR.

3 A CRUSADER AND TANK TRANSPORTER OF THE 9TH LANCERS. LOGISTICS AND THE AVAILABILITY OF ARMOUR PROVED A KEY FACTOR IN THE DESERT WAR AND LED TO LONG ADVANCES FOLLOWED BY EQUALLY RAPID RETREATS.

1	3
2	

HUMBERS OF THE 12TH LANCERS IN A DESERT LEAGUER. AFTER THE ADVANCE AT THE END OF THE CRUSADER OFFENSIVE AT THE END OF 1941 THE REGIMENT OCCUPIED POSITIONS SOME 80 MILES FORWARD OF THE MAIN DEFENSIVE POSITIONS ON THE AGHEILA BEND.

covering a frontage of about 30 miles. Observation was the principal task and for the 12th this was very much a troop leaders' and crew commanders' war. At its worst, life in a tank is described by the 9th Lancers historian who records the month spent on Ruweisat Ridge in July 1942: '*During this time our reserves of energy and mental stability were drained to the dregs. The man in the tank suffered most. He had to sit inside a furnace for fifteen hours a day, without proper meals or sufficient water, and had to watch the haze like a lynx and never relax his guard against sudden death. In leaguer, in the blessed cool of the night, he had first to maintain his tank, to fill it, to load it and to change the batteries of his wireless set before he could roll up in his blankets.*'[10]

The Crusader offensive was in full swing as the Regiments disembarked at the end of November and immediately collected, modified and painted equipment with a brief moment to acclimatise to life in the desert and, crucially, acquire the Eighth Army's non-issue uniform. On 6th December the 12th Lancers began the 400-mile journey west to join the 7th Armoured Division in the latter stages of Crusader. As it joined the Division, orders came to scout forward to cover the hook south of the German position at Gazala and then head across the desert via Msus to Agadabia. First contact came on 16th December as the 7th Armoured Division's move caused Rommel to break clean from his position though, with contact lost, the 12th were soon pushed on to the next possible line of defence, the Sidi Brahim-Antelat ridge inland from the coast south of Benghazi. They had orders to report on any enemy in the passes through it. Second Lieutenant Bishop recalled, '*for the next three days we were constantly on the move, often crawling and bumping over going only fit for a goat, in a wind so cold that overcoats, gloves and balaclava helmets were the fashion.*' The air situation, never favourable in France, soon became a major, and enduring, preoccupation: '*We were much bothered by a single Messerschmitt 110 that liked to fly low over my car, machine-gunning as it went.*'[11] No other enemy were encountered and on 22nd December patrols fanned out onto the plain beyond and headed west and north-west towards Benghazi. Inexperience in the desert, inadequate maps and frequent enemy contact now all combined with the difficulty of negotiating the various passes and defiles to confuse the battle picture. This was only clarified on the following day when large formations of enemy were reported and engaged as they withdrew towards the Agheila bend.

CHOR ES SUFAN

On Christmas Eve, the 12th withdrew to Msus and came under command of 22nd Armoured Brigade which was tasked with punching its way past Agedabia and round the Agheila bend. Christmas Day was spent '*coldly and unhilariously*'[12] at Saunnu and on Boxing Day the advance began, though, with petrol critically short, only C Squadron could move and that only when once all the petrol had been collected from the other squadrons. With enough fuel eventually found, the Regiment advanced past Agedabia and around towards Agheila, scouting and providing flank protection until they, and the rest of the Brigade, became embroiled in heavy fighting in the Chor es Sufan area on 28th December. Over the next few days enemy counter-attacks were delivered both on the ground and from the air, costing the Regiment 56 men killed or captured – the sense of anger mounting when their reports were questioned by higher formation. With the Brigade checked and then pushed back, the Regiment at one time reduced to squadron strengths of 12, 10 and 11 armoured cars, finally established a line of observation line from Agedabia to Haseiat

A 9TH LANCERS CREW WITH A RADICAL SOLUTION TO LONG HAIR, THOUGH THEIR SQUADRON LEADER, MAJOR STUG PERRY, PROVED LESS THAN COMPLIMENTARY ABOUT THE IMPLICATION THAT THE REST OF HIS SQUADRON WAS LICE-INFESTED.

and then 10 miles west along the Wadi Faregh as the Crusader offensive ground to a halt. German activity continued to be reported to the Regiment's front, though this, and the earlier counter-attacks, were to prove screens behind which Rommel was withdrawing his main forces to refit. The screens finally withdrew under cover of a sandstorm on 6th January, confirmation coming from the 12th Lancers when they found the positions deserted. One troop leader had to lead his vehicles forward on foot in order to guide them through the murk.

Both sides now began to prepare for the next phase by building up their forces, with the Axis enjoying the benefit of short, secure supply lines. The Allies found themselves in exactly the opposite situation and under the illusion that it would be they who would go onto the offensive as the 1st Armoured Division began to arrive, expecting to advance through the 7th Armoured Division and on to Tripoli.

On 9th January 1942 the 12th Lancers, taking six days' rations on the 30 armoured cars that still ran, advanced for three days to the area of Mn Burruei over 70 miles of rough country where large concentrations of Axis troops were observed and reported. The terrain and enemy air and ground activity rendered a fixed observation line impossible to maintain and forced continuous patrolling, increasing the wear on the vehicles and reducing the two squadrons the Regiment was able to field to only eight vehicles each by 15th January. Other shortages indicated the degree to which the Allies' supply lines were stretched, especially in remote forward locations in the *'weird landscape of the Burruei Basin… some eighty miles' difficult going in advance of our transport. Rations and water became short, and during the ensuing eight or nine days, I have never been so hungry or thirsty in my life.'*[13] Priority went to fuel resupply and desperate measures were called for as the water ration reduced to half a gallon a man for all purposes. Abandoned vehicles became a potential source of supply, with one officer reportedly finding, *'Already drained by AJ Clark Kennedy'* [a fellow troop leader] chalked on the side of a derelict, while Freddie Hunn recalled of another wreck: *'We immediately drained the radiator, the brown rusty liquid flowing into the water container like lava from a volcano. A brew of tea was quickly made, the taste of which was beyond description… Later, the Sergeant who had commanded that hulk asked what the brew tasted like, the answer being "Horrible but wet" to which he replied "Not surprising." His crew had drained the radiator on three occasions, washed and shaved in the water and returned it back.'*[14]

The 12th Lancers were withdrawn from the line to refit on 20th January, just one day before the offensive that they had been observing the build-up for was launched. By this time the 9th Lancers had been in the area of Msus since early January and, after a period of training hindered by inadequate supplies of fuel, now found themselves caught up in what had originally been intended by Rommel

LIEUTENANT COLONEL RONALD MACDONELL ASSUMED COMMAND OF THE 9TH LANCERS FOLLOWING THE WOUNDING OF LIEUTENANT COLONEL CHRISTOPHER PETO IN FIGHTING NEAR ABBEVILLE. HE LED THE REGIMENT FOR THE NEXT TWO YEARS, INCLUDING GAZALA AND THE DEFENCE OF EL ALAMEIN. HE DIED IN ITALY WHEN, AS A BRIGADE SECOND-IN-COMMAND, HIS TANK WAS HIT AT CORIANO RIDGE.

to be a spoiling attack but, exploiting early success, rapidly developed into a full-blown offensive. Facing him, the British had refused to believe reports of the enemy's increasing strength and had left *'the untried and, as far as the desert went, untrained 1st Armoured Division with only one of its armoured brigades [the 2nd] totalling 150 tanks... widely dispersed in the forward area'.*[15] Across the British position logistics continued to be precarious while no plans had been made for defence.

The surprise achieved by General Rommel was complete. Agedabia was rapidly captured, with three enemy columns thrusting north-eastward and threatening to push the 1st Armoured Division completely aside. In this confused situation, 2nd Armoured Brigade, 10 miles east of Antelat, was ordered south-west to intercept what was thought to be a small enemy column moving from Agedabia to Antelat. The 9th, in the van of the Brigade, met the flank of a large force late in the morning of 23rd January, having earlier been warned by the 12th, on their way back to Sidi Barrani, that several allied armoured cars had been captured and might be used by the enemy. The Brigade, less the Bays who been detached to deal with enemy in the rear areas, had orders to avoid becoming decisively engaged and the 9th were therefore to piquet the column and prevent them interfering with the withdrawing British forces, a task successfully completed though with a few tanks lost by mid-afternoon.

> 'We emerged from Saunnu and Msus and Cherruba with a feeling of frustration and bewilderment...'

The Regiment now turned north to act as a rearguard but with shortage of fuel a significant consideration. The echelon was instructed to stand by at Msus as, with darkness approaching, the 9th entered the Saunnu Depression only to discover as it was halfway across that a large enemy force had formed up on the escarpment to their front and were blocking their intended route. Orders to break out to the north-east went unacknowledged by the attached artillery who, *'unable to resist such a massed target'*, began to engage the enemy while the rest of the Regimental Group, in a series of running fights, made it to the northern escarpment and turned to face the enemy. By now the tanks were almost completely without fuel, the artillery was exposed in the Depression and a large enemy formation lay between the Regiment and safety. In a series of violent counter-attacks in which several enemy guns were destroyed but a number of the Regiment's tanks were lost, the fight continued until darkness saved them. To the rear, the guns had been overrun by German Mark IVs which had attacked into the Depression, while a number of the tanks had run completely dry and stopped, requiring the Regiment to tow almost a quarter of its fleet to an emergency leaguer a couple of miles to the north.

Cut off from the Brigade by radio jamming, the four most damaged Honeys were emptied in order to provide enough fuel for a five-mile move by the rest of the Regiment, with 2am the cut-off time at which the drained Honeys would be destroyed if no help had arrived. As 2am approached and with the noise of the German leaguer plainly heard through the night, the order was given to destroy the tanks. A new sound, however, brought a stay of execution. Initially thought to be a night attack, it turned out to be the A Echelon arriving in the nick of time with precious fuel: *'We almost wept on their necks. Petrol! Hundreds of gallons of petrol and even some mail. Once more the echelon had not failed us.'*[16]

Able to move once more, and fortunate that the German main effort had now been switched towards Benghazi at a critical moment when General Rommel might have trapped all the British forces inland, the 9th Lancers moved to Msus to rejoin the 2nd Armoured Brigade. A strong attack almost immediately forced a rapid move northwards to Charruba in what became known as the Msus Stakes. By now, the Regiment had been reduced to 10 Cruisers and 10 Honeys and, as enemy action and automotive failure reduced this even further, the Brigade formed a Composite Regiment on 26th January for the defence of Charruba. Commanded by the 9th Lancers, the Bays and 10th Hussars provided a combined squadron to augment what was left of the Regiment, while A Squadron dismounted from its few remaining tanks and withdrew. Over the next few days stragglers moved in from the south and refurbishment took place. After an inconclusive sally by the Division on the 29th January to intercept a German column on the Msuns-Mekili road, 2nd Armoured Brigade withdrew south-east of Mekili, where E Battery and C Company, 1st Rifle Brigade, rejoined the Regiment and they were able to rest and take stock from their recent experiences: *'We emerged from Saunnu and Msus and Cherruba with a feeling of frustration and bewilderment and a wish to be allowed to meet the enemy again soon on proper terms.'*[17]

THE GAZALA LINE

For the British formations inland, the imperative was now to maintain contact with those forces on the coast to prevent a German hook encircling them as the withdrawal to the next defensive position continued. Over the next few days, the 2nd Armoured

Brigade fell back by night and faced west during the day, until the 9th Lancers, by now numbering 47 tired and battered tanks following the reappearance of A Squadron, arrived at the Gazala line on the night of 3rd February. From impassable heights at Ain el Gazala on the coast, the line stretched 50 miles into the desert at Bir Hacheim and, although relatively weak as a natural position, it was heavily mined in the centre, with strongpoints behind which armour could manoeuvre. More importantly, it formed the only defendable location between Agheila and the Egyptian border and would be vital if Tobruk was to be held.

Neither side was yet strong enough to allow the campaign to continue immediately and, while both sides prepared for an offensive, the 12th Lancers, re-equipped by the beginning of March and supported by a Guards column and eight Valentine tanks, moved forward as part of the screen in front of the British main defensive positions. Their sector, which covered a huge area (a tour of A Squadron's line took seven hours to cover 66 miles) faced north and at right angles to any line of advance or retreat and represented, Lieutenant Colonel Burne noted, *'Another bottleneck. Two German Panzer Divsions on my right and right rear, with my left being cut off by an Italian sortie from Mechili: the box completed by mines behind me.'*[18]

For the next few weeks the 12th became involved in a series of attacks and counter-attacks as each side attempted to gain control of the virtual no-mans-land that existed to the west of the Gazala Line. It would allow the Germans freedom to bring their forces forward unobserved, the dominating feature of Haqfet Eleba, with its view to the coast at Tmimi, becoming particularly hotly contested. Increasingly large enemy attacks pushed the 12th and the Free-French forces grouped with them back so that, by the end of March, the Tmimi–Mechili track along which Rommel had to bring his forces for the assault on the Gazala line could no longer be observed. Moved further south, the 12th adopted for the last time the routine of a static line of troop and squadron positions in the desert as, throughout April, the enemy prepared the ground for their assault by steadily pushing forward and capturing the dominating features with the Regiment involved in intense skirmishes as they attempted to retain what favourable ground for reconnaissance was left. A final enemy push on 27th April forced them back a further ten miles, before the 12th moved back to refurbish in early May, leaving C Squadron behind to come under command of 22nd Armoured Brigade in the 1st Armoured Division (both of which were commanded by ex-12th Lancers, Brigadier Carr and Major General Lumsden) to familiarise itself with its new position and the minefields of the Knightsbridge Box.

Behind this reconnaissance battle, which the 9th Lancers' war history light-heartedly characterised as *'the armoured cars played "Tom Tiddler" to their hearts' content with the German six-wheelers'*[19], everything else, including B vehicles, was dug in and extensive, wild but morale boosting, anti-aircraft machine gun fire maintained. Efforts were also being made to solve the problem of overmatched tanks, a problem exposed not only in their recent engagements but proved in a test conducted by the 9th Lancers on a captured German Mark III using the 2-pounder on the Crusader and the 37mm on the Honey. At 400 yards, barely a dent was made, and even at 100 yards only the lower plate was breached. First-hand experience confirmed that the German 50mm and 88mm guns in particular could rip through British armour at considerable ranges, due to their superior sights and lethality. To close the gap in quality, more artillery was given to armoured brigades, while tactics altered to fire smoke to allow ranges to be reduced – though this often ended up silhouetting the attackers and could lead to more casualties. Better news arrived with the arrival of the Grant tank, of which B Squadron took delivery of the first batch. Its 75mm gun could deal with the Mark IV. With over

1 B SQUADRON, 9TH LANCERS, RECEIVED GRANT TANKS ARMED WITH A 75MM GUN IN THE HULL AND A 2 POUNDER IN THE TURRET JUST BEFORE THE GAZALA BATTLES. *'THE 9TH EMERGED FROM KNIGHTSBRIDGE DESPERATELY TIRED BUT CONFIDENT. B SQUADRON IN ITS BATTERED OLD GRANTS HAD DESTROYED NEARLY 40 PANZERS... PROVING THAT BRITISH TANKS, MEETING THE AFRIKA KORPS ON LEVEL TERMS, COULD MORE THAN HOLD THEIR OWN.'*

2 DESPITE THE SUCCESS OF THE GRANT, BY THE END OF THE FIERCE BATTLES AT GAZALA 2ND ARMOURED BRIGADE HAD TO FORM A COMPOSITE REGIMENT FROM ITS THREE TANK REGIMENTS. THE 9TH LANCERS ONLY ABLE TO PRODUCE TWO TROOPS OF GRANTS AND FOUR CRUISERS.

a month of specialist and combined arms training completed, 2nd Armoured Brigade took up position on the escarpment north-east of the Knightsbridge cross-tracks on 24th May, by now at full strength with RHQ, A and C Squadrons in Crusaders and B with 13 Grants, as increased levels of activity indicated an imminent German offensive.

The German attack, *'among the most reckless and costly fought during the desert war'*[20] began with heavy air attacks and pressure on the centre, followed by a flanking movement to the south of the Gazala Line on the night of 26th/27th May that surrounded the French Brigade at Bir Hacheim and hooked the German armour northwards behind the fixed defences. The 15th Panzer Division made straight for the Knightsbridge Box held by 201 Guards Brigade and the 2nd and 22nd Armoured Brigades of the 1st Armoured Division, while 21st Panzer Division overran 4th Armoured Brigade of the 7th Armoured Division and threatened to cut off the entire Allied line. Although the German bid for a quick and annihilating victory was to fail, due to the shock of the losses sustained and the lack of fuel and ammunition, over the following two weeks, in of the enemy anti-tank screen destroyed, the two squadrons came through the smoke screen covering their approach and punched through the remaining anti-tank guns, destroying the position completely and moving onto the lorried infantry with devastating effect. *'Tank commanders were dropping grenades right and left and using their pistols and tommy-guns at point-blank range'*.[22] The enemy withdrew, a German divisional staff officer later admitting that the battalion had been wiped out, leaving several guns, including four 88mms, along with many dead and over 100 prisoners.

Over the next few days German ground forces, supported by intense Stuka attacks, continued to try to break the British position. While achieving considerable success in defence and counter-attack, the British continued to sustain losses as the lines of anti-tank guns took their toll amongst the 9th Lancers and elsewhere. On 29th May the fighting was the stiffest so far. The 2nd Armoured Brigade position formed a triangle with the guns in the centre and the apex to the north against the southern flank of the Knightsbridge Box and, with heavy shelling beginning at 5.30am, the

'Tank commanders were dropping grenades right and left and using their pistols and tommy-guns at point-blank range'

an area that became known as 'the Cauldron' on account of to the intensity of the fighting, Rommel managed to overcome the Allies and force them into further retreat.

In the confusion of the initial days of the battle, C Squadron, 12th Lancers, watched the flanks of 22nd Armoured Brigade and then sent troops to each of the brigades in the area (including 2nd Armoured) on liaison tasks, but, while some successes were achieved (a single troop captured 78 Italian prisoners), the Cauldron was not a good place to be in an armoured car. Bruce Shand, by now commanding A Squadron, recalled the early stages of the battle: *'We were now frantically busy on the wireless as I had to send my troops round onto the enemy flanks as well as attempt to gain contact with the 7th Armoured Division. All this, and the thickening dust, prevented us from seeing all the battle but the little we did see was very thrilling... The next three days or so were very strenuous and critical, with fierce fighting day and night. An incredibly thick dust storm delayed the issue for some hours, during which trying to find the enemy was made extremely unpleasant...shortly after we located him the storm lifted and our tanks could again attack.'*[21]

The situation for 2nd Armoured Brigade nearby was equally confused, the 9th's first serious engagement taking place as they supported an artillery attack on an enemy column, joining in with B Squadron's Grants and E Battery to considerable effect, and sending out A and C Squadrons to attack from the flanks. With much first German assault began soon afterwards. In confused and almost continuous fighting, attacks came first from one direction, then the next, British squadrons being moved from regiment to regiment to assist each other, while the Grant tank's powerful gun proved its worth against the Mark IIIs and IVs. In the grinding fight, which included a Regimental attack to relieve pressure on the 10th Hussars, A Squadron was reduced to five tanks and C to six, while B Squadron, whose Grants were all still intact, was by now critically short of ammunition, one replenishment by the echelon having to be brought forward and conducted under cover of a smokescreen until detected and engaged at the cost of further casualties. At dusk, the Regiment leaguered in battle order, three officers and 11 men having died, but with at least 13 enemy tanks destroyed by the Grants, only one of which had been lost.

Rommel's initial blitzkrieg had been held and his logistic situation was precarious, leaving the initiative with the Allies who in their turn tried to destroy the salient that had been created with a series of armoured attacks thrown against the ring of German armour and anti-tank guns. On 30th May the 2nd Armoured Brigade, despite its low numbers of tanks (the Bays were down to 16, including five Grants, the 10th Hussars to one Grant and two cruisers), was to assault a part of the line on which 35 enemy tanks had been sighted earlier. The 9th were to lead with the Bays in reserve. Cresting the ridge on which the Germans could be seen, the Regiment immediately ran into heavy fire from 88mm anti-aircraft guns positioned amongst wrecks put out to give an impression of greater numbers. With mounting casualties and ammunition running low, a withdrawal under smoke was ordered, the Regiment by now reduced to two severely damaged and ineffective tanks in A Squadron, 11 Grants in B Squadron and four cruisers in C Squadron.

Despite these heavy losses, the 9th Lancers were ordered to attack again, this time with A Squadron of the 3rd County of London Yeomanry and a composite squadron from the remainder of 22nd Armoured Brigade under command, and with more than 60 guns in support. General Lumsden told the Commanding Officer that if the Germans could be broken here the Gazala Line could be restored. Smoke to screen the attack had blown away by the time the crest was reached and again the Regiment came under sustained and accurate fire, one hit on his tank forcing the Commanding Officer to move to another. With no chance of success, a counter-attack inbound and Stukas attacking, the Brigade Commander once again ordered a withdrawal, both attacks, it was discovered later, having been launched against 36 tanks and 90 guns.

The landscape was, by now, a sea of debris and tracks: '*the desert on which we had been fighting for the past three days was by this time an incredible sight. Every yard of it was criss-crossed with tracks and pock-marked with shell-holes, while everywhere lay piles of empty cases. Slit trenches and gun pits had been dug all over the place and round the circumference lay the wreckage of our own and enemy tanks, burnt-out armoured cars and the skeletons of lorries and trucks. Every puff of wind raised a white, powdery dust.*'[23] On 31st May, in line with 4th and 22nd Armoured Brigades, the 2nd Armoured Brigade formed a composite regiment, led by the Bays. To help, the 9th Lancers could only produce two troops of Grants as by now A Squadron had no tanks left and C were down to four 'almost useless' Cruisers. What remained of the Regiment moved back to the B echelon where, despite the losses that had been suffered, they were at least able to take some comfort from their performance: '*The 9th emerged from Knightsbridge desperately tired but battle-hardened and confident. B Squadron in its battered old Grants, had destroyed nearly forty panzers…proving that British tanks, meeting the Afrika Korps on level terms, could more than hold their own.*'[24]

Elsewhere, with the Cauldron battle still raging, A and C Squadrons of the 12th Lancers, attached to 1st and 7th Armoured Divisions respectively, continued to observe the approaches to the Knightsbridge Box until, with his position secure following a final, failed British counter-attack, Rommel took Bir Hacheim on 10th/11th June and turned his attention to the remaining positions of the Gazala Line. With no option but to withdraw, the remnants of 1st Armoured Division and other tank formations provided what cover they could as the Gazala boxes emptied, a full-scale retreat to Egypt starting on 13th/14th June with the evacuation of the Knightsbridge Box.

SIDI REZEGH

On the same night, some 60 miles to the rear at Capuzzo, the 9th took over the last reserve of tanks, bringing their strength to three Honeys in RHQ, 16 Cruisers in A Squadron and 12 Grants and three Cruisers in B Squadron (including two troops from the 10th Hussars), while C Squadron, without tanks, moved back to Egypt. After a move forward on transporters to join 7th Armoured Division on the night of 15th June, the Regiment began an extended rearguard operation, an early action at Sidi Rezegh on 17th June setting the tone for what was to come as 45 Mark IIIs and IVs were engaged: '*the first two shots set tanks afire while others stopped and began shooting back. Within minutes both sides had settled down to a terrific slogging match. The air was filled with flying metal and cordite fumes, and soon six of seven German tanks were blazing and two of the Grants were hit and ceased firing, whilst a third went up in a great explosion. Twice the enemy faltered and broke and twice they pressed on from behind.*'[25] Finally outflanked, the 9th were forced to withdraw, a difficult operation in a Grant whose main armament was fixed in the hull and could only point to the front. Leaving A Squadron behind as a single cruiser squadron, and having handed over its serviceable Grants, what remained of the 9th moved east eventually to reach Alexandria on 24th June where,

THE RETREAT FROM GAZALA WAS COVERED BY BOTH THE 9TH AND 12TH LANCERS, THE LATTER LOSING THEIR COMMANDING OFFICER, LIEUTENANT COLONEL BURNE, WHO WAS CAPTURED IN THE CHAOS. AT SIDI REZEGH, ALTHOUGH THE GRANTS AGAIN GAVE A GOOD ACCOUNT OF THEMSELVES, THE WEAKNESS OF HAVING THE MAIN GUN FIXED IN THE HULL WAS EXPOSED.

THROUGHOUT JULY AND AUGUST 1942 BOTH REGIMENTS PARTICIPATED IN THE DEFENCE OF THE ALAMEIN LINE, THE 9TH AS PART OF A COMPOSITE REGIMENT ON RUWEISAT RIDGE, THE 12TH SCREENING THE QATTARA DEPRESSION AND ROMMEL'S FINAL ATTEMPT TO BREAK THROUGH AT ALAM EL HALFA. FRESH TROOPS AND NEW EQUIPMENT, INCLUDING THE SHERMAN TANK, WERE BY NOW ARRIVING.

almost immediately, instructions arrived to turn around and move back to the front at Fuka, 100 miles away, where enough tanks to re-equip the Regiment had apparently been found. These turned out to be seven old cruisers and four scout cars which, crewed by the 9th, were given to the Bays to move west to meet the German advance.

The 12th Lancers also found themselves intimately involved in covering the retreat from Gazala, A Squadron moving from their screening position to the north of the line through the minefields around Tobruk to rejoin the rest of the Regiment at Capuzzo as the withdrawal to the east began in earnest. Placed under command of a sequence of different divisions and brigades in delaying positions along the coast, the 12th provided a series of screens, starting at Sollum on 17th June and followed at Sidi Barrani, Mersa Matruh and Fuka, their role made more difficult by the enormous amounts of men and equipment of the Eighth Army now rushing back to the next defendable position at El Alamein. One result of the confusion was the capture of the 12th Lancers' Commanding Officer, Lieutenant Colonel Burne, when RHQ mistook enemy transport for friendly forces and realised their mistake too late to do anything other than scatter. Elsewhere much of the Regiment came close *'to the nearest thing to the end of the 12th Royal Lancers in regimental history'*, having been attacked from the escarpment that overlooked the coast road and only escaping by firing smoke that *'would not have discredited a destroyer'*[26] before withdrawing behind a hasty screen further down the road. The next day the enemy were found to be behind them and a race east, neck and neck with the enemy's armoured cars, was only called off when the enemy stopped to raid the fuel supplies at Fuka and elements of 2nd Armoured Brigade provided a more heavyweight defence. By now the Regiment was at El Daba with the uncomfortable thought that *'if you breakfasted there you could easily lunch in Alexandria'*[27]. Having provided a final series of artillery observation posts to cover the coast road, however, after two weeks of rearguards they finally came in behind the defended line at El Alamein on 30th June, by now reduced to a composite squadron. They awaited the outcome of the crucial defensive battle being fought by the 1st Armoured Division and the South Africans to stop the retreat.

RUWEISAT RIDGE

The 9th Lancers were in equally dire straits and seriously fragmented. There was no news of A Squadron, which had been detached earlier, while the two remaining squadrons were so light on manpower that any equipment available could not have been crewed. From Fuka, they again returned to Alexandria, *'feeling like the lost tribe of Israel'*, where they received a few replacement tanks and took a squadron of the 4th Hussars under command, before, on 1st July, taking delivery of all the available tanks in

Egypt, the Army Commander having ordered, *'Send up your best team – suggest 9th Lancers.'*[28] Re-equipped, B Squadron 9th Lancers, now with 12 Grants and four Crusaders, moved to join 22nd Armoured Brigade on the Ruweisat Ridge with A Squadron, 4th Hussars and a composite A and C Squadron in eight Crusaders following a day later.

The Ruweisat Ridge, running for 10 miles east to west, formed the centre of the Alamein line. To the north, sandy desert stretched for eight miles to the coast while, to the south, over another short stretch of desert lay the Qattara Depression, an obstacle impassable to armour. Arriving on 3rd July and with no time to check the weapon systems, 1st Armoured Division's Rear Headquarters gave immediate orders: *'Get down that ridge as fast as you can – there's an enemy tank attack coming in and there's very little to stop it.'*[29] The Germans had already seized the western end of the Ridge and at dusk their armour was reported to be moving along its southern side, into which B Squadron attacked. They destroyed 12 of the 30 tanks before the remainder retreated. The following day, a further series of attacks was beaten off with the assistance of some attached anti-tank guns.

Although the effects of individual actions are never easy to calculate, Major General McCreery, by then Chief of Staff of Headquarters Middle East Forces, is recorded as saying to the Lieutenant Colonel Macdonell of the 9th a few weeks later, *'You saved Egypt that evening'*. This view is reinforced in his foreword to the 9th Lancers' History, written shortly after the war: *'Many think that Egypt was saved when the Eighth Army defeated General Rommel's last big attack in the Western Desert at the end of August, 1942. Actually, Egypt was saved earlier during those first critical days of July when General Rommel drove his tanks and self-propelled guns and trucks forward along the Ruweisat Ridge in close formations, to be stopped by the 25-pounders and the remnants of the 2nd Armoured Brigade with their "thin-skinned" Crusader tanks. In this critical action the 9th Lancers took the principal part.'*[30] A perhaps less unbiased view of the whole action comes from Major General von Mellenthin, who at the time was on Rommel's staff: *'Our one chance was to out-manoeuvre the enemy but we had actually been drawn into a battle of attrition. 1st Armoured Division was given an extra day to reorganize, and when the Afrika Korps advanced on 2nd July it found the British armour strongly posted on Ruweisat Ridge, and quite capable of beating of such attacks as we could muster'*[31] John Wheeler-Bennett, in his biography of George VI, wrote: *'The actual turning point of the tide in the Second World War may be accurately determined as the first week of July 1942.'*[32]

While 3rd July may have marked the end of their advance, the Germans continued with local attacks, forcing the 9th to stay on the Ridge for the rest of the month. In what was one of the most exhausting periods of the war and under constant threat from bombers, shelling, heat, flies and sickness, attacks and counter-attacks took place on an almost daily basis, with one, a Stuka attack directed at RHQ while it was being visited by the Corps, Divisional and Brigade Commanders, injuring all three and causing the Commanding Officer to remark to the Adjutant, *'I think I'm a Corps Commander'*.[33] Casualties to men and materiel continued to come in, while the record for 23rd July (the Regiment would be withdrawn two days later) spells out the effect of the continual strain: *'It is apparent that the length of time which the Regiment has now been in the desert (seven months), combined with the constant battles and lack of sleep, is having its effect; most of us are at the extreme limit and it is getting hard even to think clearly. Yesterday, three men – all normal, stout-hearted men – went temporarily out of their minds and others were showing the same signs of mental and physical strain.'*[34]

THE BUILD-UP TO EL ALAMEIN SAW THE EXTENSIVE USE OF DECEPTION MEASURES TO DISGUISE WHERE THE BRITISH ARMOUR WAS LIKELY TO BE LAUNCHED FROM.

Both sides now settled down to rebuild their strength after the marathon battles of the last month, with changes in command taking place at every level as General Montgomery took over the Eighth Army, bringing with him an assuredness of command and an immediate boost to morale. Reinforcements arrived, the 9th receiving 137, while new officers were sent up to the Composite Regiment, which remained on Ruweisat Ridge until early September, to be *'entered to shell fire'*. Sherman tanks, with a 75mm gun in the turret, began to replace older models. This was just one sign of the balance of supply that was beginning to move in the Allies' favour. General Rommel, again operating over-extended supply lines, now faced critical shortfalls in manpower and equipment, while General Montgomery was able to draw on increasing volumes of both and make best use of the air power available to him.

THE REGIMENTAL ORDERS GROUP, 9TH LANCERS, GIVEN BY LIEUTENANT COLONEL GERALD GROSVENOR ON THE EVE OF THE BATTLE OF EL ALAMEIN.

The 12th Lancers, commanded by Lieutenant Colonel GJ Kidston since early July, had, thoughout the battle, screened the southern sector of the line from Munassib to the edge of the Qattara Depression, though mobile patrols became more limited by the increasing threat of mines and the fixed positions being adopted by both sides: '*for the armoured-car soldier, self-contained and bred for independence, the sweetness had gone out of it all.*'[35] Involvement in two raids broke the routine, however. In the first of these, B Squadron formed part of a force that struck Fuka airfield in the enemy's rear, the Squadron returning largely intact, despite having been heavily shot up on the return journey. The second raid, planned for late July using a combined arms group based on the 12th, was set to attack enemy logistic bases and airfields, but had to be abandoned when an assault in the north with which it was to coincide failed.

ALAM EL HALFA

Rommel's final attempt to break through the British line came on 31st August with the battle of Alam el Halfa. Using the same tactics as at Gazala, the Germans feinted in the centre and then hooked south, the 12th Lancers picking up and tracking the two main columns, one containing 100 tanks, with a sandstorm at one point reducing visibility to 400 yards which made '*locating and reporting Panzers never easy but always exciting*'.[36] Playing their part in the attritional battle that followed, in the B Squadron sector 22 tanks were destroyed, 19 damaged and at least a dozen had hit mines. Sergeant Bryant's recollections of the battle highlight the change in fortunes that had now taken place: '*We rejoined the Squadron who quickly established its position between our own forces and Rommel. All that day we retreated, heavily shelled by Rommel's artillery and panzers and we thought "Here we go again, how much further into Egypt are we going this time?" As evening approached we noticed a change, the shells were still going over but now a large proportion of them were going in the opposite direction, towards the panzers… As we continued to retreat we passed lines of British tanks dug into the sand… there was also a number of anti-tank guns. The German tanks had come as far as they were coming and were now driven back.*'[37] During the next three days Rommel proved unable to break through the Allied defensive positions and the Germans were forced back, allowing the 12th Lancers to raid their lines of communication in the south and, as they tracked their withdrawal and re-established the line, to remain there until withdrawn to refurbish and train in mid-September, the Divisional Commander congratulating them on a performance of the 'highest possible order.'[38]

EL ALAMEIN

Preparations for the next offensive now pre-occupied each Regiment both of which were back in the 1st Armoured Division which, along with 10th Armoured Division, formed Lieutenant General Lumsden's X Corps. Training focused on one event – a passage through a minefield breach at night – as part of Montgomery's plan to inflict a crushing defeat in a set-piece battle that would give Rommel no freedom to manoeuvre. In the north of the Alamein line XXX Corps' infantry and engineers would break through the 'Devil's

Garden' of minefields to create lanes through which X Corps' two divisions of armour would pass to cut off the German supply lines and destroy the panzer reserves. To the south, XIII Corps would attack to fix enemy forces there and prevent them reinforcing the north, while also pushing lighter armoured forces through to El Daba.

With all preparations conducted in the greatest secrecy, the 9th Lancers Regimental Group, commanded since early September by Lieutenant Colonel GH Grosvenor, moved into the desert to conduct final training and fully integrate the attached gunners and infantry. On the night of 20th October, having travelled on transporters and left behind hessian and wood decoy tanks in their previous location, they, together with the rest of the 1st Armoured Division, drove under the cover of decoy lorries that had been there for weeks and which now completely masked the armoured concentration to the north. Orders came on the morning of the 23rd October for the attack that night, the whole thing preceded by *'a real old-fashioned barrage'*.[39]

Movement to the start line commenced at 7.30pm as the 9th Lancers passed along 'Moon Track', through the Allied minefields and the first enemy minefield belt by 2am before waiting for an hour as the second enemy minefield was breached, with A Squadron's Cruisers assisting the Minefield Task Force. By dawn the minefield belts remained unbroken and the Regimental Group, with much of 2nd Armoured Brigade, found itself exposed,

BOTH REGIMENTS FORMED PART OF THE 1ST ARMOURED DIVISION DURING THE BATTLE OF EL ALAMEIN WITH THE 12TH PROVIDING SQUADRONS TO EACH OF THE BRIGADES AS THEY ADVANCED UP SUN, MOON AND STAR TRACKS. THE 9TH ADVANCED THROUGH THE MINEFIELDS ALONG MOON TRACK, THE PHOTOGRAPH TAKEN AT 0200 ON 23RD OCTOBER 1942 BEING REPRODUCED IN THIS LATER PAINTING BY TERENCE CUNEO.

A SHERMAN OF B SQUADRON, 9TH LANCERS, NEARS METEIRIYA RIDGE. THE REGIMENT HAD BEEN ORDERED TO DRIVE STRAIGHT THROUGH A MINEFIELD IN FRONT OF THE RIDGE '*WHATEVER THE CASUALTIES*'.

hemmed in by minefields and unable to manoeuvre as heavy shelling began. Vehicles started to burn as enemy guns on Meteiriya Ridge, 3,000 yards to the front, successfully engaged them, a situation endured until midday when the minefield was breached and the advance continued until, within a few hundred yards of the Ridge, yet another minefield was found with no apparent way around: '*The Brigadier ordered us to drive straight through whatever the casualties, so, after a quick check back to make certain that he really meant it, C Squadron drove into the mines.*'[40] To add to the danger, German tanks were spotted, while 88mm guns and small arms began to engage until the two leading troops got through (a troop leader had dismounted to guide and clear mines). Having engaged the enemy armour, they seized and held a section of the Ridge until the remainder of the squadron, supported by B and RHQ could secure it. At dusk the enemy withdrew, leaving 12 tanks destroyed for the loss of four of the Regiment's Shermans. That night, the 9th Lancers leaguered in the same spot, with bullets still flying about, as they prepared for the next part of the mission with success seemingly within their grasp.

It proved a false hope as attempts to advance over the following days were baulked by further defences and counter-attacks that took a significant toll across the Brigade, with neither armour nor infantry able to make significant progress. The situation was the same across the front although the assault had tied up the enemy's tactical reserve, taken a large bite out of his position and used up much of his fuel, though at a high cost to the Allied infantry which was by now exhausted. A pause was needed to withdraw the armour, reset and then attempt to push through again as on the first night, the 9th Lancer's history summing up the plan (Operation Supercharge) briefly – '*In other words to back down the hill again and take another rush at it.*'[41] In preparation, after four days spent in close contact, the 9th were taken out of the firing line to refit during the last three days of October.

The 12th Lancers' part in the opening stages of El Alamein had been less dramatic, but equally frustrating. Having moved up behind the artillery barrage along Sun, Moon and Star tracks to support 1st Armoured Division, dawn found the Regiment just to the north of the entrances to the two main minefield gaps where they remained, prevented from reaching 2nd Armoured Brigade on Meteiriya Ridge by the weight of fire from artillery and anti-tank guns. The situation persisted until 27th October, when the first patrols from each squadron reached the formation ahead of them, before being withdrawn with the rest of the 1st Armoured Division to recuperate the following day, the War Diary recording: '*Our patrols are not very useful. This is*

LIEUTENANT COLONEL GERALD GROSVENOR COMMANDED THE 9TH LANCERS FROM SHORTLY BEFORE EL ALAMEIN UNTIL MARCH 1944. HE WAS PICKED AS ONE OF A NUMBER OF EXPERIENCED COMMANDERS FOR THE NORMANDY INVASION AND WAS SEVERELY WOUNDED SOON AFTER LANDING. HE WAS LATER COLONEL OF THE 9TH/12TH LANCERS FROM 1961-1967.

…'the hammering of the panzers' had succeeded in bringing Rommel's armour to battle and reducing it significantly, causing losses the Germans could ill afford.

definitely no place for an armoured car regiment.'[42]

Operation Supercharge on 2nd November was to use similar tactics but this time with X Corps prepared to fight to achieve a breakthrough if XXX Corps failed to open a sufficient breach. The 9th Armoured Brigade were ordered to punch through the anti-tank screen – prepared to take 100% casualties if necessary – with 2nd Armoured Brigade ready to pass through and bring 21st Panzer Division to battle. The 12th Lancers were to continue to act as the Divisional reconnaissance regiment with orders, so Captain Bishop, by now the Adjutant, recalled to '*"keep going, not stopping for 88s or 105s or anything like that", which sounded slightly ridiculous, not to say suicidal.*'[43]

By dawn the infantry were on their objective and the 9th Armoured Brigade, at an appalling cost (the 3rd Hussars lost all but four of its 52 tanks), had succeeded in punching some of the way through the German anti-tank shield as far as the Rahman track in order to allow the 1st Armoured Division to begin the break-out. With the 12th Lancers fanning out in front of the Division, a troop leader described the situation as they moved forward: '*As dawn broke one's sensations were very unpleasant. In the haze of dust shapes arose. All of them were hostile in silhouette and only time told which of them were alive, which dead and innocuous. The agony of suspense felt by a troop leader approaching a cluster of enemy tanks or an anti-tank line of up to twenty guns before he could be certain, by the mere fact of his continued existence, of their abandonment can best be imagined…advancing over ground which had been fought for and captured only a few hours before, was the indescribable smell of battle, of death, of explosive and burnt material. It was most unnerving.*'[44]

In the same area, the 9th Lancers had led the 2nd Armoured Brigade advance on to the plateau of Aqqaqir where they, too, came across the wreckage of the 9th Armoured Brigade as both Regiments now found themselves engaged by the enemy's still potent anti-tank guns and armour. For the 9th the fight that ensued was '*about the worst we had ever had*'.[45] Facing a line of 88s, 105s and armour which engaged them from three sides, over six concerted counter-attacks were repulsed, with the 9th Lancers accounting for 31 tanks in a fight

1 GERMAN TRANSPORT ON THE COAST ROAD NEAR MERSA MATRUH. HAVING FINALLY BROKEN THROUGH THE AXIS DEFENCES AT EL ALAMEIN BOTH REGIMENTS, AS PART OF 1ST ARMOURED DIVISION, RACED TO CUT OFF THE RETREATING ENEMY. ALTHOUGH A LARGE NUMBER OF PRISONERS WERE TAKEN, THE ANNIHILATION OF THE AFRIKA KORPS WAS THWARTED BY BAD WEATHER AND SUBSEQUENT FUEL SHORTAGES.

2 THE CHRISTMAS MENU OF THE 12TH LANCERS IN 1942. DRAWN BY SERGEANT HIGGS THEY WERE A FEATURE OF THE NEXT THREE YEARS AND REFLECTED THE INCREASING CONFIDENCE FELT BY THE ALLIES FOLLOWING VICTORY AT EL ALAMEIN.

that was by no means one-sided: '*The terrific cross-fire was taking its toll. Two of C Squadron's Shermans were burnt out, one cruiser destroyed and five other Shermans knocked out. Our own infantry, dug-in on the battlefield, suffered terribly, being killed by shells meant for us. In that torrent of shot and shell any man who moved was killed. We did what we could for them, but our attention was taken up in fighting for dear life.*'[46] Although the breakthrough had not occurred, 'the hammering of the panzers' had succeeded in bringing Rommel's armour to battle and reducing it significantly, causing losses the Germans could ill afford. The following day continued with much the same slugging match, though signs were coming, as the German infantry began to lose their nerve, that the battle was beginning to turn. By the afternoon the 12th Lancers, who were in an observation line north-east of Aqqaqir and engaging enemy transport with direct fire, were able to report on an enemy that was finally abandoning its positions and heading west.

On 4th November the breakout by the 1st Armoured Division was led by the 12th Lancers as news began to arrive of large numbers of prisoners being taken to the south. In the brief lull, men who were exhausted after the action of the last few days and without the sound of shells to wake them, slept where they stopped, the 9th Lancers' history recording that on the following morning '*the first thing we saw… was a cold and untidy German private standing over the Colonel as he slept and saying, "I've been trying to find someone to surrender to for three hours." To which a sleepy voice replied: "Shut up and sit down".*'[47] Despite these distractions the attempt to destroy the Afrika Korps continued, with 1st Armoured Division initially

CORPORAL NICKOLLS AT EL ALAMEIN

On 27th October 1942, with the slow advance at the beginning of the battle of El Alamein grinding on, the infantry in the 9th Lancers area found themselves facing 50 or 60 enemy tanks a short distance away. With 88mm guns to the right, B Squadron moved round to the left and directly behind the infantry, where two rounds by Sergeant Edwards' gunner, Corporal Nickolls, quickly destroyed two tanks and dispersed the rest. They continued to engage the remainder of the German tanks. Edwards, dismounted and lying on a ridge, called forward Nickolls in the tank when the enemy appeared. Using his civilian skills as a poacher, Nickolls advanced slowly to avoid raising dust until he could pick off a tank and then retired again out of sight. Soon, with the assistance of the remainder of his troop, he had several Italians and Germans burning. He continued to snipe throughout the day, knocking out eight tanks from the troops' total of 11, and bringing his overall tally for the North African campaign to over 30. By chance, General Montgomery was listening in on a radio intercept as each kill in this sequence was relayed and ordered that Cpl Nickolls was to be put in for an immediate Military Medal to encourage other gunners. His efforts are remembered by the award of the Nickolls Trophy to the best gunner in the Regiment.

ordered to roll up the enemy positions to the north before new instructions arrived to break contact and move south-west before hooking up towards Mersa Matruh to intercept and destroy the enemy as they withdrew. By chance the Afrika Korps had also taken this route and the 12th was soon back in contact with the enemy. Major Shand unwittingly tried to destroy General Rommel's headquarters which, unsurprisingly, was heavily defended and led to his capture. By 7th November, both regiments were in position on an escarpment overlooking the road 45km west of Mersa Matruh, with the enemy three miles in the distance and their complete destruction seemingly certain – if only they could be got at.

This proved impossible. Torrential rain had started to fall, turning the ground to a quagmire that bogged the 12th Lancers' wheeled vehicles and prevented the fuel lorries reaching the tanks, leaving the 9th Lancers static for 20 hours. Unable to do anything but watch the Germans get away on the Tarmac road to their front, both Regiments felt the same degree of frustration. '*Below us, on the plain, there stretched many miles of German transport, guns and tanks… The [2nd Armoured] Brigade sat and fumed, watching them until it became too dark to see…the lorries arrived and tanks were filled…An hour before dawn we formed up in battle order and raced over the top and down the escarpment – but the bird had flown.*'[48] Once again there was to be no complete destruction of the enemy, which would now begin a skilfully handled withdrawal to the west.

Despite this frustration, the battle of Alamein had produced the first major Allied victory of the war, reduced the Axis' armour by 450 tanks and cost them 30,000 prisoners, of which the 12th Lancers accounted for nearly 1,000 in the four days to 8th November. This was also the day that the coast road was finally reached, a squadron of 12th Lancers letting slip a fleeing German lorry full of high-class food and other luxuries that the 9th, further along the road, managed to intercept before a small portion and a note of thanks was sent back.

Notwithstanding the extra rations, the 9th Lancers were called off the chase, the logistic support deemed incapable of maintaining more than one armoured brigade forward of Tobruk until Benghazi became operational as a port. The 12th, after a few days of rest, moved west to Buq Buq, from where they formed one of a series of raiding parties sent to harass the enemy's withdrawal. With a column consisting of over 240 vehicles and including a battery of artillery, a troop of anti-tank guns, some anti-aircraft guns, engineers and two companies of Royal Army Service Corps, complete with six days' rations and petrol for 1,000 miles, they set off on 13th November to seize Matuba airfield 200 miles to the west. Despite a successful two-day march that brought them in from the south they proved just too late, reaching the airfield to find that the enemy had fled, leaving a total bag of '*five unhappy wops*'[49], while, with the frustration of not being able to continue to advance, they watched the RAF move into the captured landing strips.

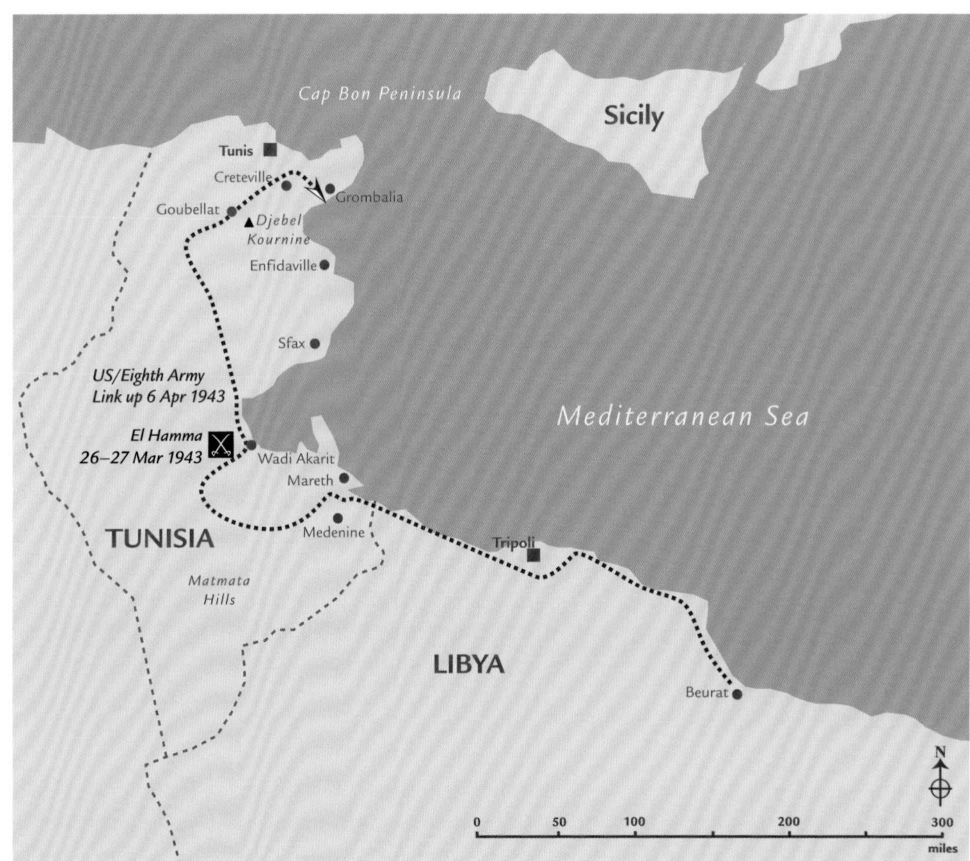

OPERATIONS FROM JANUARY-MAY 1943.

Both regiments remained in the area of Tmimi while the advance continued. The 12th rejoined it on 12th January 1943, some 600 miles further along the coast at Buerat, with contact immediately re-established before the Germans once again began to pull back, all three squadrons meeting little opposition as they tracked them west. '*The primary task was that of furnishing 'going reports' every two hours, together with the protection of the 22nd Armoured Brigade – no easy task in view of the speed with which the advance developed, the continual pressure from behind to "push on", and constant inquiries such as "What's the going like".*'[50]

Despite difficult ground and mines, both of which took a heavy toll on both armoured cars and personnel, the pursuit continued with up to 45 miles made in a day and large amounts of equipment destroyed or captured. The vital port of Tripoli was reached on 21st January and captured by 7th Armoured Division the following day, before the 12th Lancers, now under 8th Armoured Brigade, moved further west, progress slowing as a result

1 TANK COMMANDERS OF THE 9TH LANCERS. OF THE SIX, FOUR WOULD BE KILLED DURING THE WAR.

2 LIEUTENANT COLONEL GEORGE KIDSTON, 12TH LANCERS, BRIEFING GENERAL MONTGOMERY PRIOR TO THE ASSAULT ON THE MARETH LINE. CAPTAIN TIM BISHOP IS TO THE RIGHT OF THE PICTURE.

of impassable desert to either side of a road that was denied by effective German delaying tactics. Captain Bishop noted that, *'with the terrain on their side, [delay] could be successfully effected with the minimum amount of troops. One 88 could stop an army.'*[51]

MARETH LINE

Despite their presence and the deteriorating vehicle state, the Tunisian border was crossed and Medenine taken on 20th February, with the advance continuing north-west until halted by the enemy positions of the Mareth Line. At this stage in the North African campaign the noose was tightening around the Afrika Korps' neck. Operation Torch in November of 1942 had landed British and American troops along the coast from Casablanca to Tunisia but, after a successful early campaign, they had been checked and the First Army was now strung out on a line running about 150 miles inland from the coast in the north, but still 50 miles short of their final objective of Tunis. From the south-west, a Free-French force was advancing, while from the east the Eighth Army completed the encirclement, but was now faced by the Mareth Line, a pre-war French defensive position built to protect Tunisia, complete with concrete emplacements, anti-tank ditches and minefields, flanked on one side by the sea and on the other by the Matmata hills.

As preparations for an assault went on, A Squadron of the 12th, temporarily under command of the Royals, found itself in the path of General Rommel's final fling in the North African campaign at the Battle of Medenine. Launching two strong armoured thrusts on 6th March, he hoped to open up the Eighth Army's flank but, instead, with tactics that mirrored his own and with his intentions revealed through Ultra, he ran into a well-organised defence in depth in which he lost 50 tanks to well-sited anti-tank guns with infantry in support. 'A' Squadron, tracking the attack, managed nevertheless to keep up a steady stream of reports on the columns, which it then had the satisfaction of seeing destroyed by the Allied defensive position.

For the rest of the 12th, early March was spent re-equipping with Daimler armoured cars, which, although still under-powered, had lower silhouettes than the Humbers and were armed with a 2-pounder gun and 7.92mm Besa machine gun, some Humbers remaining in squadron and regimental headquarters where their larger size made command and control easier. As preparations continued, the 9th Lancers also moved up from Tmimi and arrived on 13th March.

General Montgomery's plan for the Mareth Line was strikingly similar to that used at El Alamein and aimed, again, not only to crack the position, but to destroy the enemy forces manning it using a frontal assault by XXX Corps, while the armour, including both 9th and 12th Lancers, was held together in X Corps to exploit the break-in. The New Zealand Corps was to move around the flank of the position through the Matmata hills as a secondary axis and tie up the enemy reserves. The failure of the XXX Corps assault on the night of 20th–21st March and the success of the New Zealand Corps move was to result, however, in a sudden change of axis. The 1st Armoured Division was now to follow the path taken by the New Zealand Corps and attack through them to El Hamma, thereby cutting off the enemy's line of retreat. The order required a move of 170 miles over treacherous terrain of deep sand in which the wheeled vehicles bogged, while elsewhere steep wadis and rocky outcrops caused other obstacles. To make matters more complicated, the whole operation was to be completed at night, in total secrecy, in two days.

By the morning of 26th March, the 1st Armoured Division had overcome the difficulties of the move and was in a position to attack the German position in the Tebaga Gap south-west of El Hamma, a 6,000-yard wide bottleneck through which every unit must pass to get onto the coastal plain. Following a two-hour bombing mission by the RAF, the New Zealand Corps were to attack at 4.30pm before the 1st Armoured Division, with the 2nd Armoured Brigade leading, broke through to El Hamma that night before driving to the coast road and trapping the enemy on the Mareth Line. In the Brigade the 9th would be forward right, the Bays forward left and the 10th Hussars in reserve, with C Squadron of the 12th Lancers attached as a reconnaissance element. The rest of the 12th were to provide flank protection to the divisional artillery at the rear of the column. Everyone was to take their echelons with them, loaded with five days' stores in case the road behind was closed. It was, the 9th's Commanding Officer, Lieutenant Colonel Grosvenor, conceded, *'A very bold plan; and not one, I must admit, that I felt very confident about, as I remembered only too well the desert at El Alamein littered with the burning tanks of 9th Armoured Brigade.'*[52]

Despite these misgivings and some interference from shellfire, the 2nd Armoured Brigade moved through the minefield gaps, pausing in the dark as they waited for sufficient moonlight to push on: *'It was a curious and not altogether pleasant sensation to be sitting in the middle of the German position with such a large phalanx of vehicles.'*[53] Moving shortly before midnight, the first nine miles gave little opposition as enemy vehicles, unaware of the breakthrough, were either caught where they stood, or were attacked as they moved to the front: *'it soon became*

THE LINK UP WITH THE US ARMY IN TUNISIA

The link up between the Eighth Army and the Americans of the First Army who had invaded the North African coast in Algeria and Tunisia had been heralded by interference on the net over the previous few days. The 12th Lancers' War Diary noted laconically that *'Roger [a novel part of the American voice procedure] becomes more and more conspicuous on the wireless'*[61], though the historic link up, at 3.30pm on 7th April, took place amidst scenes that no film-maker would have been proud of. *'The behelmeted Americans bundled up in warm clothes suitable to Djebel temperatures, the British in ragged bleached desert uniforms, without helmets… They said 'Hello' to each other, but did not shake hands until the movie men recalled that millions of people in America and Britain wanted their money's worth.'*[62]

A more immediate example of Allied co-operation was an attack that took place shortly after the link up, when US tanks and 12th Lancer armoured cars rescued B Squadron Headquarters from captivity. This followed an over-ambitious attack on suspected transport which proved to be a headquarters protected by tanks. The thanks given to their American allies over the next few months was not always as heartfelt as it might have been, several soldiers taking the opportunity to sell hastily gathered dust as 'genuine' Alamein sand, while another, keen to buy souvenirs was shown a Luger pistol by Sergeant Nutting with unfortunate results: *'Taking it with shining eyes one of our visitors proceeded without noticeable delay to shoot himself in the leg with it.'*[63]

THESE TWO SERGEANTS were the first to exchange greetings when British and American patrols met on the Gabes road on the afternoon of 7th April.

a competition between the two leading regiments as to who could shoot up the most vehicles and there were complaints by both regiments of poaching on their side of the road.'[54] A hastily cobbled-together screen of anti-tank guns and dug-in tanks brought the charge to a halt five miles short of El Hamma and, an hour before dawn, the Brigade received orders to consolidate the ground it had taken.

Although Grosvenor, together with many others, was sure that El Hamma could have been reached that night, the situation behind him was far from secure, with a mass of enemy, including armour, still effective – as the 12th Lancers' main body and the divisional artillery discovered at first light when it repulsed an armoured counter-attack. Despite the remaining threat, the success of the attack into El Hamma had unhinged the German position on the Mareth Line, though the halt allowed them to escape north and left Lieutenant Colonel Grosvenor to sum up the events. *'So ended a brilliant operation which just failed to achieve its object [of cutting off the whole enemy force in the Mareth area]...It was the first time that we had achieved a successful breakthrough by armour in the dark.'*[55]

The advance north resumed on 29th March, though with A Squadron, 12th Lancers, sent south-west to Kebili to link up with General LeClerc's Free-French army that had advanced from Chad to join the Allied armies. The Axis forces had by now occupied a further defensive position to the north of Mareth along the Wadi Akarit feature. After a careful build-up, this was taken on the night of 5th/6th April, the 9th helping to provide a diversion to draw enemy fire as the heights that dominated the feature were cleared by the infantry. Although depth positions once again allowed many of the enemy to escape before the exploitation force could destroy them, the fall of the Wadi Akarit position marked the beginning of a long retreat to the north to the next Axis position at Enfidaville. Behind them, the Eighth Army fanned out, with the 12th, who were providing flank protection to the New Zealand Corps on the west of the Army, linking up with the American forces on the southern flank of the First Army in the afternoon of the 7th April on the Gafsa-Gabes road. The pursuit north continued and, on 12th April, the 12th Lancers again made a further link up, this time with a troop of the 1st Derbyshire Yeomanry, the first time that British forces from the First and Eighth Armies had met.

LIEUTENANT ROBIN BROCKBANK'S ACTION ON THE GOUBELLAT PLAIN, FOR WHICH HE WAS AWARDED A MILITARY CROSS. TUNISIA, WITH ITS FARMS AND VEGETATION, REQUIRED A DIFFERENT SET OF TACTICS AND A DIFFERENT COAT OF PAINT FOR THE VEHICLES – A DISAPPOINTMENT FOR BOTH REGIMENTS WHO TOOK A PRIDE IN THE BATTERED, FADED PAINT OF THEIR DESERT CAMPAIGNING.

TUNIS

With the encirclement of the Axis forces in Tunisia complete, the First Army was designated to take the lead in the final act of the North African campaign. The Eighth Army was to fix the German position at Enfidaville and tie up their forces there as the First Army attacked from the west to capture Tunis and then advance towards Hammamet to prevent the enemy retreating into the Cap Bon peninsula from which they might escape. To give substance to this order of priorities, 1st Armoured Division, with both 9th and 12th Lancers under command, was to move to join the First Army to the west of Tunis, to come under command of IX Corps in the area of the Goubellat Plain.

As they moved in the middle of April, similar sentiments were felt by both Regiments as the scenery changed from the desert wasteland that they were so familiar with to the fertile olive groves, cornfields and neat farms growing fresh vegetables that they now met in Central Tunisia. *'The Promised Land could not have looked sweeter to the Israelites than Tunisia looked to the dusty Eighth Army.'*[56] Rather more prosaically, the changing countryside forced them to repaint all their vehicles and begin to conform, Captain Bishop commenting that *'the thing that most annoyed us was having to paint all our vehicles dark green, like those at home. Our vehicles were white, symbolic of the Desert Army. They had become a pinkish yellow and we were proud of this well-worn hue. Indeed it was a badge of honour for we had just advanced thousands of miles. We were also told to 'cut out the Arabic' which punctuated our every sentence.'*[57] Tactics had to be adjusted in the closer country where tank squadron leaders were less likely to see all their troops at once, while tales of the new Tiger or Mark VI tank were also heard. It was not just the scenery that was changing, shops and other soldiers produced equal comment: *'To those of us who had been away from England for so long it was a shock to realize exactly how far we had wandered from the accepted appearance of a British soldier. The First Army men were wearing neat battledress with blancoed gaiters, web equipment and steel helmets… Our first*

1 **THE DJEBEL EL KOURNINE** – A PHOTOGRAPH TAKEN BY FREDDIE HUNN IN 1999 DURING A BATTLEFIELD STUDY. DOMINATING THE GOUBELLAT PLAIN AND THE ROUTE TO TUNIS, THE GERMAN POSITIONS HELD UP BOTH REGIMENTS AFTER THE 1ST ARMOURED DIVISION HAD BEEN SWITCHED FROM THE EIGHTH ARMY TO THE FIRST ARMY FOR THE FINAL ASSAULT TO TUNIS.

2 **LIEUTENANT MATT ABRAHAM** WHO WITH ONE OTHER SOLDIER CLIMBED THE DJEBEL KOURNINE DESPITE ALL OTHER ATTEMPTS TO TAKE IT. ARMED ONLY WITH A REVOLVER HE TRIED TO CAPTURE SIX DOZING GERMANS 'BUT WAS COMPELLED TO BEAT A PRECIPITATE AND UNDIGNIFIED RETREAT'.

'MOUNT UP!'

9TH LANCER SHERMANS.

impressions can best be summed up in the words of a member of the leading tank crew, who took one look and said: "My God! Soldiers!"'[58]

On 22nd April, the First Army attacked along the whole of its front. IX Corps, attacking with 6th and 1st Armoured Divisions, had been ordered to advance over the Goubellat Plain and seize the dominating Djebel Kournine feature. They were then to push north-east to destroy any armour that might interfere with the V Corps attack on their left flank. As had happened so often before, the reality proved different from the optimism of the plan. After initial progress across its front, the First Army found itself checked by fierce opposition from elite German divisions while in the Goubellat Plain both Regiments found the observation obscured by the high corn and the ground intersected by small, deep wadis and numerous farm buildings that proved ideally suited to defence. Capitalising on these natural advantages, the enemy, mainly comprising the Hermann Goering Division, had established a multitude of positions protected by skilfully laid mines covered by 88mm guns. The effect proved devastating to both Regiments, with A Squadron, 9th Lancers, reduced to four tanks by 24th April.

A day later, it was clear that the attack had not achieved the breakthrough hoped for and the 2nd Armoured Brigade came to a halt in a position overlooking 'Dead Horse Farm' – so named because of the many animal carcasses putrefying in the sun – with the enemy on the other side of the bowl covering the position with both 105mm artillery and Tiger tanks, the latter destroying two Shermans and seemingly impervious to returning fire. With no infantry available to conduct an immediate combined-arms assault, the Regiment remained behind the crest, observing and containing the enemy until the withdrawal of the German armour on 7th May as the result of the successful breakthrough to the north. The 12th's experiences were no more satisfactory. There was little scope for armoured car work and, despite some individual successes, including the scaling of Djebel Kournine by a troop leader who found an enemy OP ensconced before he was forced to retreat, the 12th Lancers remained in observation until all but two of its patrols had been relieved by the end of the first week in May.

Although the attack had proved unsuccessful in achieving a breakthrough, 50 German tanks and 40 anti-tank guns had been destroyed in the offensive, losses that could be ill-afforded by the now cut-off Axis forces in Tunisia. To complete their destruction, further reinforcements from the Eighth Army to First Army at the end of April provided additional combat power for the next and final act in the campaign. To their immediate north, IX Corps would punch up the valley from Medjez el Bab to Tunis in an attack that began early on 6th May, while 1st Armoured Division resumed its stalled progress in the Goubellat Plain. This time, there was no stopping the Allies and rapid progress was made in all areas, Tunis falling on 7th May, by which time the 1st Armoured Division was racing to cut off the enemy from retreat into the Cap Bon Peninsula.

General Alexander was able to tell Churchill, 'Sir, it is my duty to report that the Tunisian campaign is over. All enemy resistance has ceased. We are masters of the North African shore'

The advance began easily enough, but the defended Creteville pass through the hills to Grombalia held both Regiments in what Sergeant Bryant of the 12th Lancers remembered was *'casually described on the BBC as "mopping up operations", they were the scenes of fierce rearguard actions by the enemy and nightmare advances by ourselves'*.[59] On 8th May, the 9th began the task of clearing the pass in fierce fighting, during which a number of Germans and 88mm guns were captured, together with 200 Italians, though, following an inconclusive duel with tanks and anti-tank guns that afternoon, the pass remained in German hands.

The hold-up was to prove only temporary and the next day enemy resistance largely ceased, with news that 6th Armoured Division had moved down the road from Tunis, cutting off their position and any withdrawal to the Cap Bon Peninsula. The 9th Lancers pushed on to find that, although Grombalia had already been liberated a few hours before, they were able to enjoy a *'positively embarrassing'* welcome from the local French, which included a magnificent breakfast. Elsewhere, the 12th Lancers' squadrons collected prisoners and dealt with the last vestiges of resistance while the sights of the victory sank in – no evacuation had been possible and there were thousands of prisoners and abandoned vehicles to be dealt with. This was Dunkirk in reverse but with no boats to take away the defeated army. While on 9th May General Alexander was able to tell Churchill, *'Sir, it is my duty to report that the Tunisian campaign is over. All enemy resistance has ceased. We are masters of the North African shore'*, for the men of both Regiments the end of 18 months of fighting meant that they could sit *'by the roadside with our mouths open and watch the prisoners go'*.[60]

ITALY

1944–1945

Citerna | Gothic Line | Coriano | Capture of Forli | Lamone Crossing | Pideura | Defence of Lamone Bridgehead Conventello-Comacchio | Argenta Gap | Bologna | Sillaro Crossing | Idice Bridgehead | Italy 1944–1945

THE SURRENDER OF THE AXIS POWERS in Tunisia resulted in the capture of over 250,000 prisoners, causing Goebbels to comment that *'our losses there are enormous. We are indeed experiencing a sort of second Stalingrad.'* For both Regiments, it meant the chance to relax, with visits to Tunis and swimming in the sea among the highlights, though a victory parade in a sweltering Tunis on the 20th May was not so welcome, a 9th Lancer remarking that, *'as usual, the only people who did not enjoy it were those taking part'*.[1] The order to hand in all the recently 'liberated' transport, including cars, trucks and generals' caravans, while probably an improvement in safety, curtailed some of the pleasure of the period, as did the move back within the month to Tripoli and the desert nearby. Here an inspection of the whole of 1st Armoured Division by the King took place on 21st June. Re-organisation and training began immediately, the 9th Lancers receiving Shermans for A Squadron to replace their Cruisers, while in July the 12th's establishment increased with the formation of D Squadron. Equipped with five troops of two Daimler armoured cars and two scout cars, each squadron was also provided with greater flexibility through a support troop of infantry in trucks and its own integral firepower from a heavy troop of two 75mm artillery pieces mounted in White half-tracks.

THE VICTORY PARADE IN TUNIS ON 20TH MAY 1943 INVOLVED BOTH 9TH AND 12TH LANCERS. *'AS USUAL THE ONLY PEOPLE WHO DID NOT ENJOY IT WERE THOSE TAKING PART.'*

1 LESSONS LEARNT IN NORTH AFRICA LED TO THE 12TH RECEIVING WHITE HALF-TRACKS WITH A 75MM GUN TO PROVIDE DEDICATED SUPPORT WHEN OPERATING BEYOND THE REACH OF ALLIED ARTILLERY.

2 THE 12TH LANCERS SOLDIERS' CHRISTMAS DINNER MENU 1943, ONE OF A SERIES DRAWN BY SGT HIGGS FROM 1942–1944

In early August 1943, both regiments returned to Tunisia *'to guard prisoners, docks and dumps'*, the bulk of the 9th initially detailed to guard a prisoner of war cage on the Algerian–Tunisian border, a simple task that was curtailed when the authorities realised that the place held only one prisoner, an Italian who did not wish to escape. A move nearer to Algiers allowed courses in England and Egypt to be taken, and, though equipment remained scarce at first, training began, initially at troop level and aimed principally at the newly arrived reinforcements – the 9th alone receiving three officers and 120 men. New drills were needed for the new equipment, Honey light tanks replacing Daimler armoured cars in the 9th's reconnaissance troop. The Regiment also perfected indirect fire from tanks using methods that were adopted across the Armoured Corps, while the 12th got to grips with the 75mm gun which, despite being an 1873 French design, proved accurate and effective. The US Staghound armoured car was also brought into the 12th's inventory, while both Regiments learnt the newly adopted US voice procedure.

The experience gained in Tunisia and the expectation of the different conditions on mainland Europe had also caused a re-evaluation of tactics, with increasing emphasis placed on combined-arms training. Troop, squadron, regimental and then divisional level exercises occupied both Regiments, the 9th Lancers' Regimental Group in January 1944 eventually involving over 1,500 men from all arms and services. Alongside tactical training, the new Commanding Officer of the 12th, Lieutenant Colonel KE Savill, also decided to concentrate on physical fitness, instituting a period of exercises before breakfast which all officers were required to attend. On the first parade everyone less the Intelligence Officer and the Quartermaster appeared, the former informing the Commanding Officer that he had joined the 12th in the war because, *'he had hunted with the 12th before the war and he thought he would like to give them a hand…in doing so he was prepared to be shot at by the Germans, wounded by the Germans, taken prisoner by the Germans, or even killed by the Germans, but under no circumstances would he stand on his head for the Germans at 6 o'clock in the morning.'*[2] A compromise was eventually reached, with all those over 32 years of age excused, which included the two concerned.

More entertainingly, tank-driving 'trials' between Churchills, Shermans and Honeys were also conducted, for which 'race-cards' were produced, with shed tracks, ditchings and several overturnings the inevitable result. Sport of all varieties, including skiing in the Atlas mountains, also filled the time, as did leave at Army-organised centres on the coast. Others took advantage of the shooting on offer, including boar hunting, as well as a pack of hounds which the 9th Lancers trained from the local hunting dogs. After such a long period on operations it was inevitable that several good parties would be enjoyed: *'C Squadron gave a farewell party to Col George [Kidston] followed by a Regimental farewell, where the Mess was severely damaged, not helped by [later Major General] Abraham's introduction of a small and greasy pig.'*[3]

Following the end of the war in North Africa, Allied strategy aimed to draw German forces away from France, where it had been agreed the decisive landings would take place. Sicily was invaded in July 1943, with landings on the mainland of Italy following in early September. It was now that the Allies discovered that Italy, despite its glamorous appeal, *'was a truly terrible place to fight a war'*.[4] The landscape was ideally suited to defence. The Appenine mountains formed a central spine running down three-quarters of the country's length. Peaks rose to over 10,000ft from which lateral spurs, with deep valleys and wide, rapid rivers in between them, ran down to the sea on both sides, making rapid movement impossible. On the 20-mile wide coastal strip, on which all the north–south roads ran, movement was also easily checked at key choke points dominated by naturally strong positions. Infrastructure was poor, with roads and tracks away from the main highways largely undeveloped and easily blocked by demolitions while, where the mountains gave way to the plains, these were dissected by rivers, canals and deep ditches, the net effect being to negate much of the advantage that the Allies had in armour and mechanised forces. The Germans kept large numbers of their strongest divisions in Italy whereas, at regular intervals during the campaign, the Fifth and Eighth Armies were stripped of combat power to feed the requirement for troops in other theatres. Further complicating the mix were the activities of the partisans and a bitter civil war that ran as a sub-plot between the ousted Fascists and their opponents. The campaign, the longest and bloodiest fought by the Allies in the West, too often turned into *'a slow and remorseless grinding battle of attrition'*[5] that was not helped by harsh winters that brought rain and snow, turning the battlefield into a muddy quagmire resembling the First World War.

GUSTAV LINE

The initial landings had been followed by rapid early progress, but hopes for an early German collapse evaporated with the Allies held in October 1943 on the Winter Line that ran across Italy. Its western end, the Gustav Line, hinged on the near impregnable strongpoint at Monte Cassino. By the time of the 12th Lancers' arrival in Italy in April 1944, several attempts to break through had failed, but with pressure mounting for troops to be released for the impending invasion of Europe, a further assault was set for early May. The plan was to punch through at Cassino before driving on to liberate Rome and then to exploit north to reach the Po valley in the north-east before maybe continuing into Austria – all to be done before the end of 1944.

As part of these preparations, on 22 April 1944 the 12th gave up their armoured cars to take up a sector of the line in an infantry role, though not before they had established contact with the Polish 12th Podolski Lancers (who would be responsible

1 THE 12TH LANCERS ARRIVED IN ITALY IN APRIL 1944 AND WERE IMMEDIATELY POSTED TO SANGRO VALLEY IN THE INFANTRY ROLE AS PART OF THE ALLIED PREPARATIONS ON A FRESH ASSAULT ON MONTE CASSINO AND THE GUSTAV LINE.

2&3 IN CONTRAST TO THE SPEED OF THE BATTLES IN NORTH AFRICA, THE ITALIAN CAMPAIGN, IN WHICH BOTH REGIMENTS SERVED AS INFANTRY AS WELL IN VEHICLES PROVED TO BE A *'SLOW AND REMORSELESS GRINDING BATTLE OF ATTRITION'*.[6] BAD WEATHER WAS A FEATURE OF THE CAMPAIGN, BOGGING IN BOTH TRACKED AND WHEELED VEHICLES AND MAKING ANY SORT OF SHELTER ATTRACTIVE.

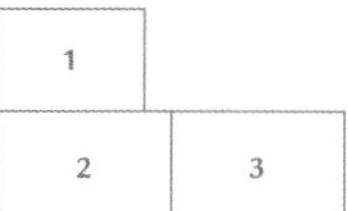

A MAP DRAWN IN 1946 TO SHOW THE ROUTE OF THE 12TH LANCERS THROUGH ITALY. ALTHOUGH CONDUCTED THROUGH ATTRACTIVE COUNTRYSIDE, THE FIGHTING PROVED BITTER AND FIERCELY CONTESTED WITH AMBUSHES AND MINED ROADS A CONSTANT THREAT TO RECONNAISSANCE TROOPS.

for the final capture of Cassino and hoist a 12th Polish Lancers pennant over it), the meeting being marked by an appropriately large party. The Regimental sector lay in the northern part of the Winter Line and covered the River Sangro valley, a feature with steep-sided mountain walls leading to a flat-bottomed valley in which small villages were scattered on the lower slopes and banks.

Enemy positions lay up to a kilometre away across the valley and, while observation posts scanned the valley by day, by night the emphasis changed to aggressive patrolling with ambushes and raids as both sides sought to gain an advantage. Patrol bases for operations of up to a week were established on the far side of the river with troops lying up by day before venturing out at night, the squadron leader in one of these rejoicing in the title *'Officer i/c all British troops north of the Sangro.'*[7] With extra instruction from 2nd Battalion, Grenadier Guards in May, these independent operations proved both enjoyable and popular: *'...for my troop a kind of stalking game in a solitary mountain kingdom of our own; and my men seemed to enjoy this more than any other kind of military activity'*, while another noted: *'A patrol had all the qualities of a poaching expedition – just enough danger to add spice and purpose, and the exhilaration of walking through lovely country in spring.'*[8] The activity was not without its dangers: mines, weather, the difficulty of constantly crossing the Sangro and a determined enemy added to logistic difficulties, with most of the resupply coming forward by mule. One officer remembered that *'our chief memories of those times in the mountains were the cold, the hunger and those awful steep walks'*.[9] The locals in the area on both sides of the River proved friendly and co-operative, providing guides and local knowledge as well as vino: *'The most important contribution to the conduct of these operations came, however, from the Italians...who knew that anything that smacked of partisan activity would draw a summary vengeance from the Germans, but whose hospitality was never wanting... Old or young they had little use for ideologies, possessing only a simple and uncomplicated hatred of the Germans. "Those", remarked an Italian as he watched shells bursting on the enemy positions, "are the chocolate drops to give them".'*[10]

The final chapter in the Battle for Monte Cassino began on 11th May 1944, with the 12th Lancers' part limited to their 75mm guns assisting in a diversionary barrage and increased foot patrolling, until, after occupying a sector further west, they were able to rejoin their vehicles at the end of the month to begin the hoped-for pursuit to the north. Under command of X Corps, orders were received to protect the open right flank of the 2nd New Zealand Division as they pushed north on the Army's eastern flank. Patrols were immediately held up, however, by fire from heavy mortars in a pattern that continued for the next few days until the pace picked up as news arrived first of the fall of Rome on 4th June and, two days later, the Normandy landings.

Despite these encouraging events, it was soon apparent that this was not to be a full-scale rout of a defeated foe but rather a planned withdrawal by a determined enemy intent on imposing the maximum amount of danger and delay, the advance taking until August to reach the next German

'The type of warfare here in Italy was completely different to that which we experienced in the desert, where we had space and room to manoeuvre.'

1 4TH TROOP, D SQUADRON, 12TH LANCERS IN ASSISI IN THE SUMMER OF 1944. THE FIGHTING THROUGH UMBRIA PROVIDING FLANK PROTECTION TO THE EIGHTH ARMY AS IT ADVANCED TO THE GOTHIC LINE WAS CHARACTERISED BY AMBUSHES, BOOBY TRAPS AND MINES. SERGEANT HIGGS, WHO DREW THE CHRISTMAS MENU CARDS, IS ON THE LEFT.

2 ELEMENTS OF REGIMENTAL HEADQUARTERS, 12TH LANCERS, IN FRONT OF A STAGHOUND ARMOURED CAR IN 1944. FROM THE LEFT ARE CAPTAINS MARK WYNDHAM, SIGNALS OFFICER; ROBIN BROCKBANK, ADJUTANT AND GEORGE KNIGHT, TECHNICAL ADJUTANT.

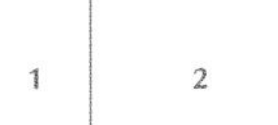

defensive belt, the Gothic Line between Pisa and Rimini, 150 miles north of Rome. Throughout these operations the 12th continued to protect the right flank of the Army as it moved, the task initially involving little movement, but rather guarding roads through and out of the mountains as slow progress continued with frequent demolitions and mines to hinder movement. All this was '*living among the sweet sickly smell of rotting horses and humans*'.[11]

By the middle of June, the Regiment had entered the more gentle countryside of Umbria and a true reconnaissance task could be carried out as they pushed on faster, a patrol on 16th June having bypassed the enemy rearguard, reaching Foligno near Assisi, to capture the bridge on the far side of town as it was prepared for demolition, dispersing the engineers involved in the task but unable to make anyone else react. '*Two Germans walked unconcernedly up behind one of the Daimlers, climbed up and looked inside. The occupants, when they felt a friendly interest close behind their necks, turned round and the shock of surprise was mutual. They pushed their visitors off by hand. A little later two German parachutist officers walked past with their hands in their pockets...In response to bellowed appeals from the troop leader they merely ambled further away. Words being useless he drew his pistol and shot one of them, unhappily, ingloriously and terribly painfully, in the backside.*'[12] With such a rude awakening, the enemy finally took an interest in the threat, engaging the troop for over an hour until British reinforcements arrived to guarantee the safety of the bridge.

The more rapid progress north proved only temporary. Assisi marked the start of another change of terrain as mines and ambushes in the woods and mountains dogged progress and German opposition stiffened as the Allies neared the Gothic Line, Kesselring having ordered the maximum delay to be imposed south of the line in order to buy time for its completion. From now on, everything that could be blown was, with mines and booby-traps planted for the unwary as an extra fanaticism and ruthlessness crept into the enemy's methods. Freddie Hunn recalled: '*A new tactic was to conceal small groups of infantry in ditches or hedgerows, armed with rocket launchers and machine guns, allow our patrols to pass, destroy the rear vehicle, thus blocking any escape and deal with those in front.*'[13] Described as the most unpleasant period experienced by the 12th '*The type of warfare here in Italy was completely different to that which we experienced in the desert, where we had space and room to manoeuvre. Our casualties higher,*

BOB MAQUIRE WAS UNUSUAL IN HAVING WON THE MILITARY MEDAL IN NORTH AFRICA BEFORE HE WAS COMMISSIONED IN THE FIELD BY GENERAL ALEXANDER, THEREBY AVOIDING HAVING TO UNDERGO OFFICER SELECTION. HE WAS THEN AWARDED A MILITARY CROSS FOR DEFEATING A GERMAN COUNTER-ATTACK NEAR CAMERINO ON 21ST JUNE 1944 BUT WAS CAPTURED FOUR DAYS LATER IN AN AMBUSH.

each commander's nerves stretched to the limit as they moved forward expecting the enemy hidden in ditches, houses or a tank just around the corner, the range too short to avoid disaster. The enemy used all sorts of dirty tricks to delay our advance; one in particular was to stretch a length of fine wire across the road, fixed to a tree on either side at a height which would decapitate the driver, passenger or commander of open vehicles travelling at speed. Later this was improved upon when a land mine would be fastened to one end of the wire...The long hot days seemed endless, with patrols lasting for as much as seventeen hours in the burning heat which left all ranks exhausted. The hours of darkness were so few and after withdrawing to a place of reasonable safety, replenish and maintain the guns and vehicles, little time was available for sleep.'[14]

Progress through what would normally be regarded as some of the most attractive parts of Italy continued, though the attentions of the enemy dulled its edge. Entering Gubbio, which had been reported as unoccupied, the Regiment discovered that 20 Germans had occupied the monastery and taken 200 hostages. Using a priest as intermediary, the Commanding Officer demanded their release, *'or take the consequences'*, though the Germans, well aware that they would not be shelled, effectively called their bluff and demanded supplies. With the situation intractable the matter was referred to the Pope, a letter being, despatched to the Vatican explaining previous relations with the Pontiff and seeking his assistance. Divine assistance was not forthcoming, however: the envoy came back with a rosary but no solution to the problem, which was handed on to follow-on forces.

A move to the west into the Tiber Valley sector at the end of July required a modification of tactics to deal with the long straight roads on raised embankments. Once again patrols continued to track the slow retreat of the enemy as it withdrew northwards into the hills and the Gothic line, contending with enemy positions, blown bridges and blocked roads as they moved. Booby traps continued to present a risk, Regimental Headquarters at one time occupying a villa near Perugia until the Commanding Officer noticed a date, a few days in the future, written on the wall by his bedroom window. Immediately ordering a search of the cellars, a large bomb was found and deactivated before the whole Headquarters went skywards. Despite the dangers, progress continued slowly, passing through Citerna and Sans Sepulcro to reach Piave San Stefano at the end of August, when a change of strategy brought fresh orders.

THE GOTHIC LINE

The 9th Lancers had moved to Italy in mid-May 1944, immediately beginning training with the rest of 2nd Armoured Brigade near Gravina in the heel of Italy. The focus was now on armoured and infantry co-operation in preparation for a campaign in which snipers and hand-held anti-tank weapons posed a constant threat and where the varying terrain would mean frequent changes of lead between the two arms. For these exercises, and to make up for the shortage of infantry, the Regiment deployed both in tanks and on their feet to ensure they fully understood the difficulties and capabilities of their infantry counterparts, while recce troop and HQ Squadron provided the enemy. Following various false alarms, a move north brought them to a concentration area near Ancona on the east coast where, in August, the 9th Lancer Regimental group was once again established with C Company of the King's Royal Rifle Corps (KRRC) and E Battery, 11th HAC. Twelve Shermans equipped with the 76mm gun were received, the 105mm Firefly version (issued at two per squadron) arriving several weeks later.

'The enemy used all sorts of dirty tricks to delay our advance...'

Their arrival with the rest of 1st Armoured Division anticipated the planned assault on the Gothic Line, which aimed to break through the mountains and into the plains of the River Po, before sweeping north to the Alps. While the intention had been to attack through the centre from Florence to Bologna using both Fifth and Eighth Armies side by side while the Poles on the Adriatic coast provided a diversionary attack, in early August a dramatic decision was taken to shift the Eighth Army to the coastal approach. Done to make best use of their weight of armour and artillery in the apparently more suitable ground on the Adriatic coastal region where the peaks were less dramatic, the change in approach required a huge, but successful, sidestep to the right to bring the Eighth Army into position. As the 9th Lancers and the rest of the Eighth Army were about to find out, the ground may have been better but it was to prove far from perfect: *'the hills were lower, and along the coast there was the flat coastal road, but the line of hills ran at ninety degrees to any proposed advance. To fight through along the Adriatic coast would involve crossing ridge after ridge after ridge. And beneath every ridge was a valley, and in those valleys were rivers – rivers that would have to be crossed.'*[15] All this had to be done quickly if the Gothic Line was to be breached before the end of the summer, when further troop reductions were expected.

If the terrain was by nature unsuitable for a rapid advance, it was even less so by the time the

THE GOTHIC LINE, ILLUSTRATING THE DIFFICULT AND BEAUTIFUL TERRAIN OVER WHICH THE REGIMENTS CAMPAIGNED.

Germans had prepared it. Facing 1st Armoured Division, leading V Corps, was a defence in depth bolstered by anti-tank ditches, concrete emplacements, wire entanglements and massive quantities of mines, which would soon dent their high hopes and careful preparations. In the face of the ground, weather and fanatical defence, *'every few miles we [the 9th Lancers] ran against a river line defended by the enemy'*[16] and despite intense battles in close country fought at considerable cost, the 9th would advance less than 40 miles from early September to mid-November, when the attack was finally halted.

To get to their jumping-off point, the 9th Lancers moved to the River Foglia in an epic journey which took over 50 hours with little or no rest, the route being so bad that tanks ended up *'mountaineering'* and frequently breaking down. Never over-faced, in the midst of the chaos and to his eternal credit, a Regimental despatch rider, having being shouted at for 10 minutes by an irate staff officer who clearly blamed him for the echelon's presence on the main approach road, set things in context by replying *'Beg pardon, sir, but in spite of the fact that I am a Lance Corporal I was not consulted before the Brigade went up this route'*.[17]

CORIANO RIDGE

Despite the exhaustion following the approach march, orders for 4th September detailed 2nd Armoured Brigade, with 9th Lancers in reserve, to lead the breakout by 1st Armoured Division as it drove northwards to cross the River Marano and then on, the impression being that the Gothic Line had already been cracked by earlier attacks. With the first part of the attack expected to be the most difficult, tanks carried timber and steel cages to drop in ditches while charges were prepared to knock down obstacles.

Despite these preparations, as was so often to prove the case in the coming fighting, the ground and enemy conspired against a rapid breakout, while faulty information failed to point out that the start line was not secure. By midday, the assault had stalled and new orders arrived to seize the San Savino-Coriano Ridge, which barred the way to the River Marano, with a full-scale Brigade attack, with the 9th in reserve. Once again this foundered amongst the steep slopes, impassable gullies and enemy firepower. New orders next instructed the 9th to capture the village of San Savino but, in trying to execute them, tanks almost immediately started to bog in on the hillsides or overturned so that, having achieved an advance of only half a mile and with darkness approaching, the attack was called off – *'In a matter of minutes the situation had changed from thrilling prospect to disillusionment'*.[18] The dramatic breakthrough had failed to materialise, while that night instructions arrived for the Regimental Group, supported by 1 King's Royal Rifle Corps, to capture the southern end of the San Savino-Coriano ridge.

After a successful probe in which elements of recce troop reached the village of San Savino, at 8am the Regiment was formed up – A and C Squadrons ready to provide fire support to B, which would make the assault. With artillery ready but no infantry present, after an hour's wait it was decided to go it alone: *'Picking its way down the steep slopes, the [B] Squadron reached the treacherous wadi at the bottom. Two tanks lost tracks, but the remainder got through and at once encountered bazooka-men hiding in vines and haystacks. This clearly needed infantry, so a halt was made.'* With the arrival of a platoon and a new fireplan, *'the second phase of our attack went in at 11 o'clock as planned. Bazookamen and snipers were much in evidence and progress was slow. Some of those who were not killed gave themselves up and were a great embarrassment on account of the inadequate infantry.'* Continuing forward, the outskirts of the village was eventually reached, with several tanks knocked out or bogged in the process and it now became a matter of holding onto the gains despite the lack of the frequently requested infantry. *'The persistent enemy began to infiltrate back down hedgerows and vines, and this demanded intense vigilance. Speed was vital; the members of B Squadron either saw the bazookaman or sniper within three seconds of his taking aim and shot him within the next two, or they were shot themselves…Until they [the infantry] should come, our position remained in grave danger.'*

Using artillery in close proximity to suppress the enemy, B Squadron remained in position until a battalion of infantry arrived that evening and they could be relieved by A Squadron. Their costly attack had captured and held the southern end of the ridge, taken 60 German prisoners and killed 30 more, losing one Sherman and two Honeys destroyed and five of the former ditched. Among the dead was Colonel JR Macdonell who had

THE VILLAGE OF SAN SAVINO SIX WEEKS AFTER THE BATTLE FOR THE CORIANO RIDGE. A STRONGPOINT ON THE GOTHIC LINE THE CORIANO RIDGE, LIKE SO MANY OTHERS, LAY ACROSS THE ALLIES' LINE OF ADVANCE TO THE RIVER PO VALLEY AND WAS THE SCENE OF 10 DAYS OF FIERCE FIGHTING BY THE 9TH LANCERS. LIEUTENANT JOICEY RECORDED THAT *'EVERY KITCHEN GARDEN WAS LITTERED WITH BRITISH AND GERMAN GRAVES'.*

commanded the 9th during the last few weeks in France and throughout the desert until Alamein. Now deputy commander of the Brigade, a shell had struck the front of the command tank, blasting the dummy wooden gun into the turret where Macdonell was working. To avoid damaging morale, the Regiment were not informed of the death of this highly respected officer until the end of the day.

For the best part of the next week, squadrons either took their place on the ridge or prepared to deal with counter-attacks, the whole time subjected to shelling and anti-tank fire which inflicted several casualties until, on 11th September, with A Squadron assisting 18th Infantry Brigade and B acting as a diversionary force, a divisional night assault was launched to secure the whole ridge and with it 1,000 prisoners. A final comment on the battle was entered into his diary by John Robson, a troop leader of the 12th Lancers, who visited the sight on 24th September: *'Went rubber necking to Savino and Coriano Ridge. Glad not in tanks, what a bloody mess. We apparently won the battle!'*[19]

Before the River Marano could be reached, yet another ridge, the Ripa Bianca, would have to be seized, a task given to 9th Lancers Regimental Group, followed by the 1st KRRC, on the afternoon of 12th September. Starting at 5pm, the inevitable minefields, covered by fire, were soon met on the forward slopes of the Coriano Ridge with three tanks receiving direct hits in the first 10 minutes and six knocked out in total leading to its postponement until the following day. An infantry Brigade with the 9th and 1st KRRC under command next re-launched the assault, which again faltered near the objective when they found themselves faced by about 10 Panthers and self-propelled guns which, despite three different approaches by C Squadron could not be moved. Shelling across the front proved accurate and continuous, the Commanding Officer, Lieutenant Colonel RSGP Perry, receiving a wound to the hand while the position was consolidated. Finally, a night attack on the Divisional left flank succeeded in crossing the Marano and allowed the Regiment to be withdrawn to reconstitute. Recovering many of the ditched and damaged tanks from the earlier engagements and receiving 15 new tanks (including six armed with 105mm guns), planning continued for the next breakthrough and its subsequent exploitation, though the experiences of the last 17 days had proved that, although *'we were still eager and determined…any mention of the Po fell on rather sceptical ears'.*[20]

The next attempt at a breakthrough came on 20th September when a ridge some six miles south-west of Rimini was attacked. Again the German defence proved impossible to break with the Bays, leading the 2nd Armoured Brigade, reduced to 18 tanks in their assault. This was also the moment that the weather, which had been perfect, even if it created clouds of choking dust, broke. Almost instantly the going was made near impossible while the flooded rivers swept away the Bailey bridges upon which re-supply depended: *'the rain … was destined to impede our every move during the next six months. It was abnormal rain. Within ten minutes the countryside was transformed into a quagmire and not a tank in the Regiment could move.'*[21] Ironically the next morning it was discovered that the enemy had abandoned their positions and withdrawn over the next river, though the weather now rendered pursuit impossible.

While in the leaguer, quickly christened 'Muddy Field', news came that the 1st Armoured Division was to be broken up and its elements sent to provide intimate support to the infantry divisions. One small comfort was that the White Rhino flash was to be handed to the 2nd Armoured

VETERANS OF THE ITALIAN CAMPAIGN AT CORIANO CEMETERY IN APRIL 2004 DURING A BATTLEFIELD STUDY AND CELEBRATION OF THE 60TH ANNIVERSARY OF THE LIBERATION OF BOLOGNA. FROM LEFT TO RIGHT: DEREK PRIDDEY-SMITH 12L, LEN PORTER 27L/12L, MARK WYNDHAM MC 12L

Brigade, to whom it had originally belonged. The Brigade would move to 46th Division with 9th Lancers forming part of 128th Infantry Brigade consisting of three battalions of the Hampshire Regiment, who sent officers over to familiarise themselves with armour and sort out minor tactics. The change of formation coincided with the appointment of General McCreery, who had commanded the 12th Lancers before the war, as the Commander of the Eighth Army. General McCreery had decided to change the direction of attack further inland, beginning a series of left hooks through the foothills of the Apennines in a north-westerly direction following Route 9. This would concentrate his forces closer to the Fifth Army and exploit the better going of the less-flooded plains away from the sea.

At a tactical level, this change of direction made little difference. Rivers still had to be crossed in the face of a determined opposition, with torrential rain making many tracks impassable. Crossing sites suitable for tanks became not only difficult to find, but near impossible to maintain. Despite the problems, the River Marrechia was crossed with the River Fiumicino the next obstacle, though here, despite the use of Arks (a Churchill tank bridge), and a considerable amount of indirect fire from the Shermans (B Squadron fired 2,000 rounds in 30 minutes in one barrage), it was only on 10th October, after four days of trying, that the 9th managed to get five tanks across to support the infantry, which had earlier succeeded in securing a lodgement in the village of Montilgallo. The frustrations were obvious: *'We manned fifty-two Sherman tanks, which were useless because they could not even cross a ploughed field. Our patience was severely tried.'*[22]

With the ground unsuitable for further armoured movement (even on tracks, culverts frequently collapsed), the 9th reverted to 2nd Armoured Brigade and, less the few 105mm close-support tanks, were taken out of the line, completing their conversion to 76mm tanks (from the mix of 75s and 76s), practising with Arks and fascines while reflecting on its recent experiences: Working with dismounted infantry formations *'demanded a quite different technique from anything we had known before… armour is taught to go into battle at a few minutes' notice and to act with speed … But there is nothing impromptu about mutual co-operation, when emphasis must always be placed on detailed preparations. We saw that we should have to plan for a week before capturing two square miles of Italy, instead of receiving half an hours' notice to pursue without limit. The tempo would be reduced to the slowest.'*[23]

The 12th Lancers were by now also operating in the same part of the theatre, having been affected by the earlier decision to move the Eighth Army to the Adriatic coast. After a circuitous journey from Piave San Stefano to the area of Urbino, they initially protected V Corps' left flank until moved north to

LANCE CORPORAL CAMPION, 12TH LANCERS, *'WASHED AND SHAVED'* IN A FARMHOUSE AT BAGNACAVALLO. THE 12TH MORE OR LESS PERMANENTLY PUT ASIDE THEIR VEHICLES FOR FIVE MONTHS DURING THE WINTER OF 1944–1945. BOTH REGIMENTS WOULD DISCOVER THAT, ALTHOUGH DIGGING IN WAS IMPOSSIBLE DUE TO THE HEIGHT OF THE WATER TABLE, FARMHOUSES WERE AN OBVIOUS POINT FOR ARTILLERY TO AIM AT.

Coriano in expectation of a breakthrough following the fall of Rimini on 18th September, C Squadron even going so far as to practise using the American Greyhound armoured cars which, although not without fault, were capable of crossing the Class 9 bridges that it was planned would replace blown structures. Even more agile was the Regiment's Mounted or Cavalry troop, which had been in use for much of the Italian campaign having been formed by using captured German transport animals: *'It was always possible to capture enough to fill up two three-tonners, nose to tail and send them to any squadron that got held up by a blow in the road or difficulties in getting out to the flanks.'*[24]

With hopes dashed and then temporarily raised again by the possibility of further progress north of the River Ronco, the 12th remained in the area, conducting training until ordered out of their armoured cars and onto their feet on 26th October to take over 4,000 yards of the line along the River Ronco at Forlimpopoli (which inevitably became 'Falling Properly') near Forli. Ordered to protect the right flank of the 4th British Division in the infantry role, this employment would last for over five months, throughout which the armoured cars were semi-permanently laid aside. With the high water table in the area precluding digging in, requisitioned houses offered both observation and mutually supporting defended locations over the flood banks and the rivers at the enemy positions which varied in range between 200 and 1,000 yards but, in one spot, came as close as 12 yards. Welcomed by several highly accurate artillery engagements, Robson noted, *'at one point 72 shells landed on or around the house in 20 minutes. Shaving interrupted by a complete fir tree entering the house by an upstairs window. Less hidden than when we came as they have now blown down all the trees.'*[25] The arrangement did, however, have other advantages: *'Being able to live inside a building and to cook a meal while holding a front line position considerably reduced the effects of fatigue, and it was possible to maintain this form of life until the enemy began systematically shelling each house individually. But by this time it was spring and a roof was no longer needed.'*[26]

The 9th, which had been out of the line since 18th October, joined the 12th in the area on 2nd November as they, too, came under command of 4th British Division for the next series of attacks across the numerous river lines. Unlike the 12th, they were to remain in their vehicles for the assault to break out of the bridgehead secured over the River Ronco, to then reach the River Montone and capture the aerodrome at Forli. With squadrons again acting in intimate support to the three battalions of the Hampshires in 128th Brigade, a night advance on 7th November succeeded in clearing stiffening opposition before eventually reaching the river south-west of Forli early on 9th November, with the town falling soon after. The momentum of the advance now quickened, with a crossing achieved in the early hours of 13th November. C Squadron and recce troop pushed on with the 2nd Hampshires to exploit north-west to Villagrappa. Moving at speed in spite of the cratered roads and resistance from self-propelled guns, machine gun posts and defended houses, all of which were systematically destroyed with the improving infantry-tank co-operation, progress continued for the next two days, before the 128th Brigade was relieved and C Squadron rejoined the rest of the Regiment at Forli on 16th November. *'The cycle of our winter's adventures had thus been repeated twice. Every few miles we ran against a river line defended by the enemy, and on each occasion we followed the same principles, the same procedure, varying only in the particular...Yet compared to our efforts in September there was a large and heartening improvement at little cost. Though the teeming rain hindered us at every turn, gradually we were conquering Italy.'*[27]

LAMONE CROSSING

Progress towards Bologna continued, with the 9th Lancers, still with 128th Brigade, called on to become 'gunners' to thicken up the next fireplan before crossing the Cosina Canal and the River Marenzo south of Faenza. The latter was through a chaotic and hard-fought bridgehead, before the River Lamone came within reach at the end of November. Reconnaissance showed that a full-scale assault would be required to secure a crossing and dislodge the enemy on the far bank, a feat to be made more difficult by the disappearance of an Ark bridge over the recently crossed Marenzo, which had been swept away by the torrent. An improvised ropeway provided a temporary solution but left those troops forward of the Morenzo exposed to enemy fire from the far bank of the Lamone and at the end of a very tenuous supply line.

Part of a wider Fifth and Eighth Army scheme to fix the German divisions in Italy and prevent them reinforcing the Rhine, the plan to cross the Lamone was set at the highest level. From the 9th Lancers, C Squadron was split among the three battalions of the Hampshires to provide intimate support as they established a bridgehead a few miles south-west of Faenza and would then climb to seize the villages of Olmatello and Piduera. The high ground in between them, which dominated the river line with its ravines and tracks built on knife-edges, was largely unsuited to armoured manoeuvre.

At 7pm on 3rd December the Hampshires crossed the Lamone accompanied by a heavy artillery barrage supported by B and C Squadrons, the former also taking part in a diversionary action to draw the enemy's fire a mile to the north of the actual crossing. By dawn, Olmatello had been taken but the infantry could go no further without tanks in support, C Squadron being unable to reach them until a double Ark had been put in the river and craters on the far bank over-bridged. Two tanks eventually made it up the single track to the village, which had to be cleared of enemy and mines, early on the afternoon of 6th December. To their west, further along the ridge, other elements of C Squadron had also managed to reach the infantry, eventually getting a troop up a mile-long goat track before, having been forced to withdraw in the face of a strong German counter-attack, they managed to take the village of Piduera on the morning of 7th December. For his efforts, Sergeant Corbett earned a DCM in the fighting. *'B Company [of the infantry battalion being supported] still required assistance as the Germans were counter-attacking from the priest's house. The only available tank, Sgt Corbett's, set off back along the track with smoke covering it. He reached the hamlet in safety, expecting to be met by B Company, but there was no one except Germans in sight. He proceeded to fire about six shots into the priest's house while being engaged from all sides by Spandaus. Then his 76mm gun failed because a cartridge case became stuck in the breech, but without hesitation Sergeant Corbett charged straight through a wall of the house. Half of the roof and a wardrobe fell on to his tank, damaging the gun beyond repair. As the tank was driven through the parlour door it was covered with falling plaster and drapery. In fifteen minutes Sgt Corbett had used up all his machine gun ammunition, but he backed his tank alongside the church door and fired his tommy-gun through it, killing three Germans while his operator fired through the turret. It was not until all his ammunition, including grenades, had been exhausted that he withdrew to Casa Nova.'*[28] Within five minutes, B Company, who had been driven out as Sergeant Corbett arrived, reported they had taken the hamlet and 30 prisoners.

Although a fresh infantry brigade had by now relieved the Hampshires, resupply for the two forward tank troops in Olmatello and Piduera proved highly demanding, with everything coming forward via a three-mile journey on foot while, to the rear, all the tracks and roads across the Corps area were knee-deep in mud or under water. Despite constant bombardment and a concerted counter-attack along the four-and-a-half mile length of the position from Piduera to Faenza, the ground was held, C Squadron being relieved by A Squadron on 10th December, the troop in Piduera having spent over 60 hours in their tanks under almost constant engagement and leaving behind a hamlet with only three rooms left intact.

B Squadron had also been heavily engaged, half the squadron providing support to 169th Brigade's advance up the west bank of the Lamone to capture Faenza itself. Passing through the bridgehead on 7th December, the advance captured a vital crossroads to the south-west of the town that controlled the two routes into the town from that direction. Both, it was discovered, were dead straight, mined,

1 A SHERMAN FROM B SQUADRON FIRING IN THE INDIRECT FIRE (ARTILLERY) ROLE. THE CAGE OR FASCINE FIXED TO THE REAR OF THE TANK WAS USED TO HELP CROSS THE NUMEROUS SMALL DITCHES IN NORTHERN ITALY.

2 MAJOR DEREK ALLHUSEN NEAR 'HARRY', A CROSSROADS NEAR FAENZA HELD BY A TROOP OF TANKS OF THE 9TH LANCERS FOR FIVE DAYS IN NOVEMBER 1944. IN FULL VIEW AND UNDER FREQUENT ATTACK IT WAS, ACCORDING TO LIEUTENANT JOICEY, *'BY FAR THE MOST UNPLEASANT TIME I HAVE EVER HAD'.*

1
2

THE BACK PAGE OF THE 12TH LANCERS' CHRISTMAS MENU 1944. FOR BOTH REGIMENTS THE WINTER, A PARTICULARLY COLD AND WET ONE, WAS SPENT AWAY FROM THEIR VEHICLES IN TRENCHES AND BLOCKHOUSES.

surrounded by minefields and covered by tanks, anti-tank weapons and observed artillery fire so that, with the half-squadron reduced to a troop and infantry losses high, the plan to capture Faenza was called off. The tanks were now ordered to remain in position to hold the crossroads, a task carried out with crews rotating every 24 hours at night. Their positions were subjected to fire on fixed lines as well as counter-attacks until the attack to the next river-line, the Senio (in which A Squadron acted in support of 10th Indian Division), allowed them to pull back, though by now only one of the three tanks had sufficient power to start.

While less spectacular, the 12th had also been heavily involved in the V Corps drive up Route 9, initially putting in a deception plan to the east of the main attack on Forli by successfully using smoke, boats and hammering on steel girders to convince the enemy that a bridge was being built in preparation for a crossing in strength. As the advance continued, squadrons filled in to guard the open right flank and mop up enemy positions, using armoured cars where possible but frequently having to dismount to clear buildings on foot while, at other times, providing close reconnaissance for the various formations they found themselves subordinated to. Any pauses during the advance required them to occupy a sector in the line in the infantry role again.

By 15th December, it was clear that only limited further progress would be made during the winter and that, despite everyone's best efforts, the combination of the weather and fanatical German resistance would ensure that the war in Italy would drag on into 1945. Having advanced 30 miles as the crow flies and assisted in crossing five major rivers and many other more minor obstacles, the 9th were taken out of the line and moved back to Pesaro on the Adriatic coast where they arrived on 20th December. The shortage of infantry in Italy was by now critical, with further demands being made on manpower to feed other theatres. With no prospect of armour advancing over the winter, regiments re-roled. The 9th, with one troop of tanks retained for each 'company', adopted a position in the line opposite Alfonsine from 15th January until 4th March 1945, while the 12th, already very familiar with the task, moved to several sectors of the line close to the Adriatic near Ravenna and

...despite everyone's best efforts, the combination of the weather and fanatical German resistance would ensure that the war in Italy would drag on into 1945.

Lake Commachio, where boat patrols among the marshes proved a novelty, while also maintaining a partisan base behind the enemy lines.

For both Regiments, a routine of raiding, shelling and patrolling became the norm, with positions based once again on mutually supporting farmhouses which were secured at night to act as strongpoints against the enemy and listening posts sent forward to warn of attack. Sniper rifles were issued to the 12th, although Major Speke, seeking duck and snipe in the flooded area, found a 12-bore shotgun a useful tool when confronted by a brace of Germans, one of whom was captured. Various troops were attached to other forces that appeared in the line, including the Jewish Brigade, a platoon commander from which was next encountered when a cordon and search for terrorists was being conducted two years later in Palestine. The winter proved particularly wet and cold, with the flooded areas freezing over and preventing planned amphibious operations to set up patrol bases behind the enemy positions. The Germans, for their part, refused to let up, one 12th Lancer squadron holding off 200 German infantry for four hours and inflicting 70 dead and 45 prisoners, while a 9th Lancer farmhouse was subjected to an hour-and-a-half's bombardment in which 25 out of the troop of 28 were injured.

More positively 'LIAP' or 'Leave In Addition to Python' was announced (Python being six weeks' UK leave for troops), effectively relaxing the time required to qualify from five years' continuous service overseas. For both Regiments, nearly all those serving qualified, the initially flurry of excitement eventually settling down to four or five men being sent away every three weeks. Four days' local leave in Florence and Rome also started to be taken, while a day's racing was also organised by the Pack Transport Group at Cesana which 60,000 people were reported to have attended, proving *'an excellent example of the British ability to combine healthy amusement and serious fighting, a way of life incomprehensible to the Hun'.*[29]

THE ARGENTA GAP

The spring of 1945 brought with it the opportunity to attack again, with the weather expected to improve and the German army by now desperately short of fuel and supplies as a result of the air interdiction that had effectively isolated them in Italy. The Eighth Army would assault on two axes on 9th April. V Corps, supported by a deception force in the Adriatic and an amphibious assault across Lake Commachio, would drive through the narrow Argenta Gap between Lake Commachio and the flooded areas to its south-west, while simultaneously the Polish Corps would pass along the north of Route 9, skirting the southern edges of the floods, to relieve Bologna. Five days later, with the Germans drawn to defend against the Eighth Army push, the Fifth Army would attack from the Apennines to sweep around the north-western flank of the German defences, link up with the Eighth Army and cut off the German line of retreat to the Alps. Both assaults would draw on the massive air and artillery firepower available.

THE 'PRIVATE ARMY' WAS A NEW COMBINATION OF ARMOUR AND INFANTRY, THE LATTER CARRIED IN 'KANGAROO' CARRIERS MANNED BY THE 4TH HUSSARS.

Withdrawn from the dismounted role in late March, the 9th Lancers began training with their new infantry formation, the 78th Division, while continuing to provide fire support to the infantry in the line, Lieutenant Colonel KJ Price taking over command from Lieutenant Colonel Perry, who had succumbed to diptheria. New equipment, particularly the Kangaroo, an infantry carrier based either on a turretless Sherman (which carried one section) or a Priest self-propelled artillery piece with the gun removed (which carried two sections), required new thinking, for they finally allowed the infantry to keep up with the tanks and to arrive safely and fresh, on the objective and seemed to offer the ideal basis on which to fight a rapid advance without ponderous set-piece attacks. While commonplace by today's standards, this was a revolution at the time, and training in all-arms attacks from squadron/company upwards was hastily arranged and practised, with air power fully integrated and delivered from a cab rank above in under a minute.

Part of the V Corps drive through the Argenta Gap, the 9th Lancers' part in the coming battle was dependent upon an initial assault by the infantry over the Rivers Senio and Santerno, which guarded the approaches to the Gap through which 78th Division, with most of 2nd Armoured Brigade under command, would assault before exploiting north to the Po. With the initial assaults successful, the Regiment moved forward to Lugo on 11th April to join 38th Irish Brigade, marrying up with 2nd

1&2 A SKETCH MAP SHOWING THE ROUTE OF THE 9TH LANCERS DURING THE ASSAULT THROUGH THE ARGENTA GAP.

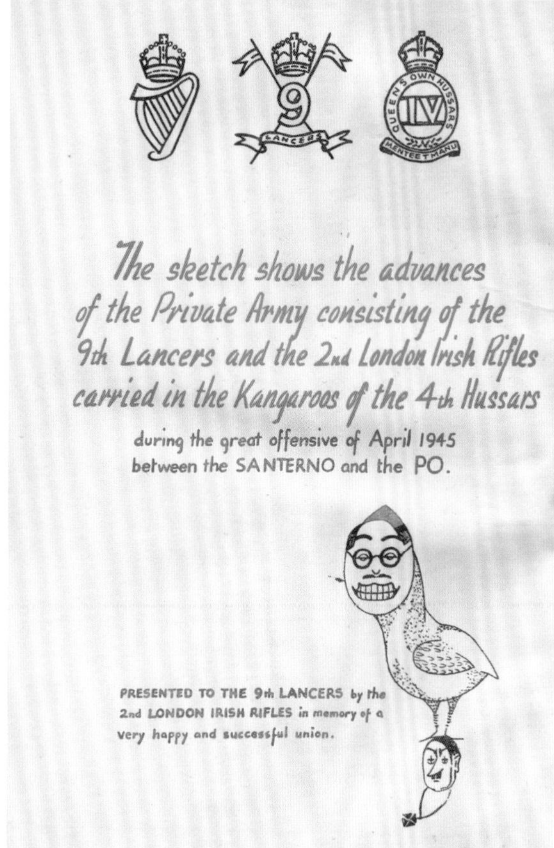

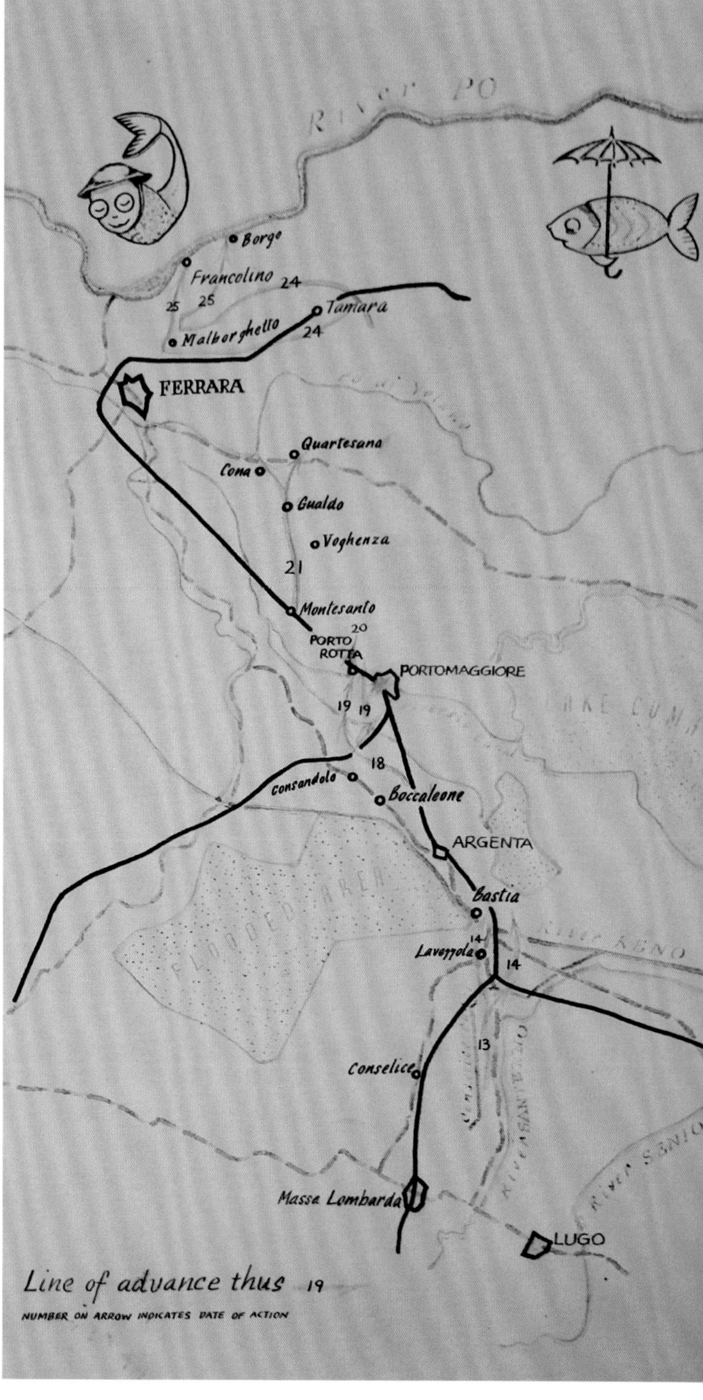

London Irish Rifles, flail tanks from 51st Royal Tank Regiment and A Squadron 4th Hussars to crew the Kangaroos, as well as engineers, gunners, doctors and ambulances, the whole lot forming a private army of 210 vehicles.

Crossing the Santerno on 13th April, the Regimental Group was finally launched at midday, moving north along the west bank with a squadron/company group leading. The light opposition was swept aside by combined arms assaults until the enemy, wires and trees forced the infantry to dismount and the pace to slacken, while operations to deal with the various rivers and canals in their path had the same effect. With a bridgehead established over a canal two miles short of the River Reno, the Group leaguered for the night, with the infantry Commanding Officer giving orders for defence and patrolling before the details for the next day, when armour would again lead, were given by the 9th. The following day, the Reno near Bastia was reached quickly. With the crossings blown, the infantry managed to secure a lodgement on the far bank. With no bridging available due to the unexpectedly rapid advance, however, they were driven back across the river.

Forced to wait while Argenta itself was secured and flanking formations caught up and broke across the Reno, the 9th stood poised for a repeat of the previous action to exploit rapidly out of the bridgehead, their mission starting on the morning of 18th April when, with fighting still going on in Argenta itself, they skirted east of the town to come up behind the leading battalions and begin to drive northwards. First contact with the enemy was almost immediate and from then on relentless. Tanks, anti-tank guns, artillery, machine guns and snipers took their toll as the column, with exposed flanks and fighting every inch of the way, pushed north, the infantry frequently dismounting to deal with enemy panzerfausts and strongpoints, while the RAF provided indispensable help from the cab rank above. With blown bridges over ditches circumvented by bulldozing, or by using fascines, and with other critical bridges bounced, a brief halt was called to deal with prisoners and provide a bridge guard before the advance continued, this time with three squadrons up as enemy artillery positions were encountered and dealt with. *'We had to fight every yard of the way. The country was difficult to cross owing to the innumerable ditches which had to be filled in with bulldozers, and the London Irish were constantly dismounting to destroy bazookamen and strongpoints.'*[30]

By dusk, a further canal had been reached and, while tempted to push on, the Regimental Group was cluttered with captured equipment and prisoners, while the ground behind them was far from clear of enemy. Once again, command fell to the infantry as all around the destruction wrought by the Group continued to explode and burn. *'It was a very big thrill indeed to sit in the middle of this ring of fire and to realize the extent of the destruction wrought by the 9th Lancers Group and to know that we had burst the Argenta Gap wide open.'*[31] The echelon now arrived to replenish the Group, having itself captured 30 prisoners, before departing with the rest in their empty lorries, while, throughout the night, a further 125 enemy were captured by patrols, adding to the tally for the day of four tanks and two armoured cars destroyed, 33 artillery pieces captured or destroyed, together with a similar number of assorted lorries, 450 prisoners, 12 horses, two Alsatian dogs and a pony and trap.

Blown bridges over the double canal west of Porto Maggiore prevented a similarly rapid advance until a deliberate brigade operation created a crossing and allowed the Regimental Group to set off once again on 21st April, with the aim of capturing the bridge over the River Po di Volano at Cona some five miles from their start line. Despite the continuing opposition and the difficulty of the ground, by dusk the objective was within a mile and a half away and the decision to keep going was made – an unusual occurrence for armour in a war fought without the use of night-vision devices. Amid confused fighting that raged until midnight, B Squadron/Company Group succeeded in capturing three bridges over a tributary to the east of Cona, while the bulk of the Regimental Group neared Cona itself, the infantry riding on the back of the tanks when moving and dismounting when static to provide protection from bazookas. Moving slowly in the dark, every house and likely building was engaged, while also avoiding becoming bogged in ditches or moving on roads, a danger brought home 1,000 yards short of Cona when a battery of 88mms fired straight down the road into the approaching noise, missing the column that was to a flank but landing close to the echelon that had to keep to the road.

In Cona, pandemonium erupted *'The Germans were in all the houses, hedgerows and fossas firing for all they were worth. Bazookas shot this way and that, exploding against houses and trees like fireworks. One tank was hit, luckily not fatally, though one Irishman was killed and several others wounded. The noise was terrific with the fire from our tanks and the merciless spray from German machine guns.'*[32] Despite the confusion, the bridge, though wired for demolition, was captured intact, the fighting in the town lasting until 3am, when a pause could be taken as higher headquarters worked out where best to develop the advance.

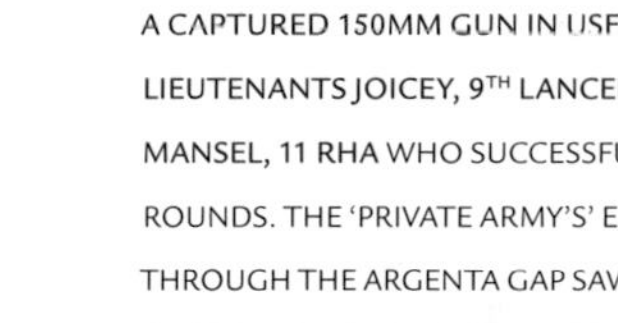

A CAPTURED 150MM GUN IN USE BY LIEUTENANTS JOICEY, 9TH LANCERS, AND MANSEL, 11 RHA WHO SUCCESSFULLY FIRED 100 ROUNDS. THE 'PRIVATE ARMY'S' EXPLOITATION THROUGH THE ARGENTA GAP SAW THE CAPTURE OF 33 GUNS AS THE GERMAN FRONT LINE WAS BROKEN.

'The Germans were in all the houses, hedgerows and fossas firing for all they were worth. Bazookas shot this way and that, exploding against houses and trees like fireworks.

A major obstacle to the north of Cona now forced a side step to another bridgehead four miles to the north-east. The Regimental Group was ordered to move north and then strike seven miles due west to cut Route 16 running from Ferrara to the Po at Pontelagoscura, and thereby cut the German lines of retreat. On the afternoon of 22nd April, the breakout from the bridgehead began, the ground and enemy hindering movement and slowing progress to only 3,000 yards in the first three hours until, by 6pm, a broader front could be opened up. In the last hour of daylight a major tank battle over open ground began which *'on the wireless sounded like a flashback to the days of Knightsbridge and El Alamein'*,[33] Corporal Nickolls ending his war with 'a right and left' and damaging a third, while the battle also saw the 9th suffer its last fatal casualty of the war. Though still short of Route 16, new orders arrived to change axis in the hope of capturing reported enemy pontoon bridges at Francolino and Borgo on the River Po three miles to the north. Disengaging under fire by the light of burning tanks and farmhouses, the Regimental Group finally reached the river at dawn, though with no pontoons seen. This final assault was to prove the 9th's last of the war. Along with various other guns and mortars, 10 enemy Mark IV panzers had been destroyed and two captured intact, while a further 11 were found abandoned at the Po. Two hundred and thirty prisoners had been captured and more continued to come in as the local inhabitants fêted the Regiment.

SHERMANS AND KANGAROOS OF THE 'PRIVATE ARMY' IN THE CLOSING STAGES OF THE ADVANCE TO THE PO.

1 D SQUADRON, 12TH LANCERS, WAIT AT THE RIVER PO ON 22ND APRIL FOR BRIDGING TO BE PUT IN.

2 GENERALS MCCREERY AND FREYBERG. MCCREERY HAD TAKEN OVER COMMAND OF THE EIGHTH ARMY IN OCTOBER 1944 AND FREYBERG COMMANDED THE 2ND NEW ZEALAND DIVISION, TO WHICH THE 12TH LANCERS WERE ATTACHED FOR THE FINAL MONTH OF THE WAR.

3 BY 28TH APRIL 1945 ANY CO-ORDINATED GERMAN RESISTANCE IN ITALY HAD COLLAPSED, LEAVING THE 12TH LANCERS ENCUMBERED WITH LARGE NUMBERS OF PRISONERS, THE REGIMENT TAKING THE SURRENDER OF 1,200 IN ONE DAY ALONE.

VENICE AND TRIESTE

The Allied offensive, to the relief of the 12th Lancers, brought an end to their long period as infantry and they reverted to armoured cars on 31st March, with a 3in mortar troop now established to provide more integral firepower and White scout cars added to squadron headquarters as command vehicles. On 12th April, the Regiment moved to Cotignola to come under the command of 2nd New Zealand Division and Major General Freyberg, with whom it would stay for the rest of the war. '*Tough, self-reliant, disciplined, and tenacious, the men who comprised it had their own high standards of courage and efficiency, their own private pattern of loyalty and affection. To live up to one and to be accepted by the other were not easily achieved. But within a month the Regiment, wearing the Fern Leaf sign of the Division, had accomplished both.*' The sentiment was reciprocated: '*Had we not known something of British cavalry regiments from desert days,*' wrote a Divisional Staff Officer of the Division, '*we might have put down Colonel Savill as 'just another Pommie'…Yet like so many of his kind in the desert, he turned out to be the extremely efficient commander of a very efficient regiment, which was, in the pursuit that now lay ahead, to write one of the more spectacular pages in its history.*'[34]

Part of the Eighth Army's second axis astride Route 9 towards Bologna, the New Zealand Division's path lay to the north of the road with six river lines to cross before the Po might be reached. The 12th initially provided flank protection as they crossed the Santerno on 13th April, meeting similar scenes as the 9th Lancers who were on the same river to the north: '*Just north-west of Massa Lombarda we came hard up against it. We received considerable shelling. The town and surroundings were littered with bodies – more than I'd seen since Alamein. It was very close fighting: not much elbow room.*'[35] For the next few days, progress continued against stiff opposition as the River Sillaro, the Gaiana Canal and then the River Idice were crossed in succession, the 12th providing flank protection both on foot in vehicles as well as assistance in the fireplan from its 75mm guns and mortars. Despite Bologna's capture on 21st April, stiff opposition continued beyond the River Idice, preventing the Regiment from obeying Freyberg's order of '*Get your regiment out in front, and – don't forget – whips out*'.

Only on 22nd April did progress begin to gather pace as a link up was made with the US Fifth Army and a bridge over the Reno south of Cento was captured intact, the Regiment fanning out the next day and reaching the River Po at last light, having captured significant amounts of equipment and personnel. A day's pause ensued as bridges were put in and, on the 25th, the race now began to prevent the escape of the German army from the north of Italy, with the 12th screening the whole of the V Corps front. A series of rapid advances on a broad front ensued, crossings over the next series of rivers being recced and bridges, if present, held until the infantry could take them on.

The Germans, although now incapable of a co-ordinated defence, continued to fight ferociously and were either bypassed or destroyed. Pauses only

came as bridges were brought forward to get the troops across while, by 28th April, the complete disintegration of the enemy now led to a change of plan. From their position at Este, all three squadrons received the order *'Objective Padua – Bum on'.* The city was entered, with 9th New Zealand Brigade, at 3am as the Commanding Officer, whose driver had been killed beside him earlier in the day and was to prove the 12th's last fatality of the war, tackled his orders for 29th April: *'Tomorrow you will send one squadron to occupy Venice and take the rest of the Regiment on to Trieste.'*

These orders reflected the strategic importance placed on Trieste and the disputed region of Istria in which it stood. If liberated and held by Tito and his Communist Yugoslav partisans, it stood little chance of remaining part of Italy in post-war Europe. The more immediate concern for those receiving the orders was how to execute them as the city was off any maps possessed by the 12th, was the other side of the Adriatic and was almost as far as the Regiment had come since the start of the battle.

B Squadron made for Venice the following morning, fighting through the remnants of a panzer division as it retreated across their front, while in the chaos a troop was even charged by some cavalry. Reaching the causeway to the city at 2pm, the Squadron Leader overtook the lead troop halfway down to gain the honour of being the first Allied soldier into the city. He had strict orders from Freyberg to secure the Danielli Hotel, where he had spent his honeymoon. John Robson, who accompanied the force, recalled their entry: *'Left armoured cars at end [of the causeway] with strict instructions to keep all other allies out until we reported it 'clear'. Commandeered a gondola and had a most unsavoury journey, with a bolshie gondolier, being sniped at from the church spires by the 'fascisti'. Reached the Danielli before the prospective Town Major of 56th Div. He was coming with a flotilla by sea, so called for support. New Zealand infantry arrived and took up position on hotel steps with fixed bayonets and 'repelled' invaders. Remained for champagne with partisans, the management and some of the PPA. Slept luxuriously.'*[36] He later added that, while press releases had already announced that 56th Division had entered Venice first, General Freyberg was unconcerned so long as the Danielli was secured as a rest camp for his troops.

Further east, other troops had moved on, crossing first the River Sile and then, with 9th New Zealand Brigade, defeating more determined opposition, including a German naval vessel that capsized *'and lay there with its foghorn making a noise reminiscent of a cow having a very difficult labour'*[37] as they reached the Piave. Across the broadly spread Regiment, prisoners poured in and were soon a major headache, with 1,200 captured on the 29th alone. Two troops provided half the bag, having persuaded 600, equipped with eight artillery pieces, to capitulate after a brief fight, the indignity of surrendering to such a small force nearly causing the German commander to renege on his promise. Ferried across the Piave on the afternoon of the 30th April and using atlases and guidebooks in place of maps, the dramatic advance continued with enemy of all shapes and sizes encountered as they sought to flee in all directions until the River Isonzo, which marked the border of the disputed region of Istria between Italy and Yugoslavia, was reached at midday on 1st May. Even now the pursuit continued, the intact bridge having its charges made safe by a support trooper lowered on a rope to allow the advance to proceed.

The change in country brought about a change in attitude, the enthusiastic welcome of the Italians giving way to sullenness from the Yugoslavs who

1 CORPORAL BRAITHWAITE AND TROOPER MARTIN IN THEIR DINGO ARMOURED CAR ENTER VENICE WITH B SQUADRON, 12TH LANCERS, ON 29TH APRIL 1945. THE FIRST TROOPS INTO THE CITY THEIR ORDERS FROM GENERAL FREYBERG WERE TO SECURE THE DANIELLI HOTEL AS A REST CAMP FOR HIS TROOPS.

2 SOLDIERS OF THE 12TH LANCERS WITH PARTISANS TOWARDS THE END OF THE WAR.

1	2

'The young officers of the Lancer Regiments were there [at the Cesena Races] in force and all dressed in immaculate clothes . . . If you are very young and beautiful you don't get a Military Hair Cut but grow your hair in tasteful curls as below . . .

. . . Age probably 20, plus a D.S.O. or M.C.'

[To Nicholas Ardizzone, 1945]

1 **THE RACE TO TRIESTE TO TAKE ITS SURRENDER** BEFORE TITO AND THE YUGOSLAV COMMUNISTS COULD SEIZE IT REQUIRED THE 12TH LANCERS TO PUSH ON, CROSSING RIVERS BY FERRY WHERE NO BRIDGES EXISTED.

2 **THE LAST DAY OF THE WAR.** LANCE CORPORAL CAMPION AND LIEUTENANT WALLER, 12TH LANCERS, HALTED NEAR DVINO CASTLE OUTSIDE TRIESTE.

3 **CESANA RACES IN 1945.** A CROWD OF 60,000 DEMONSTRATED *'THE BRITISH ABILITY TO COMBINE HEALTHY AMUSEMENT AND SERIOUS FIGHTING'*[40] (COPYRIGHT EDWARD ARDIZZONE 1945).

1	2
3	

remained resentful of further foreign interference in their business, to such a degree that D Squadron were stopped by partisans at Monfalcone who insisted that the road to Trieste was clear of enemy and that they had no need to go on. Ordered on by General Freyberg, who was travelling close to the leading cars, German opposition was soon encountered and a squadron attack required to clear them, though by now many of the enemy proved keen to surrender to the British rather than face an uncertain future at the hands of Yugoslavs.

The 12th, by now spread out over an area 60 miles by 20, was on the limit of its communication and logistic ability, the echelon guided by the Regimental numeral scratched on the walls of abandoned houses to show the route taken as the race for Trieste continued. With elements of German resistance still to be contended with, the 12th pressed on, the troop leader on the coastal road accepting the surrender of the garrison at Miramar on 2nd May, from where it was suggested that he should be escorted to Trieste to negotiate the surrender of the whole area. In the city chaos reigned. The Germans had walled themselves into the Citadel and Law Courts, having been ordered, as part of the peace negotiations with the Allies, not to surrender to the Fourth Yugoslav Army, which had fought to this point at considerable loss. They were, however, prepared to surrender to either the British or New Zealanders. The Yugoslavs, however, appeared unwilling to let them off so easily until *'a soldierly compromise was arrived at. The New Zealanders shelled the buildings; the Yugoslavs attacked them; the Germans surrendered in them'*[38]. In the immediate confusion, as Communist witch-hunts began, Major Abraham was persuaded to 'sign for' the City of Trieste in a large book handed to him by the City Fathers.

The surrender of Trieste marked the end of the 12th's 23 day advance in which 220 miles had been covered and 3,500 prisoners captured. They were almost immediately employed rounding up stragglers and scouting possible positions, should it be necessary to defend against the Communists as that night came the announcement of the unconditional surrender of all German forces in Italy and the South Tyrol.

The 9th Lancers had remained where their last great push had brought them on the banks of the Po but, for both Regiments, the news of Germany's total defeat brought a certain sense of unreality. *'For over six years the 9th Lancers had done nothing but study the best methods of killing Germans. Now there was no-one left for us to kill. . . . One could throw one's hat in the air and shout, but somehow that was inadequate. In a matter of minutes life had changed and it was difficult to adapt oneself to the fact that the last six years were finished. This does not mean that we regarded the news as anything but wholly good, for we had everything to be thankful for, but it was beyond our immediate grasp to recognize it for what it was.'*[39]

COLD WAR

1945–1960

THE REGIMENTS' HISTORY from the end of the Second World War, although absent of the major conflict that is the normal catalyst for military adaptation, saw some of the greatest changes they had so far faced. While a post-war period of retrenchment inevitably occurred, a new threat already existed that drove defence thinking and affected the Regiments' operational experiences. In Europe, the Soviet Union's presence kept the British forces stationed in Germany at the forefront of military thought and ensured that the Royal Armoured Corps, and most especially the tank regiments, would spend long periods in the country. Elsewhere, other communist-backed insurgencies hurried the withdrawal from Empire and called for emergency augmentation of the permanent garrisons to ensure a smooth exit, placing a premium on the wide utility of armoured-car regiments. Finally, the challenge of terrorism in the United Kingdom needed yet another set of skills to be demonstrated, testing the flexibility of the Regiments' soldiers as they adapted to the infantry role.

1 **THE DISBANDMENT PARADE OF THE 27TH LANCERS IN AUGUST 1945.** FORMED ON A NUCLEUS OF THE 12TH LANCERS IN 1940, MANY OF ITS OFFICERS AND SOLDIERS WERE ABSORBED INTO THE 12TH TO TAKE THE PLACE OF THOSE LEAVING THE ARMY OR GOING ON LEAVE.

2 **THE END OF THE WAR ALLOWED MANY IN BOTH REGIMENTS TO RETURN TO BRITAIN** FOR THE FIRST TIME SINCE LEAVING IN SEPTEMBER 1941 UNDER A SYSTEM KNOWN AS 'PYTHON'. SERGEANTS FROM THE 9TH LANCERS PREPARE TO START THE SIX-DAY JOURNEY ACROSS EUROPE.

A DAIMLER ARMOURED CAR OF THE 12TH LANCERS IN VIENNA DURING THEIR DUTIES AS AN OCCUPYING POWER FROM AUGUST TO DECEMBER 1945.

Associated with this variety of demands was a change in the nature of the operational postings undertaken by each regiment. Prior to the 1970s, almost all postings were to a country where there was a strong colonial past, a permanent garrison and the infrastructure to allow for a 'normal' pattern of life, including sport, recreation and families, this despite the counter-insurgency operations that might be happening as a backdrop. The IRA campaign that began in 1970 created a different model, with troops removed from their conventional role and deployed for four-month and later six-month 'emergency' tours to conduct intensive operations from secure bases. Such deployments meant that normal life was suspended, with families left behind in whatever station they happened to be in, the pattern enduring to the present day.

Two more obvious but related changes were also faced and overcome. The first was the end of National Service, through which many otherwise reluctant soldiers came into contact with the Regiments. The second was the amalgamation of the two founding Regiments in 1960, a response to Britain's diminishing requirement for a large army based outside Europe as well as financial stringency.

ITALY AND AUSTRIA.

These things were yet to come when peace in Italy in May 1945 brought with it parties and the chance to relax. Billets were found in towns and villages and villas taken for leave in which soldiers were administered by regimental cooks and other staff, *'On the whole our life was idle and very pleasant'*[1]. Demobilisation, although anticipated, was yet to be announced and, despite an increase in home leave, the routine of peacetime soldiering and training began. It was to prove short-lived. Two weeks after Germany's surrender, news of fighting in Yugoslavia and of the Communists' occupation of the area around Trieste caused a large Allied force to prepare to reassert control while political negotiations took place. Both Regiments were detailed for rear-area security duties, providing permanent guards and quick-reaction forces for the base dumps and stores until the scare died down with no action required.

Local leave was granted with the only condition that return was on time, the result being that 'local' came to include Amiens, the Riviera and Vienna. Others indulged in riding, fishing (using radio aerials and other improvised rods), mountaineering and swimming. Those leaving the Army underwent an extensive education programme to prepare them for civilian life, while the leave system to return to the United Kingdom began to kick in. Complex rules on 'Python' and other sorts of leave were amended or brought in, augmented by a local invention of 'Lollipop' or 'Lots of local leave in place of Python'. The effect achieved was disruption on a grand scale, the 9th Lancers alone containing 258 men qualifying for Python by virtue of having served over four (reduced to three) years abroad so that, on 27th August the Regiment emptied, despite the arrival of 100 reinforcements from the 12th and 48th Battalions of the Royal Tank Regiment. Similar losses in the 12th were made up by drafts from the recently disbanded 27th Lancers, including the new Commanding Officer, Lieutenant Colonel Andrew Horsbrugh-Porter, who with many others from the 12th had formed its nucleus in 1940, with other additions from the 46th and 78th Divisional Reconnaissance Regiments.

The 9th Lancers remained in north-east Italy taking in new recruits and, in 1946, Comet tanks, though a more welcome addition were some of the wives who arrived in April and *'heralded an increase in social activity and brought a more civilised touch to life'*.[2] Their routine was disturbed only by a parade in Trieste on 2nd May to celebrate the first anniversary of its liberation before, in June, activity in Yugoslavia required their attention. Once again, a show of force ensured that Tito, who had gone to Moscow early in May, would be discouraged from organising a coup after the imminent elections, the effect being achieved by moving the whole brigade, by now on a war footing, towards Trieste. Although the political storm passed quietly, the deployment was not completely without incident, a Comet getting caught and completely submerged by a flash

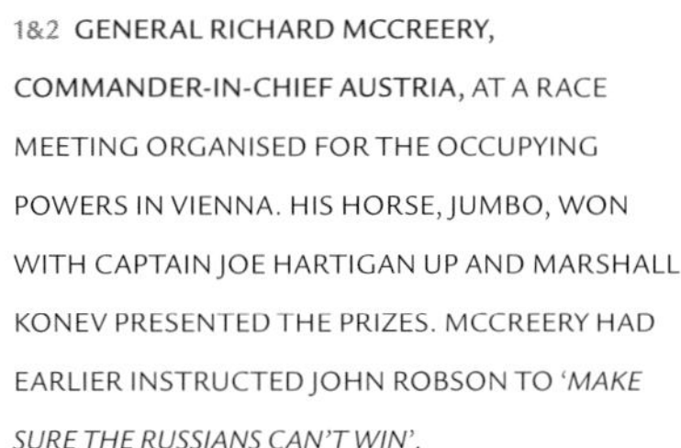

1&2 **GENERAL RICHARD MCCREERY, COMMANDER-IN-CHIEF AUSTRIA,** AT A RACE MEETING ORGANISED FOR THE OCCUPYING POWERS IN VIENNA. HIS HORSE, JUMBO, WON WITH CAPTAIN JOE HARTIGAN UP AND MARSHALL KONEV PRESENTED THE PRIZES. MCCREERY HAD EARLIER INSTRUCTED JOHN ROBSON TO *'MAKE SURE THE RUSSIANS CAN'T WIN'.*

3 **D SQUADRON, 12TH LANCERS, IN THE CANAL ZONE IN EGYPT IN MAY 1946.** BOTH REGIMENTS MOVED FROM ITALY TO EGYPT AND PALESTINE TO CONDUCT INTERNAL SECURITY TASKS PRIOR TO THE CREATION OF THE STATE OF ISRAEL.

flood in the River Tagliamento, from which the crew narrowly escaped.

The 12th Lancers' enjoyment of life in Italy proved short-lived with a move to Austria in August 1945 to join the occupying forces there. Duties included mounting checkpoints and the arrest of wanted men, especially those in the SS, which involved several dramatic raids in the small hours. Supervision of the first elections since the pre-war German occupation of Austria, in which only 20% of the population were eligible to vote as the rest were classified as Nazis, passed off smoothly. The Regiment also found themselves involved in the return of Russian and Yugoslav prisoners to their own side, the repercussions of this seemingly straightforward activity being felt again in the late 1980s when Lord Aldington, in 1945 the Brigadier General Staff of V Corps, sued Nikolai Tolstoy and Nigel Watts for libel. The two writers had alleged that he and others involved in the repatriation knew what awaited the prisoners and that these operations *'were achieved by a combination of duplicity and brutality without parallel in British history since the massacre of Glencoe'.*[3] Many of the 70,000 prisoners (including women and children) had been shot or sent to the gulags, accused of having fought on the German side or just as plain traitors. In a case that inevitably caught the public eye, Aldington proved the libel and in doing so cleared all those involved of knowing participation in the massacres.

With their sector of occupied Austria next to the Russians', the Regiment faced other difficulties from their recent allies who made frequent attempts to rustle cattle to augment their rations, some of which were foiled by patrols on skis in which several shots were fired. Relations were uneasy and when General McCreery, Commander-in-Chief Austria, organised a race meeting for all four powers to compete in, he reminded the 12th Lancer on the committee to *'write the race conditions [to] make sure that the Russians can't win!'*[4] On the day, McCreery got his way and his horse Jumbo, with Captain Joe Hartigan up, took the prize.[5]

PALESTINE

Austria proved a regrettably brief interlude, for skiing and shooting abounded, but more trouble had occurred across the Mediterranean and, by 13th January 1946, the 12th Lancers were once again in the Middle East, this time preparing to deal with Britain's responsibilities as the holder of a mandate in Palestine. The dilemma facing the Government had been caused by the Balfour Declaration of 1917, which bound Britain to establish a nation state for

TO PROTECT THE RAIL SYSTEM FROM JEWISH NATIONALIST ATTACKS, C SQUADRON, 12TH LANCERS, BECAME AN ARMOURED RAIL CAR SQUADRON USING TWO ADAPTED MARMOT HARRINGTON ARMOURED CARS WITH A HALF-SECTION OF INFANTRY IN THE MIDDLE.

the Jews in Palestine and allowed for increasing Jewish immigration, while at the same time guaranteeing the rights of the Palestinian Arabs. The particular threat now facing the British was the possibility of another uprising by the Arabs in the face of unrestricted Jewish immigration (a rebellion had only been ended in 1939 by the intervention of 17 British battalions), while any cap on inflow would bring trouble from the Zionists. To the latter, a sovereign state was the only acceptable solution and, since the end of the war, their increasing militancy had forced the employment of British troops to stabilise the situation while a political solution could be found. By the time of the 12th's arrival, three divisions were being used in rotation, two on operations in Palestine, the third in the Suez Canal Zone resting and retraining.

Based initially in the same camp in Egypt that they had occupied in November 1941, the 12th's hastily learnt counter-insurgency training was first practised with the suppression of a number of Egyptian nationalist riots in Alexandria, the rules of engagement being sufficiently robust to allow the armoured cars to be electrified to stop rioters climbing on them. In May, once again led by Lieutenant Colonel Peter Burne, who had previously commanded the 12th until his capture during the withdrawal to El Alamein in 1942, the Regiment moved to join the 6th Airborne Division in the Southern Sector of Palestine. Based around Tel Aviv, the four squadrons were tasked principally with the provision of escorts for anything of value ranging from money to arms, ammunition, explosives or VIPs. Additional duties included a plethora of other internal security tasks such as checkpoints, patrols, quick-reaction forces, searches and cordons. The maintenance of the curfew called for unusual measures to be employed, with Captain John Robson recalling that *'Most people were playing fast and loose with the curfew. Having shouted 'Lech Hubiter' (Go back to your homes) at them and having located a handy vat of gentian violet, we would duck them in it and leave the district inhabited by purple people for three weeks; it stopped the curfew breaking although the new MPs back home thought it cruel.'*[6] Most notable amongst the operations was the cordon for Op Agatha, which netted a haul of 600 guns and, in the aftermath of the bombing of the King David Hotel, Op Shark, a 36-hour operation in which Tel Aviv was sealed and searched.

Despite the success of these operations and the presence of 27,000 troops in the country, progress against the terrorists remained limited. Attacks on all forms of transport increased, requiring C Squadron to train as an Armoured Rail Car Squadron, becoming operational in September 1946 and using armoured cars fitted with train wheels to protect the railways. Their deployment was providential as in November the nationalists increased their attacks on the railways. There were 21 raids in the first three weeks of the month and the whole railway system to be kept under continuous observation. The attacks on headquarters and lines of communication continued and the Regiment was ordered to produce a new organisation, 'Phantom Force', aimed at improving the passage of intelligence between the divisional headquarters and the parachute brigades by embedding dedicated liaison

teams in the various formation headquarters, though this reduced the troops available for routine duties to a single squadron.

By the time of this latest reorganisation the strength of the 12th had already been allowed to run down and, with no reinforcements to replace those leaving at the end of their National Service, B Squadron was disbanded in November 1946. By January 1947 the Regiment could produce only one composite squadron and was some 300 men under strength, while the nationalist threat continued to intensify.

Despite these shortages, the 12th had been given an additional task of intercepting illegal immigrants arriving by boat, a duty they were joined in by the 9th Lancers, who had arrived in Palestine in March 1947 under the command of Lieutenant Colonel Tony Cooke. The 9th, still in an armoured role, had travelled to Gaza via Kassasine: *'In February this looked bleak and uninviting and it took us some time to get back into the old desert routine. The vehicles arrived shortly afterwards and we were very upset to find that most of the lorries had been broken into and a great deal of personal kit was missing…We were back again in the land of the klefti-wallah.'*[7] As if to make the point, their advance party lost six tents on one night when the locals collapsed them onto camels and walked off with them. For the 9th the principal task was guarding 12 new camps that were being constructed, although limited internal security duties were also conducted, including the provision of quick-reaction forces, cued by the Naval and RAF patrols, to respond to any landings by boat. One crash-out in particular was especially memorable: *'We were constantly receiving a 'RED' landing warning and dispatching troops to various points on the coast. On one occasion Lt Desmond McInnes-Skinner was despatched to the area of the Officers' Club and unfortunately traversed his gun at the wrong moment, hit the female showers hut, demolishing it and flushing out several beauties unadorned.'*[8]

The end of the British mandate and the decision to withdraw from Palestine to create the state of Israel was by now imminent, with violence escalating as the various Jewish factions tried to optimise their position. Both Regiments were finally able to return to England, the 12th leaving Port Said on 1st June 1947, while the 9th left

BOTH REGIMENTS HAD RETURNED TO BRITAIN BY LATE 1947, THE 9TH LANCERS RUNNING A YEOMANRY TRAINING ESTABLISHMENT AT GLENCORSE AND CONDUCTING CEREMONIAL DUTIES AT EDINBURGH CASTLE.

Despite the success of these operations and the presence of 27,000 troops in the country, progress against the terrorists remained limited.

AFTER SO MANY YEARS ABROAD BOTH REGIMENTS TOOK EVERY OPPORTUNITY TO MAKE THE MOST OF LIFE IN BRITAIN. THE REGIMENTAL CROSS-COUNTRY RACE OF THE 12TH LANCERS TOOK PLACE NEAR BARNARD CASTLE IN 1950. FROM THE LEFT: MAJOR JOHN MEDLICOTT, MAJOR ROBIN BROCKBANK, MAJOR JOHN CLARKE KENNEDY, LIEUTENANT COLONEL ANDREW HORSBRUGH-PORTER.

behind not only the empty camps in Palestine in August – which were quickly looted – but also one long-standing friend as they boarded the ships in December. '*The most veteran barrack dog Shagger was once more smuggled on board but unfortunately the effect of his dope wore off during the OC Ship's inspection. Before we sailed he was put ashore into the transit camp. We only hope that he did not take it out on the OC of the transit camp, when he realised that the regiment he had been with for six years had sailed without him.*'[9]

Both Regiments' return to Britain after over six years abroad (the 12th came back with seven officers and one warrant officer, who had deployed to Egypt in November 1941 and had not returned since) was scarcely to homes fit for heroes. Moving via temporary camps – the 9th's in Lanark required the soldiers to occupy '*damp, ill kempt nissen huts, and the officers were housed in cells of which the more malevolent German prisoners of war had been the previous occupants*'[10] – they eventually took up their new training roles in early 1948. The 9th, reduced to a cadre of 38 officers and 152 men based at Glencorse in Scotland, were to train the Scottish Yeomanry Regiments while the 12th became a Royal Armoured Corps training regiment at Barnard Castle, County Durham, after a four-month stay in Colchester. Command of the 9th had now passed to Lieutenant Colonel Sir Douglas Scott of the 3rd Hussars in March 1948, with Regimental Sergeant Major W Crook assuming his post in the same year. Two years later Lieutenant Colonel Tony Cooke took command of the 9th for a second time in February 1950, similar good fortune falling to Lieutenant Colonel Andrew Horsburgh-Porter who took over the 12th again in October 1948, a year after Regimental Sergeant Major Georgie Day had been appointed to a position he would hold until 1958. Although undemanding from a military standpoint, the role at least offered the chance to reacquaint the Regiments with Britain after so long abroad. For the 9th this meant seeing two different aspects of the country: the first in 1949 when they were issued steel helmets and revolvers and put on standby to assist at the docks strike, while a year later they performed at the Edinburgh Tattoo and formed the Guard at Holyrood Palace before moving to rejoin the Field Army in Germany in January 1951.

MALAYA

A month later the 12th Lancers' final training intake arrived before it, too, returned to the Field Army, with training beginning almost immediately for a posting to the Far East for which the Regiment sailed in early August 1951. Their destination was Malaya, where the Malayan Communist Party, whose military wing had fought successfully against the Japanese during the war, was exploiting the weakness of the post-war colonial administration with the ultimate aim of establishing a communist state. Originally intent on destabilising the economy, their campaign had soon turned to terrorism and in 1948 a state of emergency was declared following a series of attacks on European settlers and the Malayan Police. Operating from bases in the jungle, the Communist Terrorists (CTs) relied on support and intelligence from the Min Yuen, members of the Chinese squatter villages that existed on the jungle fringes for whom a mixture of terror and dissatisfaction with the status quo provided adequate incentive. To counter the CTs' increasing success, the authorities attempted to cut off this support, concentrating the Min Yuen in new, well-guarded villages while also expanding the local security forces and reinforcing the resident garrisons, the role that the 12th Lancers were to fulfil. If proof of the threat was required, it came soon after their arrival when, in October 1951, the High Commissioner Sir Hugh Gurney was assassinated when under the care of a police escort. A troop of the Regiment which he had refused to use as a close escort was the first to arrive on the scene to rescue Lady Gurney and conduct the immediate follow-up. Lieutenant Bobby Collins earned a Mention in Despatches for his actions. It was clear that '*the CTs were secure and well supplied in the jungle, they could mount ambushes at will and murder whom they liked and they were clearly well supplied with accurate information*'.[11]

The 25 officers and 470 men of the 12th Lancers, of which about 35% were National Servicemen, began an intensive five-week jungle training course following their arrival in Singapore, taking over a fleet of 120 armoured cars, scout cars and armoured personnel carriers, to start operations in October 1951. Without an area of its own, the Regiment deployed to locations throughout the western side of the country in support of the local infantry brigades, with RHQ and HQ Squadron collocated with B Squadron at Ipoh, A Squadron at Raub and C at Taiping, all with detached troops at various outstations, reflecting a campaign that would be won or lost at the lowest level. Tasks for the next three years proved the armoured car regiments' familiar range of roles, providing escorts for anything that moved, whether it be food, ammunition or VIPs. More interestingly, they also included mounted patrols, provision of fire support and, when the opportunity presented itself, operations on foot where, with the right combination of luck and intelligence, a successful ambush might result. Intelligence, as ever, remained the key to success, though here the Regiment only got the crumbs from the table, the police and then the infantry battalions getting first choice.

The assassination of Sir Hugh Gurney had set the tone for future operations and when the Colonial Secretary, Mr Lyttelton, visited in November the telegram received by the Director of Operations from the Prime Minister is reported to have said *'Lyttelton will live'*. The 12th, commanded from February 1952 by Lieutenant Colonel Charles Spencer, helped ensure that he did, though Lyttelton's memoirs recorded that *'I was shamefaced during my short visit to Kelantan…I was canned like a sardine in an armoured car'*.[12] Clashes with the Min Yuen and CTs continued along the limited routes available with convoys including a 320-mile round trip to resupply the troop at Kuantan on the east coast and the daily food convoys from Ipoh inevitably attracting frequent attention.

The arrival of the new High Commissioner, Field Marshal Sir Gerald Templer, in February 1952 marked a turning point in the campaign. The foundations for success were through the co-ordination of intelligence and the reorganisation and retraining of the police, coupled with an increasingly effective information campaign. Combining both civil and military authority in a single individual and thereby drawing together all of the arms of government, Templer introduced a civil-aid programme, promised full citizenship for the Chinese and was able to offer political independence. From a military perspective, areas were systematically cleared of CTs and declared 'White' with privileges, such as freedom from curfews, given to the inhabitants. As a result, ambushes reduced as the CTs were forced into the jungle to conduct raids from their bases. These were increasingly liable to detection from the air or by trackers and support from the villages dried up, a pattern that continued throughout 1953, in which the 12th was only contacted in 10 road ambushes.

Other activity, including large numbers of foot patrols and ambushes, continued to wear down the terrorists, though the effort expended

1 **REGIMENTAL SERGEANT MAJOR GEQRGIE DAY** (SEATED IN DECK CHAIR) CLEANS HIS KIT ON THE TROOP SHIP TO MALAYA. HE ASSUMED THE ROLE OF RSM IN 1948 AND HELD IT FOR NEARLY 11 YEARS.

2 **12TH LANCERS BAYONET TRAINING** SHORTLY AFTER ARRIVING IN SINGAPORE IN 1951.

3&4 **FOR THE 12TH THE BULK OF THE WORK IN MALAYA CONSISTED OF ESCORTS,** DURING WHICH OVER 4.5 MILLION MILES WERE COVERED. FIELD MARSHAL AND LADY TEMPLER AND OTHER VIPS TRAVELLED THE DAIMLER ARMOURED CARS WHILE THE GIRLS OF SLIM SCHOOL HAD A LESS GOOD VIEW.

1	2
3	
4	

1&2 FOOT PATROLS REQUIRED IMMENSE PATIENCE AND WERE RARELY REWARDED WITH SUCCESS. LIEUTENANT GERALD CHARRINGTON AND CORPORAL KEARNEY REST NEAR TAIPING, WHILST CORPORAL CHANDLER CELEBRATES WITH A FIND FROM A COMMUNIST TERRORIST CAMP IN THE JUNGLE.

3 THE TURNOVER OF NATIONAL SERVICEMEN MADE TRAINING A CONSTANT PROBLEM, THE 12TH LOSING 328 MEN IN 1952.

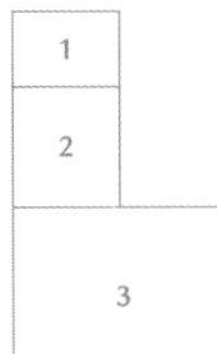

in all these activities was only rarely repaid by success, one set of statistics claiming that 1,600 patrol hours were needed to kill a single terrorist and 1,000 to capture one.[13] For the 12th, the odds were made no higher by the difficulty of keeping both infantry and vehicle skill levels high in this demanding environment when National Service induced a high turnover of personnel, the Regiment losing 328 men in 1952 as they completed their engagement.

Despite the difficulties, many successes were achieved, including the award to Corporal Hearnden of a Mention in Despatches in May 1954 for attacking a group of four CTs and mortally wounding one. A feat in itself was the Regiment's mastery of the demands of soldiering in the jungle, as the description of an ambush conducted by Second Lieutenant Anthony Arkwright indicates: '*It [the ambush] was to be half-way up a rubber covered hill overlooking a path to a culvert under the main road. The position had been occupied before as it was a known CT crossing place. The troop dropped off its APC while it was still in motion about a mile away (a standard tactic) and walked back to the position. Movement through the jungle at any time invited attack by leeches and ferocious ants which fell off the trees knocked into. The incessant croaking of tree frogs and the whirr of cicadas is unnerving to some. It is not impossible to meet a tiger. Much can therefore go wrong but on this night it didn't. Within half an hour of taking up his position the troop*

GERMANY OFFERED THE CHANCE TO CONDUCT DEMANDING TRAINING. CENTURIONS OF THE 9TH LANCERS EXERCISE DURING THE 1950S.

The incessant croaking of tree frogs and the whirr of cicadas is unnerving to some. It is not impossible to meet a tiger.

leader heard the cracking of twigs and whispering: there was light enough for him to see two figures approaching from behind and at about twenty yards he opened fire with his rifle. This was the signal for a general engagement after which a search of the ground found five food packs, a Japanese rifle and a trail of blood. The next day tracker dogs rapidly located a wounded CT… The Regiment mounted hundreds of ambushes during its time in Malaya and this is one of the very few successful ones although records of unknown CT casualties incurred in ambushes or in convoy fire fights sometimes came back through intelligence sources after several months.'[14]

The tour, which for officers, senior ranks and regular junior ranks was accompanied by their families, also provided opportunities to unwind, with polo, football and cricket played against the other garrison troops while more exotic pastimes of crocodile and pig shooting were also indulged in. Equally unusual pets were also kept, including an otter, a gibbon, a pig and a cockatoo, though what became of them when, on 1st September 1954, the 12th left Singapore is unknown. By then they had driven four and a half million miles with no significant damage to any convoy or VIP in their care.

GERMANY

The 9th Lancers began their last full posting as a separate regiment on arrival in Detmold in January 1951 to join the British Army of the Rhine (BAOR). This was a metamorphosis of the army of occupation into a deterrent to the Soviet threat as part of NATO, which had been established in 1949 'to keep the Russians out, the Americans in and the Germans down'.[15] After nearly six years in which their tanks had been little used, the arrival in Germany was eagerly awaited and the Regiment quickly slotted into the excellent barracks and the soon to be familiar round of exercises at every level up to Army Group. Command passed in November 1952 to Lieutenant Colonel Anthony Llewellen-Palmer from the King's Dragoon Guards, Regimental Sergeant Major Molly Morgan taking over his role in the previous year before handing it over to Boot Bennett in 1953.

The pattern of training, if not the intensity, was to become the norm for all future years that either regiment was to spend in Germany. Low-level training and gunnery on either Sennelager, Soltau or Hohne training areas would be conducted in the spring or summer, with formation level exercises taking place over open countryside once the harvest was complete in the autumn. An absolute right to manoeuvre anywhere without compensation being paid existed until 1954, replaced thereafter by the '443' system (the number of the form) of gaining clearance from the German authorities. Even with this system in place, large-scale exercises took

place until the end of the Cold War and, initially at least, for many German farmers the compensation on offer, along with 'Barn Money' provided for using buildings, proved an attractive incentive to allowing free rein.

With between 30% and 60% of the soldiers still National Servicemen, much of the training was inevitably repetitive, though added spice was given from 1954 by exercises practising drills that might be used in conjunction with the recently acquired tactical nuclear weapons. Until this point, NATO had believed that a conflict with Russia and its satellite states would be fought along conventional lines, with defence in depth, a policy replaced first by 'Massive Retaliation' (smaller tripwire forces triggering a massive US nuclear bombing strike into Russia) and then, in 1957, by 'Shield' which evolved, in 1968 into 'Flexible Response'. These later policies saw a balance of conventional and nuclear forces, the first sufficiently capable to buy time for negotiation, the latter graduating from tactical battlefield nuclear weapons to strategic bombers and missiles. In the scenarios, practised armoured forces, including the 9th, which from July 1955 had been commanded by Lieutenant Colonel The Honourable Christopher Beckett with Regimental Sergeant Major Des Maloney in post from 1954 to 1957, would be used either to follow up and exploit a 'friendly' nuclear strike, or to block an enemy thrust and thereby force them to concentrate for effective employment of a nuclear weapon.

In order to be able to react to any surprise attack, minimum levels of manning and equipment had to be maintained through the year, ready to 'crash out' when demanded to deploy to dummy General Deployment Positions (GDP) when Exercise Active Edge was called. Mistakes on these exercises, the site guards for nuclear dumps or the other test exercises could cost a commander or crew its name, while the large-scale exercises at divisional and corps level (familiar names that have endured) ensured that the Army understood some of the complexities and frictions of large-scale manoeuvre that can only be represented by live, rather than simulated training.

Little distinguished one year from the next in terms of military routine, although various reorganisations inevitably occurred, including a short-lived period for the 9th Lancers in an Infantry Brigade where '*the exercises were now much more deliberate*'.[16] In the late 1950s, the Conqueror tank and the Ferret Scout Car were issued, the former a heavily armed and armoured monster designed to meet the threat posed by the latest Soviet tanks but which, even though only equipped at one troop per squadron, proved too cumbersome and unreliable to be of real value.

Together as a Regiment for the first time since 1951, the 12th joined the 9th in Germany in January 1955...

For most of the Cold War the make-up of both regiments remained much as it had done before the war. National Service meant that many sons of both soldiers and officers joined their fathers' old regiment. Officers continued to be ignored on arrival, Lieutenant Nick Peto recording an initial exchange with one (un-named) Major when he arrived in the 9th Lancers' Mess in 1959: '*He had a black Labrador lying beside his chair, which sat up and wagged its tail when I entered. I went over and stroked it, at which point the Major growled "Do you like dogs?", "Yes, I do," I replied. "Well, get one of your own and stop bothering mine."*'[17] The regular routine of Germany allowed plenty of time to think up practical jokes amongst all ranks, ranging from the simplest – a trip to the stores to ask for 'a long weight' – to the more elaborate, involving an apparently out-of-control tank crushing the Adjutant's car while commanded by a hapless newly arrived subaltern. The band too was able to help out, Nick Peto arranging for his father, at that time Colonel of the 9th, to be greeted by a rendition of 'My Old Man's a Dustman' as he inspected the Lance Guard.

The lifestyle in Germany at the time has been described as '*uncomplicated and sometimes incongruously grand*',[18] and, as late as the 1950s, families lived in requisitioned houses, rent free, often with nannies and domestic staff for all ranks, while food was delivered by an army ration truck. If 'patch life' for married personnel remained close-knit and generally attractive, for single officers and soldiers Germany, and particularly some of the larger garrisons, provided a posting of mixed appeal. Although even in the late 1950s it was considered '*a good posting for young officers. We played polo in the afternoons, and trained hard with the soldiers and our Centurion tanks in the mornings*',[19] with added compensations of good allowances and tax-free cars, petrol, drink and cigarettes, there were disadvantages that after several years in the same location, took the edge off the place. The cost of travel before the advent of cheap air fares meant that getting home on a regular basis was prohibitive, with the result that social life tended to revolve around alcohol and regular trips to the seedier areas of large towns to see, and sample, the exotic shows on offer. With German linguists few and far

THE PARADE OF THE 12TH LANCERS IN 1958 COMMANDED BY LIEUTENANT COLONEL MATT ABRAHAM. FIELD MARSHAL TEMPLER PRESENTED THE REGIMENT WITH ITS FIRST GUIDON SINCE AT LEAST 1811, LIGHT CAVALRY HAVING CEASED TO CARRY THEM IN 1816 AS IT WAS FELT THEIR PRESENCE WOULD JEOPARDISE STEALTH.

between, this often represented the limit of cultural exchange, though officers who had an interest in sport such as racing, drag-hunting, polo or stalking were often well and generously looked after. Perhaps inevitably the soldiers, often with the Regiment for an entire posting to Germany, proved themselves more prepared to overcome the linguistic challenges they faced and a good many Anglo-German marriages were made.

Together as a Regiment for the first time since 1951, the 12th joined the 9th in Germany in January 1955 having returned from Malaya via Crookham. With Lieutenant Colonel John Medlicott taking over command, the following month the Regiment was posted to Harewood Barracks, Herford, before moving in March 1956 to Northampton Barracks, Wolfenbuttel. Saladin Armoured Cars and Ferret Scout Cars arrived as, for the first time since 1945, the 12th once more formed part of the Corps Covering Force with Wolfenbuttel, only eight miles from the Inner German Border, providing a popular location. The 12th also changed Commanding Officer, Lieutenant Colonel The Hon Gilbert Monckton, a 5th Royal Inniskilling Dragoon Guard, taking over when his predecessor had retired early shortly after his Adjutant, Captain Bobby Collins, had driven a car up the Hamburg to Berlin railway line after a 'good night', thereby bringing the usually highly efficient German railway system to a shuddering halt.

Amidst the routine of soldiering came highlights worth noting. On 1st June 1953 it was announced that Her Majesty Queen Elizabeth, The Queen Mother was to become the Colonel-in-Chief of the 9th Lancers, thereby beginning a relationship with the Regiment that would last nearly 50 years. For both Regiments, 1957 had brought two further bits of good news: the first, notification of the battle honours awarded in the Second World War; the second that they appeared to have escaped the defence cuts that had been recently been announced. The same year saw changes of Regimental Sergeant Majors: in the 9th Lancers Joby Hillary held the position until 1958 when he handed over to Ted Quinn, while in September 1957 Bill Frape took over from Georgie Day after 11 years in the post with the 12th Lancers. In September of the following year, in a parade commanded by the recently arrived Lieutenant Colonel Matt Abraham, the 12th received a guidon for the first time since at least 1811, light cavalry having ceased carrying them in 1816, when it was felt that their presence would jeopardise stealth. The guidon was presented by Field Marshal Sir Gerald Templer who, it is reported, had a penchant for giving them out and virtually ordered the Regiment to take it, in spite of some opposition.

AMALGAMATION

The round of amalgamations that the Regiments had considered themselves fortunate to escape was the product of the 1957 Defence White Paper, which sought to reduce MOD spending as a percentage of GDP (at 10% in 1957, compared to 2.5% in 2008), end National Service and

1&2 SARACENS AND DAIMLERS OF THE 12TH LANCERS IN CYPRUS IN 1959 DURING THE LAST STAGES OF THE EOKA CAMPAIGN FOR UNIFICATION WITH GREECE.

3 QUEEN ELIZABETH, THE QUEEN MOTHER, PRESENTED THE 9TH LANCERS WITH THEIR FIRST GUIDON SHORTLY BEFORE AMALGAMATION IN 1960 IN A PARADE COMMANDED BY LIEUTENANT COLONEL DAVID LAURIE. ARTISTIC LICENCE HAS INCLUDED THE DRUM HORSES, WITH THEIR BANNERS, WHICH WERE THE EQUIVALENT OF GUIDONS, WHICH HAD BEEN MARCHED OFF PRIOR TO THE PRESENTATION OF THE NEW GUIDON. BY TERENCE CUNEO.

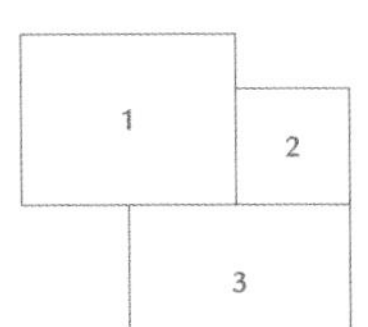

herald a reliance on the nuclear deterrent at the expense of conventional forces. For its part, the Armoured Corps was to reduce in size by eight regiments though in the initial reductions the 9th and 12th were spared. The reprieve was to prove only short lived, for on 21st January 1959 a further announcement was made that they were to amalgamate in Tidworth in 1960.

Despite the flurry of activity that the announcement brought about, the 12th moved first to Tidworth in March 1959 and from there to Cyprus on an emergency tour in early May. It arrived to find that the EOKA campaign for unification with Greece had just ended, the Greek Cypriots preferring an independent state instead (which Britain, with its Sovereign Base Areas retained, was content to grant) and that the situation was relatively peaceful. Despite this, the Regiment dispersed across the island, C Squadron establishing itself in Famagusta while the rest of the Regiment moved inland to the dismal Camp Elizabeth in Nicosia, with a troop detached to Paphos. The riot training undertaken in preparation for the tour proved unnecessary and although some operations were undertaken to prevent arms smuggling, much of the rest of the time was spent exercising on the armoured cars or making the most of the island and what it had to offer.

Unusually, Major John Clark Kennedy's pet donkey, which accompanied him everywhere, also joined in when it took a fancy to a mare donkey in a Kyrenia street and mounted her, the faggots she was carrying and old Greek lady on top of them.

The final months as separate regiments were spent in Tidworth in the summer of 1960. The 12th, having returned from Cyprus in July, celebrated Moy Day for the last time while the 9th, who moved back from Germany in June, took the opportunity to confirm their prowess at football by winning the Cavalry Cup. To add to the frenetic activity prior to amalgamation, they also received a guidon, this time from the Queen Mother on 24th July in a parade commanded by the last Commanding Officer of the 9th, Lieutenant Colonel David Laurie, who had taken over in June 1958.

Behind the scenes of these activities the last details of the amalgamation were sorted out. This culminated with the creation of the new regiment on 11th September at Tidworth Garrison Church. Having marched to the church as separate regiments, the serving members of the 9th and 12th formed up afterwards on the Lucknow Square as a single entity where new insignia was adopted and cap badges and shoulder titles changed. Commanded by Lieutenant Colonel John Clark Kennedy with Regimental Sergeant Major Ted Quinn, the new Regiment marched past the Colonel, General Sir Richard McCreery, and received a telegram of greetings from the Colonel-in-Chief, Queen Elizabeth, the Queen Mother.

The purely military elements of the amalgamation had been, almost inevitably, the easiest. Resolution of matters such as uniform and title were made straightforward by a combination of the similarity in background and by historical precedent, as well as some 'trading' by the various Regimental committees set up to oversee the process. The adoption of the title 9th/12th Royal Lancers was easy, while the decision to adopt Prince of Wales's as opposed to the Queen's Royal Lancers was taken on the basis of precedent, the first honour dating from 1768, the latter from 1830. The link to Queen Adelaide was retained, however, in the use of her cipher on the new Regiment's buttons.

INTER-NATIONAL FOOTBALLERS

Both Regiments found that National Service brought them unexpected talent on the football pitch.

Tom Finney, then aged 21, was a potential England football player at the outbreak of the war, receiving his call-up papers in 1942 and joining the 9th Lancers. *'I found it comparatively easy to drive a tank: it was on sticks for each track. We first went to Egypt, where I played for the Eighth Army against King Farouk's team. Omar Sharif played for them.'* In February 1945, with manpower critical, he was needed. An officer at Foggia interviewing him asked: *"'Have you seen any action yet?' I said, 'No.' And he said, 'Well, you bloody soon will.' The following day I was off to join the 9th Queen's Royal Lancers.'*[21] Tom Finney survived the war, playing two unofficial internationals against Switzerland before leaving Italy in the summer of 1946. Inextricably linked with Preston North End (he was known as the 'Preston Plumber'), he went on to be named footballer of the year in 1954 and 1957 and become one of England's most celebrated players, winning 76 caps and scoring 30 goals before being knighted for his services to the game.

John Charles joined the 12th Lancers in 1949, before being selected to play for Wales in 1950 at the age of 18 – their youngest ever cap. He captained Wales in 1957 and played for Leeds and Rome where he was well known for his sportsmanship. Remarkably he failed to add a Cavalry Cup Winners medal to his cabinet, being a losing finalist in the 12th Lancers' team of 1951.

THE 12TH LANCERS FOOTBALL TEAM WITH JOHN CHARLES. IT WAS BEATEN IN THE CAVALRY CUP FINAL OF 1951.

1 'CEREMONIAL DRESS OF THE 9TH AND 12TH ROYAL LANCERS' BY PAUL MAZE. ONE OF THE LAST PAINTINGS BY THIS DISTINGUISHED ARTIST, HE HAD WITNESSED THE 12TH LANCERS' CHARGE AT MOY WHEN AN INTERPRETER WITH THE SCOTS GREYS.

2 SQMS PRIDDY-SMITH AND SERGEANT WARD. ON 11TH SEPTEMBER 1960. THE TWO REGIMENTS MARCHED TO CHURCH IN TIDWORTH WHERE A SERVICE WAS HELD TO SOLEMNISE THEIR AMALGAMATION. HAVING FORMED UP AS A SINGLE REGIMENT, CAP-BADGES AND INSIGNIA WERE CHANGED BEFORE MARCHING PAST THEIR COLONEL, GENERAL MCCREERY, AS THE 9TH/12TH ROYAL LANCERS (PRINCE OF WALES'S).

3 THE OFFICERS' MESSES OF BOTH REGIMENTS AT THE TIME OF THE AMALGAMATION POSSESSED WHAT THEY THOUGHT TO BE UNIQUE PIECES OF SILVER.

1	2

3

Affiliations to the Leicestershire and Derbyshire Yeomanry, Prince Edward Island Regiment of the Royal Canadian Armoured Corps and the 12th Cavalry (Sam Browne's) of the Pakistan Army were confirmed while the two Old Comrades Associations also agreed to amalgamate. In future they would visit on the newly named MonsMoy Day, a celebration of the last charges by each Regiment. The forward-looking spirit surrounding the process is perhaps best exemplified by the signals exchanged between the two Officers' Messes both of which held silver statuettes of a Tired Hunter and a Mounted Lancer:

'From 12th Lancers to 9th Lancers:
Lancer to Lancer.
Our hunter though tired has never been gelded,
If yours is a mare the twain can be welded.
The result of the match when you have a good look
Can't fail to turn out as the best in the book.
From 9th Lancers to 12th Lancers:
Our hunter is gelded no foal can we breed,
But our Lancer like yours is well mounted indeed.
So we'll ride in half sections, knee to knee in the line
And show the whole world that there is nothing so fine.'[20]

TO THE FALL OF THE WALL
1960–1990

ALTHOUGH NO AMALGAMATION HAS EVER BEEN ENJOYABLE and the occasional niggle is still sometimes recalled, the birth of the new Regiment was eased considerably by immediate activity that left little time to brood. Mirroring its antecedents' early years, the newly created Regiment almost immediately moved to Northern Ireland to occupy bases at Lisanelly Camp in Omagh and Castle Archdale on Lough Erne, both camps ripe for demolition, with 60 families forced to live in caravans. Equipped as an armoured-car regiment with Saladins and Ferrets, their task, to be repeated frequently over the next 40 years, was to support the Royal Ulster Constabulary in the defeat of terrorism. Since its latest resumption of violence in 1954, the IRA had been trying to stir up nationalist activity through cross border raids, though in what was a largely loyalist area of the Province it had few supporters. Involved in frequent call outs and demanding a high level of training at a junior level, the role served to bond the new Regiment together, with border patrols, guards and ambushes focusing attention.

A SQUADRON MUSICAL DRIVE: BELFAST ARMY WEEK. THE FERRET SCOUT CAR WAS A RELIABLE, QUIET AND ROBUST VEHICLE USED BY THE REGIMENT IN THEATRES AROUND THE WORLD

JOHN PROFUMO, THE SECRETARY OF STATE FOR WAR, VISITED THE REGIMENT THE DAY BEFORE REVELATIONS ABOUT HIS PRIVATE LIFE BROKE. LOST IN THE NOISE CREATED BY THE SCANDAL WAS THE MAULING HE HAD BEEN GIVEN BY THE REGIMENT'S WIVES OVER THE STATE OF THE FAMILIES' ACCOMMODATION, 60 OF WHICH LIVED IN CARAVANS.

Diversions from the purely military activity came from the local population (the Regiment reportedly found 106 brides during the posting), or by the various sports available, which included hunting and racing, the latter often over the border in Southern Ireland: *'a Regimental cross-country race was organised in County Sligo each year – on these occasions it was interesting to see the Regimental flag flying in Eire and the Officers' Mess silver in use in the mess tent.'*[1] Visits, too, were numerous. The Chief of the Defence Staff, Admiral of the Fleet The Earl of Mountbatten, discovered that the Regiment was the nearest unit to his castle at Classiebawn and so regularly 'popped in', though he took exception to having a lance guard of only 10 men when he declared he was entitled to 96. John Profumo's visit as Secretary of State for War was notable for the mauling given by the Regiment's wives over the state of their housing, and was further overshadowed by revelations on the day of his return to London of his dalliance with an upmarket call girl, Christine Keeler, with links to Russian intelligence.

The benign nature of the tour was confirmed on 26th February 1962, when the IRA Council issued a statement that: *'they were ceasing active hostilities due to the lack of public support and fantastic odds against them: they particularly disliked the "armoured vehicles supplied by the British Government"'*, a back-handed compliment in which the Regiment took considerable pride.[2] The reduced threat, while allowing a first visit to the Regiment by the Colonel-in-Chief in April, spelled the end of the requirement for armoured cars in Northern Ireland and in September 1962, under the command of Lieutenant Colonel Peter Thomson-Glover and with Regimental Sergeant Major Nobby Norman, a move to the Arabian Gulf began.

ADEN

The Regiment arrived in a theatre overlaid by a complex series of treaties and sovereign possessions that covered most of the coastal lands, stretching from the town of Aden (a colony) and its surrounding protectorates, Oman and the Trucial Oman States. Pan-Arab nationalism was sweeping the Gulf, with communism providing a convenient vehicle on which to run a campaign, while the recent revolution in Yemen brought a more immediate pressure. Here, the new government was attempting to undermine the British presence in Aden and the Protectorates, with further trouble coming from internal agitators who demanded union with Yemen. The Regiment was therefore faced with a situation bearing all the characteristics of a colonial confrontation, involving the preservation of order within the Colony and Protectorates, which were now grouped together as The Federation of the Emirates of the South, while also dealing with incursions by hostile forces along the frontier.

To carry out their tasks, one squadron was kept on internal security duties and co-located with RHQ in Little Aden a few miles outside the town, while the other sent troops up country to be attached to the various battalions of the Federation Army. These observed and patrolled along the border with the squadrons rotating roles halfway through the tour. Assisting them was 13 Flight, Army Air Corps, which had been formed by the Regiment in Ulster and was, in essence, its own air wing. Operationally, the squadron on internal security duties were kept busy by a plethora of demonstrations and riots that eventually reduced in number, particularly after November 1962 when a firmer line, including the deportation of the militants' leaders, was introduced.

1 **ADEN OFFERED A NUMBER OF SPORTING OPPORTUNITIES,** MANY OF THEM CENTRED AROUND THE SHARK-NETTED AREA OF THE SEA.

2 **A SALADIN ARMOURED CAR IN ADEN.** THE 76MM GUN PROVED USEFUL IN PROVIDING FIRE SUPPORT TO THE FEDERATION ARMY POSITIONS ON THE BORDER WITH YEMEN.

3 **THE WAR MEMORIAL IN ADEN** DURING THE REGIMENT'S TOUR FROM 1962–1963.

4 **A CAREFULLY STAGED PHOTOGRAPH SHOWING A ROUTE CLEARANCE OPERATION IN THE INTERIOR OF ADEN.**

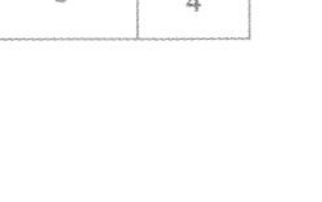

For the squadron further inland, the escalating number of incidents on the border with Yemen required troops to be despatched to support the Federation Army positions at Dhala, Ataq, Mackeras and Beihan. All of these were in isolated locations in terrain that was high, remote and inhospitable and ideal for ambushes and other attacks. Troops provided escorts, recces and mine searches, as well as maintaining a high profile among the tribesmen of the region. Resupply and reinforcement was often by air, while the increasingly belligerent activity of the Yemenis meant that by the end of the tour over half of the Regiment's sabre troops had been engaged. Although most of these actions were on a small scale, there was always the possibility of escalation across the border. The troop at Ataq in June 1963 first engaged a position of mortars, machine guns and field guns before moving a few days later to deal with an incursion at Hagar by 60 enemy infantry, supported by three field guns, three mortars, two anti-aircraft guns, a heavy machine gun and two armoured personnel carriers. In what was probably the most war-like incident of the tour, the enemy were successfully engaged by the troop firing 40 rounds from their Saladins and the supporting guns 180, destroying the village in the process and forcing the enemy to withdraw, leaving eight dead behind.

The third squadron location (rotated through B and C Squadron) was Sharjah in the Trucial Oman States, where an independent role was assumed and long-distance patrols conducted to Muscat, Oman, Qatar and Buraimi, each of which could last up to two weeks and cover 1,200 miles. Though an operational focus was provided by coastal watches to catch illegal immigrants and gun-runners, the distance to regimental headquarters of over 1,500 miles ensured that a more relaxed atmosphere could be adopted, the only blot on the tour being the death in an air-crash of B Squadron Leader, Major Raymond Lewis, and Trooper Roy Brierley.

The time spent in the Gulf proved an ideal ground for troops and squadrons to practise their military trade, responsibility resting firmly on the shoulders of the former, both in their operational duties and in more exotic forms such as exercises involving landing craft and even camels. Opportunities for escape existed, with leave, expeditions and exchanges to Rhodesia, Kenya and India, while accommodation was reasonable for the 45 families who no doubt enjoyed the sea swimming in the shark-netted bay.

THE PARADE TO COMMEMORATE THE 250TH ANNIVERSARY OF THE RAISING OF THE REGIMENT AT ACHMER HEATH, GERMANY. THE QUEEN MOTHER IS ESCORTED BY GERALD GROSVENOR, DUKE OF WESTMINSTER, WHO COMMANDED THE 9TH LANCERS FROM 1942–1943.

GERMANY

After only a little over a year, the Regiment returned to Germany in November 1963 to the large garrison town of Osnabruck to re-role as the armoured regiment in 12 Infantry Brigade Group alongside three infantry battalions, a mixture that kept the new Regimental Sergeant Major, John James, busy. The move to Germany could not have provided a greater contrast to life in the Middle East. The conversion between tanks and armoured cars was, at the time, a routine part of life as a method of breaking up the amount of time spent in Germany by armoured regiments, as well as giving everyone a chance to shine in the spotlight of BAOR where names were made or broken. Although an apparently simple process to the outsider, conversion took regiments out of the line for a considerable period of time with a loss not only of technical competence but also of the requisite mind-set for the different disciplines. In this, the 9th/12th's first experience of tanks, the Regiment was fortunately able to draw on the knowledge of those from the 9th who had served on armour before as they set about mastering the Centurion 20-pounder and three troops of Conqueror with which they were equipped.

To ensure a thorough grounding, the familiar routine of gunnery camps, exercises and inspections began, the pattern of life broken by several events in 1965 to celebrate anniversaries of the founding regiments and a re-enactment of Waterloo. To mark 250 years since establishment, a parade under Lieutenant Colonel Robin Brockbank, who had commanded since July 1964, was followed by *'revelry of the highest order'*[3] and a Tattoo for which over 150 Old Comrades joined the Colonel-in-Chief in making the journey from Britain, though only 149 returned, one member of the OCA dying during the OCA race at the sports meeting. A new addition was the formation of the Recce Squadron by combining a flight of Skeeter helicopters with the reconnaissance troop to provide improved intelligence, fire control and passenger transport. A further change came with the unlamented withdrawal of the Conqueror tanks, which had earlier been put into preservation when poor recruiting left them unmanned. While these may have been improvements, the same could not be said for the redundancies in 1967 and 1968 that resulted from a Defence Review which saw large cuts to the Territorial Army (including the disbandment of the affiliated Leicestershire and Derbyshire Yeomanry). The net result was unsurprisingly downbeat, the Journal (rechristened the Delhi Spearman from 1966) commenting on the annual exercises: *'Considering the preparation and work that goes into these exercises it is a tragedy that higher commands cannot devise them to be of more interest to the troops.'*[4]

For most, a change from Germany came with a move to Catterick in January 1969 as the training regiment responsible for adult recruits for the Royal Armoured Corps. The change in location was followed soon afterwards by a change of command, Lieutenant Colonel Mike Woodhead, who had led the Regiment since July 1966 supported by Regimental Sergeant Majors Ron Peaper and Alan Soulsby, handing over to Lieutenant Colonel Mike

1 ONE OF A SERIES OF HIGH-PROFILE PARADES DESIGNED TO SHOW THE WEST'S RESOLVE. MAJOR HUGH PYE LEADS THE BERLIN ARMOURED SQUADRON THROUGH THE STREETS OF WEST BERLIN.

2 THE CENTENNIAL ANNIVERSARY OF THE FIRST POLO MATCH IN BRITAIN WAS COMMEMORATED IN JULY 1970 BY A REMATCH BETWEEN THE REGIMENT AND THE ROYAL HUSSARS. UMPIRED BY THE PRINCE PHILIP AND LORD MOUNTBATTEN AND WITH TEAMS OF EIGHT PLAYING TWO CHUKKAS. THE REGIMENT REVERSED THE DEFEAT OF 1870 BY WINNING 3-2.

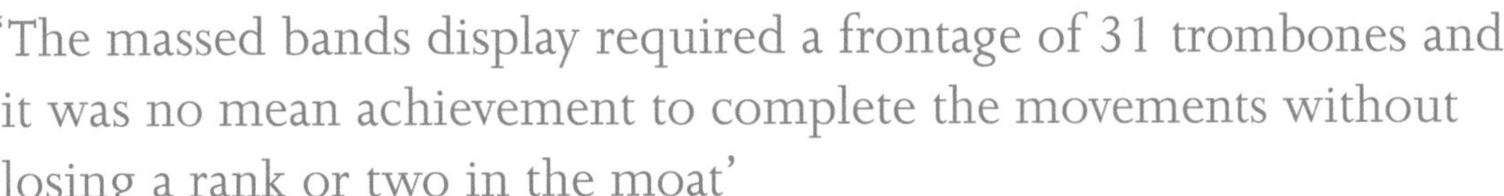

'The massed bands display required a frontage of 31 trombones and it was no mean achievement to complete the movements without losing a rank or two in the moat'

Swindells, a 5th Royal Inniskilling Dragoon Guard, with Andy Bell and then Douglas McMeeken as his Regimental Sergeant Majors. Despite the predictable routine of a training establishment, a greater sense of professionalism was ushered in while, as the only Armoured Corps regiment north of the Thames and one of very few not based in Germany, visits by anyone wishing to 'see a tank' were frequent. These distractions did not prevent other aspects of Regimental life being concentrated on, particularly re-engagement with the recruiting areas and the local community as well as a centennial re-match of the first polo match in Britain in which the Regiment reversed the original result to beat the Royal Hussars 3-2. As befitted a Regiment titled 'The Prince of Wales's', the band participated in a Tattoo at Cardiff Castle to celebrate the investiture of the Prince of Wales, though *'the massed bands display required a frontage of 31 trombones and it was no mean achievement to complete the movements without losing a rank or two in the moat.'*[5]

Catterick did not require the whole Regiment and A Squadron remained in Germany, moving to take on the popular role of the armoured squadron of the Berlin Infantry Brigade. Berlin had the feel of a location in a time warp. Politically disconnected from the West and surrounded by a belligerent East Germany with fragile land communications, it remained divided into four sectors by the Allied Powers, with the Berlin Wall the physical manifestation of the situation. Technically still on active service, the squadron received free food in their quarters and the use of British Armed Forces Vouchers instead of Deutsche Marks, while the close proximity of the threat, and the ability to step through Checkpoint Charlie to the East in uniform, provided a high-octane edge to life. One troop, complete with war-time ammunition scales, remained on alert at all times. Allowed 10 minutes to get out of camp and called on to attend any incident such as East Germans scaling the Wall, engines were kept running in cold weather to prevent the diesel freezing.

For the Berlin squadron this independent command with high-profile displays and international parades, all aimed to show off the West in a good light, had more cavalry style than military substance. There were also the distractions of the city. The stories of the time are legion, as were the fires, with the cookhouse, the officers' and the sergeants' messes all catching light at some point during the tour. The squadron even managed to produce a twenty-three gun salute at the Queen's Birthday Parade on the Maifeld as the result of a suspected mis-count by the Second-in-Command, Captain Robin Readhead,

1 FROM 1970–1976 THE REGIMENT WAS EQUIPPED WITH THE CHIEFTAIN TANK. NOTORIOUSLY UNRELIABLE IT DEMANDED CONSTANT MAINTENANCE TO BE KEPT GOING.

2 THE MAYOR OF DERBY INSPECTS THE REGIMENT DURING THE CEREMONY TO MARK THE GRANTING OF THE FREEDOM OF THE CITY IN 1972. THE REGIMENTAL MUSEUM WAS ESTABLISHED IN THE CITY SOON AFTERWARDS.

1	2

the fine being exacted in an equal number of bottles of champagne, while elsewhere 96 windows were replaced as the charges in the tank guns had not been reduced. Whether as a result of these or not, the Berlin Squadron was the first to arrive at the next posting at Hobart Barracks, Detmold in December 1970, the rest of the Regiment arriving in January 1971 to join 20 Armoured Brigade. The new and notoriously unreliable Chieftain brought with it an immense amount of work, while new tracked command vehicles and the Swingfire guided-missile system, both mounted on AFV432 chassis, were also additions.

NORTHERN IRELAND

While armoured warfare may have provided a backdrop (RHQ, B Squadron and some of HQ Squadron were selected for the newly opened BATUS training ground in Canada in 1972), for many the early 1970s is remembered for the contribution made by the Regiment to operations in Northern Ireland. IRA terrorism was again in full swing, the campaign growing out of the Roman Catholic civil rights movement which had erupted in violence in 1969. The army's commitment escalated soon afterwards when units on four-month emergency tours were committed to help the resident battalions. The numbers required proved too great for the infantry and other Arms were called on to shoulder the burden by re-roling and augmenting them in the line. For an Armoured Corps regiment, with its smaller overall establishment and different rank structure, the ORBATs to be generated for Northern Ireland and other theatres would always be a challenge and usually resulted in two squadrons amalgamating to form a single company-sized group, the special-to-theatre training burden increased by having first to master basic infantry skills.

C Squadron's tour was no exception, with A Squadron folding to join C for training and deployment. A change in command with Lieutenant Colonel David Maitland-Titterton taking over, a parade to accept the Freedom of Derby and the opening of the Regimental Museum in early 1972 all added to the complication of sending this first contingent. Having completed the recently created package of pre-deployment training for internal security skills in 'Tin City', during which Lieutenant Christopher Gundry lost an eye to a rubber bullet while riot training, the Squadron converted onto Saladin, Saracen and Ferret armoured cars and moved to Gosford Park, six miles to the south of Armagh. The four-month tour brought with it the familiar ingredients of a counter-insurgency campaign, including a mix of patrols, searches and checkpoints, mostly in conjunction with the Royal Ulster Constabulary and the Ulster Defence Regiment. Other locals were equally happy to see the Squadron who were able to run a disco every Saturday, leading to complaints from the Padre that his caravan, which stood outside the venue, *'was rocked'* during the evenings – and not by the music. The darker side to the tour was evidenced by the large number of incidents that took place (1972 proved the worst year for the army, with 129 deaths, 1,300 explosions and more than 10,000 shootings). The Squadron was fortunate to suffer only injuries rather than fatalities.

C squadron's return was followed by the deployment of B Squadron in May 1973, by which time Jake Ferguson had been appointed Regimental Sergeant Major. Once again based in Gosford Park, responsibility on operations devolved to a junior level with the usual mix of vehicle and foot patrols, route clearance, observation and endless vehicle check points (VCP), one of which provided a near miss for Trooper Watson: *'A car which turned back when it saw the VCP was followed up by a Land Rover and stopped at the Customs Post. Because the driver did not have the key to his boot he was asked to accompany the Rover back to the VCP for an identity check to be made. The driver seemed perfectly reasonable and co-operative. The driver, with Trooper Watson as passenger, then accelerated towards the Border instead of after the Rover. After a James Bond struggle in the car Trooper Watson managed to halt the car just North of the Border. Unfortunately the driver was allowed to go South due to his need for emergency first aid. The car was removed to the North. Mr Heneage under the wary eyes of a number of people opened the boot. The boot contained 1 Mauser rifle with telescopic sights, 29 detonators, 25lb of gelignite, 400lb Anfo Mix, 2000 mixed rounds of ammunition, and some detonating cord; quite a major haul. It is much to the credit of a Junior NCO that the car was followed up and stopped. It shows a good example for initiative to be shown at all levels.'*[6]

In the meantime the demands of armoured training in Germany and BATUS continued. The stresses imposed by the relentless pattern of

1&2 THE UPSURGE IN VIOLENCE IN THE 1970S SAW THE REGIMENT DEPLOYED TO NORTHERN IRELAND ON BOTH EMERGENCY AND RESIDENTIAL TOURS. ALTHOUGH EQUIPPED WITH FERRET SCOUT CARS, A SIGNIFICANT AMOUNT OF THEIR WORK WAS DONE ON THEIR FEET.

3 GOSFORD CASTLE IN SOUTH ARMAGH WAS HOME TO A SQUADRON ON SEVERAL OCCASIONS.

4 CROSSMAGLEN POLICE STATION HAD YET TO BECOME THE FORTRESS OF LATER YEARS.

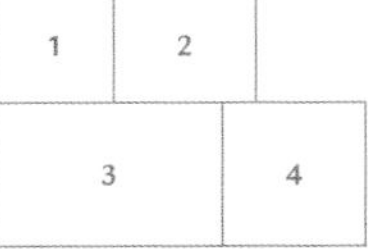

 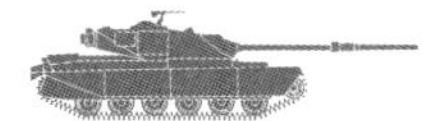

1 BELCOO FORTIFIED POLICE STATION WAS TYPICAL OF THE LOCATIONS IN WHICH TROOPS WOULD SPEND THREE WEEKS AT A TIME, UNDERTAKING PATROLS ON FOOT, IN VEHICLES OR BY HELICOPTER.

2 CULVERT BOMBS PROVED THE MOST FREQUENT FORM OF ATTACK AND THREATENED BOTH VEHICLE AND FOOT PATROLS.

operational and training activity, exacerbated by manning shortfalls, family pressures and shortages of leave led to the coining the now-familiar term 'overstretch', with the Regiment returning, as a whole, to Northern Ireland in 1975. The tour was conducted in the infantry role, two large squadrons deploying to North Armagh from January to May 1975 under Lieutenant Colonel George Vere-Laurie and Regimental Sergeant Major Bill Grant. With the IRA seemingly distracted by internal feuding and the bombing of commercial targets, the tour proved fairly quiet, although several members of the Regiment were lucky to escape with only minor injuries following attacks. One incident (an attack by two gunmen sitting in the Republic) was resolved when they were engaged by a troop of Ferrets firing machine gun across the border, as a result of which *'the gunmen ran but two cows suffered'*.[7] As ever, patrols and checkpoints formed the framework of operations by day and night, all aiming to prevent the infiltration of bombers, for which many hours were spent guarding the Royal Engineers as they sealed off the numerous border crossing points to the South, which in itself did little to endear the Army to the local population.

The return to Germany, although complete with the usual activity, proved shortlived, the Regiment returning to Northern Ireland after only a year, but this time on an 18-month accompanied, residential, tour. Lisanelly Barracks in Omagh had fortunately been rebuilt since the Regiment's last visit in 1960 and over 300 families could live a relatively normal life with only few constraints. Friendships were established and renewed with the overwhelmingly friendly local population on both sides of the border, the local packs of hounds from north and south laying on meets within 500 metres of the divide with neither the quarry, nor the pursuing field, seeming to recognize the distinction. Several wives also joined the Ulster Defence Regiment as 'Greenfinches'. For single soldiers the local population again proved accommodating, while a plane in January 1977 brought Miss 9th/12th Lancers, *'a honey blonde eighteen year old beauty queen from Leicestershire...who swept around the Regiment over a long weekend bringing charm and beauty to some dismal places'*[8] and possibly distracting it from the new Commanding Officer, Lieutenant Colonel Hugh Pye who had just arrived and Regimental Sergeant Major James Mitchell, who took over later in the tour.

> The involvement of the whole Regiment in the Belfast deployment bucked the trend of splitting up reconnaissance regiments into squadron packets for operations

Militarily the Regiment quickly dropped into the routine of the posting, providing two squadrons on operations based in troop locations across the Fermanagh and Tyrone police divisions, with the third squadron 'off', resting and training, the rotation between the various tasks taking place every six weeks. Stationed with the Regiment was XX Squadron Army Air Corps with their Skeeter helicopters. Despite their low lift capability, these proved vital on many operations, though one was

THE DEMANDS FOR RECONNAISSANCE SQUADRONS IN VARIOUS THEATRES MEANT THAT, WHILE BASED IN TIDWORTH IN THE LATE 1970S, THE REGIMENT WAS NEVER TOGETHER IN THE SAME PLACE. CYPRUS PROVIDED A CONSTANT THEME, WITH C SQUADRON PERMANENTLY ATTACHED TO THE SOVEREIGN BASE AREAS WHILE OTHERS SUPPORTED THE UNITED NATION FORCES ON THE GREEN LINE.

overwhelmed when trying to take off with the substantial figure of the Colonel of the Regiment, Brigadier The Lord Grimthorpe. Fuel had to be siphoned out to lower the overall weight before take off was achieved. Patrols and checkpoints dominated the rapid tempo of operations, as did the danger from the landmines and culvert bombs that threatened both vehicle and foot patrols and claimed the only fatality of the tour, Trooper Shaun Prendergast, who was ironically a Roman Catholic from Corby.

Responsibility and decision making, as so often, devolved down to the lowest levels of command and resulted in several successful operations, the Minister for the Army even commenting to the House of Commons after a visit, '*I witnessed the splendid work of our Security Forces in the Border area as I arrived in the area just as an operation was being mounted. I was able to see for myself the smartness of the reaction that our Security Forces can produce. This was at a little outstation under command of a 2nd Lieutenant.*'[9] Successes against the terrorists were, as usual, few and far between but quick thinking and good drills could still pay dividends if opportunities were grasped. Second Lieutenant Mark Linnell intercepted a senior member of the IRA as he was trying to cross the border illegally. Another low-level incident was more fully described: '*during the follow up [to a terrorist ambush of a school bus in which the (Roman Catholic) driver had been killed and a fifteen year old girl wounded] C Squadron found the getaway car and in the subsequent search Sergeant Beaumont's section saw two men armed with pistols asleep in a bungalow near Carrickmore. Trooper Richards climbed through a window, tiptoed across the kitchen, and let in the patrol through the back door. The gunmen were quickly arrested.*'[10]

TIDWORTH

The involvement of the whole Regiment in the Belfast deployment bucked the trend of splitting up reconnaissance regiments into squadron packets for operations and some postings, often leaving the Regimental Headquarters with no obvious operational role. What might have been bad for RHQ was generally good for those let loose on their own, with C Squadron the first to benefit from the policy when, soon after their return to Tidworth in 1977, they were permanently detached as the armoured car squadron for the Sovereign Base Areas in Cyprus. Mounted in Saladins and with headquarters at Episkopi on the south coast, troop outstations were taken on at Ayios Nikolaos and Pergamos to the east. Further denuding the Regiment, they were joined for six months from March 1978

RQMS TEBAY RECEIVES THE 9TH/12TH LANCERS' FIRST GUIDON ON 4TH MAY 1979 AT TIDWORTH IN A PARADE THAT INCLUDED A DRIVE-BY OF THE NEW FOX ARMOURED CAR.

by A Squadron who became the first of many squadrons that would in the future be sent to Nicosia to form part of the United Nations Forces in Cyprus, or UNFICYP. Patrolling the various national sectors along the 'Green Line' and buffer zone in their white-painted Ferret Scout Cars, the Squadron monitored the opposing Greek and Turkish Cypriot lines – the result of the peace treaty that had divided the island following the Turkish invasion of 1974. Inevitably these tours, which have continued intermittently, have proved hugely popular, the predictable military activity more than off-set by the weather, the other nations' hospitality and the opportunities for every sort of diversion.

For the rest of the Regiment, immediate demands of a less glamorous nature were made in December 1978 with the requirement to cover the national fire-service strike using antiquated Green Goddess fire engines loaned from the Civil Defence reserve. Deployed to Scotland by train, it was almost inevitable that at Crewe the Regiment should pass a Scots battalion heading south en route to their duties. In Scotland the Regiment was met with overwhelming friendliness and generosity, tangibly expressed by bottles of whisky left outside the barrack gates while the House of Fraser department store gave every man a £10 voucher for Christmas. Another expedition by train was less successful when the move to a firing camp in Castlemartin in Pembrokeshire saw the Regiment held in a siding in Dorking for a weekend with no one apparently able to feed, water or move them. Faced with a similar possibility for the return journey, the Commanding Officer elected to move by road once the camp had finished, to the consternation of several police forces and the staff of the Severn Bridge, who were faced by a huge convoy of armoured cars.

The industrial unrest in the country at the time saw further unusual employment when the Regiment covered for an ambulance strike using medical orderlies, including the band. While routinely trained for most eventualities, delivering babies was not an anticipated occurrence on the battlefield, so a Royal Army Medical Corps team ran courses, with those who passed thereafter carrying an umbilical cord clip in their pocket should it be required.

New equipment arrived with the Combat Vehicle Reconnaissance (CVR) series of vehicles. B Squadron became a Close (battlegroup) reconnaissance squadron equipped with the Fox Armoured Car, a wheeled variant with a 30mm cannon and 7.62mm machine gun while, in the following year, the whole Regiment converted to Medium (formation) reconnaissance, equipped with Scorpion and Scimitar tracked vehicles armed with a 76mm gun and a 30mm cannon respectively. Less war-like equipment replacement came with the presentation by the Colonel-in-Chief of a new 9th/12th Lancers guidon in 1979, to take the place of the two 9th and 12th Lancer guidons that had both been carried on parade since amalgamation.

1 THE RETURN TO GERMANY IN 1979 ALLOWED THE REGIMENT, BY NOW EQUIPPED WITH SCORPION AND SCIMITAR RECONNAISSANCE VEHICLES WITH A LOW GROUND PRESSURE, TO CONDUCT EXERCISES OFF THE MAIN TRAINING AREAS.

2 FRANCIS PYM, SECRETARY OF STATE FOR DEFENCE AND ADJUTANT OF THE 9TH LANCERS DURING THE LATTER STAGES OF THE SECOND WORLD WAR, VISITED THE REGIMENT IN MUNSTER IN 1980. 2LT LUMSDEN ESCORTS.

3 IN MEMORY OF EARLIER SERVICE IN THE VATICAN STATES, POPE JOHN PAUL II IS PRESENTED WITH A COPY OF THE 12TH LANCERS HISTORY BY MAJOR GENERALS ROBIN BROCKBANK (RIGHT) AND VISCOUNT GILBERT MONKTON IN AUGUST 1984.

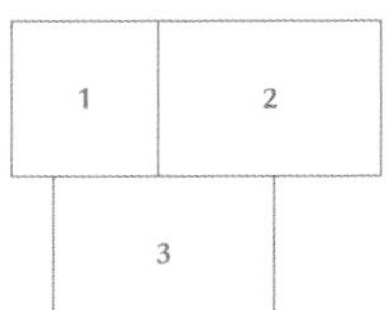

GERMANY

A move to Munster in Germany immediately after the parade saw the Regiment, following several years of dispersion, more or less back together again, less two troops that had been attached to infantry battalions for a tour in Belize, this being found to be the best way to disguise the fact that it was 90 men over strength. Once again the Regiment, under command of Lieutenant Colonel The Hon Peter Lewis, who had come from the 15th/19th Hussars, and with Regimental Sergeant Major Keith Jones, slipped into the British Army of the Rhine's familiar round. Exercises, however, proved more varied as the low ground pressure of the new vehicle meant less damage, which in turn made it easier to get permission to exercise

WOLFENBUTTEL IN WEST GERMANY WAS THE SCENE FOR THE ANNUAL LIVE OAK EXERCISES DESIGNED TO DEMONSTRATE NATO'S WILLINGNESS TO FORCE A WAY TO BERLIN UP THE ROAD AND RAIL CORRIDORS. ALWAYS SUCCESSFUL IN THEIR MISSION, THE EXERCISE WAS FOLLOWED BY AN ANGLO-AMERICAN-FRENCH DRIVE-PAST AND A PARTY OF EPIC PROPORTIONS.

over farmland. This proved the key factor that influenced the decision to make a further move in 1981, this time to Hohne, where it could remain as a reconnaissance regiment, the less attractive alternative being to re-role to tanks and remain in Munster.

Regarded by many as one of the bleakest garrisons in Germany, not least for its unhappy association with Bergen-Belsen concentration camp for which the barracks had provided some of the guards' accommodation, the move was notable for the 'postal paralysis' that afflicted the Regiment on its arrival. Caused by the inexplicable decision of the post clerk to hold onto all the outgoing mail, the blockage lasted for several months and was only discovered when Major Charlie Enderby, who was away from the Regiment, wondered why no courses had been bid for, the rest of the Regiment's life seemingly unaffected by an almost complete loss of communication.

On arrival in Hohne, the Regiment adopted a mix of two formation and one close-reconnaissance squadrons. The former were to support the division and its brigades while B Squadron, holding nearly half the Regiment's vehicles, provided battlegroup reconnaissance troops to armoured and infantry units whose integral reconnaissance troops and platoons had been disbanded. With battlegroups responsible for the training of 'their' reconnaissance troops, standards remained inconsistent while cohesion across the Regiment, the result of so many conflicting pulls on troops and squadrons, was further undermined by the deployment of a reinforced C Squadron to guard the 'H' Blocks in Long Kesh (latterly the Maze) prison in Northern Ireland for four months in July 1982. The deployment coincided with a visit by the Colonel-in-Chief and the arrival of Lieutenant Colonel Richard Nash as Commanding Officer and Regimental Sergeant Major Colin Whitehead at the end of 1984. Further reorganisation in 1983 and 1984 helped provide more balance, close reconnaissance reverting to parent battlegroups and leaving the 9th/12th free to concentrate on formation-level duties. By now a further change of location was imminent and in early 1984 the Regiment returned to Wolfenbuttel, which the 12th Lancers had left in 1958.

New additions to the order of battle came with the changed role and location. The 9th/12th now became a divisional reconnaissance regiment and grew with the creation of D Squadron as a fourth sabre squadron. Additional capability was provided to each squadron by the CVR(T) Striker vehicle, and of a Support Troop to give an infantry-like assault pioneer capability, the utility of which had seemingly been forgotten since their use at the end of the Second World War. At the same time the Regiment lost its CVR(T) Scorpion to provide close support to infantry. The leap in establishment inevitably caused a shortage of manpower but the greater coherence as a regiment brought with it considerable benefits, especially in the independent fiefdom of an isolated barracks with no military hierarchy in the vicinity.

'at Wolfenbuttel we were perpetually at four hours' notice to go to war'

Again the benefit of being able to deploy off the major training areas was felt, with Regimental training routinely conducted in Southern Germany where the novelty of British *'spahpanzers mit gummi-kettern'* (reconnaissance tanks with rubber tracks) provided more attractive scenery and more tolerant locals. One of these had lost a leg on the Russian front but still managed to hop out to a troop leader carrying a tray of coffee and schnapps and, with a broad grin on his face, declared '*Tomorrow we march on Moscow!*'

Under Lieutenant Colonel Robin Readhead, who had taken over command towards the end of 1984 with Regimental Sergeant Major Michael Todd joining him the following year, the absence of higher-level control allowed the exercise scenarios to become increasingly imaginative (an entire fortnight was spent hunting the mysterious 'Grand Duke of Rotkophia' and his followers), while troops and squadrons vied to find the best accommodation for headquarters, observation posts, hides and weekend locations. Larger, higher-level exercises still continued in the autumn in the familiar lands of the north German plain, though by now the tolerance of the locals was being severely tested with movement by heavy formations increasingly restricted. This state of affairs was not helped by Corporal Noone who, impersonating a military policeman when acting as enemy, deliberately and successfully diverted an entire armoured brigade down a one-way street causing a six-mile tail-back that took five hours to sort out.

Additions to the training cycle appeared in Wolfenbuttel, most notably those conducted with the Americans and French as part of Operation 'Live Oak' – the plan to ensure links to Berlin were maintained. These annual exercises were designed to prove intent to the witnessing Soviet Mission (SOXMIS) that the Allies would use military force to exercise their right of access to Berlin along both the rail and road corridors if they were threatened. The exercises were further seen as a test of Soviet resolve and a gauge of the political temperature. For those taking part, the exercises, for which the Regiment provided command elements and troops for both the road group and on the train, proved enjoyable, even if the idea of a battle-group-sized probe in either a train or on an autobahn forcing its way through Warsaw Pact-held East Germany probably bore little scrutiny as a sensible act of war. Perhaps inevitably the blockade was always breached and Berlin saved, a feat celebrated, according to Major Roger Burgess by *'a grandiose parade and drive past by the Tripartite Force to the sound of the combined Regimental and French Camel Corps Band… followed by an even grander NATO celebration by all the troops concerned'.*[11]

Further multi-national activity was undertaken through participation in the German Army's 'Boeselager' international armoured reconnaissance competition in both 1985 and 1986. Involving 22 teams from nine NATO nations, the competition tested both mounted and dismounted reconnaissance skills over four days and nights, but crucially was largely centred on German doctrine, tactics and equipment. Under the leadership of Major Roger Burgess, who quickly gathered that the key to success was close liaison with the local German reconnaissance battalion and intelligence gathering before the outset, the Regiment came sixth overall and the second foreign team in the first year it entered, before winning the entire competition outright the following year – the first team from a foreign army ever to do so, for which Sergeant David Williams, the patrol commander was awarded the MBE.

If success in this competition demonstrated high standards of individual and collective training, the overall scheme of manoeuvre for dealing with an attack by the Warsaw Pact was coming under increasing scrutiny. This was especially pertinent at a time when the state of the economy in Britain

1 THE REGIMENT WAS STATIONED WITHIN EIGHT KILOMETRES OF THE INNER GERMAN BORDER WHEN AT WOLFENBUTTEL AND HAD FORWARD POSITIONS OVERLOOKING IT.

2 CORPORALS KOVACS AND HOWES IMITATE EAST GERMAN TROOPS AS PART OF THE 'ENEMY' FORCE BARRING THE RAIL LINK TO BERLIN.

3 LANCE CORPORALS KERR AND HARRISON IN THE BOESELAGER INTERNATIONAL RECONNAISSANCE COMPETITION. THE REGIMENT WAS THE FIRST FOREIGN TEAM TO WIN THIS GERMAN-RUN COMPETITION.

1	3
2	

FLYING LANCERS

For a brief but golden period in the 1960s the Regiment had its own Air Troop. Aviation at regimental level was already well established in Royal Artillery Regiments that had affiliated Air OP flights for directing gunfire, but with the emergence of viable light helicopters in the late 1950s and early 1960s the concept was broadened to include armoured-combat arms.

Some postings in non-NATO theatres were also to have their own flights and, when the Regiment moved from Northern Ireland to Aden in 1962, four officers and two sergeants trained as pilots to provide the inaugural Air Troop. In the event there was no British helicopter capable of flying in the exceptionally demanding conditions in Aden, so aviation support was provided by the Auster, a light fixed-wing aircraft that was scarcely more able to cope with the conditions than the non-existent helicopters, and required some of the pilots to convert and join 13 Flight Army Air Corps, which was in direct support to the Regiment. The remaining pilots were seconded to other aviation units, the pick of which seemed to be in Kenya where they flew French-built Alouette helicopters, supporting the brigade and the Kenya wildlife service.

In Aden, 13 Flight worked with the squadrons and troops deployed to remote outstations and the British officered Aden Protectorate Levies to keep an eye on the northern border. The Auster, although adequate in the cool climate and low ground of northern Europe, proved wholly unsuitable for Aden where airstrips 'up country' were at altitudes of up to 6000 feet and mid-day temperatures over 40 degrees. After several crashes the Austers were restricted to the coastal plain which much reduced their usefulness though they did manage a link up with the Navy when landing on HMS *Bulwark*.

AN RSMS NIGHTMARE. ALTHOUGH THE RECCE FLIGHT WAS PART OF THE REGIMENT'S ESTABLISHMENT, IT TOOK A MULTITUDE OF DIFFERENT ORGANISATIONS TO FIND ITS PERSONNEL.

AN AUSTER IN THE GULF OF ADEN ABOUT TO LAND ON HMS *BULWARK*. THE DRILLS FOR DECK LANDINGS HAD BEEN WORKED OUT OVER A THERMOS OF GIN AND TONIC THE NIGHT BEFORE.

In Germany the Air Troop, though fully under command of the Commanding Officer and grouped in a Reconnaissance Squadron, took its place as part of Army Aviation BAOR which supplied instructors or 'Trappers' (so called because of their delight in 'trapping' Regimental Pilots who indulged in 'non-standard' flying practices) and second-line support. Skeeter helicopters flew the bulk of the reconnaissance tasks with the scout cars of Recce Troop while also conducting liaison flights, bringing vital (small) parts for the tanks, photography and observation for the artillery leaving longer distance liaison or recce flights to be done by the Auster. An unusual piece of flying included a pageant in Osnabruck where, with a lance strapped to the side of a Skeeter and enacting the role of St George, Captain Richard Nash jousted with a Ferret Scout Car made up as a dragon.

Flying the Skeeter in Germany in those days was not without its hazards. Nigel Willoughby, Royal Marines, remembered that two days after the completion of his conversion course his engine failed at 300 feet near Achmer Heath, 15 minutes north of Osnabruck. The only choices of landing area were a wood and a sloping cornfield. *'We ended up on our side in the latter where the aircraft rolled and noisily thrashed itself to bits. There was high octane fuel all over the place and we were keen to get out. I was on the upper side and the only injury of the day occurred when I trod heavily on my observer L/Cpl Ellison's sensitive bits as I kicked off upwards and outwards.'* Others were not to prove so lucky, Captain Stopford, on attachment to the Air Corps, dying when his Beaver aircraft crashed in 1980.

Towards the end of 1968, the Regiment left Osnabruck to become training Regiment in Catterick and thus lost its own little Air Force, several personnel staying on with 1RTR who had taken the Regiment's place. Following a farewell fly-past of our two remaining serviceable aircraft, the Skeeters left ignominiously on their final journeys by lorry, the last to leave removing the guard-room barrier as it went.

THE ALTITUDE AT THE OUTSTATIONS IN ADEN MADE FLYING IN AN AUSTER MARGINAL AS CAPTAIN CHARLES PERRY PROVED WHEN HE WAS SERIOUSLY INJURED IN A CRASH.

had resulted in severe shortages of ammunition and spares. Despite the doctrine of forward defence (with the emphasis on not yielding German ground) being altered to defence in depth, sceptics remained, not least those serving with the Regiment who could see some of the flaws with the plan. Brigadier Richard Nash later recorded: *'at Wolfenbuttel we were perpetually at four hours notice to go to war. Initially we were required to cover the entire 90-mile corps frontage until the remainder deployed. The hierarchy conveniently forgot that most of us might still be half-way to Berlin on a probe or more likely already in the bag. To suggest we could have gone to war at any time at four hours notice was pure wishful thinking.'*[12]

WIMBISH

A further arms plot move in March 1987 brought the Regiment back to England to take up residence at Wimbish, near Saffron Walden in Essex with Lieutenant Colonel Robin Searby in command, joined by Regimental Sergeant Major John Sewell. This old RAF station was an ideal location, with plenty of space, good accommodation and housing and a massive airfield with both grass and Tarmac for the vehicles to use. Located over an hour from the nearest senior officer, its proximity to both London and the recruiting area offered plenty of scope, as well as the pleasures of a return to Britain. Demonstrating 'green credentials' even before they became fashionable, the Regiment was awarded the 'British Gas Award for Energy Conservation' in 1989 and with it a cheque for £7,000, no doubt the result of the production of a report cast in 'business-speak' that listed a Board of Directors in which The Queen Mother was named as Chairman. Less happily on 10th March 1988, Major Hugh Lindsay, commanding B Squadron but previously an equerry to the Queen, was killed while skiing with a Royal party, including the Prince and Princess of Wales. He is commemorated by a prize awarded annually to a trooper or Junior NCO for outstanding sporting or military achievement.

Freedom from the minimum manning restrictions of Germany meant that a more varied diet of military activity could be pursued, beginning with the almost immediate deployment of a squadron to Cyprus. Once again back to providing the Ferret Scout Car Squadron for the United Nations in Cyprus, this first squadron was followed by two others in quick succession, while other troop-level deployments included soldiers supporting the infantry battalions in Belize. The main operational focus remained in Germany, where the Regiment continued to form a part of the order of battle and to which it travelled for the annual large-scale exercises, the final manifestation of the Cold War that was now entering its final throes. Exercise Iron Hammer in November 1988, the last great Corps-level exercise conducted by combined arms in Germany, proved bitterly cold and nearly lethal for the Regiment's civilian padre who was in the back of the RSM's Land Rover when it rolled, while the Commanding Officer enjoyed more comfort in his 'mobile home', where he entertained Dennis Thatcher and the Corps Commander.

More eye-catching military activity took place closer to home. With the USA, supported by Britain, upping the stakes by deploying nuclear-armed cruise missiles at several airbases around Britain, the Army responded to calls for assistance by the police to

ALTHOUGH BASED IN BRITAIN AT END OF THE 1980S, THE REGIMENT'S ROLE REQUIRED IT TO EXERCISE REGULARLY IN GERMANY WHERE A FAVOURITE SPORT BECAME IMPERSONATING MILITARY POLICEMEN TO DIVERT 'ENEMY' FORCES. THE CARTOON DRAWN BY MAJOR ROGER BURGESS CELEBRATES THE ACHIEVEMENT OF LANCE CORPORAL NOONE IN CREATING A SIX-MILE ARMOURED TRAFFIC JAM, WHILE EVEN THE REGIMENTAL SERGEANT MAJOR, JOHNNY SEWELL, WAS NOT ABOVE HAVING A GO.

ALTHOUGH TOURS WITH THE UNITED NATIONS SCOUT CAR SQUADRON IN CYPRUS WERE POPULAR AND MORE LIKELY TO LEAD TO INJURY THROUGH SUN-STROKE OR ALCOHOL, DANGERS STILL EXISTED AS CAPTAIN MILNE-HUME AND TROOPER MOTUM DISCOVERED WHEN THEY WERE LUCKY TO SURVIVE THE BLAST FROM AN ANTI-TANK MINE LAID OVER 25 YEARS PREVIOUSLY.

ensure that their tactical deployment exercises could go ahead. For these, the Regiment provided an outer cordon to ensure that the Greenham Common Peace Protestors – an eclectic mix of anti-establishment groups based around a 'women's group' – were kept away by intercepting them as they tried to infiltrate across Salisbury Plain. In this their task was made easier by use of the recently issued thermal imaging sights that had revolutionised operations at night, allowing the cordon to pick its moment to round up the protesters, ideally after they had been crawling about for an hour or more. Further aid to the authorities was also practised with reinforcement to the security of London's airports against terrorist attacks, and to help them clear up after the storms of 1987, which had blocked many roads in the local area. The flexibility of the British soldier was further tested in March of the following year when a squadron was deployed to guard a hastily converted training camp on Salisbury Plain that was to be used to house 300 prisoners during industrial action by the Prison Officers Association.

The weather threatened a vehicle-mounted parade for the Colonel-in-Chief in June 1987. Involving a drive-by of all the Regiment's current vehicles and a large selection of historic armour as well, the day of the visit proved dismal. The torrential rain and howling easterly wind seemed not to bother the Colonel-in-Chief who, when asked what the wet-weather programme was to be, simply replied 'We get wet'. As it was, divine intervention stopped the downpour as she got out of the car, leaving her immaculate and ready to review a damp but enthusiastic Regiment.

DETACHED DUTIES

ATTACHMENT TO OTHER ARMIES, PARTICULARLY THE SULTAN OF OMAN'S, PROVIDED AN OPPORTUNITY FOR MANY OFFICERS AND SOLDIERS TO GET AWAY FROM THE ROUTINE OF SOLDIERING ON THE WEST GERMAN PLAINS.

From the early 1960s, particularly in the Middle East, a model was implemented of British officers and NCOs on secondment leading local forces to ensure stability and influence. Members of the regiment served in Aden, the Trucial States and, in the 1970s and 1980s, with the Sultan of Oman's Armed Forces. Officers were also employed in 1981 in Zimbabwe to supervise and train the newly emerging army of that country, formed in the main from ex-guerrillas of the civil war, which had recently ended.

Both officers and soldiers also operated in various guises while detached to other units in Northern Ireland. These high-risk activities resulted in the death of Sergeant Robert Maughan who was murdered in 1979 in Lisnaskea alongside a Royal Ulster Constabulary colleague while undercover. Five years later Sergeant Paul Oram, who had earlier been awarded the Military Medal for his work in Northern Ireland, was killed in a gun battle at Dunloy while conducting surveillance of an arms dump, leaving behind a five-month-old daughter.

SERGEANT PAUL ORAM MM WHO WAS KILLED WHILE SERVING AWAY FROM THE REGIMENT ON A SURVEILLANCE MISSION IN NORTHERN IRELAND.

FLEXIBLE RESPONSE

1991–2010

THE MOUNTED PARADE IN JUNE 1989 may have given an impression that certain things were immutable, but the environment in which the Regiment existed was about to change fundamentally and bring with it fresh challenges. On 10th November the Berlin Wall, the most visible symbol of the Cold War, was forced open. The result of several years of rumbling discontent among Russia's increasingly nationalist satellite states, and the crippling cost to the Soviet economy of trying to keep up in the arms race, and the collapse of the Warsaw Pact can only be described as a victory in which the Regiment and its antecedents had played their full part.

In hindsight, the long years in Germany could easily be depicted as an extraordinarily anachronistic period. It was certainly untypical of the pressures faced by the Regiment in the conflicts of the last decade of the 20th century and the first of the 21st. While true that life was conducted at a lower tempo and training had a distinct air of unreality, perhaps even a lack of edge, the Regiment spent far longer in the field conducting training then than would be the case in the future. The successive months of troop, squadron and regimental training on Soltau or across large tracts of German countryside, with weeks of a typical year spent uncomfortably cocooned in Nuclear, Biological and Chemical (NBC) suits, brought core armoured skills to their zenith.

At a higher level, the culminating exercises at divisional, or even corps level, while sometimes lacking low-level activity or stimulation, tested both commanders and staff, who were given little quarter, especially when failing to pass a brigade or division across

THE TEMPTING PROSPECT OF A 'PEACE DIVIDEND' FROM THE END OF THE COLD WAR COULD NOT NEGATE THE REQUIREMENT FOR THE REGIMENT TO CONTINUE TO PRACTISE ITS CORE SKILLS SUCH AS GUNNERY.

 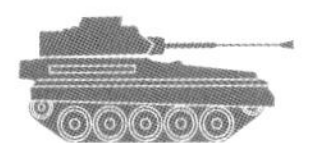

1 CAMOUFLAGED SPARTAN IN A DUST STORM, A FREQUENT AND IRRITATING HAZARD IN THE DESERT.

2 SGT MARK HARRISON'S SPARTAN PASSES AN IRAQI T62 DURING THE LIBERATION OF KUWAIT IN 1991.

a major water obstacle such as the River Weser in good order, for which summary sacking was certainly not unknown, effectively terminating their future prospects. Large-scale manoeuvre exercises routinely incurred a significant death toll, too – sometimes several fatalities in a single night of divisional manoeuvre as a result of vehicle accidents or drownings – driving home to commanders and staff an intuitive understanding of how to conduct large- scale operations, the complexities involved and the sheer scope for things to go radically wrong. The lessons learnt from training in Germany were to underpin the Army's ability to conduct the large-scale high-intensity operations in the Gulf that would confront it twice in the next 12 years, though, as the Berlin Wall came down, speculation on these sort of future conflicts seemed irrelevant to the new world order.

As with the end of all military campaigns, the Government and the public now demanded a 'peace dividend', the results of a defence review, 'Options for Change' being announced in July 1990 to produce *'smaller forces, better equipped, properly trained and housed... they will need to be flexible and mobile and able to contribute both in NATO and, if necessary, elsewhere'.*[1] With an overall reduction in the army from 155,000 to 116,000, a new structure was devised that would mean less armour (though '*it will not mean the death of the tank...The trouble is that no one at the Ministry of Defence has much idea at whom the tanks will be firing*'[2]), and with it fewer Royal Armoured Corps regiments, the total falling from 19 to 11.

The Regiment was in the right business, Lieutenant Colonel Robin Searby remarking in his foreword to the Journal of 1989 that '*the Light Armoured Forces of the reconnaissance regiments... have a great deal to offer. Their mobility, flexibility and ability to be moved far and quickly make them invaluable assets and we should have every confidence for the future,*'[3] but inevitably speculation was rife as to where the cuts would be made and how the Regiment would be affected. Consultation revolved around whether it might be better to choose a bed-fellow rather than be given one, though in the end the decision by the Director of the Royal Armoured Corps to stick to the principles used in earlier reductions spared the Regiment a second amalgamation. These principles sought to maintain the historical balance of the types of regiment in the Household Cavalry and Royal Armoured Corps, and amalgamate like with like (hussars with hussars, lancers with lancers), the whole being tempered by seniority.

Despite the relief of emerging as one of only three regiments to avoid amalgamation and the distinction of being the only remaining 'fraction', uncertainty remained. Cuts in personnel and a re-balancing of numbers by year of service had to be made across the Army in even measure, reductions and reallocations taking place in several tranches spread over the next three years. A generous redundancy package ensured that those who left the Regiment were, in the main, volunteers from cohorts that would be over the permitted establishment levels for recruitment in their years of birth, while, to fill the gaps that existed in other places in the Regiment's manning, new faces from amalgamated regiments were welcomed.

THE GULF WAR 1991

With impeccable timing, forcing even these Whitehall manoeuvres to be put on hold, Saddam

Hussein chose the end of the year to invade Kuwait and precipitate the US-led Coalition to liberate the country. Although the very earliest planning focused on light mobile anti-tank forces to deter further aggression and led to D (Guided Weapons) Squadron being put on stand-by, the British contribution was eventually based on the 1st Armoured Division in Germany and was thought unlikely to involve the Regiment. As the scale of the operation grew, almost every part of the Army was touched and the Regiment, commanded since October 1989 by Lieutenant Colonel Hugh Dickens with Regimental Sergeant Major Peter Palfreyman, eventually despatched over a quarter of its strength to the Gulf, with an equal number employed in Britain supporting the logistic effort, working in headquarters or, in the case of the band, on stand by to receive casualties as they arrived back for surgery.

The first away, and most closely involved in the fighting, were a support troop sent to bolster the 16th/5th Lancers, the 1st Armoured Division's reconnaissance regiment. Staging via Germany they arrived in Saudi Arabia on 30th December 1990 and then deployed into the desert to familiarise themselves with laser target markers and radar. They also conducted more training with night navigation and Nuclear, Biological and Chemical (NBC) training in expectation of the threat from Iraqi Scud missiles and their possible use of chemical munitions. Given the mission *'to identify and attrit the enemy tactical reserves prior to the contact battle'*[4], the battlegroup expected to move rapidly up to 100km behind the enemy forward positions and then use artillery rockets and air strikes to engage the enemy.

Passing through the initial breach on 25th February in atrocious conditions, they pushed onto Objective LEAD where at daybreak on the following day it became apparent that, in the chaos of the advance, the battlegroup was now effectively surrounded by enemy armour. Captain Rupert Maitland-Titterton, the troop leader, wrote: *'As fire continued, it became apparent that contacts were happening from all sides: to our West, tanks were escaping west TOWARDS our own screen; to our North, it was reported that 2 Battalions of T72 reinforcements were on their South, TOWARDS our Northern screen; and in our own sector there were numerous sightings as tanks and APCs tried to escape through our own screen to north. With confusion starting another contact showed a column of tanks advancing towards us from the west – thus we were surrounded. Fortunately, the column turned out to be friendly.'*[5] The subsequent battle at LEAD lasted for six hours before, after a brief halt, they moved on, further rocket strikes being brought onto other positions as the Iraqi army headed back in full retreat. Ordered to provide a further screen and then conduct rear-area security, news of the ceasefire following the short, intense conflict brought with it the requirement to guard prisoners of war, the troop finally returning to Britain at the end of March.

D Squadron, back in the order of battle at the last minute, formed part of the battle casualty replacement chain equipped initially with Ferret Scout Cars and then with some *'extremely unbattleworthy CVRs'*.[6] Although eventually creating a role for 'Ferret Force', the hundred hours of war proved uneventful for them, with many memories revolving around their early stay in the appropriately named 'Black Adder Camp' – neatly encapsulating the sense of confusion that reigned in Saudi Arabia as the Army inloaded. Individual augmentees were also employed throughout the theatre. Major Mick Underhill spent an interesting war acting as the Quartermaster for a Romanian Field Hospital which was that country's contribution to the alliance, the members of which found novel uses for anti-freeze that rendered them largely incapable of giving (but perhaps needing) medical help.

'As fire continued, it became apparent that contacts were happening from all sides…'

Though still recovering some of its vehicles from the Gulf, the Regiment, with Graham Kerridge having taken over as Regimental Sergeant Major in late 1990, moved back to Herford in Germany in August 1991. Despite the long period since the 12th Lancers' last occupation of the barracks in 1955, with the changed international situation and the implementation of the Options for Change decisions, a pattern of life familiar to many was resumed, the officers even managing to get banned from the nurses' mess of the British Military Hospital in Hannover on their first night in the country. The novelty of an open border to the east brought a surge of 'road-trips' to Berlin, Prague and beyond, while military and non-military tourism uncovered countries, clearly destitute from years under communism, struggling to come to terms with the new world order. Operationally, certain aspects of life remained unchanged, C Squadron again finding the guard for the Maze prison in Northern Ireland in 1992. The requirement to meet the minimum manning strength for this operation forced A and D Squadrons to be thinned out, leaving B the only one available for operations. As Yugoslavia disintegrated, they trained for deployment.

1 A SCIMITAR OF B SQUADRON IN BOSNIA IN LATE 1992 AS PART OF THE FIRST DEPLOYMENT OF BRITISH FORCES TO THE AREA.

2 THE RESTRICTIVE MANDATE OF THE DEPLOYMENTS TO BOSNIA UNDER UNITED NATIONS LEADERSHIP ALLOWED THE WARRING FACTIONS TO CONTROL MOVEMENT AS THEY SAW FIT.

BOSNIA

The decision to send troops to Bosnia had been taken in the autumn of 1992 as the deepening humanitarian crisis caused by war between Croatia, Serbia and the other states of the former republic of Yugoslavia prompted the international community, despite severe doubts as to a force's role and precise status, to act through the United Nations. The British contribution to the United Nations Protection Force was set at an armoured infantry battalion in Warriors, with a reconnaissance squadron attached, the first deployment of British troops coming from the Cheshire Regiment and B Squadron. In an expedition that caught the attention of the world's press, the green of the squadron's Scimitars was changed to white and shipped to Split where, in November, the men and their vehicles married up, a photograph of a troop using green golf umbrellas to ward off the rain generating a lively correspondence in the Times. This proved an indicator of the media circus that would follow the tour, as much as highlighting the fact that no cold-weather clothing or equipment had arrived.

This first deployment to Bosnia on 'humanitarian support operations' involved a wide variety of operations that proved the utility of armoured reconnaissance once again, particularly in difficult country with undeveloped infrastructure and in atrocious weather conditions. The squadron frequently managed to deploy their vehicles when the infantry's Warriors were often confined to their operating bases. Based at Vitez and then Kladanj but with much wider responsibilities, the Squadron's primary tasks included humanitarian aid convoy-escorts, the delivery of aid directly – '*delivering blankets and stoves to a mental hospital north of Sarajevo was an eye-opener to all*'[7] – and the negotiation of local ceasefires to allow the movement of refugees. Inevitably the skills and ethos of reconnaissance troops rapidly expanded their role to wider patrolling activity, locating the warring parties' front-lines or finding the latest atrocity, before reporting it back to give the UN commanders some degree of initiative. Living in derelict factories, with little or no sanitation, inappropriate kit and with expeditionary infrastructure unheard of, this, the first of Britain's new operations of choice, was to expose the requirement for rapid investment in many areas if the commitment was to be sustained.

With neither of the warring sides welcoming the UN deployment, the threat facing the force ranged from booby traps, mines and indirect artillery and mortar fire on 'Bomb Alley' and elsewhere, through to direct-fire machine-gun and main armament engagement – all of which was always 'the other side's fault'. To add to these direct threats, on several occasions when they had made it through to cut-off Muslim enclaves, troops found themselves effectively held hostage by the inhabitants who remained fearful that, without a British presence, they would be massacred by the opposing forces. These fears often proved real as the Squadron's uncovering of a massacre at Amici and elsewhere would bear out. Such activity, and the removal of refugees, would introduce to the world a sinister terminology. An article in the Journal described a convoy leaving Tuzla for Srebrenica: '*It was a pitiful sight, two thousand frightened women, children and old people crammed into eighteen open trucks for a fourteen hour journey.... This evacuation was no more than organised "ethnic cleansing". The second convoy the*

Squadron escorted was blocked at the Bosnian front line with mines and RPGs, whilst the rear of the convoy sat on the Serb front line. Both sides threatened to open fire whilst the UN and refugees sat in the middle. If anything typified the situation in Bosnia this was it.'[8] Throughout the tour, with the UN's limited mandate (the rules of engagement would only allow force to be used in self-defence), one hand was tied firmly behind their back, leading to a sense of frustration made more acute when taking casualties, and one that reinforced the perception in Britain that troops had been deployed into someone else's war with no more of an aim or instruction than that 'something must be done'.

Operations in Bosnia continued to demand reconnaissance soldiers, with troops from the Regiment bolstering other units, while, from May to October 1995, an augmented RHQ, two sabre troops and the echelon deployed to the Balkans to command the British Cavalry Battalion or BRITCAVBAT, Lieutenant Colonel Martin Rutledge and Regimental Sergeant Major Fred Reid taking under command New Zealand and British infantry and a squadron of the Queens Royal Lancers. The deployment of this 9th/12th-led battlegroup provided a vivid demonstration of how the earlier expectations of a post-Cold War peace dividend had singularly failed to reflect the realities of newly emerging security threats. Cobbled together at the last moment, most of the Regiment had to remain behind in England to sustain the unglamorous RAC Centre Regiment role at Bovington, while the demands for reconnaissance skills necessitated a composite battlegroup to form up under RHQ to deploy into a supposedly fairly benign and well-understood theatre.

Based at Zepce and with an area of operations that initially covered much of north-west Bosnia, including the Maglaj finger, a Muslim and Croat area surrounded on three sides by Bosnian Serbs, the tasks, risks and frustrations looked familiar to those who had been on other tours, while those new to the operation learnt *'a great deal about the United Nations and the Balkans'*.[9] The situation the battlegroup encountered on arrival was, however, entering a new phase, with an emphasis on outright conflict between the warring factions and, almost literally at the moment of handover between the Household Cavalry and the 9th/12th, a Bosnian Serb tank shelled the sub-unit base in Maglaj. Amazingly, although the incident caused some serious casualties, far greater numbers were avoided by an accident of timing, the shell impacting on the dining hall that earlier had been full of soldiers. While mass casualties might have had a significant political impact and transformed Britain's future posture in the Balkans, the response was to fire a substantial amount of 30mm cannon from Scimitars as well as numerous guided missiles.

The incident not only demonstrated the desire of the warring factions to test the newly arrived battlegroup, but to set the tone for the tense next few months, giving a salutary reminder of the parlous position it was in. Under the command of a Germany-based brigade, few in the battlegroup knew each other, or had properly trained together before deploying, while a complacent attitude in London, the weak UN mandate and the inevitable resource constraints meant that the Regiment had

'ETHNIC CLEANSING' ENTERED THE LEXICON AND FOUND SQUADRONS PATROLLING DESTROYED VILLAGES AND ASSISTING THOSE WHO WISHED TO LEAVE.

SCIMITAR IN UNITED NATIONS COLOURS IN BOSNIA.

only limited ammunition stocks and no echelon support. In considerable haste, elements of the Household Cavalry had to return to Bosnia to reinforce the battlegroup and provide at least some rudimentary capability to manoeuvre and fight. Maglaj was further fortified and the armoured infantry company under command had to be withdrawn from its base in the north after persistent artillery harassing fire close to its camp. In a *'situation [that] was by turns tense and farcical'*[10] freedom of movement across the area was restricted, particularly by the Bosnian Muslims, with logistic resupply often fragile, travel only becoming easier to achieve once NATO's campaign of air-strikes finally added teeth to the UN mission. In the event, the manifest deficiencies and difficulties faced by the Regiment escaped discovery, the air-strikes eventually curbing Bosnian Serb activity, but it had not been a comfortable period for the battlegroup which, quite justifiably, felt that they had been left unnecessarily exposed by decisions back in the UK and elsewhere.

Despite the challenges, towards the end of this tour signs of progress and a return to a limited degree of normality were becoming evident, with schools, water, electricity and telephones restored in some areas, the presence of the UN force having an effect in its own right. The involvement of NATO was, however, to prove the critical factor in rebuilding the Balkans, as the air-strikes in support of the UN ground operation finally forced all sides to the negotiating table. The resulting Dayton Agreement of December 1995 produced a plan with agreed boundaries that would be implemented by NATO ground troops prepared, if necessary, to use lethal force.

The final tour to Bosnia as a Regiment followed the implementation phase of the Dayton Agreement, B and D squadrons, together with a squadron of tanks from the Royal Dragoon Guards forming a battlegroup based at Mrkonic Grad from December 1997 to June 1998 under command of Lieutenant Colonel Nick Everard with Regimental Sergeant Major Mark Harrison having recently taken over from John Pearce. With NATO's overwhelming presence felt by all sides, and green painted vehicles having replaced white, a true 'peace' was in evidence, the main threat coming from unexploded munitions, the driving conditions and the local brew, *slivovic*. By now, operations focused on assistance to non-governmental organisations and humanitarian groups, though many of these so-called 'tree-huggers' proved wary of association with the military, as together they tried to reassure and restore the battered country, rehouse displaced refugees, regenerate the local economy or locate mass graves. Militarily, the requirement for a force capable of fighting was already an insurance policy designed to keep the lid on the former warring factions, which not only allowed force protection measures to be reduced, but broadened the role to include weapons collection and anti-trafficking activity. Once again, the lighter, more agile reconnaissance squadrons proved the work horse, showing presence and intent without causing undue damage, an attribute that would ensure that the Regiment would have to continue to supply squadrons to Bosnia well into the future. Appropriately enough, the last formation British reconnaissance squadron to conduct operations in Bosnia was B Squadron, which left in 2003, almost exactly 10 years after its initial involvement.

NORTHERN IRELAND

While the initial B Squadron deployment to Bosnia had been taking place at the end of 1992, the remainder of the Regiment, commanded since April 1992 by Lieutenant Colonel James Short with Bob Hartwell as Regimental Sergeant Major, was by now complete as C Squadron returned from guarding the Maze in Ireland. It soon began what was thought to be its last training season as a reconnaissance regiment. Amid the headlines of amalgamations and redundancies, Options for Change planned to reduce the number of regular reconnaissance regiments to just two, a decision that even at an early stage was questioned by the

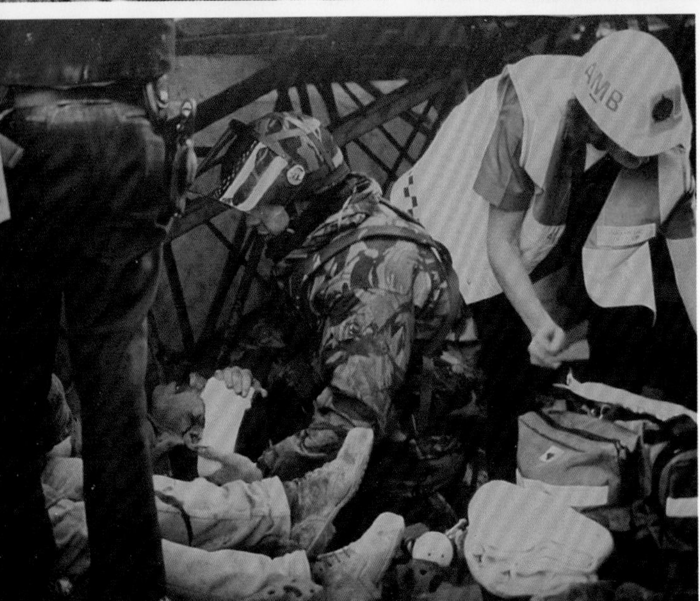

House of Commons Defence Committee and which scarcely reflected the emphasis on flexibility and deployability that was supposed to characterise Britain's reorganised Armed Forces. As a result, the Regiment was instructed to re-role to Challenger tanks and move to Paderborn in Germany in July 1994, though prior to this they were to fit in another six-month tour to Northern Ireland.

The location for this, their final tour to the Province, was to Belfast city centre, occupying a tough area that had always been the preserve of the infantry. Though regimental-sized deployments by Armoured Corps units to Northern Ireland had been commonplace up until the late 1970s, the small size of such regiments' establishments and the cost of conversion to the infantry role, both in terms of cash and skill-fade, had resulted in their cessation, with only squadron-sized groupings, such as the Maze guard force, being found. The return of the Royal Armoured Corps to the hardest parts of Northern Ireland front line was, therefore, looked on with interest by those who doubted their ability to cope and (though would never say it), were possibly looking for a less than glittering performance. Unfortunately, they had not only chosen the wrong Regiment, but also the wrong ground on which to make their point, the urban patrolling of Belfast suiting the 9th/12th's soldiers' aptitude for agility, inquisitiveness, quick wit and good humour better than the rural landscape of South Armagh might have. These natural attributes were reinforced by extensive pre-deployment training that saw several blocks in Herford being converted to a security force base from which to practise patrolling.

The 'patch' that the Regiment, reinforced by a battery of air-defence gunners, was to take on from July 1993 to January 1994 was one of the busiest and most demanding in the province. Consisting of a mainly loyalist population, including the hard-line Shankill Road, it also contained the two nationalist enclaves of the Ardoyne and New Lodge, neatly separated by the Regiment's base at Girdwood Barracks. The most frequent threat came from the 'coffee-jar' bomb, a home-made

1 A FOOT PATROL IN SUPPORT OF THE ROYAL ULSTER CONSTABULARY IN THE NATIONALIST ARDOYNE ESTATE IN BELFAST. THE MAIN THREATS TO THE REGIMENT CAME FROM THIS ESTATE AND THE NEW LODGE AREA.

2 THE REGIMENTAL AREA OF RESPONSIBILITY CONTAINED A MIX OF NATIONALIST AND LOYALIST ESTATES WITH INTER-SECTARIAN VIOLENCE A CONSTANT PRESENCE. A BUNGLED IRA BOMBING OF A FISH AND CHIP SHOP ON THE SHANKILL ROAD SAW THE BOMBER AND 10 OTHERS KILLED IN THIS INCIDENT.

3 TROOPER PAYNE ASSISTS WITH CASUALTIES.

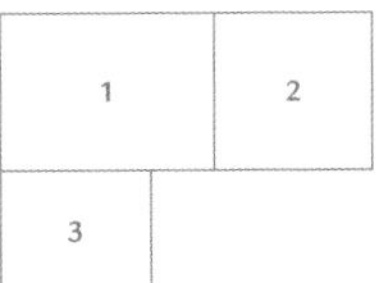

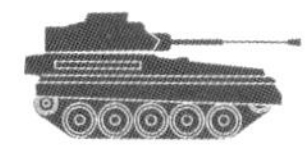

A FOOT PATROL IN THE NATIONALIST ARDOYNE ESTATE, BELFAST. THE OBSERVATION TOWER AT THE OLD PARK POLICE STATION CAN BE SEEN ON THE HORIZON. IT WAS MANNED BY MEMBERS OF THE REGIMENT.

 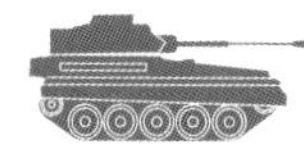

1 CORPORAL ANREW DYNES WHO WAS AWARDED THE MILITARY CROSS FOR CATCHING AN IRA TERRORIST AFTER AN AMBUSH. HE WAS THE FIRST CORPORAL AND THE SECOND SOLDIER TO HAVE BEEN AWARDED THE MEDAL AFTFR IT WAS OPENED UP TO SOLDIERS AS WELL AS OFFICERS.

2 THE INSIDE OF THE SOLDIER'S ACCOMMODATION AT GIRDWOOD BARRACKS, BELFAST.

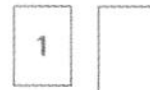

hand grenade made of high explosive and shrapnel packed into an empty jar that could then be thrown or dropped from one of the blocks of flats in the area with little chance of the perpetrator being caught. Small off-route mines and rocket-propelled grenades presented the principal threat to vehicle patrols, with shootings at foot patrols not uncommon.

The Regiment's mission continued to be to 'support the RUC in the defeat of terrorism'. In practice, this meant escorting RUC policemen, either on foot or in armoured Land Rovers (the 'Snatches' that would later receive such bad press in Iraq and Afghanistan), as they went about their business using well-developed 'multiple' patrolling, several squads of four soldiers using the streets and alleys around the policeman to provide him with close protection and cut off any terrorist escape routes. In addition, two permanent observation posts were manned looking into the nationalist areas, one of which, set on top of a tower block in the New Lodge, could only be re-supplied or visited if a large-scale operation was mounted to secure it. The difficulty of doing so meaning that several soldiers did not emerge from its confines for the entire tour.

At this late stage in the campaign, IRA tactics and security were highly sophisticated and any demonstrable success was difficult to come by, intelligence reports of an aborted attack often being the only metric. The action therefore of Corporal Andrew Dynes, a member of the Commanding Officer's vehicle patrol that had just been ambushed, who chased and caught the gunman, one of the main 'players' in the Ardoyne IRA, was especially noteworthy. For his prompt action Corporal Dynes was rewarded with the Military Cross, the first to be given to a Corporal and only the second to a soldier following the opening up of this award to soldiers as well as officers.

While the direct threat to soldiers' lives came almost exclusively from the nationalist areas, the boundaries of the communities represented fault lines, with assassination and attack by shooting and bombing a regular occurrence that the security forces were there to prevent. The intense levels of violence, particularly across the sectarian divide, that were seen during the tour were, in hindsight, a precursor of the announcement of the ceasefire that would come within a few months of the tour's end. They signalled an attempt by the IRA and others to gain leverage in the secret talks that were already ongoing during the tour which would lead, slowly, to the normalisation of life in Northern Ireland and the end of the military campaign.

In all that they faced, the soldiers of the Regiment, as so often before and afterwards, showed a level of courage and restraint that seems remarkable. They lived cooped up in a converted TA centre with accommodation in 'submarines' (mortar-proof concrete shelters where soldiers lived crammed 10 to a room). There were few welfare facilities and limited contact with home. They daily faced a situation in which the law seemed only to apply to one side, the rules of engagement being interpreted in such a way that 'coffee-jar' throwers could not be engaged because they had never been shown to kill anyone. It is, perhaps, surprising that no more than a single occurrence took place where an individual lost control. In this incident a soldier, part of a patrol designed to prevent loyalist reprisals, engaged several suspected members of the IRA who were attending the wake of a terrorist who had blown up himself and 10 innocent civilians in a fish and chip shop on the Shankill Road.

Prior to their tour in Belfast, the Regiment had been subjected to order and counter-order in the 'post-Options' reshuffle, the latest convulsion of which caught it by surprise on its return to Herford. The demands of Bosnia, amidst other factors, had proved that the reduced number of regular reconnaissance regiments could not work and the Regiment was therefore not to re-role. The planned posting to Paderborn (to which a number of families had already moved) was cancelled at short notice. The 9th/12th Lancers would return to the United Kingdom as a training regiment at Bovington and Lulworth in the summer of 1994, while B Squadron, by now nearly fully trained on tanks following its return from Bosnia, moved to Warminster to provide the Demonstration Squadron of 15 Chieftain, and later Challenger 1, tanks and a close reconnaissance troop for all the courses and exercises run on Salisbury Plain.

THE MOVE BACK TO BRITAIN IN 1994 SAW THE BULK OF THE REGIMENT AT BOVINGTON AND LULWORTH PROVIDING TRAINING SUPPORT. B SQUADRON WAS FORTUNATE TO BE BASED AT WARMINSTER IN A MORE FULFILLING ROLE ON CHIEFTAIN AND THEN CHALLENGER 1 TANKS.

1 ALTHOUGH NATO FORCES COULD GUARANTEE THE SOVEREIGNTY OF KOSOVO, TERRORIST ACTIVITIES CONTINUED, A BUS BOMB IN FEBRUARY 2001 KILLING 12 AND WOUNDING 40, WITH MEMBERS OF C SQUADRON THE FIRST ON THE SCENE TO DEAL WITH THE AFTERMATH.

2 THE KOSOVO FORCE (KFOR) DEPLOYMENT IN EARLY 2001 INVOLVED LONG HOURS TRYING TO INTERCEPT GUERRILLAS PASSING BETWEEN KOSOVO AND MACEDONIA. LIEUTENANT PETER CORCORAN (PICTURED) WAS LATER TO BE SERIOUSLY INJURED WHEN HIS SCIMITAR DROVE OVER A MINE, KILLING TROOPER ADAM SLATER.

For those in Dorset, the attraction and stability of the location only partially offset the thankless and repetitive role (which was in the process of privatisation) that they found themselves in, each squadron's differing duties and widely varying establishment making Regimental cohesion difficult to achieve. The Colonel of the Regiment, Major General Mike Swindells remarked that it was *'not what many young soldiers imagined they might have to do when they joined the Army'*.[11] Even the requirements of the operational tour to Bosnia in 1995 would only lead to a few of the Regiment taking part, the Commanding Officer, Martin Rutledge, noting with *'regret that we are unable to release more soldiers to participate'*.[12] B Squadron in Warminster enjoyed a more fulfilling posting with a proper squadron structure, plenty of track miles and ammunition to be expended on well-resourced exercises, with RHQ at some distance and only the infantry battalion to which they worked to impress.

The news that the Regiment was to reform as a reconnaissance regiment in April 1997 could not come soon enough, the lack of recruits while at Bovington having left a scar across the establishment that would take years to grow out. A sudden inflow of new recruits proved big enough only to bring the Regiment to three depleted squadrons, while an untidy extraction required A Squadron to remain in Dorset. Although the new location at an old RAF station at Swanton Morley in Norfolk included a huge grass airfield and plenty of space, it required a considerable amount of work to turn it into a satisfactory base for an armoured reconnaissance regiment. The initial refurbishment made good some of the accommodation before a major investment, as the Regiment which was about to leave for Germany, built both new vehicle lines and the Army's first 'Z Type' accommodation – single rooms with en suite ablutions for all ranks.

The MonsMoy celebrations of July 1998, which were attended by the Colonel-in-Chief, saw A Squadron rejoin the Regiment and marked

the end of the reorganisations set in chain by Options for Change, which had resulted in the Regiment's dispersal for over four and a half years. With Lieutenant Colonel James Mackaness assuming command, the Regiment turned to a new role – the provision of training support to troops exercising in Canada. The British Army Training Unit Suffield or BATUS, while still a live firing area, by now required the presence of an enemy or opposing force (OPFOR) to play a thinking enemy using equipment fitted with lasers to represent the effects of direct and indirect-fire engagement. Although an excellent training package, the requirements for the OPFOR required those providing it to remain in Canada for up to, and in some cases over, six months, demanding the same separation from families as an operational tour and a duty that the Regiment picked up in 1999, 2002 and 2007.

The seven years spent in the United Kingdom were by now drawing to a close and were fittingly marked by a final visit by the Colonel-in-Chief in her centenary year to present a new guidon.

The seven years spent in the United Kingdom were by now drawing to a close and were fittingly marked by a final visit by the Colonel-in-Chief in her centenary year to present a new guidon. On a perfect day, the efforts of Regimental Sergeant Major Phil Kerr were rewarded, while behind the scenes the added difficulties of dealing with A Squadron's recent return from six months in Bosnia were neatly juggled with the move back to Germany that was to take place three weeks later.

The return to Hohne in August 2000 brought with it not only the added competition of garrison life but also the demise, after 17 years in the ORBAT, of D Squadron which was disbanded as part of a wider reorganisation. The once familiar routine of life in Germany had by now been shaken by the operational spur of deployments to Bosnia and Kosovo, the latter country imploding as the former settled down, nationalist forces on both sides being checked only by NATO intervention in 1999. Reconnaissance soldiers again proved at a premium and C Squadron deployed in early 2001 to monitor the border and stabilise areas where the Serb and Kosovar nationalists continued to fight, their first week of what was supposed to be a quiet tour being ripped apart by a culvert bomb in Podujevo, which killed 12 civilians on a bus. Although aiming at each other rather than the NATO forces, dangers persisted in form of unexploded ordnance. A deeply laid mine in a previously cleared area detonated when the ground had softened, destroying a Scimitar and killing the driver, Trooper Adam Slater, on the Kosovo-Macedonian border.

For those not committed to operations, exercises continued to provide the military challenge and the new Commanding Officer, Lieutenant Colonel Jamie Martin and his Regimental Sergeant Major, Stephen Cunningham, planned a return once again to Bavaria in 2001. With everything in place and the troops on the trains and heading south, the ambitious exercise proved stillborn when the outbreak of foot and mouth disease in the United Kingdom called it to an early halt. More satisfactorily, the training programme later that year involved a divisional-level exercise in Oman, with added interest provided for both the participants and the worlds' media by the terrorist attacks in New York in September 2001 and the resultant speculation that this was not a coincidence of events but a stepping stone prior to an invasion of Afghanistan.

IRAQ

Against the background of tension with Iraq over Saddam Hussein's alleged possession of weapons of mass destruction, Regimental Headquarters, recently returned from seven months in BATUS, began contingency planning in December 2002 for possible operations in the Middle East as part of the 1st Armoured Division. The decision not to mount an attack from Turkey in the north of Iraq brought a change of requirement for forces,

C SQUADRON – SHEFFIELD 2003. THE NATIONAL FIREMAN'S STRIKE IN 2002/2003 REQUIRED THE REGIMENT TO MOVE TO SOUTH YORKSHIRE TO PROVIDE EMERGENCY COVER USING A VARIETY OF EQUIPMENT INCLUDING GREEN GODDESS FIRE ENGINES, SOME OF WHICH WERE OVER 50 YEARS OF AGE.

THE LACK OF PREPARATION FOR THE POST-INVASION PHASE OF THE IRAQ WAR SAW THE REGIMENT UNDERTAKE A NUMBER OF TASKS TO COVER GAPS LEFT BY OTHERS. THE OPERATIONS OFFICER, CAPTAIN JAMES MATHESON, ATTEMPTS TO TEACH THE CIVIL SERVANTS OF BASRA COUNCIL WHILE CAPTAIN MATTHEW EVERETT NEGOTIATES IN A CAMP FOR PILGRIMS FOR THE HAJJ AS THEY ATTEMPT TO TRAVEL OUT OF IRAQ FOR THE FIRST TIME.

but it remained a considerable shock when the commanding officer was informed in early 2003 that the Regiment would not be part of the final invasion package, the military logic directing that there was no requirement for a divisional reconnaissance regiment. This was a deeply disappointing and frustrating time, the more so as the other elements of 7th Armoured Brigade departed and the barracks emptied around them.

Fortunately for the Regiment and the author, who assumed command at this time with Regimental Sergeant Major Lee Barnett, there was little time to brood as the build-up to invasion progressed elsewhere. Distraction came from a national firemen's strike that had been rumbling on in Britain for some months and to which the 9th/12th now deployed. Training occurred both in Germany and England before, with a diverse mix of other cap-badges and fire engines, including Green Goddesses of over 50 years of age, the Regiment took over responsibility for the whole of South Yorkshire in preparation for the next wave of strikes. Not a hose was to be fired in anger however for, with everyone in position, the strike was called off, leaving the Regiment to repair back to Germany wondering what might come next.

The disappointment of missing out on initial phase of the war in the Gulf would probably have been less keenly felt had the Regiment known how familiar it was to become with southern Iraq. Within weeks of the return to Germany, C Squadron were earmarked to deploy in the reconnaissance role with 20th Armoured Brigade in October 2003, while Regimental Headquarters would also go, but as part of Brigade Headquarters running Civil Affairs and Information Operations. By late summer it was becoming apparent that more forces were going to be needed and A Squadron, prised out of yet another planned tour to Bosnia, joined the order of battle – the Commanding Officer, in a somewhat surreal moment, receiving the instruction over a mobile phone when shopping in a well-known high-street store.

By the time of their arrival in southern Iraq, the initial euphoria that had greeted the defeat of the Iraqi army and the toppling of Saddam Hussein had, to a large extent, evaporated and been replaced with a feeling that the Coalition's promises, either made or hinted at, had not been delivered. Fuel, water and power, to say nothing of lawlessness and unemployment, were a constant source of friction. The summer months before arrival had shown that trouble could flare up almost instantaneously, either as a result of a spontaneous grievance or as an orchestrated event. With only the Ba'ath party as a model to draw on, a vacuum existed with the Iranian-backed, largely fundamentalist parties proving better able to represent and exploit the concerns of the people. On the Coalition side the military, used to dealing with Balkan-sized issues, found themselves largely overfaced by the sheer

scale of the problem posed by the city of Basra and its two million inhabitants, broken infrastructure and complete absence of indigenous security forces. On the civilian side it was soon apparent there were neither plans nor resources to get the country back on its feet. Many of those who might normally have been interested in this sort of work stayed away either because they disapproved of the operation or felt unsafe.

Despite the ominous potential from this tinderbox, the threat was deemed sufficiently low, at least for the first few months, to allow patrolling in a mixture of soft-skinned vehicles and Scimitars as A Squadron, with a battlegroup to the south of Basra, took on responsibility for an area of operations along the border with Kuwait. Tasked with interdicting smuggling and keeping an eye on the key border crossing points, their activities gave rise to several incidents, including one where the 'Ali Babas', as the locals called any criminal, were found hiding in rolled-up carpets that their family were sitting on. C Squadron, with a battlegroup just outside the northern town of Al Amarah, took on a more conventional reconnaissance role in a large area of empty desert drained by Saddam, which had once been the home of the Marsh Arab tribes and which, to the east, continued to bear the largely unhealed scars of the Iran/Iraq war. With their close proximity to the Iranian border, much of which had never been properly defined on the ground, C Squadron also put out an extensive reconnaissance screen, bolstered by unmanned air vehicles and electronic warfare teams to maintain observation on weapons trafficking suspected of coming across the border. RHQ formed a part of the enlarged brigade headquarters, and ran media and information operations as well as the military efforts to help rebuild the economy and provincial governance.

By early 2004 violence was increasing and a major reorganisation took place to concentrate elements of the army on rebuilding the corrupt and wholly ineffective Iraqi judicial system. With no civilian agencies able to do the work, C Squadron and others received two weeks' training and found itself in charge of reforming Basra's law courts and prisons. Like so much of the nation's bureaucracy, this had fallen apart following the Coalition's decision to dismantle all levels of Ba'athist bureaucracy. Equally daunting tasks were faced by others: the Regimental Second-in-Command, Major David Pritchard, took on responsibility for the Border Police and the crossings into Iran, the doctor found himself the Chief Advisor to the Basra Minister of Health, while the Operations Officer found himself planning (aborted) elections and teaching the Iraqi Civil Service, amongst other skills, how to take minutes of a meeting. Further grit came from the sense of *schadenfreude* among many in the media and the public that things were going wrong in this unpopular campaign, while instances of mistreatment of prisoners by American and British troops and a catalogue of stories of inadequacies of both thinking and of kit pervaded.

By the time the Regiment returned to Hohne in April 2004 the security situation across Iraq had worsened and continued to deteriorate. Attacks on Coalition troops by well-armed local militias flexing their muscles to gain status or intimidate others had increased, while sectarian violence between Sunni and Shia Muslims escalated in scale, rendering the combined efforts of the Coalition and the newly formed Government of Iraq seemingly futile. The Regiment returned to southern Iraq 18 months later, with Lieutenant Colonel Charles Crewdson in command and with Regimental Sergeant Major Bernie Winter having taken over from Steve Buckley. Although the situation that faced them was more stable and equipment had improved, the theatre was essentially hostile with force protection the over-riding consideration.

Forming the first Formation Reconnaissance Battlegroup to deploy to Iraq, Regimental Headquarters took under command in October 2005 both B and C Squadrons together with a squadron of the Scots Dragoon Guards in Challenger 2 tanks. The area of operations spanned a large area south of Basra containing over a million people, the Iraq/Kuwait border and the strategically vital Al Faw peninsula, through which much of Iraq's oil flows. Routine patrolling formed the basis of operations, with major effort put into building the capability of the Iraqi security forces, which by now included a nascent army. More classical formation reconnaissance skills were also put into practice by C Squadron, who again deployed into the desert for a lengthy period to provide observation and also to act as a quick reaction force ready to assist the Iraqis who had by now taken over responsibility for security in certain areas. A Squadron, detached to Brigade Headquarters, led and formed half of the Brigade Surveillance Company to produce detailed surveillance information on insurgents for others to exploit.

Despite the ominous potential from this tinderbox, the threat was deemed sufficiently low, at least for the first few months, to allow patrolling in a mixture of soft-skinned vehicles and Scimitars…

BY THE END OF THE REGIMENT'S FIRST TOUR TO IRAQ THE LARGELY BENIGN SITUATION HAD CHANGED AS POLITICAL AND RELIGIOUS GROUPS USED VIOLENCE TO GAIN STATUS AND POWER, THE COMMANDING OFFICER AND HIS TACTICAL HEADQUARTERS BECAME INVOLVED IN A RIOT ORGANISED BY A PARTY CALLED 'GOD'S REVENGE'.

REGIMENTAL PATROLS IN SOUTHERN IRAQ DURING 2005/06. THE PRIMARY THREAT HAD BY NOW EVOLVED INTO HIGHLY ACCURATE AND EFFECTIVE ROADSIDE BOMBS.

After a quiet beginning to the tour as a constitutional referendum and national elections were held, the insurgents predictably increased their levels of activity. Corruption, inefficiency and intimidation made the task of reforming Iraqi security forces difficult enough but by now the insurgents had perfected increasingly lethal roadside bombs that could defeat all but the most heavily armoured vehicle using infra-red sensors to trigger them. The numerous strikes killed one member of the battlegroup and injured several others. With every casualty putting greater pressure on the Government in Britain, the difficult act of balancing risk against mission success was summarised by the Colonel of the Regiment, Major General Robin Searby: '*The intention of the insurgent is to force the troops to expend most of their efforts in protecting themselves, thus taking them away from their primary task of promoting stability in Southern Iraq; to make them become cautious and inward looking. A balance has to be struck… but the spirit and manner in which it [the task] is carried out depends on the combined will and determination of the individual components – the soldiers. The Regiment passed that test very well indeed.*'[13]

THE REGIMENTAL BAND

Considerable passion has always been raised by the Regimental bands and their role. One of the earliest examples of the debate comes from 1814, when Frederick Ponsonby, who was trying to re-establish the band of the 12th Light Dragoons, was curtly told by the Colonel of the Regiment (who would have had to fund it) that *'I am sorry you should think of giving way to the ill-considered wishes of my Regiment respecting a band. I should prefer their taste for discipline to that for Music, if a bad band may be so called.'* Both Regiments nevertheless maintained mounted bands, giving up their horses on mechanisation and merging on amalgamation before suffering a series of cuts that substantially reduced their numbers.

Beyond the provision of military music the band's justification latterly rested on their role as medical orderlies, a task that they carried out for the last time in the 1991 Gulf War. They also formed the backbone of the Regimental rear party when on exercise or other operations to free up manpower from an otherwise small establishment. While overseas the Band was often an important way of making contact with the local community, whether in Germany or, for the 12th Lancers Band, in Malaya where local villages were given concerts as part of the Hearts and Minds campaign, the bandsmen travelling in open lorries with rifles and machine guns augmenting their instruments. For the Regiment, ignoring the self-evident adage that *'a parade without a band is like a pee without a fart'*, the band integrated into every part of life and added considerably to morale.

THE BAND OF THE 9TH/12TH ROYAL LANCERS ON THE STEPS OF THE ROYAL MILITARY ACADEMY SANDHURST.

THE MOUNTED BAND OF THE 9TH LANCERS, ABASSIA, 1923.

The Regimental band ceased to exist on 1st July 1994 after 159 years of continuous service and following a review by the Corps of Army Music at Kneller Hall. Based on the apparent requirement for a minimum size of band to create 'proper' (perhaps 'loud') military music, the individual cavalry regiments' bands were deemed too small, ignoring both the fact that they had, up until then, been performing to everyone's satisfaction; indeed the last report by Kneller Hall had graded them 'excellent'. The effect disbandment might have proved difficult to quantify, and could be measured only in terms of operational capability in their capacity as medical orderlies, while other, intangible benefits, such as their representational value and effect on morale were ignored. The band's successor came into being at the beginning of August 1994 in Bovington as the Band of the Royal Lancers (effectively a shared arrangement with the Queen's Royal Lancers), for which some sheet music and instruments were bought by the Army, the remainder of the property being transferred to the PRI. A further review of military music implemented in 2006 produced further cuts and reduced the Royal Armoured Corps to two bands, of which the Light Cavalry Band is the closest link to its Regimental predecessors.

THE REGIMENT'S FINAL TOUR OF IRAQ IN 2008 SAW THEM UNDERTAKE A MULTITUDE OF TASKS INCLUDING RIVER PATROLS, THE DEVELOPMENT OF THE PORT OF UMM QASR AND, CRUCIALLY, THE IMPROVEMENT OF THE IRAQI ARMY.

The groundwork put in place by these operations, the increasing capability of the Iraqis themselves and a backlash against the Shia militias had begun to bear fruit when the Regiment next returned to Basra in April 2008. Considerable confusion persisted until the very last minute as to the precise employment that the Regiment would undertake, until eventually Lieutenant Colonel Tim Robinson and Regimental Sergeant Majors Ken Hayes and then Robert Millar could confirm that A Squadron would be responsible for improving the Iraqi Marines capability and developing the port of Umm Qasr. More idiosyncratically, they would also command an (unmanned) surveillance balloon. RHQ and C Squadron were to train the brigade's troops as they staged through Kuwait, before the Squadron turned its hand to river patrols in boats to deter attacks onto the main British base that were being launched from the network of waterways that surrounded it. RHQ with the remainder of B Squadron and an amalgam of other units joined the programme to mentor an Iraqi Army brigade. Split into specialist advisory groups to develop each area and level of command, the mentors provided support and advice, living and working with the Iraqi army to ensure that high standards were met and a shared commitment was being seen to be made. It involved, in a change to the situation of only a year or two before, '*small teams, sometimes as few as four travelling in Iraqi vehicles, following the Iraqi Army around the city [of Basra], cajoling, advising and supporting with surveillance, reconnaissance and strike capability*'.[14] As with any such operation, success is difficult to quantify although all this water-based activity did result in imports through the port quadrupling during the tour.

THE DUKE OF YORK AND MEMBERS OF THE OLD COMRADES ASSOCIATION DURING HIS FIRST VISIT TO THE REGIMENT AS COLONEL-IN-CHIEF, HOHNE, JULY 2004.

Despite the ominous potential from this tinderbox, the threat was deemed sufficiently low, at least for the first few months, to allow patrolling in a mixture of soft-skinned vehicles and Scimitars…

The investment in Iraqi forces had also been deemed to have been a success and within a few weeks of the Regiment's departure in October 2008 the withdrawal of all but a few British forces was announced and largely complete within six months. A deeply unpopular campaign amongst the British and world population, Iraq had tested the Army and the Regiment not only in terms of pure numbers, but also in the skill sets that it required of its soldiers who, while rarely in the limelight, proved once again their ability to work both off and on their vehicles in any number of complex situations.

If Iraq provided the Regiment's operational focus, soldiering in Germany continued to offer the chance not only to benefit from the opportunities of a cheaper, more extravagant lifestyle but also from the greater cohesion brought from a close-knit community often centred on the Messes and squadron bars, the latter reinstituted in the face of some doubt from the chain of command. External forces continued to be felt, most notably the Defence White Paper published in 2003, which not only spelt the end of the infantry's traditional structure of single battalions but saw the 9th/12th's order of battle reduced to two sabre squadrons and affiliated to a brigade rather than a division. Although partially offset by the subsequent creation in 2006 of a new, small squadron containing radar, specialist liaison teams, tactical air-control parties and a chemical-reconnaissance capability, the Regiment, which at the time of writing had been commanded since July 2009 by Lieutenant Colonel Will Fooks, stood at an almost unsustainably small number of 292 soldiers, with a further 70 attached from other arms with which to face the challenge of operations in Afghanistan for which it was then preparing.

There is, beyond those currently serving, a wider part that makes a vital contribution to the

HER MAJESTY QUEEN ELIZABETH THE QUEEN MOTHER

Her Majesty Queen Elizabeth The Queen Mother agreed to be Colonel-in-Chief of the 9th Lancers in 1953 and on amalgamation with the 12th continued to be the Colonel of the present Regiment, presenting it with its first guidon in Tidworth in 1978. She made many visits to the Regiment that were always, happy and memorable occasions, whatever the weather. Her last occurred in July 2000, two weeks before her 100th birthday when she presented a new guidon.

Her involvement extended beyond the purely ceremonial and she took a keen interest in all aspects of regimental life, though with a particular fondness for horses, presenting more than one to the Regiment and running several of her stable in the Grand Military Gold Cup as the Colonel-in-Chief of the Regiment. Renowned for her quick wit on visit to the Regiment in 1965 she asked to see the polo ponies and asked the groom, Edward Smith, one of their names. *'Unable to remember the Commanding Officer said "It's Sierra isn't it Smith!" The royal party moved on about 15 feet, the Queen Mum stopped, came back and whispered in my ear. Her Majesty's actual words were "Never mind Trooper Smith these Argentinean names are a bugger to remember."'*[15] At her funeral on 10th April 2002, the Colonel of the Regiment acted as an escort to the gun carriage, with a number of other Regimental personnel attending the service.

HER MAJESTY QUEEN ELIZABETH, THE QUEEN MOTHER, WAS COLONEL-IN-CHIEF OF THE 9TH LANCERS FROM 1953 AND THEN OF THE AMALGAMATED REGIMENT UNTIL HER DEATH IN 2002.

THE STRONG LINKS TO THE REGIMENT'S RECRUITING AREA WERE DEMONSTRATED IN A SERIES OF HOMECOMING PARADES IN 2009 IN LEICESTER, DERBY AND NORTHAMPTON.

sense of what it means to be a 9th/12th Lancer. His Royal Highness Prince Andrew, the Duke of York, has been the Regiment's Colonel-in-Chief since 2003. Renewing an association that had existed from flying helicopters from the Regiment's at one-time affiliated ship, HMS *Brazen*, his first visit, conducted over a period of 24 hours in July 2004, took the form of a mounted and dismounted parade in blazing sun. The visit was attended by many families and Old Comrades from the Regimental Association and co-ordinated through Regimental Home Headquarters, which provide a vital link to the 'home base'. Increasingly called on to assist with care of families, veterans and casualties, Home Headquarters and the Museum also represent the Regiment in the community, the feelings of which were most clearly demonstrated on return from Iraq in 2009, when tens of thousands lined the streets for parades in Leicester, Derby and Northampton.

These then are the parts that make the Regiment so formidable and allow its serving soldiers to face up to adversaries of all kinds, including the most dangerous, of which George Bernard Shaw observed *'the British soldier can stand up to anything except the British War Office'.* Based on a profound sense of belonging and pride, the 9th/12th Lancers have proved over time that they, and the Regimental system that they embody, are *'still the best way of raising, grouping, training, and leading men in action devised by any army'.*[16]

BIBLIOGRAPHY/FOOTNOTES

JW Bryant, *Some Thoughts at Sunset,* unpublished

David Chandler (General Editor), *The Oxford Illustrated History of the British Army*, Oxford University Press, 1994

Paul Collier, *The Second World War (4), The Mediterranean 1940–45*, Osprey, 2003

The Delhi Spearman, *Regimental Journals of the 9th/12th Royal Lancers*

Christopher Hibbert, *The Great Mutiny, India 1857*, Penguin, 1980

Richard Holmes, *War Walks*, BBC Books, 1996

John Keegan, *The Second World War*, Hutchinson, 1989

Henry de la Falaise, *Through Hell to Dunkirk,* published in the USA, 1941

Fremont-Barnes, Gregory, *The Boer War 1899–1902*, Osprey, 2003

Fremont-Barnes, Gregory and Fisher, Todd, *The Napoleonic Wars, The Rise and Fall of an Empire*, Osprey 2004

Philip Haythornethwaite, *British Cavalryman 1792–1815,* Osprey 1994

Hunn, Freddie, *recollections of service with 12th Royal Lancers 1939–1945,* unpublished

James Holland, *Italy's Sorrow,* HarperPress 2008

Allan Mallinson, Light Dragoons, *The Origins of a New Regiment*, Leo Cooper 1993

The Marquess of Anglesey, *A History of the British Cavalry 1816 to 1919*

Volume 1, *1816–1850*, Leo Cooper, 1973

Volume 2, *1851–1871*, Leo Cooper, 1975

Volume 3, *1872–1898*, Leo Cooper, 1982

Volume 4, *1899–1913*, Leo Cooper, 1986

Volume 7, *1914*, Leo Cooper, 1996

Volume 8, *1915–1939*, Leo Cooper, 1997

Charles Messenger, *The Tunisian Campaign,* Allan, 1982

Peter Newark, *Sabre and Lance, An Illustrated History of Cavalry,* Blandford Press, 1987

David Owen, *Balkan Odyssey,* Victor Gollancz, 1995

Nick Peto, *Peto's Progress,* Long Barn Books, 2005

John Robson, *War Diary 14th August 1943 to 3rd May 1945,* unpublished

Hugh Sebag-Montefiore, *Dunkirk,* Penguin, 2006

Bruce Shand, *Previous Engagements,* Michael Russell (Publishing), 1990

Peter Simkins, *The First World War, The Western Front, 1914–16*, Osprey, 2002

Peter Simkins, *The First World War, The Western Front, 1917–18*, Osprey, 2002

Hew Strachan, *The First World War*, Simon and Schuster, 2003

Philip Warner, *The British Cavalry,* J M Dent and Sons, 1984

Barney White-Spunner, *Horse Guards,* Macmillan, 2006

1715–1792

1 SHEPPARD | page 5
2 OXFORD ILLUSTRATED HISTORY OF THE BRITISH ARMY | page 103
3 STEWART | page 10
4 STEWART | page 25
5 STEWART | page 24
6 SHEPPARD | page 37
7 OXFORD ILLUSTRATED HISTORY OF THE BRITISH ARMY | page 99
8 SHEPPARD | page 26
9 SHEPPARD | page 27
10 STEWART | page 15
11 SHEPPARD | page 30
12 STEWART | page 20
13 STEWART | page 20
14 STEWART | page 19
15 STEWART | page 21
16 ANGLESEY, Vol 2 | page 95
17 MALLINSON | page 10

1792–1811

1 OXFORD ILLUSTRATED HISTORY OF THE BRITISH ARMY | page 137
2 STEWART | page 42
3 STEWART | page 4
4 STEWART | page 47
5 STEWART | page 47
6 STEWART | page 53
7 STEWART | page 53
8 STEWART | page 56
9 STEWART | page 72
10 STEWART | page 77

1811–1815

1 STEWART | page 65
2 HAYTHORNETHWAITE | page 16
3 NEWARK | page 95
4 OXFORD ILLUSTRATED HISTORY OF THE BRITISH ARMY | page 147
5 LETTER FROM WELLINGTON TO EARL OF LIVERPOOL, Lorvao, 20th September, 1810, War Times Journal | Internet
6 STEWART | page 66
7 STEWART | page 68
8 STEWART | page 70
9 SHEPPARD | page 67
10 STEWART | page 90
11 STEWART | page 72
12 STEWART | page 73
13 STEWART | page 75
14 STEWART | page 77
15 STEWART | page 78
16 STEWART | page 80
17 SHEPPARD | page 91
18 SHEPPARD | page 90
19 STEWART | page 83
20 FREMONT-BARNES AND FISHER | page 234
21 STEWART | page 87
22 STEWART | page 87
23 STEWART | page 87
24 STEWART | page 90
25 STEWART | page 94
26 STEWART | page 96
27 STEWART | page 98 and NEWARK | page 96

1815–1857

1 ANGLESEY, Vol 2 | page 74
2 STEWART | page 110
3 ANGLESEY, Vol 1 | page 135
4 ANGLESEY, Vol 1 | page 141
5 ANGLESEY, Vol 1 | page 151
6 MALLINSON | page 93
7 MALLINSON | page 93
8 MALLINSON | page 92
9 SHEPPARD | page 109
10 SHEPPARD | page 112
11 SHEPPARD | page 112
12 ANGLESEY, Vol 1 | page 278
13 ANGLESEY, Vol 1 | page 279
14 ANGLESEY, Vol 1 | page 282
15 SHEPPARD | page 122
16 STEWART | page 125
17 STEWART | page 122
18 STEWART | page 130
19 STEWART | page 133
20 STEWART | page 139
21 STEWART | page140
22 STEWART | page 140
23 STEWART | page 144
24 STEWART | page 143
25 HANSARD, House of Commons Debate, 7 August 1896, Vol 44 | c97
26 STEWART | page 119
27 NEWARK, Sabre and Lance | page 72
28 PHILIP WARNER | page 154
29 ANGLESEY, Vol 2 | page 416
30 STEWART | page 124

1857–1880

1 SHEPPARD | page 132
2 SHEPPARD | page 133
3 HIBBERT | page 283-288
4 SHEPPARD | page 134
5 SHEPPARD | page 135
6 ANGLESEY, Vol 2 | page 160
7 ANGLESEY, Vol 2 | page 161
8 SHEPPARD | page 139
9 SHEPPARD | page 146
10 SHEPPARD | page 147
11 ANGLESEY, Vol 2 | page 189
12 STEWART | page 150
13 ANGLESEY, Vol 2 | page 286
14 ANGLESEY, Vol 2 | page 301
15 ANGLESEY, Vol 2 | page 315
16 SHEPPARD | page 387
17 SHEPPARD | page 161
18 SHEPPARD | page 161
19 SHEPPARD | page162
20 ANGLESEY, Vol 3 | page 227
21 SHEPPARD | page 167, 168
22 SHEPPARD | page 167, 168

23 ANGLESEY, Vol 3 | page 233
24 ANGLESEY, Vol 3 | page 233
25 ANGLESEY, Vol 3 | page 235
26 SHEPPARD | page 170
27 SHEPPARD | page 174
28 SHEPPARD | page 175
29 SHEPPARD | page 176
30 ANGLESEY, Vol 2 | page 148
31 ANGLESEY, Vol 1 | page 269

1880–1914

1 STEWART | page 170, quoting G W HOBSON, Some 12th Lancers | page 207
2 SHEPPARD | page 190
3 SHEPPARD | page 192
4 DELHI SPEARMAN, 2002 | page 82 The Stellenbosching of Colonel Gough, David Ramsay
5 STEWART | page 185
6 SHEPPARD | page 193
7 SHEPPARD | page 192
8 CONAN DOYLE, The Great Boer War | page 158
9 ANGLESEY, Vol 4 | page 84
10 ANGLESEY, Vol 4 | page 125
11 SHEPPARD | page 198
12 NEWARK | page 237
13 ANGLESEY, Vol 4 | page 140
14 STEWART | page 198
15 STEWART | page 198
16 SHEPPARD | page 204
17 ANGLESEY, Vol 4 | page 169–170
18 STEWART | page 214
19 STEWART | page 213
20 STEWART | page 220
21 ANGLESEY, Vol 4 | page 236
22 STEWART | page 203
23 NEWARK | page 241
24 ANGLESEY, Vol 4 | page 407
25 ANGLESEY, Vol 4 | page 397
26 MALLINSON | page 157
27 ANGLESEY, Vol 4 | page 433
28 ANGLESEY, Vol 4 | page 431
29 STEWART | page 238
30 ANGLESEY, Vol 4 | page 423
31 ANGLESEY, Vol 4 | page 484
32 STEWART | page 239
33 STEWART | page 236
34 ANGLESEY, Vol 4 | page 498
35 ANGLESEY, Vol 4 | page 500, 501
36 ANGLESEY, Vol 4 | page 502
37 CORELLI BARNETT quoted in ALAN MALLINSON | page 160
38 BROCKBANK AND COLLINS page 31

1914–1918

1 ANGLESEY, Vol 8 | page 282
2 ANGLESEY, Vol 7 | page 129
3 ANGLESEY, Vol 7 | page 120
4 HOLMES | page 107
5 SHEPPARD | page 237
6 ANGLESEY, Vol 7 | page 123
7 ANGLESEY, Vol 7 | page 124
8 ANGLESEY, Vol 7 | page 124
9 HVS CHARRINGTON, The 12th Royal Lancers in France 1914–1918, App 1
10 SIR H GOUGH, The Fifth Army | page 35
11 STEWART | page 256
12 ANGLESEY, Vol 7 | page 178
13 ANGLESEY, Vol 7 | page 189
14 SHEPPARD | page 244
15 ANGLESEY, Vol 7 | page 191
16 ANGLESEY, Vol 7 | page 193
17 STEWART | page 258
18 SHEPPARD | page 254
19 SHEPPARD | page 257
20 STEWART | page 265
21 STEWART | page 266
22 SHEPPARD | page 258
23 STEWART | page 267
24 STEWART | page 268
25 ANGLESEY, Vol 7 | page 216
26 SHEPPARD | page 262
27 STEWART | page 270
28 SHEPPARD | p267-268
29 BUCHAN, FRANCIS AND RIVERSDALE GRENFELL | page 234
30 ANGLESEY, Vol 8 | page 17
31 SHEPPARD | page 274
32 DELHI SPEARMAN, 2003 | page 74
33 STEWART | page 284
34 STEWART | page 285
35 STEWART | page 285
36 STEWART | page 285
37 STEWART | page 290
38 SIMKINS, Volume 3 | page 41
39 STRACHAN | page 301
40 STEWART | page 298
41 SHEPPARD | page 300
42 SHEPPARD | page 302
43 STRACHAN | page 313
44 STEWART | p306

1918–1939

1 OXFORD ILLUSTRATED HISTORY OF THE BRITISH ARMY | page 272
2 BRYANT | page 22
3 SHAND | page 17
4 BRYANT | page 9
5 STEWART | p313
6 ANGLESEY, Vol 8 | page 334
7 STEWART | page 320
8 STEWART | page 328
9 BRYANT | page 24
10 HOLLAND | page 14
11 ROBSON | page 38
12 9TH LANCERS HISTORY 1936–1945 | page xx
13 9TH LANCERS HISTORY 1936–1945 | page xxv
14 ANGLESEY, Vol 8 | page 334
15 ANGLESEY, Vol 8 | page 318
16 STEWART | page 320
17 9TH LANCERS HISTORY 1936–1945 | page xix
18 9TH LANCERS HISTORY 1936–1945 | Introduction page xxiii

1939–1940

1 STEWART | page 348
2 STEWART | page 350
3 HUNN | page 4
4 SHAND | page 42
5 BISHOP | page 47
6 SHAND | page 44
7 HUNN | page 7
8 BISHOP | page 51
9 STEWART | page 359
10 SHAND | page 53
11 BISHOP | page 59
12 STEWART | page 364
13 STEWART | page 368
14 HUNN | page 13
15 BISHOP | page 67
16 STEWART | page 371
17 BISHOP | page 67
18 SEARBY, Corps Recce Study Period, 14 May 1985
19 9TH LANCERS HISTORY 1936–1945 | page 5
20 9TH QUEEN'S ROYAL LANCERS 1936–1945 | page 10
21 2 LT DEC STEEL quoted in 9th Lancer History | page 19
22 9TH LANCERS HISTORY 1936–1945 | page 25
23 HUNN, page 27
24 STEWART | page 374
25 THE DELHI SPEARMAN, 2006, Volume 11, No 9 | page 119
26 THE DELHI SPEARMAN, 1990 | page 152

1941–1943

1 STRAWSON | page 8
2 BISHOP | page 127
3 HUNN | page 30
4 HUNN | page 33
5 SHAND | page 94
6 BISHOP | page 97
7 HUNN | page 53
8 9TH LANCER HISTORY | page 45
9 9TH LANCER HISTORY 1936 | page 72
10 9TH LANCERS HISTORY | page 93
11 BISHOP | page 69
12 STEWART | page 381
13 BISHOP | page 73
14 HUNN | page 49
15 STRAWSON | page 93
16 9TH LANCERS HISTORY 1936–1945 | pages 51-2
17 9TH LANCERS HISTORY 1936–1945 | page 58
18 STEWART | page 386
19 9TH LANCERS HISTORY 1936–1945 | page 61
20 KEEGAN | page 331
21 SHAND | page116, 118
22 9TH LANCER HISTORY | page 70
23 9TH LANCERS HISTORY 1936–1945 | page 76
24 9TH LANCER HISTORY | page 77
25 9TH LANCERS HISTORY 1936–1945 | page 82
26 BISHOP | page 90
27 BISHOP | page 90
28 9TH LANCER HISTORY | page 87
29 9TH LANCER HISTORY | page 88
30 9TH LANCERS HISTORY 1936–1945 | page xv
31 STRAWSON | page 116
32 STRAWSON | page 121
33 9TH LANCER HISTORY | page 99
34 9TH LANCERS HISTORY 1936–1945 | page 104
35 STEWART | page 397
36 STEWART | page 399
37 BRYANT | page 39
38 BISHOP | page 102
39 9TH LANCERS HISTORY 1936–1945 | page 109
40 9TH LANCERS HISTORY 1936–1945 | page 111
41 9TH LANCERS HISTORY 1936–1945 | page 117
42 STEWART | page 401
43 BISHOP | page 110
44 STEWART | page 402
45 9TH LANCERS HISTORY 1936–1945 | page 118
46 9TH LANCER HISTORY | page 119
47 9TH LANCERS HISTORY | page 121
48 9TH LANCERS HISTORY | page 122
49 BISHOP | page 114
50 STEWART | page 408
51 BISHOP | page 123
52 9TH LANCERS HISTORY | page 128
53 9TH LANCERS HISTORY | page 130
54 9TH LANCERS HISTORY | page 130
55 9TH LANCERS HISTORY | page 131
56 9TH LANCERS HISTORY 1936–1945 | page 136
57 BISHOP | page 142
58 9TH LANCERS HISTORY 1936–1945 | page 137
59 BRYANT | page 5
60 9TH LANCERS HISTORY | page 147
61 STEWART | page 414
62 STEWART | page 415
63 BISHOP | page 142

1944–1945

1 9TH LANCERS HISTORY 1936–1945 | page 149
2 ROBSON, My Memoirs | page 37
3 ROBSON | page 3
4 HOLLAND | page 29
5 COLLIER | page 58
6 COLLIER | page 58
7 STEWART | page 423
8 STEWART | page 423
9 STEWART | page 425
10 STEWART | page 424
11 ROBSON, My Memoirs | page 39
12 STEWART | page 428
13 HUNN | page 100
14 HUNN | page 101, 102
15 HOLLAND | page 293
16 9TH LANCERS HISTORY 1936–1945 | page 212
17 9TH LANCERS HISTORY 1936–1945 | page 183
18 9TH LANCERS HISTORY 1936–1945 | page 184
19 ROBSON | page 13
20 9TH LANCERS HISTORY 1936–1945 | page 191

21 9TH LANCERS HISTORY 1936–1945 | page 194
22 9TH LANCERS HISTORY 1936–1945 | page 201
23 9TH LANCERS HISTORY 1936–1945 | page 205
24 ROBSON, My Memoirs | page 44
25 ROBSON | page 14
26 THE DELHI SPEARMAN, 1990 | page 132
27 9TH LANCERS HISTORY | page 212
28 9TH LANCERS HISTORY 1936–1945 | page 224
29 REGIMENTAL JOURNAL, 1990 | page 135
30 9TH LANCERS HISTORY | page 260
31 9TH LANCERS HISTORY 1936–1945 | page 262
32 9TH LANCERS HISTORY 1936–1945 | page 269
33 9TH LANCERS HISTORY 1936–1945 | page 273
34 STEWART | page 449
35 STEWART | page 450
36 ROBSON | page 18
37 DELHI SPEARMAN, 2002 | page 78
38 STEWART | page 463
39 9TH LANCERS HISTORY 1936–1945 | page 278
40 REGIMENTAL JOURNAL, 1990 | page 135

1945–1960

1 9TH LANCERS HISTORY 1936–1945 | page 279
2 9TH QUEEN'S ROYAL LANCERS 1945–1960 | page 21
3 DAILY TELEGRAPH, obituary for Lord Adlington, 8 December 2000
4 ROBSON, My Memoirs | page 56
5 REGIMENTAL JOURNAL, 1989 | page 147
6 ROBSON, My Memoirs | page 63
7 9TH QUEEN'S ROYAL LANCERS 1945–1960 | page 24
8 9TH QUEEN'S ROYAL LANCERS 1945–1960 | page 26
9 9TH QUEEN'S ROYAL LANCERS 1945–1960 | page 27
10 9TH QUEEN'S ROYAL LANCERS 1945–1960 | page 28
11 BROCKBANK AND COLLINS | page 25
12 BROCKBANK AND COLLINS | page 28
13 MALLINSON | page 282
14 BROCKBANK AND COLLINS | page 34
15 MALLINSON | page 293
16 9TH QUEEN'S ROYAL LANCERS 1945–1960 | page 38
17 PETO | page 44
18 MALLINSON | page 294
19 PETO | page 49
20 9TH QUEEN'S ROYAL LANCERS 1945–1960 | page 42
21 HOLLAND | page 493, 494

1960–1990

1 BROCKBANK | page 29
2 BROCKBANK | page 29
3 BROCKBANK | page 48
4 BROCKBANK | page 52
5 BROCKBANK | page 62
6 REGIMENTAL JOURNAL, 1974 | page 21
7 BROCKBANK | page 79
8 BROCKBANK | page 88
9 BROCKBANK | page 89
10 BROCKBANK | page 91
11 COLONEL RIS BURGESS, correspondence, 16 October 2009
12 BRIGADIER RICHARD NASH, correspondence, 11 February 2009

1991–2010

1 HANSARD, 25 July 1990 | column 468
2 MICHAEL EVANS, Defence Editor, the Times April 1990
3 REGIMENTAL JOURNAL, THE DELHI SPEARMAN, 1989 Commanding Officer's foreword
4 A BRIEF RESUME OF 'BOOT TROOP' 9TH/12TH LANCERS – Captain Rupert Maitland-Titterton
5 A BRIEF RESUME OF 'BOOT TROOP' 9TH/12TH LANCERS – Captain Rupert Maitland-Titterton
6 REGIMENTAL JOURNAL, 1991 | page 32
7 REGIMENTAL JOURNAL, 1993, B Squadron notes | page 16
8 REGIMENTAL JOURNAL, 1993 | page 75
9 REGIMENTAL JOURNAL, 1995 | page 5
10 REGIMENTALJOURNAL,1995 | page 12
11 REGIMENTAL JOURNAL, 1995, Colonel of the Regiment's foreword | page 4
12 REGIMENTAL JOURNAL, 1994, Commanding Officer's foreword | page 3
13 REGIMENTAL JOURNAL, 2005 | page 3
14 9TH/12TH LANCERS COMMANDING OFFICER'S UPDATE LETTER, dated 5 February 2009
15 REGIMENTALJOURNAL,2002 | page 75
16 OXFORD ILLUSTRATED HISTORY OF THE BRITISH ARMY | page 375

INDEX

N

O

P